THE VERDI-BOITO
CORRESPONDENCE

✺ THE VERDI-BOITO CORRESPONDENCE ✺

Edited by Marcello Conati & Mario Medici
With a New Introduction by Marcello Conati

English-language edition prepared by
William Weaver

THE UNIVERSITY OF CHICAGO PRESS

Chicago & London

ernational de recherche sur la Presse musicale
gia, is one of the world's leading Verdi
rst director of the Istituto di studi Verdiani in
ing translator of Pirandello, Calvino, and Eco.
s, he has published *Verdi, A Documentary*
Verdi Companion.

THE UNIVERSITY OF CHICAGO PRESS, CHICAGO 60637
The University of Chicago Press, Ltd., London
© 1994 by The University of Chicago
All rights reserved. Published 1994
Printed in the United States of America
03 02 01 00 99 98 97 96 95 94   5 4 3 2 1

ISBN (cloth) : 0-226-85304-7

Originally published as *Carteggio Verdi-Boito*
© 1978 Istituto di Studi Verdiani (now Istituto Nazionale di Studi
Verdiani), Parma

This publication has been supported by grants from the National
Endowment for the Humanities, an independent federal agency, and from
the Italian Ministry of Foreign Affairs.

The first Italian edition of the *Carteggio Verdi-Boito* was published under the patronage of
the "Premio Raffaele Mattioli," with the financial contribution of the Banca
Commerciale Italiana. It was edited by Mario Medici and Marcello Conati, in
collaboration with Marisa Casati.

Library of Congress Cataloging-in-Publication Data

Verdi, Giuseppe, 1813–1901.
    [Carteggio Verdi-Boito. English]
    The Verdi-Boito correspondence / edited by Marcello Conati and
Mario Medici ; English language edition prepared by William Weaver.
        p.   cm.
    Translation of: Carteggio Verdi-Boito.
    Includes index.
    ISBN 0-226-85304-7
    1. Verdi, Giuseppe, 1813–1901—Correspondence.   2. Boito, Arrigo,
1842–1918—Correspondence.   3. Composers—Italy—Correspondence.
4. Librettists—Italy—Correspondence.   5. Opera—Italy—19th
century.   I. Boito, Arrigo, 1842–1918.   II. Conati, Marcello.
III. Medici, Mario.   IV. Weaver, William, 1923–
ML410.V4A4   1994
782.1'092'2—dc20   93-22598
                                                         CIP

♾ The paper used in this publication meets the minimum requirements of the American
National Standard for Information Sciences—Permanence of Paper for Printed Library
Materials, ANSI Z39.48-1984.

✺ CONTENTS

❧ PREFACE

Letters are not written to be translated. In most cases, they are not writ-ten to be read by anyone but the recipient. So when the translator con-fronts them, he is faced by a number of peculiar problems not normally involved in the translation of, say, a novel or an essay or a poem. The writers of letters—however cultivated they may be—often disregard spelling, quote inaccurately, punctuate according to their private rules or whims. Sometimes they write a kind of shorthand, confident that their intended reader, the addressee, will understand what they mean. Readers and translators a century later may well be puzzled, but that is the price they pay for intruding.

Novels and essays and poems are translated in order to reproduce and convey a literary experience, a cultural achievement. Letters are translated as a rule for biographical and historical reasons, to tell us something about the writer and his correspondent, about their work and their world. Verdi and Boito, at the time of their correspondence, were important figures: Verdi was internationally famous, Boito was well known in Italy and—as the association with Verdi pro-gressed—was to become a celebrity, too, at least in Europe. Though there was a thirty-year difference in their ages, they wrote each other almost as equals. If Boito at times is deferential, it is because of Verdi's seniority and his position of moral authority, not simply because of his fame.

A translation of their letters must not only give the information contained in them (which is fascinating and, in the history of opera, essential) but must also retain the elements of their contrasting person-alities: Boito's tactful patience, Verdi's prickly mistrust, fortunately ac-companied by a genuine inner warmth. Both men were intensely private, and the rare occasions when a drop of emotion spills onto the page assume surprising and affecting significance.

The original correspondence has been published, in a generously annotated edition, by the Istituto di Studi Verdiani in Parma (1978), ed-ited by Mario Medici and Marcello Conati with the collaboration of Marisa Casati. The present English-language version, while it includes every surviving document (even one letter, indicated as "letter A," that surfaced after the Italian publication), is aimed at a less-specialist audience. All the vital information from the Italian publication has been retained (and some information has been added, for the benefit of the Anglophone reader), but here the notes are interspersed among the letters with the intention of creating a fluent narrative. More than an edition of the correspondence, this volume is meant to be an account of a collaboration, which turned into a deep and special friendship between two artists.

The Italian edition faithfully and rightly reproduces misspellings and eccentricities of punctuation. After considerable inner debate, I have decided to correct tactfully almost all of these. It would be absurd deliberately to misspell a word in English and then follow it with an irritating, pedantic (*sic*). I was tempted to make an exception for the name of Shakespeare, which both Verdi and Boito tended to spell in aberrant, varying ways; but in the end I decided to forgo what would have amounted to an only mildly funny private joke.

As for punctuation, I have closed quotations and parentheses the writers left open. I have changed Verdi's beloved dashes into ordinary periods or into colons or semicolons as the sense prompted, and I have added or subtracted commas when clarity suggested such revisions. On occasion I have also broken up some of Boito's long sentences, while trying to suggest, when it seemed appropriate, the younger writer's tendency to verbosity. To remind the reader that these letters were sometimes written in haste, I have occasionally left the writers' abbreviations.

Salutations and closings are always a problem for translators. Verdi's letter of 15 August 1880, which practically initiates the collaboration, begins "Car. Sig.r Boito." His next opens with "Car. Boito," a greeting that remained unvaried, except for a "Cariss. Boito" and, on one emotional occasion, became "Caro Arrigo." Boito almost always addressed Verdi as "Caro Maestro" or "Carissimo Maestro" or "Carissimo Maestro mio." Both signed their letters formally: G. Verdi and A. Boito (only three times Boito exceptionally signed himself Arrigo). It is hard to judge the emotional weight of a closing: in some languages, an apparently passionate expression like "I kiss your hand" is sober and conventional in meaning, while the understated "affectionate greetings" can have a deeper personal undertone. Verdi frequently ended his letters with something like "I clasp your hands." This I have usually translated as "I shake your hands," though no English letter would end that way. For that matter, Anglo-Saxons shake hands less frequently and with less meaning than Italians. Similarly, "affettuosamente" has sometimes been rendered with the anodyne "warmly." As I said above, this is not a literary translation; and I believe the closings of these letters can tell us something. I have tried to gauge the depth of their significance and transmit it. In any case, these closings have no exact English equivalent and, on occasion, a rendering fairly close to the original, while unidiomatic in English, can be informative.

Titles of works and names of characters can make the translator hesitate. On the most immediate level, when should *Otello* become *Othello*? The obvious answer is when the name refers to Shakespeare's hero and not Verdi's. But should *Die Meistersinger* be translated into Italian (especially if it is a translated performance that is being mentioned) and become *I maestri cantori*? Clearly it should not be translated into *The Master Singers*. In preparing this volume I have not set myself hard and fast rules, but have dealt with these—and other—questions individually, adopting each time the solution that sounded right in the context.

A word about Italian prosody, since it figures prominently in the correspondence. Italian verses are measured—and denominated—by the number of their syllables. *Quinari* are based on five syllables; *senari*, six; *settenari*, seven; *ottonari*, eight; the less-popular *novenari*, nine; *decasillabi, endecasillabi*, and *dodecasillabi* have ten, eleven, and twelve. This "syllable count" ideally assumes an end-of-line stress on the penultimate syllable and elision of all consecutive vowels from word to word. The actual number of syllables can be smaller or larger, however, if the final word is stressed instead on its final or on its antepenultimate syllable. An example: "Se resto sul l_i_do (accent on 5) is a *senario*, "Quest'onta laver_ò_" (accent on 6) is a *settenario*, while "La donna è m_o_bile" (accent on 4, elision of "-na" with "è") is a *quinario*, even though each line has six syllables.

Classic Italian verse was generally in *endecasillabi*. When the verses did not rhyme, they were called *versi sciolti*, which is usually translated as "blank verse," though the two are not quite equivalent. For that matter, even without a profound knowledge of Italian metrics, the reader will grasp Boito's and Verdi's intentions.

In the following pages, quotations of verse are given, when opportune, first in the original Italian, followed by a literal translation in square brackets. I emphasize the word "literal." Here, more than elsewhere, the meaning of the individual word is important, so I have tried to be as precise as possible and, sense permitting, to follow the Italian word order, ruthlessly sacrificing also rhyme and meter. Longer Italian scenes are printed in a special appendix. I have made no attempt to beautify these translations; they are meant to serve as guides, as trots.

Verdi and—to a lesser degree—Boito were sometimes inconsistent not only about spelling but also about capitalization, paragraphing, underlining. I have frequently italicized titles not italicized by the composer or the librettist; similarly, I have lowercased some words (act, scene, impresario), while leaving others in uppercase (Art, Music), when the capital letter clearly had significance for the writer.

The illustrations of this volume provide some samples of Verdi's and Boito's handwriting. The older man's is more impetuous, harder to read: Boito wrote with a kind of prim clarity (he hated to break a word and would compress or expand the last word on a line so as not to use a hyphen). But Boito was a man of contradictions: while his writing tended to be fussy, he often—as he admits—found himself without paper and would write on anything he found close to hand: a bit of letterhead from a hotel where he was no longer staying or, once, even on the blank sheet torn from the Verdi letter to which he was replying.

For most of the period of this correspondence, Boito lived in a large, then-modern building in Via Principe Amedeo in Milan. He shared a spacious apartment with his brother Camillo (who had separated from his first wife in 1867) and, after Camillo's remarriage in 1887, also with his sister-in-law, the much-loved Madonnina. But Boito had his own refuge in the same building, a study on the roof, with a splendid view (in his last years he moved the study to the ground floor, for greater convenience). Much of the year he spent visiting friends or escaping to hotels or to mountain localities to find peace and quiet. He had numerous friends, the closest being the conductor Franco Faccio and, almost as intimate, the writer Giuseppe Giacosa. But Boito was eternally available, and was constantly called upon to help someone or to sit on a board or to act as host to a foreign visitor.

Verdi, on the contrary, led a more secluded life, with—until her death in 1897—his wife Giuseppina constantly at his side, ready to act as shield or secretary or lightning rod. For some years they had spent the worst of the winter months in Genoa and, in summer, a month at the spa of Montecatini. After about 1870, the Verdis began making regular extended stopovers in Milan en route to Genoa or Montecatini. There they stayed always at the Grand Hôtel Milan, where (as Conati recounts) the collaboration with Boito was sealed and where, in 1901, Verdi died. While Verdi spent months in the isolation of his Villa Sant'Agata, amid the flat fields of the Po Valley, he was a devourer of newspapers and pressed his correspondents for news of the musical world. Eventually Boito became a favorite reporter for him.

Today's reader is inevitably surprised by the rapidity of the Italian postal system in the last century, and by the punctuality of the trains.

Verdi and Boito could write frequently and receive prompt answers; thus the letters have at times the give-and-take of conversation, those unbridled conversations between close associates, where a moment of gossip can be followed by the most profound insights into their shared art.

⟡FOR THE MOST PART, Boito's letters to Verdi are in the archive of the Villa Sant'Agata, while Verdi's to Boito are preserved in the Istituto Nazionale di Studi Verdiani in Parma. These surviving originals were used by Mario Medici and Marcello Conati in preparing the Italian edition of the correspondence. Sometime between 1940, when Piero Nardi finished his invaluable life of Boito, and 1973, when the descendants of Boito's literary executor donated the Verdi-Boito letters to the Istituto, a few additional documents from Verdi to Boito were lost; and thus, in some cases, the texts that follow are based on Nardi's transcriptions (for that matter, generally scrupulous).

In preparing this English-language edition of the correspondence, I have received unstinting assistance from many colleagues and friends. The Istituto Nazionale di Studi Verdiani in Parma has participated wholeheartedly in the project from the outset, and I would particularly like to thank the director, Pierluigi Petrobelli, and Marisa Di Gregorio Casati. I am also happy to thank Gabriel Dotto, formerly of the University of Chicago Press and now of G. Ricordi & C., for following my work from the beginning and for countless, invaluable suggestions (in particular for guiding me through the snares and pitfalls of Italian metrics). Anna Herklotz, for the University of Chicago Press, has been over every line of the text many times with patience and insight, and she has made me rethink and often modify a number of decisions and choices. As always, many friends—Verdians and not—have been pressed into service; I gladly and gratefully acknowledge the help of George Martin, Mary Jane Philips Matz, Kazuo Nakajima, Andrew Porter, and my Italian neighbors Licia and Pippo Greghi.

William Weaver

ᴥ INTRODUCTION
THE VALUE OF TIME

It is in vast spaces that certain men are fated to meet and understand each other.

—Giuseppina Verdi

ᴥ Background

In thanking you for the excellent job done for me, I take the liberty of offering you, as a token of my esteem, this humble watch. Accept it wholeheartedly, as it is offered wholeheartedly. May it remind you of my name, and of the value of time.

Greet Faccio for me, and glory and good fortune to you both!

This document, dated 29 March 1862 (preserved in the Istituto Nazionale di Studi Verdiani), marks the first encounter of Boito and Verdi, which took place in Paris in the spring of that year, resulting in the two men's fortuitous collaboration on a cantata for the Great London Exhibition. Verdi's little note belongs to the prehistory of the real artistic partnership between the two men; and it was a long prehistory, lasting almost fifteen years, as the destinies of the two men seemed fated rather to diverge in opposite and apparently irreconcilable directions.

It was not, actually, the basic ideological positions of Verdi and Boito that were irreconcilable. Maintaining a facade of gruff disinterest, the aging Verdi was keenly alert to contemporary cultural developments, while Boito, as a young man, was an outspoken member of the *scapigliati* [literally, "disheveled"], an iconoclastic group of Bohemian artists. And also the younger musician, after playing the "game of not belonging to his own society" for a while, later—once he had established his career—strategically assumed a more conservative cultural position.

If anything, the difficulty lay in the characters of the two men. Both harbored a profound mistrust of human relationships and social contacts. But what principally worked against any idea of an artistic collaboration between them was a double incompatibility of ideas as well as character: an objective and almost insuperable practical difficulty created by the artistic personalities of the two men. A collaboration, in fact, would have to be based on a creative association between peers, at least in plotting the drama, in conceiving the structure of its action, in choosing and developing its poetic concepts. Boito was a gifted poet, but, more important, from the outset of his career he had made no secret of his profound devotion to the renewal of the musical theater, and one requirement of this renewal was that the author act in the double capacity of poet and composer. Boito promptly put this conviction into practice, in his *Mefistofele* in 1868 and, later, in his projected *Nerone*. But, without making any public declarations, Verdi had also been moving in a similar direction from a very early stage in his career, from the time of *I due Foscari* at least. Subjugating the librettist—especially when it was Francesco Maria Piave[1]—to his dramaturgical ideas, writing down in his own hand, scene by scene, the dramatic outline of the opera, establishing its poetic concepts, Verdi considered the librettist's duty was then merely to translate these concepts into verses suitable to be set to music. True, Verdi often expressed his ambition to collaborate with a real poet.[2] But after the death of Salvatore Cammarano—the only librettist (except for Temistocle Solera and perhaps Andrea Maffei) whom he accepted as a genuine collaborator in establishing the dramaturgy of a text[3]—the composer had in effect occupied the librettist's territory and asserted his authority over the entire creation of an opera. The poet became simply the versifier.[4]

When we study more carefully the documents of the Verdi-Boito

1. Verdi wrote to Piave on 14 February 1845, at the time of *I due Foscari:* "I must tell you frankly (and let this be a secret, and I mean a secret) that since the two of us are far from each other, and as I may need at times some changes in meter or wording, or I may have to make some cuts, [. . .] you must leave me the freedom to make such revisions as I consider opportune, always with your permission, however" [F. Abbiati, *Giuseppe Verdi* (Milan: Ricordi, 1959), 1:554].

2. "When will the poet come who will give Italy a vast and powerful opera, free of every convention, various, uniting all its elements, and above all, new!!" he wrote on 18 January 1854 to Cesarino De Sanctis [A. Luzio, ed., *Carteggi verdiani* (Rome: Accademia d'Italia, 1935), 1:23].

3. Cammarano also felt the necessity of a unified concept; on 11 June 1849, at the time of *Luisa Miller,* he wrote to Verdi: "If I weren't afraid of being called Utopian, I would be tempted to say that to achieve the possible perfection of an opera, a single mind should be author of both the verses and the notes" [*I copialettere di Giuseppe Verdi,* ed. G. Cesari and A. Luzio (Milan, 1913), p. 473].

4. In this sense the letter-contract with Somma regarding *Un ballo in maschera* is exemplary: "I agree to versify *Gustavo III di Svezia* from the version that you will hasten to send me. You will provide me with the scenario; for the musical meters it would be well for you to annotate in the margin the form of the stanzas, of the verse, and the number of verses for each stanza, so that I can more easily give you the poetry that suits you. For this reason, I beg you to be abundant in your instructions" [Abbiati, 2:450].

correspondence, it gradually appears inevitable that the two men would come together sooner or later on the pathway of art. This encounter was effected not so much by their spiritual impulses, however, but rather by the subtle and farsighted intuition of the patient, tenacious publisher and composer, Giulio Ricordi. In the crucial years of the greatest ideological divergence between the two artists, and especially at the time of the significant juxtaposition of *Mefistofele* and *Don Carlos* in 1867 and 1868, the young Ricordi was quick to detect and act upon the original poetic talent in the former work, while he found in the latter an invincible artistic self-renewal. A close friend of Boito's since his young manhood, Ricordi must be given credit for having reconciled and brought together these two antithetical personalities, thus to achieve a collaboration of supreme value to opera.

These introductory pages are intended to reconstruct, on the basis of the many surviving documents, the fifteen-year period that precedes the working partnership between Verdi and Boito.

☙From the Cantata to the "Sapphic Ode"

Boito was in Paris with his friend Franco Faccio. Both of them had just completed their studies at the Milan Conservatory, and—thanks to some influential patronage[5]—they had been awarded traveling fellowships from the Italian Ministry of Education. They had also been supplied with numerous letters of introduction: to Rossini, Berlioz, Gounod, and Verdi (though Boito's older brother, mentor, and stimulator, the architect Camillo, wrote at this same time a letter of implacable criticism of *Un ballo in maschera*).[6] The two youths were also presented to Costantino Nigra, ambassador to France, the man charged

5. Also on the recommendation of Giovannina Lucca, the Italian publisher of the works of Wagner [R. De Rensis, ed., *Franco Faccio e Verdi: Carteggi e documenti inediti* (Milan: Treves, 1934), p. 12].

6. He wrote to Arrigo from Florence, September 1861: "I went to La Pergola a few evenings ago to hear the much hailed and praised *Ballo in maschera*... It's a dreadful opera, my dear, written without thought, without knowledge, with no loftiness of concept or manner. It no longer has the vulgar invention of Verdi's first operas [. . .]: it is a fragmentary work, stolen from here and there, of a talent now worn out and buried. [. . .] in sum, it is a work for the Arena, like its libretto" [P. Nardi, *Vita di Arrigo Boito* (Milan: Mondadori, 1942), pp. 87–88]. And the letter of 12 January 1862 from Milan states: "Filippi and I argued at length and heatedly at Countess Maffei's, and it seemed a joke when I said that, far from being profound and meditated, the music of *Ballo in maschera* was trivial, lighter, and more wretched than anything else written by Verdi. In short, this opera to me is like a seamstress wearing the skirt and cloak of a great lady" [Nardi, p. 88].

with designating the Italian composer to write a work for the London Exhibition. When Rossini declined the invitation, Nigra naturally turned to Verdi, who, after Rossini, was Italy's most widely performed composer. Verdi had arrived in Paris in February, returning from a futile journey to St. Petersburg, where a soprano's indisposition had postponed until autumn the premiere of *La forza del destino*. Verdi had always firmly refused to write occasional pieces (his only, understandable, exception was in 1848 when, at Mazzini's urging, he set some patriotic verses by Mameli); but this time, unusually, he consented. Nigra may also have suggested Boito as the possible author of a cantata text. Ambassador and poet shared an interest in Freemasonry (Nigra, Boito,[7] Faccio, Giulio Ricordi, and many other leading Italian cultural figures of liberal sentiments at the time were Masons or sympathizers); and, further, the young Arrigo had some experience in the genre, having supplied the words for a "patriotic cantata," *Il quattro giugno,* and for a "mystery" entitled *Le sorelle d'Italia,* both set jointly with Faccio and successfully performed as part of their final examinations at the conservatory in 1860 and in 1861.[8]

◅THE HANDS OF THE WATCH given Boito by Verdi to recall the value of time (the same watch perhaps that we see the poet examining intently in a photograph taken many years later in his study in Via Principe Amedeo in Milan)[9] were to describe countless revolutions before the partnership with Verdi began to develop, initially with great circumspection, then more comfortably, until it was consolidated in a sincere, devoted, enduring friendship. Two years after the cantata for London, Boito sent Verdi an inscribed copy of his fairy tale in verse, *Re Orso* [King Bear], and in his brief dedication he echoed Verdi's earlier note to him: "To Giuseppe Verdi, so that he may remember my name. Milan, 20 December 1864." [10] As far as time was concerned, its value was something Verdi had long known well.

7. Boito was a Mason, though it is not certain he was already one at the time of his first journey to Paris. As for Nigra, Grand Master of the Grand Orient of Turin, minister plenipotentiary and then ambassador to Paris from 1860 to 1876, his contribution to the unification of Italian Masonry is well known.

8. The Milanese press comments on these cantatas can be read in De Rensis, *Faccio e Verdi,* pp. 6–10.

9. The photo is reproduced in C. Gatti, *Verdi nelle immagini* (Milan: Garzanti, 1941), p. 206.

10. Nardi, p. 167. Nardi was the first to reveal the copy of the poem still in the library at Sant'Agata.

Meanwhile, between presents, between inscriptions, events had taken place that, if anything, were bound to widen the gap separating the two artists. Italian political unification, finally achieved, led to a restlessness among members of the younger generation, who now dreamed of a rejuvenation of Italian culture, a renewal of taste, a receptiveness towards the most advanced achievements of contemporary European culture. An intellectual impatience, particularly among the young Milanese artists, inspired iconoclastic attitudes destined to shock the solid middle class, clinging to established cultural values, recent and less recent, to Alessandro Manzoni and to Verdi. As for the repeated anti-bourgeois declarations of Boito, of his friend the poet Emilio Praga, and others, a critic has observed that "the 'bourgeoisie,' in this case, is not so much a class as a category of literary taste, and the *scapigliati* had no 'platform' designed to oppose it, or even a code, however disarticulated, of their own moral values."[11] The young rebels wielded blows left and right, without a specific target; their activity was dictated by the necessity to stake out a territory where they could rediscover independence of ideas and action. They were impelled by a desire to destroy stagnant situations, by an aspiration towards everything new, by the need to escape from "the confines of the old and the stupid," in Boito's words. The innovatory spirit of these young rebels breached even the walls of the well-fortified Verdi camp, arriving in the salon of Countess Clara Maffei, old friend and confidante of the composer's early, Milanese years. Towards Franco Faccio, now, the countess felt a maternal protectiveness. And besides her salon, Verdi's publishing firm was infected, thanks to Tito Ricordi's son, the enthusiastic Giulio, who in October 1862 founded, with Boito and Faccio, the pioneering Società del Quartetto di Milano. When Tito Ricordi invited Verdi to become the president of this new society (whose concert activities began only in the summer of 1864), the composer declined in a letter dated 3 October 1863:

> As for the Società del Quartetto, please leave me out. You know that when it comes to music I am a jackass, and I am totally unable to understand what the learned call classical. I will stop here, because you might blush at your composer if I uttered all those truths that, to safeguard my own honor, I will leave unwritten.
>
> [Abbiati, 2:744]

11. M. Lavagetto, in *Arrigo Boito: Opere* (Milan: Garzanti, 1979), p. xiv.

Four months previously, the countess, perhaps prompted by Boito, surely with the aim of stirring interest in her protégé Faccio, had ventured to inform Verdi about the young men of her salon:

> Among the people I see every evening are Boito and Faccio, those two young men whom you received so courteously; they remember you with the warmest gratitude, and they—along with Carcano and Tenca—beg me to send you their greetings... Faccio will soon present his first opera... What is your opinion of his ability? Boito has talent but still wavers between poetry and music, and to succeed in both fields is virtually a miracle. These past few evenings the two youths played *La forza del destino* and *Un ballo in maschera* for me, in their entirety.
>
> [Abbiati, 2:754–55]

The composer's reply is dated 31 July, three months before the premiere of Faccio's *I profughi fiamminghi* and Boito's "sapphic ode." Verdi indicated that he was already informed on the artistic tendencies of Clarina's two young favorites:

> Last year in Paris I saw Boito and Faccio often and they are surely two young men of great intelligence, but I can say nothing about their musical talent, because I have never heard anything of Boito's, and of Faccio's music I have heard only a few things he came and played for me one day. In any case, as Faccio is going to present an opera, the public will pass judgment. These two young men are accused of being very warm admirers of Wagner. Nothing wrong there, provided that admiration does not degenerate into imitation. Wagner exists and it is useless to reinvent him. Wagner is not a wild animal as the purists claim, nor is he a prophet as his apostles claim. He is a man of great intelligence who enjoys taking difficult paths, because he is unable to find the easy and more direct ones.
>
> [Abbiati, 2:755]

❧THE YEAR 1863 for the Lombard *scapigliati* was a time of great fireworks, both in the musical and the spoken theater, with a new play and a new opera. This was the year of *Le madri galanti,* a play written jointly by Boito and Emilio Praga, presented in Turin, a disastrous failure; and of *I profughi fiamminghi,* Faccio's opera on a libretto by Praga, given at the Teatro alla Scala in Milan in November. It was the year, too, of a "sapphic ode, with glass in hand" entitled *All'Arte italiana* [To Italian

Art], improvised by Boito during a lively party at which all the leading *scapigliati* were gathered to celebrate the success of Faccio's opera.[12] One stanza of the poem goes:

> *Forse già nacque chi sovra l'altare*
> *Rizzerà l'arte, verecondo e puro,*
> *Su quell'altar bruttato come un muro*
> *Di lupanare.*
> [Perhaps the man is already born, modest and pure, who will set art erect once more on that altar, befouled like a brothel wall.]

As many writers have already remarked, it was perhaps not Boito's intention to launch a personal attack on Verdi: to be sure, in the impetus of an improvisation, fired by the celebratory enthusiasm of the moment, Boito did not realize the searing effect the invocation would have on the older composer. But it is obvious all the same that the words could not help but wound the musician, alive and active and, at that time, the most prestigious representative of Italian art in Europe. In fact Verdi—who read the ode in the review *Museo di famiglia*,[13] where the proud author promptly had it published—considered the poem a direct blow. And Verdi was not a man to forgive and forget an insult. On 13 December, replying to Countess Maffei, who had begged him to send a "word of encouragement" to Faccio, Verdi made no secret of his feelings, quoting some verses of the ode in his letter:

> For almost two weeks I have been going here and there like a madman [. . .], and for this reason I haven't answered your letter, or Faccio's. I must also tell you, with my usual frankness, that the latter puts me in an awkward position. How can I answer him? A word of encouragement, you say; but what is the need of such a word for someone who has already presented himself to the public and allowed it to be his judge? Now the matter is between them, and all words become futile. I know there has been much talk about this opera, too much, in my opinion, and I have read some newspaper articles, in which I

12. Faccio himself, on 16 November, had informed Verdi: "The Signora Contessa Maffei has urged me to inform you of the happy reception of my first opera. You can imagine that, in writing these lines, I am filled with that awed shyness that the very small man feels in the presence of the very great [. . .]. The countess has promised to win your indulgence for this letter that I make bold to send you. I beg you also to accept the best wishes of my Boito, who, like me, is working and hoping" [De Rensis, *Faccio e Verdi*, pp. 29–30].

13. Issue dated 22 November 1865.

found grand words about *Art, Aesthetics, Revelations, Past, Future,* etc., etc., and I confess that (great ignoramus that I am!) I understood nothing. For that matter, I do not know Faccio's talent, or his opera; and I do not want to know it, so as not to have to discuss it, or express an opinion on it, things I loathe because they are the most useless things in the world. *Discussions* never convince anyone; and *Opinions,* most of the time, are erroneous. In the end, if Faccio, as his friends say, has found new paths; if Faccio is destined to restore art to the altar now *befouled like a brothel wall,* so much the better for him, and for the public.[14]

The next day, Verdi did write to Faccio, with a sarcastic reference to another stanza of the "sapphic ode" ("Italian Art! Thou, who in the great times, wert teacher to a Northern land, with the holy harmonies of Pergolesi and of Marcello"):

> If the public, this supreme Judge, looked benevolently on your first work, and its reception was good, as you declare, then continue with firm spirit the career you have undertaken, and add to the great names of Pergolesi and Marcello another glorious name, your own. I wish the same for your friend Boito, whom I beg you to greet for me.
>
> [De Rensis, *Faccio e Verdi,* pp. 30–31]

A reply that was like a slap—to Faccio directly, and indirectly to Boito. For Verdi, accustomed to theatrical battles and newspaper polemics, the question could be put only to the arbiter he had always considered supreme in musical matters: the public. Apparently Faccio did not interpret the older man's reply offensively, at least if we can judge by the draft made by Verdi's wife, Giuseppina, on 23 December, of a letter to Francesco Maria Piave, now employed at La Scala and a regular visitor to the Maffei salon:

> Verdi is unable to answer you, as he has a diseased eye, almost closed, though it opened wide when he heard from you about how overjoyed Faccio, the countess, and others were at those replies that, as you well know, took their time in coming! It requires a very benevolent determination to interpret them so!... I can say no more![15]

14. The quotation on which this translation is based comes from the photocopy of the autograph, in the archive of the Istituto di Studi Verdiani (now the Istituto Nazionale di Studi Verdiani), Parma. This source is cited hereafter in the text and notes with the acronym ISV. This letter appears in Abbiati (2:763), but with slight differences.

15. F. Walker, *L'uomo Verdi* (Milan: Mursia, 1964), pp. 550–51.

❧A *Scapigliato* in Action

The new year, 1864, found Boito totally engaged in literary, dramatic, and musical polemics. His first pulpit was a regular column entitled "Cronaca dei teatri"[16] in a new weekly, *Il figaro,* founded and edited by Praga and by Boito himself. The publication was short lived,[17] but in the following July Boito began contributing comments on the experiments of the Società del Quartetto to its newly founded *Giornale della Società del Quartetto,* published by Ricordi, with Alberto Mazzucato as editor.[18] Some of the reports in *Il figaro* concern operas of Verdi performed at La Scala in that period, notably *I lombardi alla prima crociata,* discussed in the number dated 7 January 1864:

> [It is] an opera that no longer stands up so boldly and confidently. Time gave it a first layer of dust, and then the later discoveries of Verdi himself, and of others as well, have revealed to the public the existence of a more serious, more complete, more genuine art. [. . .] "You have to be wall-eyed," Verdi said when he wrote *Lombardi.* "You have to be wall-eyed, with one eye on the public and one on art," and for those days this was a brave notion, for there were many who trained both eyes on the public. [. . .] But today the time has come to gaze straight ahead, to look art squarely in the face, with both pupils wide, serene, confident. This is why *Lombardi* has aged, this is why *Rigoletto* is still young and is enrapturing the Parisian public at the Théâtre Lyrique.[19]

In the review of 11 February the subject is *I vespri siciliani,* presented for the first time at La Scala in its original version (but translated into Italian):

> It would have been better to leave this opera in its old guise, as *Giovanna de Guzman,* and let us go on hearing it always as it was first heard in our country; we would have all been better off. A splendid, epic story would then have remained untouched, awaiting a more vast and more Italian conception; and Verdi's great music, freed from the hollow tragedy considered only in its historical aspect, would have

16. All thirteen of the "Cronaca dei teatri" columns are included in A. Boito, *Tutti gli scritti,* ed. P. Nardi (Milan: Mondadori, 1942), pp. 1092–1157.

17. It ceased publication with the issue of 31 March 1864.

18. Boito's reports are available complete in Boito, pp. 1158–77.

19. Boito, pp. 1094–95. In this report there is also a reference to *Un ballo in maschera,* mentioning, however, only the performance [Boito, pp. 1095–96].

had a commonplace libretto not without some efficacy, a pretext to
give an embodiment to his notes.

[Boito, p. 1118]

Boito then, discussing the musical function of verse, broached a revealing idea that shows his awareness of the necessity to make the metrics of Italian opera more supple, to meet the demands of musical rhythm and dramatic expression:

> And yet, though a bit faded as a whole, this opera of Verdi is admirable in its details; it has some exquisitely elegant harmonies and some elegance of rhythm not frequent in the other operas of the great composer; French verse, less measured than ours, with vaguer and softer accents, helped the music by relieving it of the tedious singsong of symmetry, the great quality and the great defect of Italian prosody, which almost inevitably leads to poverty and commonplace rhythm in the musical phrasing.

[Boito, p. 1119]

Whether Boito considered Verdi's operas dated or timely, the guarded remarks of the young *scapigliato* indicate a sincere respect for the composer's art, and this should have attenuated, if not allayed, the provocation of the invective hurled in the "sapphic ode." Boito's articles in the *Giornale della Società del Quartetto* seem more daring in their commitment to the struggle for a total renewal of the Italian culture of the period. Paradoxically, the experiments in instrumental music carried out by the Società del Quartetto came to assume for Boito the significance of a kind of gymnasium where the new generation of composers could better be trained for the supreme test: opera. His intentions were particularly explicit in the review dated 14 May 1865, discussing quartets by Bazzini and Faccio, winners of a competition sponsored by the Società del Quartetto of Milan:

> Today music is all for opera. Its temple is the theater, its altar the stage, its worship, its ritual, its faith, that great modern rhapsody that transforms history into tragedy, legend into poem, chronicle into drama. An immense activity is concentrated around opera; all the fervid believers in art, all the brave supporters of progress cooperate in this solemn activity. Meyerbeer rises from the grave to give our age yet another opera.[20] Wagner loudly proclaims to all Europe his *Tristan und Isolde*. Opera is the latest thing in music; Shakespeare is the latest

20. Reference to *L'Africaine*, posthumous work of Meyerbeer.

thing in musical drama. Impressive sign! Does art now touch Shakespeare? Good, then art is uplifted. Great labors are suited only to great strength; to touch the Alpine peak is the eagle's craving. If today musical drama ventures to touch Shakespeare, it is a sure sign that today musical drama is worthy of Shakespeare. [. . .] The great and true mission of all the quartet societies is, in fact, to preserve religiously the relics of instrumental art, their aim is to be the teachers of the *past* to the young and to the public; to strengthen erudition. We learn from our fathers so that we can work for our children. Let us practice the Symphony and the Quartet in order to be able to face Opera.

[Boito, pp. 1172–73, 1177]

Prescient words, which at that moment referred to the imminent production in Genoa of Faccio's second opera, *Amleto* [Hamlet], for which Boito himself had supplied the libretto. But, in hindsight, these words seem to herald Verdi's future *Otello* and *Falstaff*.

◄§VERDI, FOR HIS PART, showed no inclination towards "quartettism," at least not for the moment. In late November of that same 1864,[21] he declined Giulio Ricordi's request to dedicate a quartet to him:

With all due appreciation for your kindness, I must nevertheless ask you to understand my apologies, for I cannot accept the dedication of your quartet. It would be against my inveterate rule, which I have promised myself to follow strictly. And besides, my dear Sig. Giulio, printing together on a title page *Quartet* and *Giuseppe Verdi* is a horrible discord! Your courtesy has erroneously inspired you to want to dedicate your quartet to me, but if you reflect, you yourself will perhaps be pleased that I have not accepted.

[ISV]

At the end of the following month, on 20 December 1864, Boito's *Re Orso* arrived, with the inscription already quoted. In the opinion of one authoritative Verdi biographer, this inscription shows "that Boito was not conscious of having irreparably offended" the composer.[22] Did Verdi send some reply to the reverent dedication of the poet of his London cantata? No trace of any has been found among Boito's papers, nor is there any reference in Verdi's correspondence. The only possible sign

21. The draft of this letter, published in Luzio, *Carteggi*, 4:242, is dated 28 November 1864.

22. F. Walker, *The Man Verdi* (Chicago: University of Chicago Press, 1982), p. 455.

might be the composer's rejection, at that time, of Boito's possible collaboration on the revision of *La forza del destino* that Tito Ricordi was urging. Verdi did not contemplate working again with Piave, author of the verses for the original St. Petersburg version of the opera. The composer wanted some other, perhaps more "creative" poet. In a letter dated 17 December 1864, Tito ventured:

> I see that the idea of revising the denouement means a great deal to you, and I am very pleased. I also will take care to find some poet suitable for the task. Would Boito be able to do it?
>
> [ISV]

And then, on 30 December, the publisher insisted, cautiously:

> When I spoke with Carrion[23] about your *Forza del destino*, he told me that he would take it upon himself to have the libretto revised by Gutiérrez[24] in Madrid. How does this strike you? Boito would write beautiful verses, but as far as imagination goes, perhaps he would not satisfy you. Marcello[25] and Ghislanzoni[26] would be more creative... but... is it a good idea to put ourselves in their hands?
>
> [ISV]

The composer's reply was curt, as at that same time he was involved in the revision of *Macbeth* in French for the imminent production at the Théâtre Lyrique in Paris. The letter is dated 1 January 1865:

> Isn't it a poor idea to write to Gutiérrez when in Madrid there is the Duque de Rivas,[27] to whom I can write whenever I choose?... But neither Gutiérrez nor the duke would achieve anything. For a thousand reasons it would be a mistake to turn to Ghislanzoni or Marcello, nor

23. Emanuele Carrion, Spanish tenor, then engaged at La Scala.

24. Antonio Garcia Gutiérrez, Spanish dramatist, author of *El trovador* (1836) and of *Simón Bocanegra* (1843), among others. Both plays became the subjects of Verdi operas.

25. Marco Marcelliano Marcello, composer (pupil of Mercadante) and pianist, was especially a journalist. In 1854 he had founded the music and theatrical magazine *Il trovatore* in Turin. He was a music critic and a prolific librettist, having begun this latter activity in 1838, collaborating with Gaetano Rossi on the text of Mercadante's *Il bravo.* He gained fame with the librettos of *Tutti in maschera* (Pedrotti, 1856) and *Michele Perrin* (Cagnoni, 1864).

26. One-time baritone, journalist, and man of letters, Antonio Ghislanzoni had recently taken up the profession of librettist, with *Maria Tudor* for Kaschperoff (Teatro Carcano, Milan, 1859) and *La sposa di Toledo* for Benvenuti (Teatro Canobbiana, Milan, 1864).

27. Author of *Don Alvaro o La fuerza del sino,* the drama on which the libretto of Verdi's *La forza del destino* was based.

would Boito do. Wait and see, in the end I'll find something; meanwhile, if you like, hire out the opera as it is.

[ISV]

A previous, fleeting reference to Boito, a few days before the arrival of the inscribed *Re Orso,* can be found in a letter to Piave dealing with the revision of some verses of *Macbeth:* "I read about the Boito business. Who is in the wrong?" [Abbiati, 2:805]. On 11 December 1864, the old librettist had informed Verdi about the matter:

This morning there was a duel between Sig.r Boito and a certain Sig.r Verga.[28] This is what caused it: The other evening at the Caffè Martini some people were talking about music. One man said he was enamoured of the overture of *Le pardon de Ploermel;*[29] Rovani,[30] who was present, added that the most beautiful overture in the world is the one to *Guglielmo Tell,* and that he couldn't bear to have another preferred to it. Then, realizing that Boito could overhear, he went on to say that he loathed all musical Germanisms, which certain Croats nowadays want to import into Italy to the detriment of the Italian school. Everyone understood his reference, and many imprudently looked at Boito. He remained silent, then when Rovani stood up to leave some minutes later, Boito begged to have a word with him and asked if Rovani had meant to include him among *those modern Croats.* Rovani replied that it was for Boito's own conscience to decide if he could so be considered, and with this he raised his voice. Boito begged him not to shout; Verga, who had been drinking with Rovani before, now came into the dialogue, saying that Boito needn't bother to teach them the tone in which they should speak; others in the party echoed him, and Verga puffed some cigar smoke in Boito's face. Outnumbered, Boito said to Rovani: "As for you, I advise you to drink less and go to bed earlier; and Signor Verga will have my answer tomorrow," and he turned his back on them and left the café amid the taunts of the group. Yesterday

28. No connection with the Sicilian novelist Giovanni Verga, then only twenty-four, living in Catania, and at the outset of his illustrious writing career.

29. Meyerbeer's opera, performed in Paris in 1859, better known as *Dinorah.* It had not yet been performed in Italy (the Italian premiere took place at the Teatro Pagliano, Florence, in March of 1867), but the overture had already been heard in concerts.

30. Giuseppe Rovani (1818–1874), Milanese writer of strong liberal sentiments. He was a contributor to the *Gazzetta di Milano* and the author of two popular books: a novel, *Cento anni* (One Hundred Years), and a volume on aesthetics, *Le tre arti,* concerned with the affinity of poetry, music, and the figurative arts. Rovani is considered the spiritual father of the *scapigliatura* movement.

he sent his seconds, and this morning the duel took place. Fortis tells me its only consequence was a slight wound on Boito's hand. I wasn't present at the scene, but it was told to me by someone who was there.

[Abbiati, 2:772–73]

Piave's vivid sketch of the night life of Milan's literary cafés confirms that the young Boito possessed not only a hot temper but also a certain style. No further comments by Verdi on the matter have survived. Style or not, and despite inscriptions and duels, the composer did not forge the "sapphic ode," and, above all, he did not forget that Giulio Ricordi, his publisher's son, was a sponsor of the battles of the *avveniristi* [literally, "futurists," i.e., Wagnerites] and the *quartettisti*. Tito Ricordi expressed to Verdi the fear that the "storm clouds from the North" would bring Wagnerian water to Italian land (this was just before the Genoa premiere of Faccio's *Amleto*), and Verdi wrote an explosive reply on 3 May 1865, two weeks after his revised *Macbeth* had been given in Paris:

> You complain about the storm clouds that come to us from the North?!! You are wrong. Personally, I doff my hat, and bid them come ahead, since they are welcome. I have always loved and desired progress, and if the coterie (allow me to use this word in the most kindly sense) created in Milan, to which your Giulio belongs and whose, perhaps involuntary, accomplice you may be, can manage to uplift our music, I will cry *Hosanna!* I too want the music of the future; that is, I believe in a music for the future, and if I have not been able to write it, as I wanted to, the fault is not mine. If I too have befouled the altar, as Boito says, then let him clean it and I will be the first to light a candle there. Long live the coterie then; long live the North, if it brings us light, and the sun.

[Abbiati, 3:14]

The coterie mentioned in this letter was, at that very moment, involved on a broad scale in promoting Faccio's new opera; and Verdi's affirmations aroused the wrath of the young Giulio, who shared Boito's temper. He replied promptly to Verdi with words that may not have been actually disrespectful but were certainly bound to stir things up still further. The letter did not reach the composer, perhaps intercepted by Tito Ricordi and Eugenio Tornaghi, manager of the publishing firm, both of them quick—in case their intervention failed—to alert Verdi's wife, to prevent the missive from reaching the maestro's hands. Answering Tornaghi on 8 May, Giuseppina could not repress a little sermon for the benefit of the publisher's son:

Giulio, who has great talent, should remember that he also has a wife and children, and that two plus two make four, and that no matter how agile one may be, an ill-timed leap can cause a broken neck.

[Abbiati, 3:16]

Giulio was to draw suitable conclusions and avoid ill-timed leaps, as subsequent events and documents reveal. On 21 May,[31] Verdi, replying to Piave, who was shocked by the advance publicity being stirred up for Faccio's *Amleto*,[32] again harped on the "befouled altar":

Don't be alarmed by this Babylon (as you call it) about the music of the future. This, too, is all very well, and must be as it is. These so-called apostles of the future are the initiators of something great, sublime. It was necessary to *wash the altar befouled* by the swine of the past. That takes a pure, virginal music, *holy, spherical!* I look up and wait for the star to show me where the *Messiah* has been born, so that I, like the Magi, can go and adore him. *Hosanna in excelsis*, etc.

[Luzio, *Carteggi*, 2:355]

◆§THE COMPOSER'S ATTITUDE REMAINED FIRM. Though not mentioned by name, the author of the "sapphic ode" reappeared two weeks later in another letter from Verdi to Piave, echoing a recent report in the *Giornale della Società del Quartetto* of 7 May 1865 on the discussion of a parallel, "the parallel that, in fact, exists between the Beautiful and the Sublime," based on a comparison between a Mendelssohn quintet and a quartet by Mozart. Always eager to express his personal aesthetic convictions, Boito had let his enthusiasm run away with him:

Mozart is melodious, sweet and inspired, but indefinite; and yet more nobly simple and more greatly pure than the other. And, indeed, the Sublime is simpler than the Beautiful. The Beautiful can be incarnated in all varieties of form, the most bizarre, the most multiple, the most disparate; only the great form is suited to the Sublime, the eternal, universal, divine form: the spherical form. The horizon is sublime, the sea is sublime, the sun is sublime. Shakespeare is spherical, Dante is

---

31. 24 May according to Abbiati, 2:825.

32. According to Walker (*Man Verdi*, p. 457), "Piave's letters at this time [. . .] reveal a thoroughly unpleasant side of his personality and show that no one more than he stoked the fires of Verdi's resentment against 'the musical Camorra of the future.'" The observation is not unfounded; still, the English biographer underestimates Verdi's independence of judgment as he revealed to friends and confidants his own puzzlement about the attitudes of the new generation.

spherical, Beethoven is spherical; the sun is simpler than the carnation, the sea is simpler than the brook, the Adagio of Mendelssohn is spherical and simpler than the Andante of Mozart. And therefore more powerfully conceivable.

[Boito, pp. 1169–72]

The clever Antonio Ghislanzoni, himself a *scapigliato*,[33] who was shortly to become Verdi's collaborator in the revision of the ending of *La forza del destino* and the versifier of *Aida*, could not refrain from commenting slyly in his *Rivista minima* on 15 May:

I no longer dare walk past a pumpkin without baring my head; and, thinking of that luminous idea of Boito's, that the Sublime is simpler than the Beautiful, and that the sun, since it is spherical, is simpler than the carnation, I am almost led to suspect that a pumpkin is more sublime than the sun.

[Nardi, p. 177]

From Milan the dutiful Piave informed Verdi about both articles, Boito's review and Ghislanzoni's commentary. And the composer answered him on 3 June:[34]

I laughed a lot over Ghislanzoni's article, but not as much as I did over the original one. My God! What if I were also one of the "sphericals!" How inspired I was when I refused to be honorary president of the Società del Quartetto! Me, "spherical?" The terrible thing is that with the paunch I am developing the epithet would not be entirely amiss. "Spherical... focal point... the sun more sublime than a carnation!" Fine things!! Too bad I don't understand them. So Faccio's opera in Genoa was a great success? That's what they write me. I know that all the "sphericals" (as Ghislanzoni calls them) were there, and there was also the "Great Pontiff,"[35] as you would say. This is all very well, but I ask myself: Wouldn't it have been possible to do things a bit more quietly?! Was it necessary to turn half the world upside down because of an opera?[36] Is this also "spherical" behavior? All joking aside, if Faccio

33. For his enthusiastic opinion of Boito's poem *Dualismo,* see Nardi, pp. 148–49.

34. Inserted by Abbiati in 2:777–78 in a context of documents dating from the spring of 1864, this letter can only have been written in 1865.

35. Reference to the composer and music critic Alberto Mazzucato, professor of counterpoint and aesthetics at the Milan Conservatory.

36. Similarly, in a letter of 14 June to his friend Count Opprandino Arrivabene: "You must have heard about Faccio's opera. Who can tell anything about it, in the midst of all

has had a genuine success, may the work endure and become popular. But I am afraid he has abandoned or will abandon the "sphericals" and will become an apostate. There is no middle course. "Spherical, focal point, carnation" are all fine things, but to write music one very simple thing is needed: *Music*. What do you think? For that matter, if Faccio succeeds, I will be sincerely pleased. Others perhaps might not believe these words. Others. But you know me, and you know that either I am silent or I say what I feel.

✺*Mefistofele* and *Don Carlos*

The year 1866 was characterized by apparent silence on both sides. Meanwhile the Third War of Italian Independence broke out, and both Boito and Faccio took part in it, as volunteers with Garibaldi. That summer, after the war's inglorious end—which nonetheless restored the Veneto (Boito's native region) to Italy—the volunteers returned to Milan, where Boito resumed intensive work on *Mefistofele*, the opera he had conceived in his conservatory days.[37] Verdi, residing in Paris, was entirely occupied with the composition of *Don Carlos*. After repeated postponements, this work had its premiere at the Opéra in March of 1867. At the beginning of that summer, when the composer had returned to Italy, Countess Maffei ventured yet another attempt—this time with Giuseppina Verdi as go-between—to make peace between her old friend and her young protégés Boito and Faccio. On this occasion too she added to her own words a letter from Faccio himself. But again the effort failed. Reporting the outcome, Giuseppina wrote to the countess on 21 June (the letter survives):

> I am replying at once, to thank you and to return the letter of Faccio, who is right when he says *that certain things soil us when we talk about them.* So let's leave this gossip, these nasty stories, and all this pettiness where they were, or where they were born. I followed your advice and didn't show the letter to Verdi, who, on the very rare occasions when he talks about things or about people who once displeased him, always says: "What's the need to go into it?!" And after these words,

---

the fuss and with that *entourage?!* Couldn't things be done a little more quietly? I believe, however, that if Faccio really has talent and can succeed, he must break away from the Professors, Conservatorians, Aestheticians, Critics, and neither study nor listen to music for ten years" [A. Alberti, *Verdi intimo: Carteggio di Giuseppe Verdi con il conte Opprandino Arrivabene* (Milan: Mondadori, 1931), p. 57].

37. Cf. Nardi, pp. 57, 72, 91.

> his mouth shuts, and there is no way of going any further. What can
> be done?[38]

Actually, in Giuseppina's draft, which also survives, the words attributed to Verdi are written in his own hand, and are much less generic: "I have always tried to avoid useless things, things I don't like and people I do not completely trust" [Luzio, *Carteggi*, 2:26].

☙On 27 October 1867, *Don Carlos* was given its Italian premiere at the Teatro Comunale in Bologna, conducted by Angelo Mariani. The event caused a great stir in Milanese artistic and cultural circles, among the same people who, a short time later, would attend performances of the same opera at La Scala conducted by Mazzucato during the Carnival season. The *avveniristi* and the *scapigliati* did not conceal their interest and their admiration. Having seen the opera in Paris on his way to Poland, Boito had voiced some reservations about it, echoed in a letter from his brother Camillo;[39] but Filippi (critic of *La perseveranza*), Ghislanzoni, Mazzucato, and others were now unstinting in their praise. And they were joined by the "rebel" Giulio Ricordi, who had followed the Paris rehearsals, representing the family firm.[40] In this latest work of Verdi's, the young publisher sensed a new artistic direction, in certain ways coherent with those ideals Arrigo had proposed, however confusedly, a few years earlier. Was this a conversion? That is how Piave considered it, in a letter to Giuseppina Verdi of 12 November 1867 (his last, perhaps, before the paralysis that struck him and made him an invalid for the rest of his life):

38. *Quartetto milanese ottocentesco: Lettere di Giuseppe Verdi, Giuseppina Strepponi, Clara Maffei, Carlo Tenca e di altri personaggi del mondo politico e artistico dell'epoca* (Rome: Archivi Edizioni, 1974), pp. 164, 166.

39. Written on 23 April 1867: "If your score [*Mefistofele*] can be ready before Carnival, I have no doubt that you can give it at La Scala, especially since the management has cleared out, tail between its legs. Mazzucato's influence is on the rise, I believe, and it would be a good idea for you to write him. Since you allowed me to decide the wisdom of giving him or not the letter on *Don Carlos*, neither I nor Mancini, whom I permitted to read it, thought it useful to deliver it. Mazzucato, who is a bit of a gossip, would perhaps have mentioned it to Ricordi or to others, and people would have turned on you, though your letter was written quite calmly and the criticisms seemed true and pondered" [Nardi, p. 237].

40. "Stupendous, but quite difficult..." Giulio Ricordi wrote from Paris [letter of Clara Maffei, 27 February 1867, to Franco Faccio in De Rensis, *Faccio e Verdi*, p. 57].

I'm not at all surprised by the conversion (genuine or false) of the Apostles of the Future. Who, except the blind, can deny the light of the sun?

[Abbiati, 3:150]

Conversion (only of the *avveniristi?* Or, on an artistic level, also of Verdi?) seemed to be the order of the day. For that matter, the "Apostles" had by now already taken their place in the leadership of the "cultural establishment." The future was in their hands. But it was also—as *Don Carlos* was there to prove—in Verdi's.

◆§EIGHTEEN SIXTY-EIGHT WAS THE YEAR OF *Mefistofele* and a direct confrontation between Verdi and Boito, with La Scala as their arena. Preceded, in January, by the separate publication of its libretto,[41] Boito's opera opened at La Scala in an atmosphere of incredible expectation on the evening of 5 March, three weeks before the local premiere there of Verdi's *Don Carlos. Mefistofele* was conducted by Boito, to whom Mazzucato had been forced to cede his baton at the suggestion of Filippi. Perhaps, taking Wagner as his example, Filippi wanted to see in Boito a realization of "a complete trinity: poet, composer, and conductor."[42]

The enormous fiasco of *Mefistofele* is a familiar part of operatic history and need not be described here. The evening got off to a promising start, helped perhaps, according to one spectator,[43] by the exaggerated applause of a clique of aristocrats and wealthy bourgeois concentrated in the boxes, all friends and admirers of the composer, along with the court of the "sphericals."[44] It is worth quoting the opinion Giulio

41. This was a rather unusual procedure as far as the Italian operatic theater was concerned. The publication of the *Mefistofele* libretto was intended not so much to swell the advance publicity as to follow Wagner's example (the German composer published his librettos years before the operas were composed and performed), allowing future spectators to study and better comprehend a work with some unconventional, unfamiliar aspects. Received with great interest by the critics, the poem of *Mefistofele* prompted mixed opinions, but largely favorable.

42. Letter from Mazzucato to Mariani, 24 February 1868, in Nardi, p. 250.

43. Broglio in *Palcoscenico,* 8 March 1868: "[After the first part of the second act] for all the rest of the performance there was nothing but persistent dissent, between the disapproval of the stalls and the noisy applause of all the female pleiad that peoples the first and second rows of the boxes." And in the issue of 15 March: "Boito was really assassinated by his fanatical admirers, who, ignoring his own plea, wanted to *force the public's hand* to create a triumph, and in this way they aroused a reaction as strong as it was deplorable" [Nardi, p. 273].

44. See Nardi, pp. 279–94; and also G. Tintori, "Un libretto rivelatore," *L'opera,* nos. 14/15 (1969): 11–14.

Ricordi expressed in the *Gazzetta musicale di Milano* at the conclusion of his critical analysis, for this opinion was the basis of the continuing, stubborn operation of the publisher, now determined to bring about Boito's collaboration *as poet* with Verdi. Ricordi wrote:

> Boito has certainly written an opera that is not without many merits, but also not without many faults. Now are the latter due to his inexperience of the stage, of theatrical effect? [. . .] Well, with all the sincerity inspired by my warm and heartfelt friendship for Boito, I dare say to him clearly: You will be a poet, a distinguished man of letters, but never a composer of works for the theater.[45]

The failure of *Mefistofele* had a profound effect not only on Boito's career but also on his personality. There can be no doubt that this event affected his activity as an artist and as an intellectual. The impetuous and iconoclastic character of the early artistic battles gave way to a more reflective, distrustful, and—especially—detached attitude: "His innovatory impulse [. . .] seems somehow tamed" [Lavagetto, p. xi]. On the one hand he concentrated on his opera *Nerone*, which he was never to finish, and on the other he dissipated his energies in a thousand different activities: librettos for other composers (Ponchielli, Catalani, Coronaro, Dominiceti), which he signed with the anagram Tobia Gorrio; the translation of operas by Wagner, Weber, and Glinka; not to mention countless committee meetings, consultations, official missions. His poetic vein also dried up, and he withdrew more and more into himself, concentrating on the worship of the great men of the past (Dante in poetry, Shakespeare in the theater, Palestrina and Bach in music). He began to avoid what was new, the very area for which he had fought so many battles, and he seemed almost to fear any movement that might undermine firmly established categories. Still his generosity, his loyal self-sacrifice, were to remain distinguishing aspects of his complex personality: his devotion to Verdi offers a splendid example of these qualities. But Boito the man grew more and more remote, erecting

---

45. *Gazzetta musicale di Milano,* 15 March 1868. Several commentators had expressed similar opinions. See that of the *scapigliato* Iginio Tarchetti in *L'emporio pittoresco,* 15–21 March 1868: "Signor Boito should believe that the evidence he has provided in literature is considerably superior, and this failure would be a genuine stroke of luck for Italian letters if it were to make him resolve to cultivate them and to proceed only along that path, where he could become supreme." Also C. M. in *Cosmorama pittorico,* 15 March 1868, wrote: "A strange thing, as the composer is strange: in the text, also written by him, there is more poetry, more vitality than in the music; which leads us to believe that Signor Boito will prove a better poet than composer."

a wall of tetchy, almost obsessive isolation around his private life.[46] In the end his friendship with Verdi was to be virtually the center of his existence.

◆§ VERDI'S ONLY SURVIVING REFERENCE to the news of the *Mefistofele* fiasco is a brief mention in a letter of 12 March to his French publisher Escudier: "I won't say anything to you about *Mefistofele;* you must already know about its results and the scandal of the third night" [Nardi, p. 313]. A week earlier, on 6 March, when he probably was not yet aware of the opera's outcome, Verdi had written to his old friend, Count Opprandino Arrivabene:

> I know, too, that there is a *music of the future,* but I think at present and will continue to think next year that to make *a shoe* you need some *leather* and some *skins!...* What do you think of this stupid comparison, which means that to make an opera you must first have music in your body?!... I declare that I am and will be an enthusiastic admirer of the *avveniristi* provided they make some music for me... in whatever form, with whatever system, etc., but it must be music!... [. . .] Rest assured. I may very well lack the strength to arrive where I want to go, but I know what I *want.*
>
> [Alberti, pp. 82–83]

Meanwhile, he resisted the repeated invitations of his publisher, of the impresario, and of the interpreters to come to Milan and supervise the rehearsals of *Don Carlos.* It was not only the fiasco of *Mefistofele* that restrained him, but also his fear that, thanks especially to that fiasco, things in the theater were in a state of confusion. When Giulio Ricordi insisted that "this is the opportune moment," Verdi, exploded in a letter of 13 March:

> So "this is the opportune moment"?!!... Idiots!... What?!... Am I a man to sit on the ruin of others? I am one of those who go straight ahead,

---

46. In an obituary of Boito published in the Trieste paper *Lavoratore* in 1918, the composer Antonio Smareglia recounted an episode dating back to 1870. Told by Faccio to go to Boito and ask him for his copy of the Bach *St. Matthew Passion,* "I rang the Maestro's bell. I heard the sound of slow footsteps approaching, a faint metallic click, and from the peephole of the door I saw peering at me the eye of the Maestro, who didn't want any visitors. I waited a few moments, then the door opened. Arrigo Boito, with an army rifle held against his right shoulder and aimed at me, said curtly: 'What do you want?' 'Maestro Faccio, my teacher, would like you to lend him the *St. Matthew Passion,* which he wants to read and which I also hope to hear...' 'So you want to know Bach?' 'Of course!' 'Then come in!'" [M. Smareglia, *Antonio Smareglia nella storia del teatro melodrammatico italiano* (Pola, 1934), pp. 324–25].

not looking to left or right, a man who does what he can, what he believes in, who does not want *opportune moments* or supporters or protectors, or *claque,* or *réclame,* or cliques. I love Art when it is presented in a worthy way, and not the scandals that have just occurred at La Scala. If there is one thing in the world that I am happy about it is that I did not go to Milan at this moment.[47]

❧AN EVENT THAT TOOK PLACE in that late March, shortly after *Mefistofele* and *Don Carlos,* seems to have initiated the process of Boito's gradual reconciliation with Verdi.[48] The Minister of Education Broglio wrote a public letter to Rossini that, in the circumstances, was far more disrespectful to Verdi and his fellow composers than the imprudent "sapphic ode."[49] Indignant, Verdi sent back the title of Commander of the Crown of Italy, which he had just received;[50] and the author of the "sapphic ode" himself (also directly affected by the minister's odd observations) gave Broglio a highly effective and ironic drubbing in the columns of the Milanese paper *Il pungolo.* In the issue of 21 May, Boito published a "Letter in Four Paragraphs"[51] that Frank Walker rightly considers the most witty and amusing of all Boito's prose works. The second paragraph includes a view of Verdi:

> Your Excellency lacks not only the most elementary notion of diplomacy, but even of common politeness, insulting Verdi and Mercadante only a few days after the king had bestowed new honors on them. God forbid that I should ever think of diminishing the august figure of Rossini, but still I cannot diminish the history of Italian opera. "After Rossini what have we had?" Your Excellency asks. Eh, nothing; from 1829 till now only trifles have been produced! *Nugaeque canorae!* In '31,

47. ISV. This letter appears in Abbiati (3:166), but with slight differences.

48. For the whole incident, see Abbiati, 3:190–210.

49. "Among the responsibilities of my ministry there is also music, to which I am as passionately devoted as I am, alas, ignorant of it. Now what is the state of music in Italy, or rather, in the world? [. . .] After Rossini, or in other words, for the last forty years, what do we have? Four operas of Meyerbeer and... How can such serious sterility be remedied?" [Abbiati, 3:191–92].

50. "I have received the diploma that names me Commander of the Crown of Italy. This order was established to honor those who, with arms, or in literature or sciences or the arts, have benefited today's Italy. A letter to Rossini from Your Excellency, though *ignorant* in music (as you yourself say, and I believe), decrees that for forty years no opera has been written in Italy? Why then am I sent this decoration? There is certainly a mistake in the address, and I am returning it" [Alberti, p. 88].

51. Published in Boito, pp. 1285–92, and in Abbiati, 3:203–10.

for example, there was *Norma,* a trifle that inspired Rossini to say: "I will compose no more," and he kept his word. Then in '35 *I puritani,* another trifle! Then in '40 *La favorita* and in '43 *Don Sebastiano: nugaeque canorae!* In '51 *Rigoletto* and in '53 *Il trovatore,* and all of Verdi's theater, fascinating, glorious, fertile! And since you were kind enough to mention Meyerbeer to us, why didn't you mention Halévy, Gounod, Weber, Wag——? (Don't take fright.) As Your Excellency can see, there's something for every taste. But Your Excellency calls this history sterile. [. . .] I must tell you that Rossini is the greatest jokester that ever existed, and this is proved in the reply that Your Excellency received, a reply that, apart from the fact that it took its own good time in arriving, spatters irony like ink. In choosing to act more like a theater critic than like a minister, Your Excellency has got himself into a tangled mess. Yesterday a trick of Rossini's, today a rebuff from Verdi, who has sent back the cross of the Crown of Italy.

And in paragraph three:

As far as the question of musical decadence goes, Signor Minister, I am in a position to dispel your fears. I must inform Your Excellency, first of all, that Verdi is alive and well and is still writing. Further, Your Excellency should be informed that in Italy there are numerous young people who are thinking and studying and working intrepidly, and I can also assure you that this incessant work will surely produce good fruit, such as is born from strong belief and stern conscience.

[Boito, pp. 1290–91]

Boito's "letter" gained the attention of Verdi's friend and confidant Angelo Mariani, who wrote to Tito Ricordi about it on 23 May:

I have just this moment received your letter of yesterday with *Il pungolo.* I liked Boito's letter very much; congratulate him for me.

[Abbiati, 3:193]

And if Mariani read Boito's words, it is more than likely that Verdi read them as well. But was the "sapphic ode" forgotten? Not in the least, as we will see.

IN THE COURSE OF THAT SUMMER the question of revising the denouement of *La forza del destino* arose again, in view of a possible production at La Scala. Ghislanzoni now, rather than Boito, was the poet suggested by Ricordi for the necessary adjustments. Paying a visit to Sant'Agata at the end of May, Giulio Ricordi took the writer along with him for a first encounter with Verdi. It had been more than twenty years since the composer had seen Ghislanzoni[52] (at that time a promising baritone). But Verdi did not take up the work of revision until autumn, agreeing at that time to Ghislanzoni's collaboration and arranging for a production the following winter at La Scala, committing himself to supervise the rehearsals. On 24 January of the new year, having completed the revision, Verdi went to Milan, returning for the first time in twenty years to the city and to the theater that had witnessed his debut and his early triumphs. A month later, 27 February 1869, the new *Forza del destino* was given, conducted by Franco Faccio. This peace with Milan and La Scala also comprised an effective reconciliation with Faccio, a total reconciliation that was to be sealed a year later when Verdi, in February of 1870, asked Camille Du Locle (one of the librettists of *Don Carlos*) to intercede with Victorien Sardou and obtain permission for the younger musician to set the French writer's drama *Patrie!*[53]

Meanwhile, encouraged by the success of the new *Forza del destino* and by Verdi's happy collaboration with the former *scapigliato* Ghislanzoni, Giulio Ricordi began to dream of a *Nerone* by Verdi on Boito's libretto. The publisher did not dare speak of it directly with Verdi; at first he merely hinted to Giuseppina, in a letter from Milan on 5 March 1869: "I have in mind a great and important project. To see it fulfilled I will need your valuable advice and help" [ISV]. Giulio's next letter is not known, but its contents—concerning an opera to be written for La Scala—can be inferred from a drafted reply by Giuseppina, dated 23 March:

> Now we come to the important part of your letter of 18 March. In a roundabout and very delicate way I sounded out the mood, tested the ground; but it is sad for me to tell you, dear Giulio, that at least for the present, I am convinced we cannot obtain anything of what you and Milan were wishing for. Time is pressing and Verdi feels a certain prostration after that *nervous* fever of the staging of an opera; he needs calm, and no mention of theaters; he needs, so to speak, idleness. In the end, idleness becomes a need for pleasure! Add to this the thought

---

52. Ghislanzoni has left a vivid account of this visit: "La casa di Verdi a Sant'Agata," published in the *Gazzetta musicale di Milano*, 26 July 1868 (reprinted various times, including M. Conati, *Interviste e incontri con Verdi* [Milan: Il Formichiere, 1980], pp. 66–78).

53. "Would you like to help me perform a good deed? It concerns a young composer, among our best, who has written an *Amleto* and whose name is Faccio. This young composer would like to set Sardou's *Patrie!* but he would need the permission of the play's author. He has turned to me, thinking that I know Sardou; and so I turn to you" (10 February 1870) [ISV].

of Bologna[54] and, further, the commitments with other theaters, if he were to decide to compose. All these reasons rob me of the courage to ask him for a formal *encounter* to propose the important matter you have charged me with. I am sure he would answer me with a laugh, and with one of those curt, polar-bear remarks that are best avoided. [. . .] What you must prevent is a letter from the city government offering him a contract—he seems ill to me and this would perhaps put him in a bad humor. [. . .] The matter must not be broached *officially,* but you must be content, if anything, to write him privately, as a friend.

[ISV]

Accepting Giuseppina's advice, Giulio Ricordi addressed Verdi directly, "as a friend," to inform the composer of his "dream." Ricordi's letter has not survived, but the composer's answer, dated 1 April, states:

I have never been a saint, but I know about dreams, though I explain them in my own fashion. I have the presentiment that yours is not, for the present, a good dream!

[Abbiati, 3:261]

This is perhaps the moment when the matter of the Boito collaboration, stubbornly pursued by Giulio Ricordi, began to move away from the area of pure ideology—though the "sapphic ode," as we will see, was to persist still in Verdi's memory, along with his dislike of *quartettismo, avvenirismo,* the pushing of instrumental music, and the proclamations about art that, with all the rest, seemed to characterize the position of the *scapigliati* and the younger generation. The question was now moving in a different, more fertile direction. The chief problem that the shrewd Giulio Ricordi now faced was to overcome the obstacle mentioned at the outset of this essay: namely, the artistic independence of the two men. On the one hand there was Verdi, virtual author of the librettos of his operas, who relegated the librettist only to the role of *versifier;* and on the other hand there was Boito, at once poet and musician, with his own deep-rooted convictions about musical drama.

Despite Verdi's reply, Giulio would not give up. He went on, patiently weaving his plot and waiting for the right moment. Much of the year was spent, meanwhile, on the "mass for the dead," Verdi's projected collective requiem with which Italy's composers would honor the memory of Rossini, who had died in November of the previous year.[55]

54. She was referring to the Mass for Rossini.
55. For the genesis of this Mass and its failure to be performed, see especially

The plan, as is well known, came to nothing, chiefly because of the in-dolence of the committee established to carry out the project.[56] Ricordi himself was a member of the committee; but Verdi unjustly accused Angelo Mariani of not having done everything necessary for the real-ization of the project. This episode of the Mass for Rossini was fated to spoil forever the close friendship that until then had bound composer and conductor.[57]

◂The Dream of *Nerone*

At the beginning of the new year the figure of Nero again appeared, but this time it was Verdi who evinced a certain interest in the Roman emperor. Contemplating negotiations with the Opéra for a new con-tract, he mentioned Nero in a letter of 23 January 1870 to Du Locle. After asking his correspondent to send him some writings of Wagner, Verdi continued:

> Please send also *Acte et Néron*. I still believe that *Nerone* could be a subject for a grand opera, naturally written in my own way. In that way it would become impossible for the Opéra, but very possible here.
>
> [Abbiati, 3:328]

The search for a suitable opera subject suggests the composer's intention, three years after *Don Carlos*, to return to the theater. On 3 February he wrote to Giulio Ricordi:

> Answering you the other day, in my haste "il meglio mi scordavo" ["I forgot the best," a quotation from Rossini's *Barbiere*]:
>
> 1. To thank you for the translation of the Piave Album [. . .]
>
> 2. To tell you that as far as writing an opera is concerned, it is not the task of composing that weighs on me, but rather I am held back by the difficulty of finding a subject to my liking, a poet *to my liking*, and a performance that would be new and *to my liking!*
>
> And, for that matter, for what country would I write? France?! Poor me! Every time I have set foot in those theaters I have always had

---

M. Girardi and P. Petrobelli, eds., *"Messa per Rossini": La storia, il testo, la musica* (Parma: Istituto di Studi Verdiani; Milan: Ricordi, 1988).

56. It is worth recalling that the impresario Scalaberni, publicly justifying his behavior in a letter to the *Monitore di Bologna,* lamented the absence, among the composers chosen, of younger musicians like Boito, Dall'Argine, Faccio, and Marchetti. Cf. Abbiati, 3:328.

57. Walker, *Man Verdi,* pp. 350–59; also C. M. Mossa, "Una 'Messa' per la storia," in Girardi and Petrobelli, pp. 11–56.

a fever; I can't contemplate what would happen now that I have become more difficult.

[Abbiati, 3:330]

Giulio Ricordi, who had had Nero in the back of his mind for so
long, was naturally excited by the composer's interest in that emperor.
Verdi himself spoke to Giulio about the subject when the publisher
made a brief visit to Genoa between 8 and 9 February. On his return to
Milan, Giulio wrote to the composer immediately, on 10 February:

> Today, with some adroit questioning, I managed to find out that Boito
> has not begun setting *Nerone,* whose libretto he has not yet finished.
> Now it is a matter of finding a way to discover what ideas he has on
> the issue: if he is counting absolutely on that subject—but without giv-
> ing away what this is all about. From a few words spoken to me by a
> third party, I infer that he has dealt with the subject from a point of
> view that is *different from the one you mentioned to me.* To be sure, *Nerone*
> is a splendid, grand, interesting subject; and before shelving it,
> Maestro, don't you think it's worth making an attempt in this direc-
> tion? We exchanged only a few words about it, because, from what
> Boito himself has told me, it seemed that not only was the libretto fin-
> ished but that he had also begun setting it. Now, according to this re-
> cent information, this is not so. Please let me know what you think
> about this.

[Abbiati, 3:330–31]

Verdi replied on 14 February:

> A drama for music is a very difficult thing! The more I think about it,
> the greater the obstacles loom. It is surely not impossible to find a his-
> torical event suitable to be set to music, but the difficult part is turning
> this event into the drama itself, adding the action, that is. Both in Nero
> and in Alaric we have great scenes, characters, costumes, spectacle,
> etc., etc., but a *creation* would be needed, such as, for example, Fidès
> in *Le prophète,* or Valentine in *Les Huguenots.* No mere bagatelle!
> Write Madrid for me and have the following two dramas sent:
> The *Venganza catalana* of Gutiérrez
> *El zapatero y el rey* of Zorrilla.

[Abbiati, 3:331–32]

After Giulio urged Giuseppina to encourage the composer's plan to
write a new opera, she replied on 24 February:

You make yourself very clear in Italian, in Milanese dialect, and God only knows in how many other languages!... You also know how to apply as required hot or cold sauces, sweet or spicy, artistic, diplomatic, for your talent, "it must be agreed," is great, subtle, and multiform.

Though my female vanity is flattered by a masterly hand, and though, as an artist and an Italian, I have the greatest desire that Verdi be persuaded to take up his pen once more, I still have enough common sense to declare that no hints of mine will have any weight on the scales of *yes* and *no,* though you, and many others, could or can believe the opposite.

[Walker, Uomo Verdi, pp. 566–67]

◄§THE *NERONE* PROJECT FADED OUT, at least for the moment. But, almost suddenly, the project of *Aida* took shape that spring. After some highly secret negotiations between Draneht Bey, representing the viceroy of Egypt, and Du Locle, the two men brought up the matter with Verdi. Giulio Ricordi was totally in the dark. Only when the agreement was virtually concluded and the libretto completed was he informed, by a letter dated 25 June, in which the composer, having rapidly summarized the story of the negotiations, asked Giulio to approach Ghislanzoni, to *versify* the libretto:

Now the libretto must be considered, or, rather, the versification, because at this point only the verses are needed. Would Ghislanzoni be able and willing to do this job for me? It would not be original work: explain that clearly to him; it is only a matter of making the verses.[58]

"A poet to my liking," the composer had written a few months before: in other words, a *versifier.* Therefore he turned to Ghislanzoni, who had already proved his worth with the revisions of *La forza del destino.* The Franco-Prussian War caused the Cairo premiere of *Aida* to be postponed for a year; meanwhile, at the beginning of 1871, as Faccio's opera *Amleto* was about to be staged at La Scala (and as singers were being sought for both the Cairo and the Scala *Aida*), the *Nerone* project surfaced again, thanks to the stubborn Giulio Ricordi. On 26 January, after some meetings with Boito (probably during the *Amleto* rehearsals), the publisher sent Verdi a long letter; this can be considered the moment when the foundations of a working partnership were laid, if not for *Nerone,* then for something else:

58. G. Carrara Verdi, "Preliminari di *Aida,*" in *Biblioteca 70,* 2 [1971]:15.

I have sent you a libretto of *Amleto,* and this prompts me to mention immediately a *great project!!* for, as you know, I am a greater ruminant than an ox!!... Now then: Two or three times you mentioned *Nerone* to me... and I saw that this subject did not displease you. Yesterday Boito came to see me and *bang!* I fired the shot. Boito asked me to let him think about it overnight, and this morning he was here and we talked at length about the matter. The conclusion is that Boito would consider himself the most *happy,* the most *fortunate* of men if he were to write the libretto of *Nerone* for you; and he would gladly and immediately give up the idea of writing the music himself. Boito told me frankly that he felt he would be able to fulfill all your requirements, that he would never work with more enthusiasm, more impetus, than for this project, as it represents that *very rare* combination of poet and composer both convinced of the beauty of the subject, and that he feels there is no more vast or beautiful subject than this *Nerone,* so suited to the genius of Verdi. I am perhaps too involved, and too insignificant to be able to utter a word on the question!... But if I had the courage, I could not refrain from begging you with all the power of my spirit to take this proposal into serious consideration, to keep this idea alive, for it would give Italian Art a new musical masterpiece, perhaps one of its greatest! I now know the role you play in the fashioning of a libretto, and Boito under your direction, would work well, very well!... and similarly, it would be hard to find a versifier more splendid and more elegant than he, both in form and content. But in any case this is a matter to be approached very calmly, and only when the time seems opportune to you. In the meanwhile, however, it might be well if you could write me something about it, also so that Boito can make his plans; I don't have to say that the most scrupulous silence is necessary. I *dare* (there's a method in my madness) hope for the best!... and with full knowledge I can send you a word of commendation for this young man gifted with a truly special talent, and who would deserve great fortune. It's a pity I can't go on, as I would have much to say to you concerning some precious confessions that, in a moment of enthusiasm inspired by the idea of doing *Nerone* for you, Boito made to me this morning on the subject of your musical qualities.[59]

So the *poet* Boito was cynically demoted by his friend Giulio to the rank of *versifier* (though a "splendid" and "elegant" one); the very role that Verdi, since the days of his collaboration with Piave, had assigned

59. A. Luzio, "Giuseppe Verdi e i suoi editori di Francia e d'Italia," part 2, *Nuova antologia* (February 1939):259–60.

to librettists. In his obstinate determination to achieve the long-standing dream, Giulio Ricordi managed to arrive at a first substantial result: demolishing the poet's independence and thus removing, as least as far as the future was concerned, the chief obstacle to the collaboration. Walker baldly states there is "something monstrous about Ricordi's ready sacrifice of his friend's cherished ambition"; and it is true, as Walker further observes, that "no praise could be too high for Boito's own conduct on this occasion. The fact that nothing came of the project in the end does not detract from the magnanimity of his renunciation in Verdi's favour of his long-cherished dream [Walker, *Man Verdi*, p. 466]. Once the poet was persuaded, Giulio Ricordi still had to persuade the composer. The arguments employed by the astute publisher in his latest letter could well have opened a crack in Verdi's disposition. But the time was not yet ripe. Still in the process of launching his most recent opera, *Aida*, the composer would not commit himself, merely remarking by return mail:

> I cannot answer you today about the *Nerone* business! I haven't a minute to waste. Great project, you say! Quite true, but is it feasible? We shall see!
>
> [Abbiati, 3:358–59]

Nevertheless, Ricordi insisted on 29 January:

> The *Nerone* business is such an important thing that it must be considered seriously. Now *Aida* is still on the hob, so, as I understand very well, this is not something to be decided *à tambour battant;* and further, once decided, it will take time to conclude. Still I thought it was opportune actually to mention it, since in the happy event that it can be arranged, it would be pointless for Boito to continue working, and, similarly, it would be an immense, immeasurable, irreparable harm if you, liking the subject, had dismissed the idea out of a more than kindly consideration for Boito. I have merely kept the idea alive, and there is time and space to entertain it and ponder it; but surely if you write *Nerone*, it will amaze the world, for I truly would not know where to find a more beautiful subject, or more beautiful situations, or passions more suited to making your portentous genius shine!
>
> [Luzio, "Verdi," pp. 260–61]

Verdi replied on 30 January:

> Now I will write you about *Nerone*. I don't have to tell you again how much I love this subject. And, similarly, I don't have to add how pleased I would have been to have as my collaborator a young poet

whose abundant talent I have had occasion to admire, most recently in this *Amleto*. But you know my situation and my commitments well enough to understand what a grievous concern assuming this new burden would cause me. I am in quite a singular position. I lack the courage to say: "Let's do it," nor do I dare renounce such a beautiful project. But tell me, dear Giulio, couldn't we leave this matter in abeyance for a while, and come back to it later on? I have an opera awaiting its destiny. I have a commitment, as you know, with Du Locle: a commitment that will probably come to nothing, but in view of the sad wartime events at present, I would never dissolve this agreement without the consent of my poor friend. I have some other little things to deal with, etc., etc. So let's get these nuisances off our backs, then we will be able to concentrate exclusively, persistently on the great subject. I would not ask Boito to remain at my disposal. Heaven forbid! I would not have that at any price. Let him go on with his work, as if we had never spoken. Later, if the thing is still feasible and suits us both, we will pick it up again and settle it in a few words. I also desire, in all this, the greatest secrecy.

[Abbiati, 3:359–60]

Verdi was cautious, perhaps afraid of a close confrontation on the artistic plane with the author of *Mefistofele* before having carefully studied every aspect of a collaboration that would be unusual for him. After all, Boito was no Ghislanzoni, still less a Piave. For the moment the question was shelved. And in the end there was to be no further talk of a *Nerone* to be set by Verdi, despite some additional effort by Giulio Ricordi.

◄§ON 9 FEBRUARY 1871, Faccio's *Amleto* was a failure at La Scala, chiefly because of a flawed performance determined by the indisposition of the tenor Tiberini, the protagonist. With the failure of *Amleto* (which had enjoyed an authentic success a few years earlier in Genoa), the *avvenir-isti* lost their chance to avenge on the stage of the Milan opera house the disaster of *Mefistofele*. Faccio, disheartened, withdrew the score. On this occasion Verdi too was genuinely saddened, as he now held Faccio in high esteem (and had expressed, as we have seen, a flattering opinion of Boito's text). The older composer wrote on 11 February to Giulio Ricordi:

I was very sad to hear about *Amleto!* Oh, the theater! Oh, the theater! There really seemed to be some kind of curse on this *Amleto!* Faccio must not lose heart for this; and I praise your continued faith in that young man, though I have never heard or seen a note of his opera. Tiberini, if he is ill, should go to a milder climate for three or four weeks, and, if he is a sincere artist and feels some friendship for Faccio, he should sing Amleto, perhaps at the end of the season, for at least two or three evenings. It would be a true misfortune if this does not happen, and you should use all your influence to see that it does.

[ISV]

Three days later Faccio himself wrote Verdi:

Giulio read me part of a letter of yours that referred to the unhappy outcome of *Amleto:* that kind and precious evidence of your interest in me was a tacit and healthful comfort, for which I thank you with moved and grateful spirit. [. . .] what most saddens me is the realization that the total absence of Amleto in this *Amleto* prevents me from receiving the public's opinion on that one performance of my opera, as far as the flaws in my music go. I don't know if I can dare ask you to take a look at some excerpts of *Amleto* that Giulio is bringing to your house. The stern judgment of Giuseppe Verdi would be invaluable for me and would give me food for thought even after an easy success in the theater.

[De Rensis, *Faccio e Verdi,* pp. 116–17]

Meanwhile, just after the *Amleto,* the conductor Eugenio Terziani resigned from La Scala to return to the Teatro Apollo in Rome. He was succeeded by Faccio, who had won himself an excellent local reputation as a conductor since the autumn season of 1868 at the Teatro Carcano, under Giulio Ricordi's management. This assumption of power on the part of an ex-*scapigliato* in Milan's leading opera house constituted another essential column of the edifice Giulio was slowly constructing to realize his cherished dream of Boito's collaboration with the reluctant maestro.

◆≤WHETHER BECAUSE OF THE POSSIBLE COLLABORATION with Verdi, towards which Giulio Ricordi was pushing him, or because of a need to overcome his disorientation after the fiasco of *Mefistofele,* Boito had meanwhile set aside the libretto of *Nerone* in order to undertake something else. In the spring of 1871, his interest as poet and composer became focused on a new theatrical idea: *Ero e Leandro,*[60] a simple story

---

60. Nardi (pp. 337–41) established, on the basis of some letters to Arrigo from his brother Camillo, the precise period of this new artistic enterprise.

quite unlike *Mefistofele* and *Nerone*. He quickly completed the libretto[61] and began setting it. But he was soon distracted by, and to some extent personally involved in, a profoundly significant artistic event being prepared in Bologna: the staging of a Wagner opera for the first time in Italy. *Lohengrin,* conducted by Angelo Mariani, opened on 1 November amid ardent debate about the "prophet of the future." Despite a strong hostile faction, the opera had a warm success. Though Boito at the time of the "sapphic ode" had called Wagner "a false apostle [. . .], a false precursor, one of those dangerous propagators of ill-said truths, ill-thought, ill-heard, one of those ravers who, though they have an idea of light, spread darkness, pompous sowers of sensational confusion, ruiners of theories with practice, and of practice with theories, minds swollen with vanity rather than nourished with knowledge,"[62] now the young Italian wrote the composer about the happy event, and Wagner thanked him with a public "Letter to an Italian Friend About the Performance of *Lohengrin* in Bologna."[63]

Verdi, his curiosity aroused, went to a later performance of *Lohengrin,* on the evening of 19 November. In the darkness of box number 23 of the second tier, he made notes in his copy of the vocal score, still preserved at Sant'Agata, jotting down his impressions of the work and of the performance.[64] Boito was also present that evening. A Bologna reporter seized this opportunity to imagine and describe a meeting, which then actually took place, as we will see, quite accidentally, not in the theater but at the Bologna train station after the opera's end.

Here is the story as it appeared in the *Gazzetta dell'Emilia* on Tuesday, 21 November:

> *Verdi's modesty.* We have already reported, in the previous issue of this paper, how on Sunday evening at the Teatro Comunale, at the end of the second act of *Lohengrin,* the entire, numerous audience stood up to hail the illustrious Maestro Verdi, who was in a second-tier box; and we reported also that the illustrious Maestro, though the applause

61. Indirectly confirmed by a letter of 10 May from the painter Luigi Chialiva: "I can't tell you how much I enjoyed reading your work. I find it very beautiful indeed... Now that the libretto exists, it is the music's turn, and I am convinced that this will correspond fully to the poetry" [Nardi, p. 338].

62. "Mendelssohn in Italia," in *Giornale della Società del Quartetto,* 1864; reprinted in Boito, p. 1256.

63. Published in *La perseveranza,* Milan, and in the *Monitore di Bologna,* and reprinted in other periodicals, including the *Gazzetta musicale di Milano,* no. 47, 19 November 1871: 393.

64. Listed in Abbiati, 3:508–11.

went on for several minutes, did not show himself to the public because of that exquisite delicacy and immense modesty that are his.

To some friends who questioned him on the matter, the Maestro replied laconically: "It is not a habit of mine, even if it had been one of my own operas."

That same Sunday evening, as we had announced, Maestro Boito was also in the Teatro Comunale. Speaking with Verdi, he said he had already seen some parts of *Aida,* which will be staged during the coming season at *La Scala* in Milan, and turning to other friends present, he added: "Verdi, in this latest opera, has become young again, he has gone back to the days of *Rigoletto,*" to which words Verdi replied with singular modesty: "Wait till *Aida* has been staged before praising it."

We have chosen to report the above in order to dispel any malevolent interpretation of the most reserved behavior of Verdi on Sunday evening at the Teatro Comunale.

In reading this article, Verdi was alarmed not so much by the invention of an encounter in the theater as by the possibility that Boito might have been allowed more than just a curious glance at the score of *Aida,* which was being prepared just at that time at the firm of Ricordi. He hastened to ask Giulio for an explanation (letter dated 23 November):

> Read this little article. What it says is partially true. Boito (whom I saw for a moment at the station) did not say those words to me, however; he said them at the club or in some society. So Boito has seen the opera!... and Filippi has also seen it!! You are wrong to show *Aida* to outsiders. Advance opinions are worthless and do no one any good. Besides, you should always distrust such opinions, whether they come from friends or enemies. Further, I absolutely do not want *réclame.* For better or worse, let the public judge on opening night. What is done is done, but from this moment on, I beg you, seriously, let there be no talk about *Aida,* and let no one examine it and judge it. Don't worry: either *Aida* will be effective and there will be no need of *réclame;* or it will not be, and these premature judgments will swell the *fiasco.*
>
> [Abbiati, 3 : 507–8, 513]

Giulio then published, in the *Gazzetta musicale di Milano,* a denial to satisfy the composer:

> The *Monitore di Bologna*[65] has supplied its readers with a canard concocted with great imagination in last Monday's issue. [. . .]

---

65. Actually, as we have seen, it was the *Gazzetta dell'Emilia* of Tuesday. The *Monitore di Bologna* contains no reference to the subject in the issues of November 1871. Probably

Here is the actual truth:

Signor Boito conversed with Giuseppe Verdi in the waiting room of the Bologna station at 3 A.M., after the performance of *Lohengrin*. The conversation chiefly concerned the difficulty of sleeping on the train.[66]

At the same time, the publisher sent an explanation to the composer. The contents of the letter are unknown, for, like many other letters of this period, it is missing. Verdi's reply of 26 November, however, gives an idea:

You attached too much importance to my last letter; but you did very well to write me so *frankly*. In this way things are always made clear.

There must be no gossip about this business, but this is how things stand. In Bologna Boito said he had seen *Aida* or *at least various pieces and he had found them good*, etc... This was told me by people who had heard Boito's words, whether at the club or in some society, I don't know. Filippi wrote to Clarina that he had seen *Aida* and he liked it, etc., etc... I was naturally led to believe that you had let those two read the opera. If that is not the case, then they were wrong to say so.

But let's say no more about it, and I beg you not to speak of it with Clarina or Filippi or Boito. Write *"closed"* on this account.

[Abbiati, 3:513]

⬥The Return of *Mefistofele*

On 24 December *Aida* triumphed in Cairo. Seven weeks later, on 8 February 1872, the opera was given at La Scala, where it was conducted by Franco Faccio. This was thought to be Verdi's farewell to the theater. And after this presumed farewell any projected collaboration with Boito seemed out of the question. But not to Giulio Ricordi, who was still capable of slyly and patiently awaiting the opportune moment. In this period Verdi was carefully guiding the first steps of his new opera, going personally to stage it in Parma, and then in Naples, seizing this opportunity to develop and consolidate the reform of performance practice he had initiated with the revised *Forza del destino* at La Scala. Boito meanwhile was engaged in composing *Ero e Leandro*. He was working on it still in the winter of 1873. In the following spring the music apparently was already "completely or almost completely writ-

the editor of the *Gazzetta musicale di Milano* commented on the news item sent by Verdi without any indication of the source, and simply attributed it to the most authoritative paper of Bologna at the time.

66. In the "Rubrica amena" (lighter news), no. 49, 3 December 1871: 405.

ten" [Nardi, p. 367] and the opera would soon be performed,[67] perhaps in Bologna; but then the whole project was suddenly abandoned, probably because a revival of *Mefistofele* seemed in sight and because Boito had also become occupied with writing a libretto for Ponchielli, *La Gioconda*. The libretto of *Ero e Leandro* was eventually ceded to Bottesini (1879), then to Luigi Mancinelli (1896). Only two melodic numbers were saved by Boito from the music he had written for this opera: an "offstage chorus of sailors in the distance," published by Ricordi under the title *La notte diffonde* as a barcarole for four mixed voices with piano accompaniment; and the duet of Ero and Leandro, "Lontano, lontano, lontano," which was inserted into the third act of the definitive version of *Mefistofele*.

In March 1873 *Lohengrin* was a failure at La Scala, despite Faccio's care in preparing the performance. After the fiascos of *Mefistofele* and *Amleto*, this third failure seemed to deny the *avveniristi* any chance of gaining a foothold on the Milanese stage. Now they turned their attention to Bologna, the cradle of the Wagner cult in Italy, where the previous November a second Wagner opera, *Tannhäuser*, again under the baton of Mariani, had been warmly received. And Bologna seemed to encourage Boito's lingering hope for a possible revival of *Mefistofele*.

On 22 May Alessandro Manzoni died in Milan. This death inspired Verdi to compose a "mass for the dead," of which he already had in his files the *Libera me* written for the abortive Mass for Rossini. On 3 June he wrote to Giulio Ricordi:

> I would also like to demonstrate the affection and veneration I felt and feel for that Great Man [. . .].
>
> I would like to compose a mass for the dead to be performed next year on the anniversary of his death.
>
> [. . .] Do you think the city government would assume the expenses of the performance? I would pay for the copying of the music, and I would conduct the performance myself, both at the rehearsals and in church.
>
> If you believe the thing is possible, speak to the mayor about it.
>
> [Abbiati, 3:643–44]

---

67. Chialiva to Boito, 7 March 1873: "I hope that by now la Lucca has offered you some acceptable terms for the purchase of your opera, and that the negotiations for the performance of your *Mefistofele* have progressed. [. . .] I was very happy at what you tell me about the tasks of expanding the opera and of orchestration. If you had almost completed the orchestration when you wrote me your letter, by now you must have finished it completely" [Nardi, p. 367].

Mayor Belinzaghi agreed to the proposal, but in the course of the city council meeting called to discuss it, some representatives expressed their opposition. In particular, Councillor Mussi pointed out that "the city government was forbidden to assume responsibility for solemnities of any faith. Verdi should be thanked, [. . .] but the city should not take part in the execution of a religious ceremony." Boito, a city councillor since the previous July, supported the mayor's motion, pointing out that this was not a religious act but a homage to a most eminent citizen. The motion he presented was couched in these terms: "The city council, in thanking the illustrious Maestro Verdi for his noble offer, charges the administration to convey these sentiments to him and to provide for the carrying out of the proposal." The motion was approved by an overwhelming majority.[68]

It was probably during this year that Boito wrote a libretto for Cesare Dominiceti (1821–1888), *Iràm,* which was later found in the archives of Casa Ricordi [Nardi, p. 361]. "As a lighthearted comedy of intrigue, it is a remarkable precedent for Boito's *Falstaff* libretto," wrote Nardi, who discovered the text. "It is as if Boito were practicing already the famous alliterations that, with certain verses of *Falstaff,* arrive at those extremes beyond which you enter the realm of music."[69] There is no evidence that Dominiceti actually wrote an opera with this title; if it was in fact composed, it was certainly never performed.

On 22 May 1874, the anniversary of Manzoni's death, Verdi's *Messa da requiem* was performed in the Church of San Marco in Milan, then repeated at La Scala. And in the course of that same year, the negotiations for a revival of *Mefistofele* in Bologna grew more intense; thus Boito worked on revising the opera whenever he could take time from his other commitments, including the *Gioconda* libretto and the abovementioned *Iràm.* As he wrote on 24 September to Tornaghi:

> The negotiations for the Bologna *Mefistofele* seem to be reaching a conclusion. The score, as it is now, has to be copied a second time.
>
> [Nardi, p. 370]

And to Giulio Ricordi:

> I have already written Dominiceti to tell you and Ponchielli of my return. In ten days, at most, I will be in your arms with four acts that are boiling and bubbling in my brain. They would have been long cooked

68. Proceedings of the session are summarized in Nardi, pp. 368–69.

69. Nardi, pp. 362–63. The libretto of *Iràm* is reprinted in its entirety in Boito, pp. 821–76.

if the Bologna *Mefistofele* had not interrupted my work in vain. The third is already almost complete. Don't make me lose time copying the first and the second; I need to have everything before my eyes in order to complete the action properly.

[Nardi, p. 371]

The revival of *Mefistofele* in Bologna was finally set for 1875, to inaugurate the traditional autumn fair season. But meanwhile, in the early spring of the new year, Ricordi proposed to Verdi a revival at La Scala of his *Simon Boccanegra*, a neglected work whose score had been lying for years in the publisher's warehouse. A few years earlier, at the time of *Aida*, Ricordi had made a similar suggestion, which Verdi rejected.[70] Nor did Verdi change his mind now. On 3 March 1875 he replied:

You speak to me of *Boccanegra,* for which there would be an excellent cast with la Mariani and Pandolfini, etc., etc., but the opera is sad, and the effect is monotonous. My old operas should not be considered. The only one I would be inclined to now is always *Aida.*

[Abbiati, 3:743]

The mounting nervousness in the tone of Verdi's letters to Ricordi in this period derived from financial questions, largely about royalties that had not been paid. There was serious tension between the composer and the firm, and it soon led to a grave dispute that almost caused the rupture of the thirty-year-old bond between Verdi and Casa Ricordi. On 4 April 1875, Verdi wrote Giulio, who had just urged the older man to return to the theater again, to complain of the performance of *Aida* in Rome and all the "chatter" that was being heard about the opera. In the letter he summed up some recent (and less recent) negative attitudes towards him: the single whistle at La Scala after the first act of *La forza del destino*, the accusation of having become an imitator of Wagner, the "sapphic ode," and in conclusion:

I can take only as a joke your sentence *"The total salvation of the Theater and of Art lies in you!"* Oh no, have no fear, there will never be any lack of composers, and I too will repeat what Boito said in a toast to Faccio after his first opera... *"perhaps he who will sweep the altar has been born."*

[Abbiati, 3:749]

---

70. To Giulio Ricordi, 15 December 1870: "I replied at once with a telegram to tell you to give *La forza del destino*. As for *Boccanegra* or *Macbeth*, I would be for the new *Macbeth* because I do not believe you have a good actor for *Boccanegra*" [ISV].

l

The stubborn memory of the offense caused by the "sapphic ode" here seems to toll the death knell of Giulio's persistent dream. Meanwhile, the author of that ode continued on his way: the Bologna revival of *Mefistofele* was in the future; and though he was still at work on the laborious completion of *La Gioconda,* Boito could not resist accepting a commission for a new libretto, *Pier Luigi Farnese,* for Costantino Palumbo.[71] He wrote this composer on 12 June 1875:

> These past weeks I have been terribly busy: I must tell you that they want to try my *Mefistofele* again at the Teatro Comunale in Bologna towards the beginning of October. So you will understand all the concerns and tasks that have fallen on my back: go over the score, find the performers, keep an eye on the copyists, deal with agents, correspondence, excursions, fracas, etc.
>
> [Nardi, p. 374]

The revision of *Mefistofele* almost seems inspired by Verdi's remark quoted many years before in Boito's review of *I lombardi:* "You have to be wall-eyed, with one eye on the public and one on art." For this new version, enriched with melodic additions, Boito sacrificed—whether out of personal conviction or as a concession to the public—the two pieces that had aroused most hostility in the Milan audience: the symphonic intermezzo and the Imperial Palace scene. On 4 October 1875 the new *Mefistofele* was given in Bologna, this time without all the journalistic fuss that had preceded the Scala premiere. On the first night the success was fair, and it grew as the work was repeated, until the final performances were virtually a triumph. As a result, the opera was quickly taken up by other theaters (Venice, Turin, Rome) and soon entered the normal Italian repertory. This success of *Mefistofele* gave Boito new confidence, and he resumed the composition of *Nerone.* On 22 November 1876 he wrote to Count Luigi Salina:

> My new opera sprouts a new leaf almost every day [. . .] and if I didn't have to go to Turin and Rome to watch over the fate of *Mefistofele,* thus losing a precious couple of months, I perhaps could have *Nerone* finished for the coming year. But in our art, in our way of doing things, the already finished and performed opera is the natural enemy of the opera that is being written: the former slows down the latter.
>
> [Nardi, p. 416]

71. Scheduled for the autumn of 1891 at the Teatro Costanzi, Rome, Palumbo's opera never got beyond the dress rehearsal because of a dispute between the composer and the publisher Sonzogno, "nor was it ever staged" [Nardi, p. 376].

During the Bologna performances of *Mefistofele* Verdi did not stir from Sant'Agata. The work may or may not have aroused his curiosity. The fact is that during this period relations between him and Casa Ricordi were strained. Giulio could have informed him about Boito, and would no doubt have liked to, but he knew this moment was totally inopportune. Only a few months before, the composer had reminded him of the "befouled altar." Then finally, towards the end of 1875, the serious quarrel between Verdi and the publishing firm was settled.[72] During the dispute Giulio had kept a discreet distance, leaving all the discussion to his father Tito and to the business managers of the firm; now the young Ricordi could go back to weaving his web.[73]

◄No COMMENTS BY VERDI ARE RECORDED immediately after the success of the revised *Mefistofele* in Bologna. A thank-you note from Verdi to Giulio, headed only Paris, 1 June, may date from 1876:[74]

> You have sent me *Mefistofele.* Thank my *one-day poet* for having remembered me again for a moment.
>
> [ISV]

At this time Verdi seemed many miles away from the temptation to pick up his pen again. With *Aida* and the *Messa da requiem* he considered his career as a composer ended. Now he confined himself to keeping an eye on the progress of his creations and, whenever necessary, sustaining them by going to conduct them in person: to Paris, London, Vienna, Cologne. But he did not fail to follow closely every artistic event of any

72. Verdi announced this to his friend and adviser Piroli, 29 December 1875: "I have settled things with Casa Ricordi. The firm will pay me 50,000 lire. It is not all they owe me, but that isn't important. The trouble is that we will not have the same relations as in the past" [ISV].

73. After a long silence, Giulio Ricordi wrote to Giuseppina on 23 December: "I have done nothing in my life except bear on my back the mistakes of others, and pay the penalties others should have paid. On the one hand, I am happy that such a painful question has been settled amicably from the economic standpoint; on the other hand, I cannot personally say I am happy about the moral aspect of the matter, for I feel deeply how much I have lost personally!... and how certain honorable friendships are beyond price. And I feel a double sorrow, as in all conscience I know I have done nothing unworthy!..." [ISV].

74. Certainly not from 1879, as Abbiati (4:82) supposes. The date of the reproduction of the autograph is almost illegible; so are the postmarks, but they seem to suggest 1875, thoroughly credible since in June of that year Verdi was in Paris, preparing to leave for London. But Giulio Ricordi was in Paris as well. Furthermore, by that date the new edition of the Boito score, about to be performed in Bologna, had not yet been published.

significance. When *Mefistofele* was given in Rome, he wrote to his friend Count Arrivabene for news. The answer is dated 6 March 1877:

> Here is the truth about the reception given *Mefistofele*. First let me say there is no contradiction between the fiasco in Milan and the applause in Bologna, Turin, Venice, and now Rome. Enlightened by the Milan outcome, Boito has greatly altered his opera, removing many oddities, and he has even changed a baritone into a tenor. After the Bologna applause he revised the score still further. Here Ricordi and the *avveniristi* had prepared a triumph, but even without them the score would have garnered applause, because the prologue was a big hit, despite some moments of weariness, and so was the second part of the quartet and a duet, and some phrases here and there. He has not removed all the oddities, but he reveals a strong talent, more odd than original, or at least an odd originality. In [Gounod's] *Faust* there is more sound judgment, here there is more fire, even if it is short-lived. [. . .] I haven't mentioned Boito's abominable verses, because I am not writing you as a literary man, and besides I do not know the poetry and the language of the future.
>
> [Alberti, pp. 194–98]

The composer observed, on 21 March 1877:

> Now it is difficult to say if Boito will be able to give Italy some masterpieces! He has much talent, he aspires to originality, but he proves rather odd. He lacks spontaneity and he is short of melody; many musical qualities. With these tendencies he can have some success with a subject as odd and theatrical as Mephistopheles. Nero is harder![75]

"He has much talent," but "he is short of melody"... a sharp, stern judgment from a man who had never lacked for melody—and perhaps the most accurate of the opinions expressed of Boito the composer. But was Verdi familiar with *Mefistofele*? Perhaps he had read the score. As his earlier letters indicate, he believed that any judgment of an opera should be made in the theater. In March of 1879 *Mefistofele* was performed in Genoa, Verdi's winter residence, and this time he seized the opportunity to go and hear it with his wife. On 30 March 1879 he wrote to Arrivabene:

75. Alberti, p. 201. His opinion of Boito's opera was not to change greatly even in later years, at the time of the *Otello* collaboration. See below, page 82, for Verdi's remarks as reported by Ponchielli.

You speak to me of music, but I give you my word of honor, I seem almost to have forgotten what it is, and the proof is that the other evening I went to hear *Mefistofele* and I got it all wrong. For ex.: I had been told that the Prologue in Heaven was a burst of inspiration, of genius... but hearing the harmonies of that number based almost always on dissonances, I thought I was in... surely not heaven. You see what it means not to be *dans le mouvement!!*

[Alberti, p. 226]

Giuseppina had written to Teresa Stolz on 20 March:

We have seen Mephistopheles in the company of Faust. The latter seemed seriously indisposed,[76] so I couldn't properly understand what they were saying between themselves, especially as behind those big clouds of the Prologue in Heaven there was a hellish *tapage*. [. . .] So much for me. Verdi, whose hearing is keener than mine, probably understood everything.[77]

In those same days, at the urging of Giulio Ricordi, who for some time had been impatiently badgering his friend about the collaboration with Verdi, Boito went to call on the composer. His report of that visit survives in an undated letter that Ricordi transcribed some months later in a letter to Verdi:

I went to call on him yesterday morning: I didn't dare bring up the matter that means so much to us, because, not having seen him for so many years, I thought it presumptuous to speak to him of things he didn't mention to me. He was extremely cordial, and I am very grateful to him for the perfect way he received me, nor could I have expected anything more. Among the very great musicians I have met (and they include Rossini, Meyerbeer, Wagner), Verdi is the one who stimulates my interest most vitally.

[Luzio, *Carteggi*, 4:201]

The matter that meant so much to Giulio Ricordi, and that Boito with wise discretion chose not to mention during his Genoa visit to the composer, perhaps involved the libretto of *Otello*, on which in all likelihood Boito had already begun working. Certainly the stubborn publisher was still harboring the project of presenting *Simon Boccanegra*

---

76. The opera had been given at the Teatro Carlo Felice, conducted by Giovanni Rossi, with Armando Castelmary (Mefistofele), Carlo Carpi (Faust), and Adele Garbini (Margherita).

77. From Giuseppina's letter book, in Walker, *Uomo Verdi*, p. 576.

anew, perhaps in a revised version. At the beginning of that spring of 1879—a decisive year, as we shall see—after a conversation in Genoa with the composer, who gave vague hints of assent, Giulio ventured to send him the full score. Verdi replied on 2 May:

> Yesterday I received a big package, which I presume is a score of *Simon!*... If you come to Sant'Agata six months from now, or in a year or two, or three, etc., you will find it intact, as you sent it. I told you in Genoa that I loathe useless things. True, I have done nothing else in my life, but in the past there were attenuating circumstances. Now nothing is more useless for the theater than an opera of mine... and... and it is better to end with *Aida* and with the *Messa* than with an *arrangement*...
>
> [Abbiati, 4:82]

⮬Towards the Collaboration

"You will tell Giulio that I am preparing the chocolate." This indirect reference to *Otello* in a letter from Boito to Casa Ricordi's manager Tornaghi in July 1879, and a later reference dated 24 August, also to Tornaghi ("Tomorrow or the day after, I will begin the first verses of the last act. *Everything will be finished on time*" [Nardi, p. 462]), mark that point where the prehistory of the Verdi-Boito collaboration becomes instead the true beginning of its chronicle. For a while, however, the exchange of documents remained indirect: letters from Giulio to Verdi, to Giuseppina, and to Boito, letters from Verdi and from Boito to Giulio and to Tornaghi, and letters from Giuseppina to Giulio. Gradually the knots tightened.

⮬IN JUNE 1879 VERDI ACCEPTED AN INVITATION to conduct his *Messa da requiem* at La Scala for the benefit of flood victims. The performance took place on 30 June. That same evening, after the concert, the Scala orchestra, conducted by Faccio, serenaded the composer under the windows of his suite in the Grand Hôtel Milan (Boito was in the crowd with his friend Giuseppe Giacosa). Verdi was visibly moved. On one of the days immediately following, the Verdis dined with Giulio Ricordi and his wife, perhaps also with Faccio, and "some friends." Giulio's long-awaited opportunity had come; and this strategic dinner effectively initiated the *Otello* project. Giulio would later recall that evening:

> The idea of the opera came up during a dinner among friends, at which I chanced to bring the conversation around to Shakespeare and to Boito. At the mention of *Otello* I saw Verdi stare at me with suspi-

cion, but with interest. He had surely understood, had surely vibrated. I thought the time was ripe. Franco Faccio was my able accomplice. I was mistaken. The next day, when on my advice Faccio took Boito to Verdi with the scheme of the libretto already drawn up, the maestro, after examining it and finding it excellent, was unwilling to commit himself. [. . .] I urged Boito to finish it. But when I wrote Verdi that I would make a quick trip to Sant'Agata with the poet, I received a firm letter in reply.[78]

Between the Milan dinner and the announcement of the visit to Sant'Agata, another episode intervened; apparently marginal, it offers a glimpse of a Verdi no longer reluctant to pick up his pen, and it may therefore have convinced Giulio Ricordi to step up the pace. At the end of August the *Gazzetta musicale di Milano* had published a chapter of the memoirs of the sculptor Giovanni Dupré, who described his encounter with Verdi in Florence in 1847 and then quoted Rossini's opinion on the composer of *Macbeth:*[79]

> [Verdi] has a melancholy, serious character; his colors are dark and sad, and they spring spontaneously and abundantly from his talent. He is much to be admired for this very reason, and I hold him in the highest esteem. But it is also beyond doubt that he will never write an opera semiseria like *Linda [di Chamounix]*, still less an opera buffa like *L'elisir d'amore.*

Verdi read this article and on 26 August wrote to Giulio Ricordi:

> I read in your *Gazzetta* Dupré's words about our first meeting, and the sentence pronounced by Jove-Rossini (as Meyerbeer used to call him). Imagine! For twenty years I have been looking for an opera buffa libretto, and now that I have, you might say, found it, with that article you inspire in the public a wild desire to boo my opera even before it's written, thus damaging your own interests and mine. But have no fear. If by chance, by misfortune, by fate, despite the great sentence, my evil genius were to lead me to write this opera buffa, I repeat: have no fear... I will ruin another publisher!

> [Abbiati, 4:88–89]

The composer's reaction gave Giulio a chance to relaunch his cherished project and carry it closer to achievement. He replied on 28 August, in a contrite and embarrassed tone:

---

78. Giuseppe Adami, *Giulio Ricordi e i suoi musicisti* (Milan/Rome: Treves/Treccani/Tumminelli, 1933), p. 64.

79. No. 34, 24 August 1879: 293–95. The chapter is reprinted in Conati, pp. 14–22.

The pleasure I always feel when I see an envelope addressed in your hand was, this time, choked off when I read your letter, which left me in a state of indescribable emotion. [. . .] I no longer know what world I'm in, and you must have some compassion on me... Further, I was about to write you that I was planning to make a dash to Busseto with a friend in the first half of September, and I was going to ask if we would be welcome! But now what shall I do?... I really lack the courage, and I don't know how to say it to you...

[Abbiati, 4:89]

The composer's reply was written on 4 September:

That mention made in the little piece by Dupré, I thought, could have no purpose appearing in your *Gazzetta*, unless it was meant to say to me: "Take care, Sig. Maestro, never to write an opera buffa again." Therefore I felt I had to say "I will ruin another publisher." If I do write this opera buffa and you want to ruin yourself, so much the worse for Casa Ricordi.

A visit from you here will always be welcome, in the company of a friend, who would obviously be Boito. Allow me, however, to speak to you very clearly on this subject, and without ceremony. A visit from him would commit me too far, and I absolutely do not want to commit myself. You know how this *chocolate* project was born... You were dining with me among friends. We spoke of *Othello*, of Shakespeare, of Boito. The next day Faccio brought Boito to my hotel. Three days later Boito brought me the sketch for *Otello*, which I read and found good. Write the poem, I said; it will always be good for you, for me, for another composer, etc., etc...

Now, if you come here with Boito I will find myself necessarily obliged to read the libretto that he will have completed and will bring with him.

If I find the libretto completely good, I will find myself somehow committed.

If, finding it good, I nevertheless suggest some revisions that Boito accepts, I find myself still further committed.

If, even if it is very beautiful, I don't like it, it would be too hard to express this opinion to his face!

No, no... You have already gone too far, and we must stop before there is gossip and unpleasantness. In my opinion, the best course (if you think so and it suits Boito) would be to send me the finished poem, so that I can read it and express calmly my opinion without any of the parties becoming committed.

Once these quite prickly difficulties have been smoothed out, I
will be very happy to see you here with Boito.

[Abbiati, 4:86–87, 90]

Giulio answered by return mail on 5 September 1879; his was a long
letter, which will be quoted here in its entirety because it explains the
lack of any contact between Boito and Verdi after the *Nerone* project had
faded out, from the time of *Aida* up till then:

Ever since the production of *Aida* at La Scala, we—Faccio, Boito, and
I—speak much and often of you, and of how happy Boito would have
been to write a libretto for Verdi. Some years have gone by, unfortunately, but this idea has never abandoned us!... and we have longed in
vain for a suitable moment!... Boito had his *Mefistofele* performed, and
afterwards he set to work on *Nerone*. He wrote me then that he would
no longer do librettos for anyone... but if he could write a libretto for
Verdi, he would put aside any other work, in order to have such an
honor and such good fortune. But the occasion had not yet arisen!...
Nor did I ever have the courage to say a word about this to you, for
when I find myself in the presence of Verdi, I feel such great awe that
I lose my bearings completely!... Further, to tell you the truth, this tu-
nic of Nessus I have to wear as publisher always puts me in an am-
biguous position!!... for, out of a sense of delicacy, I am always afraid
you may believe it is the *businessman* who is speaking!!... and that re-
volts me. Of course, it would be supremely ingenuous to say to you
that an opera of Verdi does not make a fortune in the material sense!!...
But this thought is a hundred times outweighed and, I must say, over-
shadowed by the immense, ineffable emotion I feel at the thought of a
work that will make your name still more glorious, if that were possible, and will make that beloved Italian Art shine with new light!...
remaining an eternal part of the history of music. Moreover, these
ideas of mine were and are always shared by Boito and Faccio; and in
their daily visits we have never failed to look at the portrait I keep in
my study, exclaiming: "But that man there, will he really not compose
any more?..." And here talk and more talk, which served to excite me
more and more and to keep my hope alive.

This may explain to you the true, warm, frank friendship that
binds us, me, Boito, and Faccio, and how grieved I was that a man like
you, Maestro, could not know Boito as he truly is. I know, if my
memory does not fail me, that Boito has done you some wrong; but
with his nervous, eccentric character, I would bet that he was unaware

of doing it, or could never find the way to undo it. The fact remains that, in our frequent meetings, Boito has always spoken to me of Verdi with veneration and enthusiasm; otherwise he would not be my friend; and I can tell you that, in my knowledge of many private matters of his, Boito has always seemed to me a straightforward and honest man, a perfect gentleman, in short. When he went to Genoa, I encouraged him to present himself to you; he was afraid of importuning, etc., etc.; but finally he mustered his courage and told me he would go and see Verdi and would try to say something about what we had been thinking of for some time. [There follows the letter of Boito to Giulio, quoted above, page *liv*.]

Your visit to Milan—may it be blessed a hundred times—was finally the fortunate occasion that we had wished for. I don't have to tell you what it gave rise to; but from me you can have the proof of everything I told you, because Boito, the day of your departure, broke off all other work and has concerned himself solely with the libretto. Having gone to Venice for his health, he wrote me these words: "Never fear: I have tried resuming work these past few days, exploiting the morning hours when my neuralgia gives me some respite. Even without making any special effort, the job will be finished in August. The hardest aspect of the task is condensing into rapid dialogue the vast sublimity of the text. Rereading what I wrote in Milan, I found much to cut, much to pare. I know for whom I am writing and I want to do the best I can."

Then yesterday morning Boito's latest letter arrived: "I am applying to this work a whole special rhythmic construction (in the lyrical part) that, I believe, will greatly interest our Maestro, and it will be a considerable surprise to you and a powerful incentive to the achievement of that project that means so much to us. But this idea came to me late, and now I must redo all the lyrical part of the second and third acts. My health is perfectly recovered, and I can have the whole work revised and completed by the 9th or 10th of this month. I believe I have found a form that will serve admirably Shakespeare's text and its musical illustrator!..."

But, you will say to me, it seems to me you are all leaving one person out of your reckonings!!... No, Maestro... If we write and we talk like this among ourselves, it is because we are talking and writing of something we have been pondering for several years, and for which the intensity of our desire is so great that it gives body to a ghost. The aim is this, but it has never occurred to one of us to exploit words exchanged with you as a promise, a commitment!... That would show lack of respect for you!... Nor has Boito, in undertaking this work, done it with the idea that it was something certain and settled. He knows the situation, and clearly.

The Maestro, however, will ask me: Then why all this urgency?... And here again I can tell you the reason. Boito was hoping to finish by the beginning of August; but in poor health, he went to Venice and that caused a delay. The conspirators who were to come to Busseto were three: Boito, Faccio, and I. Faccio is under contract to Madrid in the autumn, and is leaving, I believe, on the 15th or 16th of this month. He also had a very great desire to go to Sant'Agata before his departure, to greet Verdi, and then leave with the consolation of great and happy news!!... if that were possible. Or, in any case, with the pleasure of having seen you.

However, I can only consider *absolutely right* what you say to me in your most welcome latest letter, and I will write Boito about it. If our project can be reconciled also with your views, and we can come in time before Faccio's departure, we would be happy!!!... To be honest, Maestro, this is acting a bit too much *sans façon!*... But surely we have not deceived ourselves in counting on the cordial hospitality of Verdi and of his worthy wife!... If the thing were then to take more time, I will be sorry for Faccio's sake, but so be it!... Boito and I will await your orders!... And in whatever case, Maestro, you are and will be perfectly *free!!*...

[Luzio, *Carteggi,* 4:200–202]

In fact, things did "take more time": the official reason was Boito's neuralgia, which prevented him from working serenely; but he was also tormented by the concern to present a piece of work that would satisfy the composer. Giulio Ricordi wrote Verdi on 17 September 1879:

Boito writes me today from Venice that he has finished the work and is copying it, but with such trepidation that now he would like to do it all over again from the beginning!... for the thought of presenting it to you gives him no peace, and he is afraid of being unable to do a worthy job. In any case, he will himself be in Milan next week and will deliver his manuscript to me. Following your instructions, I will send it to you, so that you, at your leisure and in complete freedom, will be able to examine it. If I were fortunate enough to be pious, now would be the time for me to light candles to the Madonna and prostrate myself before God, so that our most ardent prayers might be granted!...

[Abbiati, 4:94]

In actual fact, the libretto was not yet entirely finished. Boito sent a note to Tornaghi dated 21 September:

> If this week I don't hand over the strangled Desdemona to Giulio, I'm afraid he will strangle me.[80]

On 29 September 1879 Giulio wrote to Verdi:

> Boito arrived yesterday evening with the completed work. I am not sending it on at once because he is recopying it and, at the same time, he will redo two scenes that do not completely satisfy him. He has delayed a bit because he has suffered a great deal from a facial neuralgia that prevented him from working. He hopes he has faithfully followed and condensed Shakespeare's ideas, and he dares hope to obtain your approval.
>
> [Luzio, *Carteggi*, 4:263]

Five days later, 4 October, Giulio wrote Verdi again:

> Having told you that Boito would send his manuscript today, I feel it my duty to inform you by telegraph of a brief delay of four days, also on behalf of Boito, who is very sorry. But he is again tormented by his facial neuralgia, [. . .] hence these few days' delay, which he hopes you will forgive him, considering the cause. I am also involved, Maestro, because I can no longer live in peace!... and am in constant agitation!... Ah! If ten years of my life could be spent for one of yours, yes!... how gladly I would give them.
>
> [ISV]

A letter from Boito to Giulio was perhaps written at this time; Ricordi sent it on to Verdi:

> I am much more distressed than you. Today I got up at seven-thirty and went to my desk. I work as much as I can, but until yesterday noon the abscess tormenting me had not burst and I could not work with that inferno in my mouth. I hope that abscess was the final stage of my ailments. I have nothing in my mind but the idea of finishing the work well and as soon as possible. No other enterprise in my life has caused the anxiety and agitation I have felt in these months of intellectual and physical struggle.
>
> You must not think that the libretto can be finished by the day after tomorrow. The abscess made me lose three days; I have gone back to work only today, so three days must be added to Thursday. The fate

80. R. De Rensis, ed., *Lettere di Arrigo Boito* (Rome: Novissima, 1932), p. 84.

that has warred against this work will be defeated. For the rest, no matter what happens, even if V. no longer wants me as a collaborator, I will finish the work and in the best way I can, so that he will have evidence that, though assailed by physical suffering, I have devoted to him four months of my time with all the affection he inspires in me. For this I would not ask, God forbid, any material compensation either from him or from you, if things work out badly. It would suffice for me to give V. proof that I am truly far more devoted to him than he believes.

[Luzio, Carteggi, 4:203]

Walker rightly comments: "Much more than the many thousands of words contributed by Ricordi, it was the transparent sincerity and selfless dedication of Boito that were decisive in the end" [Walker, *Man Verdi*, p. 475].

Meanwhile, the impatient Ricordi—whether or not with Boito's knowledge we do not know—sent already a part of the libretto to Verdi. And while on the one hand Verdi seemed far from capitulation, and on the other Boito was hesitant, tormented by constant second thoughts, tortured by the desire to perfect what he had already done, Giulio pressed Giuseppina for help. On 7 November Verdi's wife sent Giulio a splendid letter, which contains an incisive view of Boito's character. The letter also reveals Giuseppina's sensitivity:

Now we come to the serious part of your letter. I know Boito very slightly, but I believe I have divined his character: nervous, highly excitable! When gripped by admiration, capable of boundless enthusiasm and perhaps also at times, in contrast, capable of excessive dislikes! But all this in brief fits and only when the struggle is between mind and heart, or rather between opposing passions or powers. The loyalty, the fairness of his character soon prevail and restore a balance among all his faculties. Steadfast in friendship and, at the same time, mild and docile as a youth, when his fibre is not, so to speak, *tweaked.* I say all this so that you will *understand* that I believe I have *understood the man;* hence I am not surprised by his feverish state at the present hour. In the hope of bringing a bit of calm, I will whisper into Giulio's ear a little secret, on condition that it remain secret.

Towards the 20th of this November, we will come to Milan to spend a few days, and in my opinion it would be best to wait for that moment, which seems most opportune to me, because without attracting any attention or arousing any curiosity, Boito could speak at length and serenely with Verdi.

Inter nos, what has been written so far of the *African* seems to his liking and very well done; surely the rest will be equally well done. So let him [Boito] finish the poem calmly, abandoning himself to his imagination (without torturing it), and as soon as it is finished, have him send it without delay or hesitation to Verdi, before he comes to Milan, so he can read it serenely and, if necessary, prepare his observations ahead of time. I repeat, the impression has been good: the revisions and the polishing will come afterwards.

I wish and I trust that it can be said "All's well that ends well," and may this also end well. Do not write or speak to Verdi about fears, desires, hesitations, and I add: don't tell Verdi, either, that I have written you about this matter. I believe this is the best way to avoid rousing in Verdi's mind the slightest idea of pressure. Let the stream follow its course, straight to the sea. It is in vast spaces that certain men are fated to meet and understand each other.[81]

The next day, 8 November, Giulio Ricordi sent Giuseppina another letter from Boito:

So as not to trouble the Maestro uselessly, I will transcribe for you a note that Boito sent me a little while ago; too bad a telegraph line has not been installed between me and him!! [. . .] "Yesterday I worked on the fourth act, and I am pleased. There is still the trio of act 3, a vital piece, that is driving me to despair!... From time to time I abandon it and proceed with some other scene, then I go back to the trio and I find it more recalcitrant than ever!... And yet I do not despair; on the contrary, I am sure I will come and see you shortly, with the chocolate all hot and ready... and how pleased we will be!..." So the chocolate is boiling, boiling, boiling!... And so am I!...

[CVB, p. xxix]

For the rest, following Giuseppina's suggestion, Giulio refrained from writing to the composer about the matter. He confined himself to sending Verdi the finished libretto. And on 18 November Verdi informed him:

I have received this moment the chocolate. I will read it this evening, because now my head is teeming with business matters.

[CVB, p. xxix]

81. M. Medici and M. Conati, eds., *Carteggio Verdi-Boito* (Parma: Istituto di Studi Verdiani, 1978), p. xxix; hereafter CVB.

The trip to Milan announced by Giuseppina took place on schedule. And, also on schedule, in great secret, the meeting with Boito (and, obviously, with Giulio Ricordi). From later documents we can deduce that it was on this occasion that Verdi, in expressing his pleasure in the quality of the libretto, purchased it, but without any sort of commitment. From this moment on, the watchword for all, and especially for Giulio Ricordi, was to maintain the most absolute secrecy about the subject.

On 18 December Giuseppina summarized the "Othellian" story for an old friend of Verdi's, Countess Giuseppina Negroni Prati Morosini:

> As chance would have it, one day in Milan the conversation turned to Shakespeare's admirable drama *Othello* (which a common hack adapted to the [opera] stage in the way everyone knows)[82] and how that commonplace hack who adapted it to the theater had done so in a way that was without poetry and without any drama and even less Shakespearian, as all know. The words were repeated to Boito, whose imagination was fired, and he presented an outline two days later and then a complete libretto. It seems that Verdi must have liked it for, after reading it, he bought it, but he placed it beside the *Re Lear* of Somma, which has been sleeping for thirty years in its folder, a deep and undisturbed sleep. What will happen to this *Otello? Se sa minga* [Milanese dialect: "There's no knowing"]. I wish that Verdi could let it sleep like *Re Lear* for another thirty years and that he would then feel the vigor and courage to set it to music for the glory of his art, skipping straight over "Nessun maggior dolore"[83] without any need to repeat that verse in any circumstance in his life.
>
> [CVB, pp. xxix–xxx]
>
> *Marcello Conati*

82. Probably referring to Francesco Berio di Salsa, librettist of Rossini's *Otello.*

83. "No greater sorrow," a reference to the off-stage song in Rossini's *Otello* (the text is in turn taken from Dante's *Divina commedia*).

❧ LETTERS

Illustrious Maestro,

In sending you the certificate of ownership of the libretto of *Otello*, I would like to tell you once again that my pen will be entirely at your disposal for any revisions that may seem necessary in the above-mentioned operatic text. Happy and proud at having been able, in this instance, to associate my name with your glory, I declare myself

your most devoted
Arrigo Boito

◄ Between the first letter from Verdi to Boito (see introduction, p. xiii) and this one from Boito more than seventeen years later, the lives of the two men followed separate and complex paths. The events of these lives and the slow, carefully orchestrated rapprochement of the two artists are described and interpreted in Marcello Conati's Introduction to this volume. Now, in the winter of 1879, after meetings and discussions, the Verdi-Boito collaboration had already begun. Indeed, Verdi had already bought the libretto (though it would still require much revision), and Boito's first letter is, in effect, a receipt.

This letter came to light after the Italian critical edition of the correspondence was published. In order to maintain the numbering of the documents in that edition, the newly discovered letter is indicated with the letter "A."

Sant'Agata, 15 August 1880

1

Dear Sig. Boito,

Giulio will have told you that I received several days ago your verses, which I wished to read and study carefully before answering you.

To be sure, they have greater warmth than the previous ones, but in my opinion a dramatic element is still lacking; and it is lacking because it cannot exist. After Otello has insulted Desdemona there is nothing more to be said. At most a sentence, a reproof, a curse addressed to the *barbarian* who has insulted a woman! And then either ring down the curtain, or come up with an *invention* not in Shakespeare. For ex. (this is only an instance): After the words "Demon, be silent," Lodovico, with all the haughtiness of a Patrician and the dignity of an Ambassador, could proudly address Otello: "Unworthy Moor, *you dare* insult a

Venetian noblewoman, my kinswoman, and you do not fear the Senate's wrath?" (strophe of 4 or 6 verses)

Jago is pleased with what he has done (strophe idem)

Desdemona laments (strophe idem)

Rodrigo (strophe)

Emilia and Chorus (strophe)

Otello silent, motionless, formidable, says nothing...

Suddenly in the distance are heard drums, trumpets, cannon fire, etc., etc... "The Turks! The Turks!!" Populace and Soldiers invade the stage. All are surprised and frightened! Otello recovers himself and stands erect like a lion; he brandishes his sword and, addressing Lodovico, says: "Come! I will again lead you to victory. Venice will then reward me *with dismissal!*..." All abandon the stage except Desdemona. Meanwhile the women of the populace, rushing in on all sides, terrified, fling themselves down on their knees, while from off stage the shouts of the warriors are heard, cannon fire, drums, trumpets, etc., all the fury of the battle. Desdemona in the center of the stage, isolated, motionless, her eyes fixed on Heaven, prays for Otello.

The curtain falls.

This would create the opportunity for music, and a composer could be pleased. The Critic would raise many objections. For ex.: If the Turks were defeated (as we are told at the beginning), how could they now fight? This, however, would not be a serious criticism because it could be supposed, and said in a few words, that the Turks were crippled and dispersed by the storm, but not destroyed. There would be a more serious objection; Could Otello, overwhelmed with grief, consumed by jealousy, dejected, physically and morally ill, suddenly be roused and again become the hero of earlier days? And if so, if glory still lures him, and he can forget love, sorrow, jealousy, why kill Desdemona and then himself?

Are these scruples, or serious objections? I have told you what occurred to me. Who knows? Perhaps you will find in this nonsense a germ from which to create something!

Think about it, write me, and believe me

your devoted
G. Verdi

p.s. Allow me to send you my most sincere congratulations for the excellent reception of *Mefistofele* in London.

    It is significant that the first word of this letter is a reference to Giulio Ricordi, grandson of Verdi's first publisher and the third of his family to head the firm. Giulio often acted for Verdi and, in bringing about the collaboration with Boito, the publisher had been an active participant, as Marcello Conati explains in his introduction to this volume.

A silence followed Verdi's acceptance of the libretto, perhaps because he had occasion to meet Boito during the winter or because he had other things on his mind: in February he had gone to Paris to prepare and conduct *Aida* at the Opéra, in French. Verdi's first surviving letter, written from Sant'Agata, where he was finally able to set to work on the opera, immediately establishes the tone for much of the ensuing correspondence. In discussing act 3, scene 7 of *Otello* (from Otello's line "Demonio, taci!" on), he comes straight to the point, expresses his reservations frankly, but with a deference unusual in his relations with collaborators. Verdi calls his new librettist "Sig. Boito" and signs himself "G. Verdi." His postscript, referring to the successful London premiere (6 July 1880, Her Majesty's Theatre) of Boito's *Mefistofele,* is an indication of how closely Verdi followed the life of the international operatic world. As the collaboration continued, he took a special, almost paternal interest in Boito's career.

Monaco (Alpes Maritimes)
Hôtel des bains
Saturday [4 September? 1880]

2

Dear, kind Signora,

I must thank you for the great pleasure I felt at learning of the kind words you wrote about me to our friend Giulio, who faithfully reported them to me. Today I received a very interesting letter from the Maestro and I have now read and reread it ten times and have pondered it. I will not be at peace with myself until I have achieved the concept as he has written it.

Still, rather than bore the Maestro with futile words while he is awaiting deeds, I shall put off answering him until I can present him with the fruit of the seeds he sowed in my mind. And that will surely be soon, as this year, fortunately, I am not tormented by the demon neuralgia, enemy of all work; and the sea bathing, which is excellent in this bay, has strengthened my physical health, on which, I believe, my good spiritual attitude is dependent.

I beg you to present my respects to the Maestro and to accept with your innate, frank courtesy my most reverent friendship.

Your most devoted
A. Boito

⊷Boito's first surviving letter is to Giuseppina Strepponi Verdi, who had written to Giulio Ricordi about Verdi's positive reaction to Boito's work. A consummate diplomat, Boito understood the importance of Giuseppina's influence on her husband. In a letter dated 7 September to Giulio Ricordi, Boito wrote: "I have done as you wished: I have written this moment to Signora Verdi" [CVB, p. 287]. So the elaborate wheels that had brought the Verdi-Boito collaboration into existence were still turning.

Busseto, 14 October 1880
Sant'Agata

3 Dear Boito,

Today I received the third finale. I have read it: divinely good!... And now what do you think about the scruples I expounded in my last letter? What do you think of the character of Otello?

Write me a word.

My wife thanks you and greets you; I shake your hand, begging you to forgive me so many nuisances.

Warmly,
G. Verdi

Milan, Monday [18 October 1880]
Via Principe Amedeo 1

4 Dear Maestro,

Your letter made my heart swell. So the third finale exists; so I have been fortunate enough to provide suitable form for the concept you were seeking. Now in my handiwork you recognize the thought you dictated to me, which I transcribed, not allowing myself to be troubled by any doubt, not even by the doubts you yourself broached. Working in this way, I showed you that I attached far greater value to the feeling that inspired you to speak than to your argued considerations about those feelings. But now you ask me for my opinion also on those considerations. This is extremely awkward for me because if, as you have seen, in my actions I have agreed with the Artist, the Maestro, now, in my words, I must agree with the Critic. When you say (I am transcribing your own words) in the letter you sent me to Monaco: "Could Otello, overwhelmed with grief, consumed by jealousy, dejected, physically and morally ill, suddenly be roused and again become the hero of earlier days? And if so, if glory still lures him, and he can forget love, sorrow, jealousy, why kill Desdemona and then himself?" When you reason in this way I am unable to find any words to contradict you, and later when you ask me, or rather, you ask yourself: "Are these scruples, or serious objections?" I must say further: *They are serious objections.* You have hit the nail on the head. Otello is like a man moving in a nightmare, and under the fatal, mounting domination of this nightmare he thinks, acts, moves, suffers, and commits his dreadful crime. Now if we conceive an event that must necessarily rouse and distract Otello from such a tenacious nightmare, we thus destroy all the sinister spell Shakespeare created, and we cannot arrive logically at the denouement. That attack of the Turks seems to me like a fist breaking the window of a room where two people are about to die of asphyxiation. That private atmosphere of death so carefully created by Shakespeare suddenly vanishes. The breath of life circulates once more in our tragedy, and Otello and Desdemona are saved. To put them back on the road to death we must seal them again in the lethal chamber, reconstruct the nightmare, patiently lead Jago to his victims; and we have only one act left in which to reconstruct this tragedy from the beginning. In other words: *We have found the end of an act, but at the expense of the effect of the final catastrophe.* Everyone knows *Othello* is a very great masterpiece and, in its greatness, *perfect.* This perfection derives (as you know better than I) from the prodigious harmony of the whole and the details, from the profound analytical portrayal of the characters, from that very rigorous and *inevitable* logic that unfolds all the events of the tragedy, from the way all passions involved are observed and portrayed, especially the dominant passion. All these virtues concur to make *Othello* a masterpiece of art. To retouch, even in just one place, a work of such beauty and wisdom cannot be done without diminishing its perfection. And if we diminish its perfection from the psychological point of view, as well as from the point of view of the action and also of the characters, the tragedy is no longer as logical, or complete, or harmonious, or inevitable as Shakespeare wanted it. When the figure of Otello is impaired so also is the figure of Jago. His immediate, direct action in the catastrophe is suddenly interrupted by an event that he has not directed, by the *only* act, the *one* event beyond his influence: a sudden enemy attack. Otello, after this entirely new and unexpected turn of events, no longer acts under the relentless domination of Jago, and instead of seeming wretchedly unhappy he seems cruel.

We have tried to improve *perfection* and we have destroyed it. This is the Critic's reasoning, and it is right. But an opera is not a play; our art lives on elements unknown to spoken tragedy. The destroyed atmosphere can be created anew. Eight measures suffice to revive a feeling, a rhythm can restore a character: music is the most omnipotent of the arts, it has a logic of its own, more rapid, more free than the logic of spoken thought and far more eloquent. You, Maestro, with a stroke of the pen can reduce to silence the most cogent arguments of the Critics. You have said that the third act is divinely good; therefore you are right, because this exclamation of yours simply reveals to me how in your mind you already see your whole idea outlined, clear and strong.

But I have rattled on too much.

To you, my dear Maestro, and to your wife my most cordial respects. I am always yours to command, ready to recast and cut and add, remember that. I am always happy when I succeed in satisfying you.

Yours,

A. Boito

&This reply to Verdi's first letter is another example of Boito's tact, his skill in handling Verdi's shifting humors. In suggesting a Turkish attack and a rousing finale, Verdi—magnificent man of the theater that he was—had in mind a traditional dramaturgy that Boito clearly wanted to leave behind. Tactfully, Boito was able to make the older man review his position. But as it happened, work on *Otello* had to be interrupted, for Giulio Ricordi had persuaded Verdi to revise his *Simon Boccanegra* (first given in Venice in 1857) for the coming season at La Scala. The original librettist of *Boccanegra*, Francesco Maria Piave, had died in 1876. Ricordi asked Boito if he would assume this ungrateful assignment. Boito readily agreed, and Ricordi communicated the good news to Verdi. Neither the composer nor the librettist realized quite how much work would have to be done on the long-neglected opera. The pace of the correspondence accelerates over the next four months until, having completed the revision, supervised the rehearsals, and attended the first performances of the new *Boccanegra* at La Scala (premiered 24 March 1881), Verdi could return to the peace of his Villa Sant'Agata and think again about *Otello*.

Genoa, 2 December 1880

5   Dear Boito,

The third finale is well done! I like Otello's fainting better in this finale than where it was before. Only I cannot find, and have no feeling for, the ensemble number! But we could even do without it. We will talk about it later, for now, as Giulio must have told you, there are other things we must deal with. I thought that in this *Boccanegra* there was much to be done, but I see that if we can find a *good beginning* for the finale, that injects variety, great variety, into the excessive uniformity of the drama, what then remains to be done boils down to a few verses here and there, changing some musical phrases, etc.

So give it a little thought and write me as soon as you've found something.

A warm handshake in haste from

yours warmly,
G. Verdi

Wednesday [8 December 1880]

6

Dear Maestro,

One idea begets another, and a mere two ideas are enough to beget doubt, which is the natural enemy of action. This is why I am appealing to you: help me shake off this hesitation and point out the path I should follow. To tell the truth, the path was very clearly indicated in the letters you wrote to Giulio and it should have been enough to make me set to work without further questions, but a man is not always master of his own brain.

This, then, is the way I would develop the Senate scene:

The most exact description from the historical point of view would be as follows:

Council Chamber in the Palazzo degli Abati.
The Doge. The Podestà. The councillors representing the nobility, the
councillors representing the populace, the consuls of the sea, the constables.

A bailiff announces a woman who is begging to speak to the Doge. The Doge orders that she be received, but he will see her only after the fate of the fatherland has been debated. The Doge announces to the Council that Toris, the king of Tartary, has sent an ambassador suing for peace with the Genoese. (See *Annals of the Republic of Genoa* by Giustiniani, tome 2, book 4.) The whole council unanimously grants peace. Then the Doge calls for an end to the war with the Republic of Venice. Rejection by the council, uproar. The Doge cries: "With the barbarians, with the infidels, you agree to peace, yet you want war with our brothers. Aren't your triumphs enough for you? Hasn't the blood shed on the waters of the Bosphorus yet sated your ferocity? You have carried your victorious banner over the waves of the Tyrrhenian, the Adriatic, the Euxine, the Ionian, the Aegean," and here we can quote the most beautiful passages of letter 5 in book 14 of Petrarch's letters. In particular where he says: "It is a fine thing to defeat the adversary by the sword, but finer still to conquer him by greatness of heart" and where he speaks so lyrically of the splendors of the Ligurian coast—provided this last digression doesn't prolong the scene too much, but it is so beautiful where he says: "And the helmsman, awed by the novelty of the sight, dropped the oar from his hands and, in wonder, stopped his boat in the middle of its course." Also, the Doge's plea must end proudly and be interrupted here and there by cries from the multitude; the populace is for peace, the nobles are for war. Heated antagonism between nobles and plebeians. Tumult outside the door of the hall, the arrest is announced of a nobleman who, sword in hand, tried to force his way into the council. Nobles and populace vehemently insist this nobleman be brought in. Enter Gabriello Adorno, who accuses the Doge of having ordered Amelia Grimaldi's abduction. Surprise and indignation on the part of the nobles; the Doge is thunderstruck and orders them to bring in the woman who shortly before had sought help and asylum in the palace. The woman is brought in. It is Amelia, who flings herself at the feet of the Doge and reveals that she has escaped her captors. Here there could be some verses in which the Doge thanks heaven for having saved Amelia, and the act would end as in the original version of the opera.

Now we go on to the exposition of the other idea:

It is based on this concept: to fuse into a single act the main numbers of the two middle acts, skipping completely scenes 10, 11, and 12 with which act 2 now ends (or rather act 1, if we count the prologue separately), and end this whole (merged) act with the terzetto with which the present penultimate act ends. Having done this, add a whole new act, not long, and put it in the place of the original penultimate act.

Let's talk, first of all, about how to achieve the merging of the two middle acts. First of all it is a good idea to simplify the events. Give up Amelia's abduction. Let's have a look then.

ACT 1

The Grimaldi Garden

Scene 1 Amelia alone

Scene 2 Amelia and Gabriele

Scenes 3, 4, 6, 7 as they stand, without scene 5, thus allowing 4 to go on to 6 without interruption and without change of setting, and then the duet between the Doge and Amelia. After the duet, Amelia slowly exits. Scene 8, very brief, follows between the Doge and Paolo. In this scene we must add Paolo's threat: He is the soul of the people's faction and will stir up a revolt if the Doge doesn't give him Amelia's hand. Steadfast, the Doge accepts the challenge and refuses to give Amelia to Paolo. Paolo exits. Amelia is still nearby in the garden; the Doge calls her to bid her farewell and embrace her in that hour of danger. At the embrace of father and daughter enter Gabriele, drawing his sword to fling himself on the Doge. Amelia defends her father. The terzetto follows, and the act ends as it does now with cries of "To arms."

Act 2 (penultimate)
The interior of the Church of San Siro (former cloister of the Benedictines), adjoining the houses of the Boccanegras

The church is full of armed men, on the loggias are crossbowmen, from the central rose window of the facade a catapult is being loaded. Outside, cries and tumult of attackers, trumpets; inside, at the altar a priest is blessing the fighters. ~~Amelia is prostrate, praying before a Madonna.~~ Gabriele is on the central loggia, beside the catapult, as lookout. Boccanegra gives some orders, some scouts enter: the Fiescos, the D'Orias, the Grimaldis have sided with the plebeian faction that is attacking the church. Faithful to Boccanegra are the consuls of the sea, with all the navy and the crossbowmen and the majority of the populace. Gabriele asks at every opportunity if he should fire the catapult (the old Genoese called catapults *trabocchi*), but the Doge is opposed. Meanwhile the doors of the church are hit with great din, the great bell rings the alarm. A message from a scout arrives, telling how the attackers are surrounded by a strong deployment of crossbowmen who sprung forth from one of the Boccanegra houses (the scouts enter and exit by a door leading directly into Simone's house.) The doors of the church seem about to be shattered. With a group of crossbowmen, Boccanegra takes his stand facing the doors; they cave in. Enter Fiesco leading a horde of nobles and populace; he wounds Boccanegra in the ~~arm~~ hand, but all of a sudden, seeing the church filled with armed men ready to fight, the attackers stop, frightened. Boccanegra, wounded, shows Fiesco the catapult threatening the attackers from above and swears that he will not fire it and no harm will come to the rebels if, in this holy refuge where they now are, they solemnly promise peace. Moment of silence. Meanwhile Paolo, who is the leader of the revolt, softly asks Pietro, who is among the supporters of Boccanegra (in order to betray him), if there is no hope left for the rebels. Pietro answers that they are surrounded by the crossbowmen and that Boccanegra has caught them in his net. Then Paolo tears the sash from his sword and spills on that sash some drops of poison from an ampoule he has taken from his jerkin, then he throws the sword at Boccanegra's feet and, kneeling, asks to bandage the bleeding wound on the Doge's hand. All the attackers now sheath their weapons. Boccanegra allows his hand to be bandaged, tells Paolo to rise, and pardons him. Meanwhile Amelia arrives through the door by which the scouts exited. Gabriele has come down from the loggia. Boccanegra solemnly superintends the swearing of a peace oath, utters the formulas of the oath himself, and declares this peace between nobles and populace shall be sealed by the marriage of his daughter Amelia to Adorno. This oath will have the dimensions required for a broad and powerful musical number. Thus the act would end.

Now let's examine the advantages of this second project: We witness the poisoning of the Doge and therefore witness an action that is connected with the final catastrophe and thus we make it more visual, more tragic. Second advantage: We dramatize an actual event (recorded in Giustiniani's *Annals,* book 4, year 1356), which adds a little local and historical color to the drama. (Those churches transformed all of a sudden into trenches, fortresses, are found in the history of Genoa.) We show the audience Boccanegra as he makes a great gesture of strength and magnanimity and is struck by Paolo's treachery at the very moment he is performing this great and generous act. Another advantage: The wedding derives logically from the event that precedes it.

But the tenor will not have a scene in which to display his virtuosity? That scene could occur at the beginning of the last act.

———————

There. I have told you everything that has come to my mind these last few days as I plunged into the reading of Genoese history. I can guess the criticisms you will have both of the first and of the second ideas.

The Senate scene may appear cold unless the patriotic and political concept that animates it is narrated and developed with enough warmth to make it dramatic. But even if this concept manages to heighten the emotion of the drama and interest the public, there is another pitfall awaiting us: the arrival of Gabriele (and then of Amelia) comes to interrupt this idea before it is completely exploited, and the question of Venice that has made such an impression on us at the beginning is left unresolved because of the new event. Then this event will be weakened and the end of the act will also suffer.

The criticism of the second project is not hard to find. A war in a church may seem perhaps fairly novel, but the theatrical effect could be problematical. We have a story already grim in itself, and the added act would not modify the general tone. That armed church is surely neither serene nor merry.

Our task, dear Maestro, is arduous. The drama that concerns us is skewed, like an unsteady table, and we don't know which leg is too short, and however we try to adjust the table, it still wobbles. In this drama I find none of the qualities of those dramas that make us cry out: *"It seems carved in stone!"* No event that is truly fated, indispensable and powerful, in other words, generated by tragic ineluctability. I except the prologue, which is truly beautiful and, in its somber unity, powerful, solid, dark like basalt. But the prologue (I refer to the poem, because for many, many years I have had no opportunity to hear the music of *Boccanegra* again), the prologue is the table's good leg, the only one that rests solidly on the ground; the other three, as you know better than I, are all unsteady. There is much plot and little content. Everything in that drama is superficial—all those events seem improvised then and there, simply to occupy the stage: they have no deep roots or strong links, they are not determined by characters, they are *semblances of events*. To set such a drama right, it must be changed.

If, dear Maestro, you could read my thoughts (and why be reticent, why lie?), you would read a great reluctance to take up this drama again with the prospect of its being performed. This drama is lacking in deep virtues as it is in lighter touches; this drama (except for the prologue) lacks both tragic power and *theatricality*.

Still, your wishes are mine, and now that I have opened my heart to you I promise to do whatever you think must be done, since you, not I, are the supreme arbiter in this situation.

Therefore I await your decision, to do either the Senate or the Church of San Siro, or to do nothing at all.

———————————

You do not feel the logic of the ensemble in the third act of *Otello*, and to tell the truth I don't feel it either; we'll do without it, so much the better. The important thing is for us to feel that the end of the act is happily achieved. In that ending I will have some verses to change.

———————————

I don't want to end this *pamphlet* without telling you of the grateful affection you stirred in my spirit by some words you said last winter in Paris to Baron Blaze de Bury, words that do me the highest honor, and which I read with emotion in one of the latest musical reports in *La revue des deux mondes*. I have restrained this expression of thanks for over a month, so as not to bore you, but now that you have given me a reason to write you, I let it go, full tilt, towards you.

Many, many greetings to your wife.

Yours warmly,
A. Boito

❧Boito twice underlines the word "pamphlet" (fascicolo) towards the end of this letter, making fun of his own tendency to verbose explanation.

The Petrarch letter Boito refers to was, originally, a suggestion from Verdi in his letter of 20 November 1880 to Giulio Ricordi [CVB, p. 290]: "I recall two stupendous letters of Petrarch, one written to the Doge Boccanegra and the other to the Doge of Venice." Actually, the first of these letters was addressed not to Boccanegra but to the "Doge and Council of Genoa." In 1352, when the letter was written, the doge was Boccanegra's successor, Giovanni di Valente. Boccanegra was reelected only in 1356.

The erudite Boito was naturally delighted by Verdi's idea, and in the final text of the libretto the first letter is briefly mentioned (act 1, scene 10; see letters nos. 17 and 18 for more exchange on Petrarch references in *Boccanegra*). Neither the Senate scene nor the proposed (and rejected) San Siro scene appeared in the original Piave libretto.

The reference to the French diplomat and music critic Henri Blaze de Bury (1813–1888) is prompted by an interview with Verdi, published 15 October 1880 in *La revue des deux mondes,* in which Verdi is quoted as saying Boito "n'est pas seulement un musicien, c'est aussi un poète dramatique et des plus remarquables."

Genoa, 11 December 1880

7 Dear Boito,

Either the Senate... or the Church of San Siro... or do nothing...

Do nothing would be the best course, but there are reasons, not so much financial as, I would say, professional, that will not allow me to abandon the idea of adjusting this *Boccanegra,* not without having first tried, at least, to do something with it. May I add parenthetically that it's in everybody's interest that La Scala *survive!* The repertory this year, alas, is deplorable! Excellent the opera of Ponchielli, but the rest? Ye gods!!!! There is an opera that would arouse great interest in the public, and I don't understand why the Composer and Publisher stubbornly go on refusing it! I refer to *Mefistofele*. This would be the propitious moment, and you would be doing a service to Art and to everyone.

———————————

The act you conceived in the Church of San Siro is stupendous in every respect. Beautiful in its novelty, beautiful for its historical color, beautiful from the scenic-musical point of view; but it would be too much of an undertaking for me, and I could not assume so much work.

Having unfortunately to renounce this act, we must stick with the Senate scene, which, if done by you, would not prove cold, I am sure. Your criticisms are just, but you, immersed in more lofty works, and having *Otello* in mind, aim at a perfection impossible to achieve here. I aim lower and, being more of an optimist than you, I do not despair. I agree that the table wobbles, but adjusting a leg or two, I believe, we can steady it. I agree also that here we find none of those qualities (always quite rare!) that make you cry: "*It seems carved in stone*"; nevertheless, I feel that in the characters of Fiesco and Simone there are things that can be put to good use.

In sum, let's have a try and let's do this finale with its Tartar Ambassador, the letters of Petrarch, etc... etc... etc... Let's try, I repeat. We are not so inexperienced that we cannot realize, even beforehand, what will work in the theater. If it is not a hardship for you, and if you have time, set to work at once. Meanwhile I will try to straighten here and there the many crooked legs of my notes and... we shall see!

With affection, I am

G. Verdi

⮦The Ponchielli opera Verdi mentions is *Il figliuol prodigo,* which was to open the Scala season on 26 December 1880. Verdi's recommendation that Boito's own *Mefistofele* should be included in the Scala program also bore fruit: the work (in its revised version) had a run of ten performances, concluding the spring season, two months after the eighteen performances of the revised *Boccanegra.*

At this point, a Boito letter—accompanying the text of the Senate scene—is missing. The Verdi letter below is obviously the reply to it.

Genoa, 28 December 1880

8

Dear Boito,

Very beautiful this Senate scene, full of movement, of local color, with very elegant and powerful verses such as you habitually write. I agree about the verses to be changed at the beginning of the third act, and this way of poisoning the doge is excellent. But, unfortunately for me, the number is very vast, hard to set to music, and I don't know if, now that I am no longer *dans le mouvement,* I will have the time to climb into the saddle again and do this, as well as revise all the rest.

Allow me now some observations simply to clarify things for myself.

1. Do you believe it necessary to let it be known at the beginning that Amelia is safe, and is *demanding justice?*

2. Do you believe the Tartary business alone is enough to make the Senate meet? Could some other matter of state be added, for ex., a successful attack by some Corsairs; and perhaps the Venetian war cursed by the Poet? Everything, obviously, must be done quickly, in a few verses.

3. If Adorno says "I killed Lorenzino because he abducted my betrothed," and Amelia says "Save my betrothed," we ruin the scene in the third act between the Doge and Amelia. The scene is unimportant in itself, but it skillfully prepares the Doge's sleep and the terzetto. It seems to me that the action would lose nothing if, when the Doge says "Why have you drawn your sword?" Gabriele were to answer "You had

> Amelia Grimaldi abducted...
> Die, base, crowned Corsair
> DOGE Strike...
> GAB.   Amelia
> ALL   Amelia
> DOGE Adorno, you defend the maid; I admire you and absolve you...
> Amelia, say how you were abducted, etc., etc.?

The rest is fine. Stupendous from "Plebeians, Patricians, Populace" to the end, which we will close with "Be he cursed!"

Answer me as soon as possible.

Sincerest best wishes.

G. Verdi

◄When Verdi refers to act 3, he means what is now act 2 (he frequently called the prologue, confusingly, act 1). As the definitive libretto shows, Boito adopted—or adapted—most of the composer's suggestions.

In Verdi's third point, he is dealing with act 1, scenes 11 and 12.

Genoa, 8 January 1881

Dear Boito,

9

Have no remorse about wasting my time. So far I've done nothing at all about the music. Now, however, I am thinking about it; indeed, I have thought about this *Boccanegra* all day, and here is what, it seems to me, could be done.

I'll skip the prologue now, though I will perhaps change the first recitative, and a few bars here and there in the orchestra.

In the first number of the first act I would cut the cabaletta, not because it's a cabaletta, but because it's very ugly. I would change the prelude, to which I would join the prima donna's cantabile, changing the orchestration and making the whole thing a *single piece*. At the end I would repeat an orchestral passage from the prelude over which Amelia would say "Day is breaking... He does not come...." or something of the sort. So write me a couple of short verses, in broken phrases... I wouldn't want those words of jealousy for Amelia!

The offstage romanza of the tenor would stay exactly as it is.

In the following duet I would change the form of the cabaletta but there would be nothing for you to do.

In scene 5 between Fieschi and Gabriele I would like a few more words in the recitative, after the verse "Consent to our wedding." If the public doesn't catch the word *"humble"* they won't understand anything. If he said, for ex.: "Listen... deep secret," etc., etc., these are always words that make the public prick up its ears. So, if you think it worthwhile, add a pair of verses, or not, as you like. What is important for me is changing the duet between Fieschi and Gabriele "Fear, O Doge." It is too fierce, and says nothing. I would prefer Fieschi, Amelia's quasi father, to bless the young betrothed couple. This could produce a moment of pathos that would be a ray of light in all the darkness. To maintain the color, also introduce a bit of *civic feeling*. Fieschi can say "Love that angel... But after God... the Fatherland," etc... All words good for pricking up ears... In sum, eight nice verses for Fieschi and the same number for Gabriele, affectionate, moving, simple, so they can be set to a bit of melody, or something that resembles a melody at least. Ah, if we could have Amelia come back on stage and then have a terzettino for unaccompanied voices! How beautiful it is to write for three voices!... Amelia and Gabriele kneeling, Fiesco between them, erect, blessing them!... But I understand that, apart from the difficulty of bringing Amelia back on stage, we would have a scene almost identical with the conclusion of the last act...

Have I made myself clear? I'm not really sure I have. Try to sense what I have been unable to say, and meanwhile send me these few verses as quickly as possible; tomorrow or the day after I will tell you about the rest. Meanwhile I will begin working on the first number of this first act, if for no other reason than to put myself *dans le mouvement* before arriving at the finale. I would like to do all the work in sequence, as if this were a new opera.

I am waiting, and believe me yours,

G. Verdi

ᴥ Again, a Boito letter, to which the above is a reply, has not survived.

Genoa, 9 January 1881

10   Dear Boito,

I continue my letter of the other day...

I don't know if I told you not to make the verses too long in the duettino between Gabriele and Fiesco.

In scene 6, instead of the trumpets that announce the Doge, I would prefer a distant chorus of hunters. What do you say?

In the new finale, the Doge's first two verses "The new day..." etc., are useless. Fix the verse that follows and leave the duet between father and daughter as it stands. Only at the end, instead of Amelia's four verses:

> Not of regal pride
> The fleeting splendor
> But the halo crowning me
> Shall be the glow of love

I would like to her say, in four similar verses, "I shall live in mystery so you will not be the target of enemies' hatred." In this way I would give greater development to the so-called cabaletta, and I would not repeat it.

Further, I would ask you to change for me the father's verse or verses, to avoid the word "aureola" [halo]. I am not difficult about words, but in a cantabile that "au... eo..." make a nasal sound, guttural and disagreeable.

Very little, indeed almost nothing will have to be done in the other acts.

I have set to work seriously. Try to send me as quickly as possible what I asked of you yesterday and what I ask today.

In haste,

Yours,
G. Verdi

VARIANTS FOR ACT 1

11

ACT 1

Before the tenor's romanza

> Dawn breaks in the sky, but the beloved's song
> Is not yet heard...
> Every day, like the dawn that dries
> The flowers' dew, he dries my lash's tears.

Addition to the dialogue between Gabriello and Fiesco, scene 5

GABRIELE   Do you consent to our marriage?

ANDREA   A profound mystery
                                         A grim secret

       Menaces the maid.
GAB.   And what?
AND.   If I speak,
       Perhaps you will love her no longer.
GAB.   My love fears no
       Shadow of mysteries! I am listening to you.
AND.   Your Amelia was born of humble stock...
GAB.   The daughter of the Grimaldis?!
AND.   No, the daughter
       Of the Grimaldis died among consecrated
       Virgins in Pisa, etc., etc., etc...

ACT 1
Conclusion of scene 5

After the *versi sciolti*

AND.   Devout warrior, the noble faith
       Of ancient times is reborn in you;
       No, your sword does not give way
       At cruel hostile hatred.

	Come to me.
(embracing	~~Bold hero~~ I bless you
him)	In love and in war,
	Be faithful to your country,
	May your angel be faithful to you.
GAB.	From your lip the sacred words
	I have gathered like a balm,
	Steadfast for my sword are
	~~I already have strong veins and~~ my wrists,
	A vast ardor fills my breast.
	Since I have been blessed by you
	My spirit languishes within me no more,
	Raging and stirring in my blood
	Are immense hate and immense love.

Variant for the Senate scene

SIMONE	Gentlemen, the king of Tartary offers you
	Pledges of peace and rich gifts, and declares
	The Euxine open to Ligurian prows.
	Do you agree?
ALL	Yes.
SIM.	But another oath,
(after a pause)	More generous, I ask of you.
SOME	Speak.
SIM.	The same voice that thundered over Rienzi,
	Prophecy of glory and then of death,
(distant	Now thunders over Genoa. Here is a message
tumult begins	From the hermit of the Sorgues, for Venice he
to be heard)	Beseeches peace...
PAOLO	Let him attend to his rhymes,
(interrupting)	The singer of the blonde Avignonaise.
SIM.	Gentlemen!
(forcefully)	
	(the tumult approaches)
PIETRO	What noise?!
SOME	Whence such cries?
	etc., etc., etc., etc.

Other variant on the Senate scene before Amelia's entrance

SIM.	Why have you drawn your sword?
(to Gab.)	
GAB.	I have slain
	Lorenzino.

POPULACE   Murderer.

FIESCHI   He had abducted

The Grimaldi girl.

SIM.   (Horror!)

POPULACE   You lie!

GAB.   That coward

Before dying told me a powerful man

Had urged him to commit the crime.

                                                    discovered
PIE.   (Ah! You are ~~lost~~)

(to Paolo)

SIM.   And his name?

(in agitation)

GAB.   Have no fear! The culprit died

(fixing the   Before revealing it.

Doge with

dreadful irony)

SIM.   What do you mean?

GAB.   By heaven!

(awesomely)   You are a powerful man!

SIM.   Rogue!

(to Gab.)

GAB.   Bold

(to the Doge,   Abductor of maidens!

rushing at him)

SOME   Have him disarmed!

GAB.   Wicked crowned corsair! Die!

(freeing him-

self and run-

ning with

Fiesco to

wound the

Doge)

AMELIA   Strike.

(entering and

putting herself

between the at-

tackers and the

Doge)

SIM. ⎫

FIE.   ⎬   Amelia!

GAB. ⎭

ALL   Amelia!...

AM.   O Doge! (o father!)

Save Adorno.

SIM.	Let no one harm him!!
(to the guards,	All pride cedes, and at the sound of her grief
who have	All my soul speaks of love.
seized Gabri-	Amelia, tell how you were abducted
ello to disarm	And how etc., etc., etc., etc.
him)	

Very small variant for my personal use and to assuage my *scrupulous conscience*

FINALE ACT 1

STANZA	His heartfelt words
FOR	Are able to calm our wrath;
CHORUS	A flight of gentle wind
	That restores the sea's peace.

(In the first manuscript I didn't like those two overlapping images of *altar* and *sea*. They canceled each other. This variant is not beautiful, I know, but it makes a bit more sense.)

VARIANTS FOR ACT 2
Variant for scenes 1 and 2 of Act 2

Scene 1
Palazzo degli Abati
Doge's chamber, etc., etc. Big chair, table, an
alcove with bed. On the table a ewer and a cup.

Paolo and Pietro

PAO.	You saw those two?
PIE.	Yes.
PAO.	Take them at once
	From their prison by the secret door
	that this key will unlock.
PIE.	I understand you.
	(exits)

Scene 2
Paolo alone

I have cursed myself!!...
And the anathema
Pursues me still... and the air still rings with it!
Reviled... cast out
By the Senate and by Genoa, here I strike
The last blow before fleeing, here I decide

Your fate, Doge, in this extreme anguish.
You, who offend me and owe to me your throne,
Here I abandon you
To your destiny
In this fatal hour.

(extracts an   Here I administer a slow, dire death.
ampoule,   There I arm a murderer for you.
pours its con- Let Death choose its way
tents into the Between poison and dagger.
cup)

ACT 2

Scene 3 (brief variant)
The above, Andrea, Gabriele from right, led by Pietro

	have you led me?
FIE.	Prisoner, in what place ~~am I~~
PAO.	In the Doge's rooms, and it is
	Paolo who speaks to you.
FIE.	Your gazes are grim!
PAO.	I know the hatred hidden in you.
	Listen to me.
FIE.	What do you wish?
PAO.	For the fray
	You prepared the Guelph host
	etc., etc., etc., etc.

Variant for scene 8 of Act 2
Doge and Gabriele, hidden
Enter the Doge, pensive; he sits

DOGE   Doge! Shall the two rebels
              Know your clemency again? A sign of fear
              Punishment would be. My throat burns...
(pours from   Even the spring's ripple is bitter to the lip
the ewer into Of the ruler... my soul is heavy... broken
the cup and   By grief are my limbs... now... sleep conquers me...
drinks)
(falls asleep) Oh Amelia... you love... an enemy...
              etc., etc., etc., etc.

Dear Maestro,

Have I guessed right? I don't know. I await your instructions and confine myself for today to greeting cordially you and your wife.

                              Yours,
                              A. Boito

◆The "voice that thundered over Rienzi" refers, like the "hermit of the Sorgues," to Petrarch; the "blonde Avignonaise" is the poet's beloved Laura. Rienzi—more usually known as Cola di Rienzo—was a fourteenth-century Roman revolutionary, who established a people's republic; he was assassinated in 1354. The Sorgues is a river in Vaucluse, France; it figures in Petrarch's work written during his exile in that area.

[ca. 9 January 1881]

12   Dear Maestro,

You see the effects of nearsightedness added to those of absent-mindedness: on my desk I find this page, which goes with the variants for the first act. No harm done; I hope you'll receive it with the rest.

Affectionate greetings,

A. Boito

◆Boito wrote this note to accompany a page of verses, originally meant to be part of letter no. 11.

Genoa, 10 January 1881

13   Dear Boito,

The two special-delivery letters with the variants arrive just at the right moment. With the four verses "Dawn breaks in the sky..." etc., I will finish the first number, which actually can already be considered finished.

The few verses added in the following scene between Andrea and Gab. are good. I am afraid the duettino will prove long and too strong. I would like right at that moment something calm and solemn, religious. It's a wedding. A father is blessing his adoptive children. I don't like the *ottonario* meter very much because of those damned two notes on the upbeat but I will avoid them, and rather than lose time I will start immediately writing this duet on the four verses of Andrea:

Come to me, I bless you

. . . .
. . . .
. . . .

Meanwhile I'll cobble up another four verses for Gabriele so I can go on working, until your verses arrive. Four verses for each will be enough. To make myself clearer: I would like Gabriele to say his strophe on his knees; so make it something religious. This does no harm, it seems to me, and, besides, this calm and that of the following scenes, will help to heighten the tumult of the finale. You say the duettino would start after the *versi sciolti*... All of it? It seems to me the duettino should start after "On earth and in heaven..." or else after:

But let not love restrain
The enthusiasm of your civic feelings

fixing, of course, the rhymes and the meter as you think best... And if you agree, we could have him say:

The Doge is coming. Let us leave
. . . .
Fiesco in [the guise of] *Andrea*

after the duettino during the blast of trumpets, or the chorus of hunters.

All the other variants are fine, and the recitative of the *poison* is excellent. Maybe we will find ourselves a bit hampered, dramatically, by Amelia's words:

O Doge (o father)
Save Adorno...

How will she say these words?... Whispered to the Doge?... That would not be very beautiful... But these are trifles, which can be fixed with a stage movement, or with a word.

Take heart then, my dear Boito, write me these four *ottonari* for Gabriele. No more than four verses each. That's enough. Send them as quickly as possible. I, meanwhile, am working...

Greetings also from my wife.

G. Verdi

[Telegram]

12 Jan 81

14

Arrigo Boito, Principe Umberto 1, Milan
From Genoa

Don't do chorus of hunters. Will write.

Verdi

◄This telegram was obviously sent before the following letter, even though the date given above, taken from Nardi's handwritten copy, is the day after that of the letter: in all likelihood the date transcribed by Nardi corresponds to the day the telegram arrived, not the day it was sent. For that matter, a delay in the delivery of the telegram could be explained by the fact that the address was wrong: "Principe Umberto" instead of the correct "Principe Amedeo."

Tuesday [Genoa, 11 January 1881]

15   Dear Boito,

As I said in the telegram I sent you this morning, I believe there's no point in doing the chorus of hunters. It would mean another musical number, and in this act (even calculating prelude–soprano aria–tenor romanza as a single number) we would already have six numbers, of which one, the finale, is very long. A *loud blast* of trumpets of *12* or *16* measures for the Doge's entrance will suffice.

Yesterday evening I did the duet between Andrea and Gabriele. The additions have required me to revise the recitative in part, and I have stopped at the words:

On earth and in heaven

I can, however, add also:

...But let not love restrain
The enthusiasm of your civic feelings

Adjust, as you think best, the end of this recitative. For the cantabile I used the four verses of Andrea:

Come to me, I bless you
. . . .
. . . .
. . . .

and I have also adjusted on my own another strophe for Gabriele so that I could finish. All I need is 4 verses for Andrea (the four quoted above could do) and another four verses for Gabriele, to be written. The number has a calm, solemn character, a bit religious, a bit old-fashioned. So I beg you to do this strophe; I will go ahead meanwhile to the finale. When the Andrea-Gabriele duet ends the trumpets will attack off stage, and meanwhile, if necessary, they can say the verses:

The Doge is coming... Let us leave, etc.

Tell me where I must stop.
In haste,

G. Verdi

◄§Andrea, here, is Jacopo Fiesco (under an assumed name). At this stage of their work on the opera, Verdi and Boito were occasionally uncertain about the names of the characters. Fiesco is also called Fieschi on occasion, and Gabriele is sometimes referred to as Gabriello. The matter is further complicated by the fact that several of the characters disguise themselves under assumed names.

[Milan] 14 Jan [1881]
Via Principe Amedeo 1

16

Dear Maestro,

I waited for the letter announced by your telegram before returning to my desk for the new variants. I received the letter yesterday and here is the result of a careful reading of everything you have written me these past few days. It seems to me that the recitative of the scene with Andrea and Gabriele should continue up to the words "On earth and in heaven," completing the verse as I will indicate, and immediately beginning the lyrical part; for ex.:

ANDREA	You are worthy of her!
GABRIELE	Let her then be united to me!
AND.	On earth and in heaven.
GAB.	Ah! You give life back to me!
(effusive)	
AND.	Come to me, I bless you In the peace of this hour; Live happily and faithfully adore Your angel, the fatherland, heaven.

(See an alternative on the back of this page)

GAB.	Pious echo of old times Your voice is a chaste enchantment; The holy memory of this hour My faithful heart will cherish.
(trumpet blasts)	
GAB.	Here is the Doge. Let us leave. He must not see you.
AND.	Ah! let the day of vengeance soon break.

Does that seem enough to you?... It does to me. Better not to mention the conspiracy of the Guelphs, I believe; it would perhaps confuse the always somewhat lazy minds of the public and would mar the clarity of the finale.

If, however, you believe it should be mentioned, nothing prevents you from retaining, just as they are, the six verses of the old libretto that come just after the trumpet blast.

One observation. It would be desirable at this point to avoid the change of scene. Three scenes in one act seem too many to me: they destroy that impression of unity so necessary to the vital organization of the act. Remember that in the whole drama this garden is the only charming scene. All the others are grave, solemn, or grim. There is too great an abundance of *interiors:* Council Chamber, Doge's room, Ducal Hall. Since at this beginning of this first act we are in the open air, let's stay there as long as we can. To one side, at the end of the garden, there can be a couple of wings representing the entrance to the Grimaldi palace. Amelia would come to meet the Doge at the doorway of the palace, and for the ensuing scene the garden would be a fairly natural setting. Furthermore, if the scene changed, there would be no reason to send Fiesco and Gabriele away from a place where the Doge, whom they are fleeing, would not set foot. But let's not waste time.

Scene 6

Doge, Paolo, etc., etc.

DOGE Paolo.
PAOLO   My lord.
DOGE   Events are spurring us on.
    It is best to leave here, etc., etc...

And so on, as written.

In this way the verse about the festive day would be patched up *as well as possible.*

Scene 7

Now I come to the "au... eo..."
    Shall we use "gloria" instead of "aureola"?

Di mia corona il raggio
La gloria tua sarà?
[The glow of my crown
Will be your glory?]

And then let's see if, when they are transcribed, the four new verses go with the old ones, where Amelia replies to her father:

AMELIA Father, you will see your vigilant
        Daughter always beside you;
        In melancholy hours

> I will dry your tears...
> We will have solitary joys
> Known only to heaven;
> I shall be the gentle dove
> Of the regal dwelling.

And for today I think I have performed my task; ready to begin again in everything that doesn't suit you.

I must inform you, dear Maestro, that Thursday I'll be leaving Milan for Padua. I will stay there a week to help them cook up *Mefistofele* and serve it hot to my compatriots. Until Wednesday evening I will be able to receive my letters in Milan, then in Padua, Albergo della Croce d'Oro. By the 29th I'll be home again.

Giulio Ricordi has been confined to bed, ill, for many days; he still isn't on his feet, but he's better.

Many, many greetings.

Yours,
A. Boito

[on the back of the folded page]

Alternative: Your voice seems an echo, a song
As if from the old days.
The holy memory of your words
My faithful heart will cherish.

These damned *ottonari*. You're right, they're the most boring singsong in our metrics. I chose them out of desperation. I didn't want *settenari* because almost the whole libretto, as far as the lyrical part goes, is in *settenari;* I didn't want *quinari* because that part was written in *quinari* in the old libretto and I thought you would be reluctant to go back to the old rhythm.

 ∿All the quotations in the above letter refer to act 1. Boito's suggestions were followed, except the alternative verses for Gabriele in scene 5.

Genoa, 15 [January] 1881

Dear Boito,

17

Everything works well, and I am doubly happy not to change scenes before the second act.

You, my dear Boito, imagine that you have finished? Quite the contrary! We will have finished after the dress rehearsal, if we actually reach it. For the present, in the duet between father and daughter there is something that should be given greater prominence. If the public misses that one poor verse "To my non-brothers" they won't understand anything further.

I would like them to say, for ex.:

DOGE	Paolo!
AMELIA	You named that wretch!... But to you,
	good, generous, I must tell
	the truth
~~DOGE~~	~~What!~~
AMELIA	The Grimaldis are not my brothers
DOGE	But—you?
AMELIA	I am not a Grimaldi
DOGE	And who are you then?

This way the attention is held, and something is understood. If you agree, write me three or four *versi sciolti*, clear and distinct. You will write beautiful verses as always but here I wouldn't mind even if they were ugly. Pardon the heresy: I believe that in the theater, just as it is sometimes admirable if composers have the talent to not make music, and to know how to *s'effacer*, so also in the case of poets, sometimes intelligible, dramatic words are better than a beautiful verse. This is only my opinion.

Another observation about the finale. Among the 2000 spectators at the first night, there may be barely twenty who will know the two letters of Petrarch. Unless we insert some kind of footnote, for the public Simone's lines will be obscure. I would like, almost as comment, after the verse

The singer of the blond Avignonaise

all to say "War on Venice!"

DOGE	It's a fratricidal war. Venice and Genoa have a
	common fatherland: Italy.
ALL	Our fatherland is Genoa

Tumult offstage, etc.

Answer me before you leave. I wish you meanwhile a good journey and good luck...

Warmly,
G. Verdi

P.S. I'm sorry about Giulio. I thought it was something less serious. I am very happy to hear he is better.

ᴖᴥThe father-daughter scene referred to above is act 1, scene 7. The finale discussed is also that of act 1.

Sunday [Milan, 16 January 1881]

18

I completely agree with your theory, dear Maestro, about sacrificing, when necessary, euphony of verse and music to effective dramatic accent and theatrical reality. You wanted three or four *versi sciolti,* even ugly, but intelligible, instead of that verse:

of my non-brothers

which is not beautiful, to be sure. I have written the four verses (I wasn't able to make them three) but I decided not to make them *sciolti* because I was afraid that, between the rhymed *settenari* that precede them and the rhymed *ottonari* that follow them, that abandonment of rhyme for only four lines would look weak to the reader.

DOGE   Paolo!
AMELIA   You named that wretch... And since
          You feel such compassion for my fate,
          I want to reveal to you the secret that enfolds me:
(after a brief
pause)
          I am not a Grimaldi.
DOGE   O heaven! who are you?

Now we go on to the Council Chamber:

PAOLO   . . . . Let him attend to his rhymes,
(laughing)   The singer of the blonde Avignonaise.
ALL THE
COUNCILLORS   War on Venice!
(then Paolo, fiercely)
DOGE   And with this horrible cry
          Between two Italian shores, Cain raises
          His bloody club! Adria and Liguria
          Have a common fatherland.

```
ALL                                    Our fatherland is
                    Genoa!
PIERO                    What is that noise?
SOME                                         Whence those cries?
                             etc., etc., etc.
```

I have avoided the word "fratricidal" war suggested in your letter so it wouldn't diminish the effect of the exclamation "Fratricides!" which bursts out before the verses of the

DOGE Plebeians, patricians!... etc.

To be sure, in the theater there will not be more than twenty people sufficiently cultivated to recognize the Doge's reference to Petrarch's two letters to the Prince of Rome, but heaven preserve us from the temptation of footnotes and commentary. Still, if we want the 20 people to become two hundred or more, we merely have to change the reference, and instead of the letters (known today to few, whereas to Petrarch's contemporaries they were very well known) refer to the canzone that we all learn in school, and alter in this way;

> inneggiò
> La stessa voce che ~~tuono~~ su Roma,
> Pria che recasse tutta alle sue mani
> Rienzi protervo la civil possanza,
> Or su Genova tuona...
>   exalted
> [The same voice that ~~thundered~~ over Rome
> Before the arrogant Rienzi took into his hands
> All civil power,
> Now thunders over Genoa...]

But the sentence becomes too prolix and too contorted for the straightforward, rapid requirements of musical delivery.

For that matter, the first version is not historically correct. Instead of:

> Vaticinio di gloria e poi di morte
> [Prophecy of glory and then of death]

it would be more accurate to say:

> Vaticinio di gloria e poscia d'onta
> [Prophecy of glory and then of shame]

but this way the verse becomes ugly, even if that doesn't matter to you or to me. I leave the choice to you. The public, in any case, is an animal that will swallow anything and doesn't care a thing for these scruples, and in this it is not mistaken.

If you need a few more drops of ink from my pen there would be time for me to receive another letter from you before my departure, still set for Thursday.

Many cordial greetings.

> Yours,
> A. Boito

Giulio yesterday was worse, but today less so. He has a congestion of the lung and they had to apply some blisters to his chest; this is something that keeps us all a bit alarmed, not so much for the present as for the future.

᭛Here Boito refers for the first time to two more letters of Petrarch, beyond the two already mentioned (see note following letter no. 6 above). These are addressed to "the Prince of Rome," whom the librettist identifies as Rienzi, or Cola di Rienzo (see note following letter no. 11 above). The final version of the passage (act 1, scene 10) reads:

> La stessa voce che tuonò su Rienzi,
> Vaticinio di gloria e poi di morte,
> Or su Genova tuona.

The Petrarch canzone that schoolchildren memorized was probably "spirto gentil."

The other changes suggested by Boito became part of the definitive libretto.

Giulio Ricordi—just over forty at this time—was to live another thirty-two years.

Monday [Genoa, 17 January 1881]

19

Dear Boito,

Just a word to say I received this morning your verses and that they are fine.

That's enough for now...

But later, I don't know.

Affectionate greetings.

> Yours,
> G. Verdi

Monday [Genoa, 24 January 1881]

20 Dear Boito,

I need another drop of your ink. *Another,* I say... I don't say *the last!*

Involuntarily I have written an ensemble number in the new finale. Obviously Simone first sings solo all his sixteen verses:

Plebeians! Patricians! Populace

. . . .

Afterwards comes this ensemble, which isn't much of an ensemble, but still an ensemble. As a rule I dislike asides because they force the artist to remain immobile; and I would like at least Amelia to turn to Fieschi, urging:

Peace... forgive... forget...
They are our brothers!

In this way the short phrase written for Amelia would have greater warmth for me. Don't forget in this new short strophe the word "pace" [peace], which suits me very well.

In the earlier narrative of Amelia, I have never been able, nor can I now, nor will ever I be able, to set properly that verse:

Non egli è di tanto misfatto il più reo
[He is not, of that misdeed, the most guilty]

and in fact, in the old score, I set (getting both verse and rhyme wrong):

Di tanto misfatto, il più reo non è
[Of that misdeed, he is not the most guilty]

To avoid such indecency see if you can fix the verse, separating the first and the second *senari.*

I've finished... for now! Heartfelt greetings.

Affectionately,
G. Verdi

Amelia's tricky line that troubles Verdi, "Di tanto misfatto, il più reo non è," does not appear in the final libretto. Both Piave and Boito used here a double *senario,* which requires a distinct close to each half to make the structure clear; even more effectively, the librettist may make an internal rhyme. In rearranging the words (to get a masculine ending on the second *senario*), Verdi ended the first *senario* awkwardly, on an elision (Di tan-to mis-fat-to_il) instead of a good clear sound.

In insisting on the word "pace" (which, in Amelia's soaring line, becomes one of the most memorable moments of *Boccanegra*), Verdi underscored the word twice. All text in this letter refers to act 1, scene 12.

31 January [1881]
Milan

21

Dear Maestro,

I received your letter in Padua, but until today I was unable to make the variant you were waiting for. I consoled myself with the thought that meanwhile you would be working on some other part of the opera.

From what you wrote me I gather that in this ensemble number the part of Amelia, after that of the Doge, has turned out to be musically the most important, and I deduced that only four verses wouldn't be enough, so I wrote eight. See if they are all right:

AMELIA TO FIESCO
Peace! Tame your haughty blood
And bend your pride!
Peace! The fatherland suffers
Through your cruel wrath.
With my lips you are begged also
By that soul, assumed among the stars,
Of the sweet departed one
Who watches you in heaven.

I would have liked to give a bit of movement to the part of Gabriele but I couldn't, and the reason is clear: If the Doge speaks to all and if Amelia is pleading with Fiesco, Gabriele has no one to speak with, since Pietro and Paolo are also talking between themselves; so he is necessarily condemned to immobility.

And now try, dear Maestro, to put in the place of the guilty verse of the old libretto the following verse:

AMELIA   V'è un uom più nefando—che illeso ancor sta.
         [there is a more wicked man—who is still unharmed.]

I realized that here you needed a masculine ending and I had to seek, several verses above, another masculine ending to make some sort of rhyme.

Now I have resumed my usual Milanese life and am at your disposal for everything you may need. Cordial greetings

from your
A. Boito

[Genoa] 2 February 1881

22   Dear Boito,

Now first of all, my sincere congratulations for the outcome of *Mefistofele* in Padua.

Eight verses are too many for Amelia. The piece is nothing but a big solo for the Doge with the addition of the other parts at the end. Amelia has only a little phrase alone. For me the first four are fine, but you may want to change the second because of the rhyme.

The verse of the narrative will do very well.

And now we come to the last act. The first chorus of this act no longer has any justification, and, before the curtain rises, I would repeat in the orchestra the music of the revolt with which the previous act ends, with offstage cries of "Victory! Victory!" When the curtain rises, the Doge would begin:

> Warrior sword, etc., etc.

Does the following scene with Pietro, Paolo, and Paolo-Fieschi remain? What if we had finished?! Heartfelt greetings.

> Yours,
> G. Verdi

☙The original eight lines for Amelia, addressing Fiesco, in act 1, scene 12, become four in the final libretto. See letter no. 26 for the nearly definitive form.

Genoa, 5 February 1881

23   Dear Boito,

We have not finished!!!!

In the first scene of the first act, after the offstage strophes of Gabriele, there have to be a few measures for the orchestra, to give him time to arrive on stage. I would prefer a brief and agitated phrase for Amelia. Actually, I have concocted on my own four *quinari* with masculine endings:

> È desso! Oh Ciel!
> Mi manca il Cor
> · · · · · · · · · ·
> · · · · · · · · · ·
> [It is he! Oh heaven!
> My heart fails me]

and I have composed the phrase. I beg you to send these four verses. Six would be even better, but no more than six.

In the new finale of the revolt scene I have taken care, despite an agitated movement in the orchestra, to make the words clearly audible: the orchestra roars, but it roars softly. It is necessary, however, for the orchestra also to make its formidable voice heard at the end, and I would like to have a big *forte* after the Doge's words "Here are the plebians..." Here the orchestra would be unleashed with all its might and to it would be added, just having entered, populace, patricians, women, etc., etc... I would then need two verses to have everybody yell. Make sure that these verses include the word "Vengeance!" For Paolo I am composing that fine recitative you added at the beginning of the second act. What a shame! Those verses, so powerful, in the mouth of a common rogue! I have, however, arranged for this Paolo to be the least roguish of rogues.

And now, tell me.

Would it be a sin beyond absolution if in the final chorus of the second act, "To arms, to arms, Ligurians," I were to add the women?

Would it be another sin if in the last scene, the death of the Doge, Maria, having become Gabriele's wife, were to enter, followed by some Maidens? Would "some" have to mean the entire women's chorus?

After this perhaps we will have finished.

Believe me ever

yours,
G. Verdi

᪥The complex plot of *Simon Boccanegra* requires that Simone's daughter Maria go under the assumed name of Amelia Grimaldi for much of the opera's duration. In the correspondence with Boito, Verdi refers to her sometimes by one name, sometimes by the other.

In the final version of the opera Maria-Amelia does appear—with the women's chorus—in the Doge's death scene, along with Gabriele, Fiesco, Senators, Pages, etc.

Saturday, Milan [5 February 1881]

Dear Maestro,

24

I repeat my old comparison with the table; now it is the fourth leg that wobbles. It must be steadied, and in doing so we must use great skill to make sure that, with this one fixed, the others don't start wobbling again. For two days now I have been thinking constantly about the fourth act. I like very much the idea of the orchestral introduction with the curtain down and the offstage cries. It is very useful: it links wonderfully the end of the third act with the beginning of the fourth, it joins the events of the last two acts in a unity of time that is rapid, terse, very dramatic. But this idea isn't enough. The scene between Fiesco and Paolo cannot remain as it is.

It will be a good idea to alter some aspects of the scene between the Doge and Fieschi. (Fieschi and the Doge have already found themselves face-to-face in a violent emotional situation two acts earlier, namely, in the ensemble.) The Doge's very first words in the fourth act must suggest in advance the catastrophe. In the old libretto, Simone, when he says "Warrior sword," is too healthy. In short, tomorrow I will send you an attempt at repair, versified, and you will decide.

I thank you, my dear Maestro, for the thoughtful words with which you begin your letter.

Until tomorrow. A heartfelt greeting.

Yours,
A. Boito

⊷As usual, in referring to "third" and "fourth" acts, Boito means the second and third acts of the definitive libretto.

His thanks, at the end of the letter, refer to Verdi's congratulations after the success of *Mefistofele* in Padua.

Sunday [Genoa, 6 February 1881]

25 Dear Boito,

Let us then fix the fourth leg, too... but you frighten me, saying that it is necessary to alter the scene between Fieschi and the Doge! If it's just a trifle, all right; but if it has to be completely redone, there is an impossible consideration: time. Enough for now. I impatiently await your letter tomorrow.

And tell me, couldn't the whole first scene be avoided? Then the Doge would appear only once in this act, when he enters, poisoned:

...My temples burn, etc.

The act would begin with the orchestra prelude and the offstage cries of "Victory"... At the curtain's rise the Wedding Chorus would be heard offstage, and the two Saints, Pietro and Paolo, could say that the Doge has won, and Gabriele is marrying Amelia....

Now I am waiting for those four or six verses, *quinari* with masculine endings, that I asked you for yesterday. Send them as quickly as you can.

In haste,

your
G. Verdi

P.S. You have written me nothing about Amelia's strophe in the new finale.

ᴥ Verdi's suggestion was followed, and the scene in question was cut.

[Milan, 7 February 1881]

26

Dear Maestro,

This time I'm the one who says we haven't yet finished. I keep your last three letters on my desk and I consult them constantly, but as far as the first scenes of the last act are concerned my ideas are still in a tangle. Various attempts have worked out badly. Still, today you prompt a thought that seems to me very practical: To open the act with the nuptial hymn in the distance (beautiful contrast with the warlike vivacity of the prelude), while on stage the very rapid but indispensable dialogue takes place between Fiesco and Paolo (the other apostle, Pietro, we can forget; nobody will notice) and this dialogue must assume a different character from that of the old libretto. Paolo must have taken an active part in the Guelphs' uprising against the Doge and he has been caught, imprisoned, and sentenced to death by the Doge himself. It's good for the Doge finally to sentence somebody, and since we have at hand a rascal who has betrayed the people's party to join the Guelphs and has committed every sort of rascality, let's sentence him to the gallows and have done with him. Vice versa, Fiesco, at the very moment that Paolo goes by between guards, heading for his execution, Fiesco, as I was saying, is freed by the Doge's order and it is right that he should be, he didn't take part in the uprising (I should hope not: he was in prison). So the condemned man and the freed one meet as the wedding hymn continues and during their dialogue Paolo reveals the business of the poison, and from the words of the two the deeds that have to be elucidated are elucidated. About fifteen verses, not lyrical, will suffice. Now we come to the scene between the Doge and Fiesco. Don't be alarmed, dear Maestro, I understand the importance of this scene, which, among other things, is the most beautiful in the drama. I said it would be a good idea to change some aspects of that dialogue, but "some" is too much; one is enough, the one that is condensed in the words "The dead rise from their graves." But I understand also the great importance of these words. I will not cut them but will add perhaps a verse or two to lead into the dialogue in a more logical way, since now in the first act we have created some actions and frictions that didn't exist in the old version. This is what the part to be changed consists of.

But, speaking of Fiesco, before I forget I must propose two very tiny changes in the scene between him and Paolo in the penultimate act, and I do this out of a desire for clarity. Instead of that word that Paolo says, "Fool, go," which is very crude and can even seem to the public ridiculous because of its vulgarity (we might as well say its *verismo*), I would say:

FIESCO You dare propose to Fiesco a crime?
PAOLO You refuse? (after a pause) Go off to your prison.

Thus we clarify this fact: *Rather than agree to any treachery, Fieschi returns to prison.* This fact is indispensable to us for a whole series of reasons. The old text said at this point: "Fieschi exits right." And in exiting right, where was he going? To prison? Apparently not. So he was accepting not Paolo's cowardly pact, but the freedom that was that pact's reward. And that was not Fiesco's way. It's useful for us to keep Fieschi from taking an active part in the Guelphs' uprising so as not to burden him with yet another offense against the Doge, and I repeat, the best way to prevent that is to keep him under lock and key.

Meanwhile, here are the shards of poetry you asked of me:

ACT 1
Scene 1

(*quinari* with masculine endings after Gabriele's offstage song)

AMELIA He comes!... love
        Flames up in my bosom.
        And my eager heart
        Shatters its bonds.

I wager those you have written are much better, but these masculine-ending *quinari* are enemies of the pen.

───────────────────

Variant of the entrance of the chorus in the Senate scene

DOGE	Here are the plebeians!
THE CROWD	Vengeance! Vengeance!
	Let the blood of the fierce killer be shed!
DOGE	Is this then the voice of the people?
(ironically)	Distant, a hurricane's thunder; close,
	Shouting of women and children...

. . . .

You notice that "Vengeance" can be repeated as often as you like and, what's more, also the following *endecasillabo*. Thus the instrumental and choral outburst can achieve its full effect; and if the strident notes of the women in the upper register find their place in that outburst, your poet's prayer is answered and the sarcastic phrase of the Doge is explained. I put that phrase there in order to face bravely the first difficulty that worried us, namely, that of having the women appear in a Senate. If we ourselves courageously point out to the public that the women are there, then no one will dream of raising the slightest objection. For that matter, it is a well-known fact that women play a leading part in popular uprisings; just think of the Paris *Commune*. But where on earth have I got to? Let's return to the libretto. Here are the four verses of Amelia for the end of the lyrical bit in the same act:

AMELIA	Peace! Restrain, for pity's sake,
(to Fiesco)	Your immense outrage!
	Peace! Be inspired by a feeling
	Of patriotic charity.

———————————

And now I'll answer your two half-serious questions. The observation I made above will show you that I don't think it censurable to add the women's voices to the warlike chorus:

To arms! To arms, o Ligurians.

Two more lines and then I've finished for today. Can Amelia in the last act be followed by her handmaidens? Of course. She is returning from church, from the wedding, with her escort of women and also, if you like, of pages.

Most cordial greetings.

I don't think I'm deceiving myself if I promise you another conversation tomorrow.

Yours warmly,
A. Boito

◄The last act of the definitive version opens and proceeds much as Boito describes it here. As Verdi accepted Boito's verses for Amelia in act 1, scene 12 (reducing them from eight to four), he also adopted the poet's four verses for Amelia in the first scene of act 1 and the verses suggested for the entry of the populace in the Senate scene. There was only one further change: "raffrena" (restrain) became "nascondi" (hide).

[Telegram]

8 Feb 81

Arrigo Boito, Principe Amedeo 1, Milan
From Genoa

27 Excellent. But remember time pressing. Tornaghi will speak with you.
Verdi

◄Eugenio Tornaghi (1844?–1915) was an important figure at Casa Ricordi, often acting as agent for its scores. At this point, La Scala and Giulio Ricordi must have been a little uneasy, as the anticipated date of the *Boccanegra* production was fast approaching.

The day after sending this telegram Verdi made a quick trip to Milan, partly to hear an *Ernani* with some of the singers who would be appearing in *Boccanegra* (Maurel, D'Angeri, De Reszké, Tamagno), but also to meet Boito and his great friend Franco Faccio—who would be the opera's conductor—in Tornaghi's office for last-minute discussions. On this occasion Boito probably handed Verdi the verses of the finale referred to in the letter below. The manuscript of these verses has not survived.

Verdi had met Faccio before (see Marcello Conati's introduction). Faccio had conducted the Italian premiere of *Aida* (La Scala, 1872), but their closer friendship was to begin with this *Boccanegra* and continue beyond the production of *Otello*, whose premiere Faccio also conducted, until the conductor's untimely death in 1891. Born in Verona in 1840, Francesco (always known as Franco) Faccio studied at the Milan Conservatory, where he formed a lifelong association with his fellow-student Boito. After beginning his career as a composer, Faccio made his conducting debut (with a performance of *Un ballo in maschera*) in 1866 in Venice; by 1871 he was appointed chief conductor at La Scala, where he remained until his fatal illness forced him to resign in 1889. Besides Verdi, he also conducted premieres of Catalani and Ponchielli, not to mention the Italian premiere of Wagner's *Meister-*

singer. He played a significant role in the launching of Giacomo Puccini, conducting in 1884 his *Capriccio sinfonico* (later to become partially incorporated into *La Bohème*), which Puccini had written for his graduation from the Milan Conservatory. Faccio's friendship with Boito will figure prominently in a later part of this correspondence.

Genoa, 15 February 1881

28

Dear Boito,

We haven't finished yet! The very, very beautiful finale that you did for me has somewhat compromised the scene in the last act between Fieschi and the Doge. In the old libretto, after the prologue they hadn't met again. Twenty-five years had gone by, because Boccanegra was elected doge in 1339 and he died in 1364. Now the Doge knows Fieschi too well, and the latter cannot *appear to him like a ghost.* It seems to me it wouldn't be hard to fix everything:

1. If we avoid saying "At his side Fiesco is fighting"
2. Fieschi should remain hidden as much as possible in the disguise of Andrea and not say "He had abducted the Grimaldi girl," nor attack the Doge, etc.
3. In the eighth scene of the second act it would be best to avoid "the two rebels," and say "the traitors" generically
4. In the new scene of the last act I would not say "The Doge proclaims you free," but... "The Doge pardons all: you are free!"

And there are other, many other little things! Give it some thought and you will find something better. Write me at once. If necessary we'll have time to talk about it when we meet.

Believe me

yours warmly,
G. Verdi

[Milan] Tuesday, 15 [February 1881]

29

Dear Maestro,

We haven't finished! The same scruples that were tormenting you were tormenting me. I accept and approve all the solutions you suggest. We will say "Beside him a Guelph is fighting," or else "Beside him an old man is fighting," or else "Beside him a patrician is fighting." You choose. The words "He had abducted the Grimaldi girl" we will have said by Adorno or by a part of the chorus. Instead of "the two rebels" we will say "the traitors," or else "the revolutionaries," whichever you like more.

We will no longer say "The Doge proclaims you free," but instead:

You are free; here is your sword...

or else:

You are free; this is your weapon...

and the official hands Fiesco's sword to him.

I believe that these little touches will suffice to arrange everything satisfactorily.

In one of my last letters where I spoke about the scene between Fiesco and the Doge, when I said some situations had changed I was referring precisely to the points you have mentioned. Indeed, I was alarmed, believing we would have to change whole passages in the scene in question, but on the other hand I realized that the solution there could then prove troublesome for the last act. I thought to save the situation by having Fiesco exclaim that verse of his (which is still useful in any case):

At last

The hour has come for us to meet face-to-face!

With this verse I meant to explain that, even if they had glimpsed each other in a stormy crowd in the scene of the Palazzo degli Abati, still after all the years that had gone by since the scene of the prologue, the two antagonists had never been "face-to-face," that is to say alone together, masters of their actions and their words, isolated and free of outside influences, of outside episodes, or to use a phrase that our Shakespeare is fond of, they had never found themselves "beard-to-beard." And this is true and the phrase about the "ghost" strictly speaking could stand *quand même.* Still, the brief changes of words we have settled on today help greatly to clarify matters.

So then, dear Maestro, until we meet again soon in Milan. A heartfelt greeting

from yours most warmly,
A. Boito

Fiesco's line, as suggested by the poet, appears in the definitive libretto just before the third scene of act 3.

The above letter concludes the Verdi-Boito correspondence about the revised *Simon Boccanegra*. By 21 February Verdi had completed his work, and on 24 February he left Genoa for Milan. In the meanwhile he had written a number of letters to Giulio Ricordi about practical details. Working in Milan, Boito often conferred with Ricordi about matters of staging and minor changes.

On 24 March, the revised *Boccanegra* had its premiere at La Scala, with Victor Maurel as protagonist, Anna D'Angeri (Amelia), Edouard De Reszké (Fiesco), Francesco Tamagno (Adorno), Federico Salvati (Paolo), and Giovanni Bianco (Pietro). Franco Faccio conducted. Verdi's friend from Parma, Girolamo Magnani, designed the sets; the costumes were by Alfredo Edel. Several of these artists were later involved in *Otello* and *Falstaff*. The opera was well received and had ten performances. Verdi returned to Genoa on 30 March, after the third night.

Milan, Thursday [31 March 1881]

30

Dear Maestro,

There is a delicate matter that troubles the sleep of some light-sleeping gentlemen. They have already approached Giulio for help to enable them to sleep in peace, but Giulio will not hear of doing what they wish and has referred them to me. I suggested chloral, an excellent soporific, to these sleepless people, but they would not drink it and will not calm down, and now they trouble my peace as well. See, dear Maestro, if you can find a way of calming them, for their fate is in your hands.

They have got it into their heads that they must read the name of Verdi in the list of donors for the statue of Bellini, and they are already eagerly anticipating this event. I do not know who allowed them to harbor this hope that after the appearance of *Boccanegra* at La Scala, surely not before, their wish would be fulfilled; and they are wakefully waiting and visibly losing weight and they refuse to take chloral and Giulio washes his hands of them and they press me, who do not want to be pressed, to speak to you about it. And yesterday I said yes, but instead I seized the opportunity of your departure to not speak to you about it, rather than trouble you with this question during the last hours of your stay in Milan. And today I will tell them you had left and I will add that I will not write you, while on the contrary I am writing you because in the end it is best for you to be aware of this situation. So therefore, without their (the sleepless ones') knowledge, I am warning you about this matter, and you can decide about it as you choose and resolve the question as you think best. It is only fair for me to add that this zeal has stirred the hearts of people who feel the most ardent admiration for you and it is the zeal of love.

I have spoken. When are we going to begin that certain correspondence? Have a fond thought for me.

Yours warmly,
A. Boito

✍Increasingly, Boito was called upon to act as buffer between some petitioner and the notoriously irascible Verdi. The verbosity of this letter is an evident smoke screen to cover Boito's own position. He was on the side of the important Milanese (Ricordi, who also wrote to Verdi on the subject, called them "distinguished citizens" [CVB, p. 305]), but he wanted to retain Verdi's respect by making gentle fun of them.

Genoa, 2 April 1881

31 Dear Boito,

Last year at about this time I was leaving Milan, and the train had hardly begun to move before I realized the mistake I and everyone had made in erecting that certain statue, etc., etc... Through Giulio I tried to repair the damage done, but failed. I thought then that the best course was to stay out of the whole thing, as far as that business was concerned. At this stage, doesn't it seem to you, dear Boito, that if I were to contribute a sum for the statue of Bellini, people might believe, or make a show of believing, that I was contributing to the one statue so that they would erect the other? You will reply that the sum for the first statue was collected at once; so be it. The fact remains, however, that I would have contributed so that the statues could be erected at the same time. My single gesture can not and would not be understood as specific, made for the statue of Bellini, and not for mine, or for both!

Already in May or June of last year I wrote to Ricordi that I was prepared to give a sum of ——— if a way were found to have no more talk of the two statues, and to convert all the money into an act of charity. It would still be the best course, the most useful, and to me the most welcome. Nevertheless, if this cannot be done, I am willing, indeed I authorize you, dear Boito, to tell the committee I will *put my name in the list of donors for the statue of Bellini,* offering the amount still wanting in order to erect it, on condition, however, that mine not be erected for the present, nor shall it be erected in the future without my permission.

Answer me as soon as possible about this, and believe me always

Yours warmly,

G. Verdi

P.S. I leave tomorrow morning for a few days at Sant'Agata. In the event you should write, address your letter *to Busseto.*

In the previous April of 1880, while Verdi was in Milan for the first performance of his *Pater noster* for 5-part chorus, and his *Ave Maria* for soprano and strings (both on texts erroneously attributed to Dante), a subscription was opened to underwrite a life-size statute of the composer to be erected in the foyer of La Scala. The necessary sum was raised in forty-eight hours, and the sculptor Francesco Barzaghi was commissioned to make the statue. Later a subscription was opened also for a statue of Bellini, but the funds were not collected so readily. In the end the Bellini figure was made by Ambrogio Borghi, and the two works were installed in the foyer on 25 October 1881 (later to be joined by already existing statues of Rossini and Donizetti). Verdi was not present, but his friend Teresa Stolz sent an enthusiastic report of the ceremony to Sant'Agata and pronounced his statue an excellent resemblance.

Monday [4 April 1881]

32

Dear Maestro,

I understand perfectly your view of the question and others, like me, have understood it. I will take care to explain it to the committee as well as you have explained it to me and you will not be troubled further about the statues.

The matter is already settled; the two statues will be erected, no one can prevent that from taking place: *What's done cannot be undone.* They will be erected and you will be able to remain personally outside of this event, without anyone finding anything to criticize.

A cordial greeting from your

A. Boito

Many greetings to your wife.

Wednesday [Milan, 25 May 1881]

33 Dear Maestro,

You must not believe I have forgotten the Moor of Venice. I have thought about him, but until now I have not had the necessary tranquillity to work at my desk. Whatever may happen this evening, I will regain this tranquillity within a couple of days, the time it will take to say good-bye to my friends who have come here from Turin. This Mephisto has made us sweat. Faccio is the one who has sweated most, but he has achieved stupendous results; all the same, Giulio and I have had our share of labor too.

In three hours' time the theater will open. I employ this half hour of rest to assure you that within a couple of days I will concern myself effectively with the Moor.

I don't know if the secretary of the committee for the Congress of Musicians sent the circular to Sant'Agata or to Genoa. In any case I am sending it to you. Dear Maestro, if you feel up to giving us some good advice, you can make a great contribution to the practical results of this congress. You will have until June fourteenth to make your ideas known to us.

You see how the Mephisto rehearsals have made an idiot of me; for some time I have had a diploma from the Concert Society of Barcelona that I must send you and only now have I found the time to make the package.

And on this little added page, dear Maestro, I send my affectionate greetings.

Yours,
A. Boito

Boito's *Mefistofele* opened that same night at La Scala, with Maddalena Mariani-Masi, Francesco Marconi, and Romano Nannetti (protagonist). Franco Faccio conducted.

A Congress of Italian Musicians was held in Milan from 16 to 22 June of that year. One of the subjects it was to consider was the question of adopting a standard concert pitch throughout Italy. Verdi had long been interested in this matter, which is later discussed in his correspondence with Boito in 1885, at the time of the International Congress of Musicians in Vienna (see letter no. 65 below).

[Telegram]

26 May 81

Arrigo Boito, Principe Amedeo 1, Milan
From Busseto
Very happy at your success. I send my most heartfelt sincere congratu-
lations, and wishes for *Nerone* soon.

34

Verdi

◀︎Boito had conceived the idea of a great opera on Nero even before
writing *Mefistofele*. He published the libretto in 1901, but the score was
still unfinished at the time of his death. For all of his adult life, the
projected work was to be his torment and, often, a convenient pretext
for escaping tedious situations.

1, Via Principe Amedeo, 17 June [1881]
Milan

35

Dear Maestro,

The siege of foreigners has not yet ended. The poor wretches who
live in Milan are subjected, during these days of expositions and con-
gresses, to the torture of formalities and social ceremony, the most stupid and cruel spiritual torture conceivable. For more than three weeks
I have been a martyr of this inhuman business, my day is destroyed,
and evening arrives without my having written even half a page.

Still, yesterday, irritated by this foolish fate, and thinking of what
you expect of me, I set to work (after having closed doors and windows)
and tried to make concrete the ideas that I have been pondering for
some time now about that particular chorus in the second act. Now this
is where I have thought it suitable to put the chorus: towards the end of
the first fateful colloquy between Jago and Otello, when Jago cleverly
presses the Moor's thoughts towards the precipice of jealousy, after
Otello's words:

Let love and jealousy be dispelled together!

the audience hears a sweet offstage chorus approaching slowly, as Jago
continues his infernal part. A little later, through the very broad opening in the center of the scene, giving onto the garden, a charmingly arranged group will appear: Desdemona, surrounded by women and by
children, who are scattering flowers and branches in her path and
around her, singing serenely. At this fateful moment of the drama, it
will be like a chaste and gentle apotheosis of song and flowers around

the beautiful and innocent figure of Desdemona. It would be desirable for the chorus and Desdemona to remain framed throughout the piece by the arch of the central opening. You, Maestro, recall the design of the set. It is octagonal, with enclosing flats:

and it is a shallow set. The chorus then (with Desdemona) should remain beyond the door, in the spectator's view, and well grouped, but no one should cross the threshold. In this case, being a bit distant from the orchestra, they could be accompanied by harps; these could be visible; the poetry speaks also of *mandòle,* so the mandolin could also be used.

On the stage, or rather on this side of the door, at the footlights, are Jago and Otello, while the sweet apotheosis of Desdemona continues.

At the beginning and at the end of this chorus and in the refrains I have tried using *senario* meter accented not like the usual verses, but rather with one strong accent and one weak, uniform: the rhythm of the verse hints at a ternary time signature. But now it's time to copy out the strophes:

CHORUS

(offstage) Wherever you look, gleam
approaching   hearts catch fire,
Rays, ~~Choruses echo,~~
Wherever you pass, descend
Clouds of flowers.
Here amid lilies and roses
As at a chaste altar,
Fathers, children, brides
Come to sing.

CHILDREN
(scattering lilies on the ground)
We offer you the lily,
Gentle stalk,
Which in the angels' hands
Was carried to heaven,
Where it adorns the radiant
Cloak and the skirt
Of the Madonna,
And her holy veil.

WOMEN AND SAILORS
(as the children sing, accompanying and harmonizing)
(While on the breezes flies
The happy song,
The agile mandolin
Accompanies its sound.)

DESDEMONA
The sky shines, the breeze
Dances around the flowers.
Joy, Love, Hope
Sing in my heart.

SAILORS
(offering Desdemona necklaces of coral and pearls)
To you the murexes,
The pearls, and the purples,
In the
~~From the~~ depths
Of the sea plucked.
Desdemona, we wish
With our gifts
To bedeck you
Like a holy image.

CHILDREN AND WOMEN
(as the sailors sing, accompanying and harmonizing)

(While on the breezes flies
The happy song,
The agile mandolin
Accompanies its sound.)

THE WOMEN
(scattering branches and flowers)
For you the
~~The harvest~~ bounteous
~~To you the willow's~~
Harvests from
~~From our~~ aprons
~~The soft frond~~
In clouds, in clouds,
~~Love, of the wave~~

We scatter on the ground.
~~Of songs, Love.~~
April surrounds
The blonde bride
~~For you the cyclamen~~
~~Your blonde head~~
~~With its fragile stem,~~
With a dewy air
~~With its delicate calyx~~
That vibrates in the sun
~~Of azure and gold.~~

CHILDREN AND SAILORS
OR ELSE SAILORS ALONE,
(while the women sing, accompanying and harmonizing)
(While on the breezes flies
The happy song,
The agile mandolin
Accompanies its sound.)

ALL
Wherever you look, gleam
    hearts catch fire,
Rays, ~~Choruses echo~~
Wherever you pass, descend
Clouds of flowers,
Here amid lilies and roses,
As at a chaste altar,
Fathers, children, brides
Come to sing.

CHORUS

§ Live happily! Farewell. Here reigns Love.

DESDEMONA
The sky shines, the breeze
Dances around the flowers
Joy, Love, Hope
Sing in my heart. ∽

and, as this chorus is going on, Otello, from the beginning, murmurs:

There she is!
AND JAGO: Keep watch.
(murmurs to him,
and repeats to him as
the chorus sings)
AND OTELLO: That singing conquers me:
(sweetly moved) No, no, if she betrays me, heaven mocks itself.

When the chorus is over, Desdemona kisses the heads of some of
the children, and some of the women kiss the hem of her dress, and she

hands a purse to the sailors, and the chorus disperses, and she (followed by Emilia) enters the hall and advances towards Otello, and the following scene begins: Desdemona: "I bring you the plea of a man who moans under your scorn..." etc., etc., etc. And the moment Desdemona utters the name of Cassio, the echoes of the chorus that still enchant Otello's spirit cease, and the terrible drama resumes its inexorable course.

Now I still have to justify to you the reason I chose the trochee-based *senario* meter for the refrain of the chorus. I didn't choose it for the slightest love of novelty, but rather because I was looking for a rhythm that could accompany with frequent notes the individual *quinario* stanzas that are interspersed.

I resort to an example because I have no better way of explaining myself:

3/4	Mĕntrĕ	all' ăură	vŏlă	lĭetă	lă căn-	z̄on	etc.
	[˘]						

3/4	Ā	tē	dēl	sā-	lī-	cē	etc.

If this chorus seems good to you, the most laborious part of the *Otello* revision is done; I will set to work on the ensemble.

Then I will again try to make some cuts in the part of Otello, beyond those already made. This last point, too, would be something indispensable for the two of us to discuss together.

I want to thank you again for the telegram you sent me after the first performance of Mephisto; I will never be able to tell you how much noble joy I received from your words.

The Mephisto at La Scala was like those fireworks that begin with a great racket and end with a wretched little pop. The public came to the theater very little. I had too serious a rival to defeat: I mean the equestriennes of the Renz Circus. But I am even too happy with my lot.

Many friendly greetings to your wife. To you, an affectionate handshake. Write me your impression of the chorus so that, if necessary, I can find some other idea before I leave for the country.

Your devoted
A. Boito

🔊The National Exposition in Milan had been inaugurated on 5 May 1881, attracting many Italian and foreign visitors.

During the rehearsals and first performances of *Boccanegra,* Boito and Verdi obviously had had ample opportunity to meet and discuss the future of *Otello.* When the correspondence resumes with this letter, Boito is already at work revising act 2, scene 3.

Sant'Agata, 23 June 1881

36   Dear Boito,

Don't cast the first stone at me for not having answered earlier your very dear and important letter.

The chorus you sent me, I believe, will do very well. I say I believe, because not having at hand the second act, I am not sure about the place that chorus is meant to occupy. In any case, that chorus could not be more charming or more elegant or more beautiful. And besides, what a burst of light in so much darkness! Concern yourself now with the finale, and go ahead and make a very extended piece, I would say *big.* The theater demands it; but even more than the theater, the colossal power of the drama requires it. The idea (which still appeals to me) of composing an *Otello* without choruses was, and perhaps still is, madness!

As for the cuts in the part of Otello, I agree, we'll make them together.

Greetings from my wife, and an affectionate handshake from me.

G. Verdi

🔊In early July Boito made a brief visit to Sant'Agata, with Franco Faccio and Giulio Ricordi, to decide about a projected performance of *Boccanegra* in Barcelona. The *Otello* libretto was also discussed.

It is probable that Boito made another visit in mid-August when, as we read in the following letter, he absent-mindedly left behind some personal effects.

The finale Verdi mentions is probably that of act 3, as Boito apparently confirms below.

Wednesday [Milan, 24 August 1881]

37   Dear Maestro,

You were probably beginning to believe that, along with my hat, sponge, and brush, I had also forgotten the grand finale of *Otello.* Not so. I was ruminating over this finale. I was ruminating, and since it is a very thick morsel, I could never manage to assimilate it into *the blood-stream of the form,* if I may so express myself. And I had a hard time achieving the result that by now is already known to you, and that is, it seems to me, the consequence of all our discussion at Sant'Agata.

The ensemble number has, as we planned, its lyrical part and its dramatic part *blended together;* it is, in other words, a lyrical, melodic piece, with a dramatic dialogue stirring beneath it. The chief figure on the lyrical side is *Desdemona,* the chief figure on the dramatic side is *Jago.* In this way, Jago, after having been only briefly overwhelmed by an event that was not within his control (the letter recalling Otello to Venice), quickly reknots, with an unparalleled rapidity and energy, all the threads of the tragedy and again makes the catastrophe *his,* and he actually exploits the unexpected event to accelerate dizzyingly the course of the final disaster. All this was in Shakespeare's mind, all this is evident in our work. Jago passes from Otello to Rodrigo, the two instruments left him for his crime, then he has the last word and the last action of the act.

See for yourself if the two parts, lyrical and dramatic, seem well blended. See also if the length of each part is well gauged. I did not economize on verses because I remembered a warning of yours: *Say all that it is useful to say, and be sure everything is explained.* In giving me this warning you felt that the dialogue beneath the lyrical piece had to be developed in order to become tragic, and you saw the problem correctly, and so I have done this. In fact, if the dialogue between Jago and Rodrigo should seem a bit brusque to you and not too clear, here are four verses that, if necessary, will complete it and conclude it.

JAGO   In deepest night I will follow his path
And study the meeting place and time; the rest is up to you.
I will be your lookout. To the hunt, the hunt! Gird on
Your bow.
RODRIGO   Yes. I have sold you honor and fealty.

There is one observation to make here. The dialogues: Jago and Otello, Jago and Rodrigo follow each other, the former first and the latter afterwards. During the dialogue of Jago and Otello, what is Rodrigo doing? Nothing. And yet his voice could create another distinct part at the beginning of the melodic ensemble and be the fifth part, until the time comes for his dialogue with Jago. In this case, I am giving you four lyrical verses that Rodrigo could sing with the others, while Otello talks with Jago and the ensemble begins:

> RODRIGO
> (For me the world grows dark,
> Destiny is beclouded,
> The angel chaste and blonde
> Flees from my path.)

On this point it could be observed: Since we have concerned ourselves with Rodrigo's attitude during the Jago-Otello dialogue, why don't we concern ourselves with Otello's attitude during the Jago-Rodrigo dialogue? No. Otello's position is indicated, indeed demanded, by the drama. We have seen him slumped beside the table after the words, "To the ground! and weep!" and slumped there he must remain, not rising for the entire duration of the ensemble, not even when he replies to Jago. He has no need to *speak* or to *sing* while Jago talks to Rodrigo. Mute, he is greater and more terrifying, more plastic. He will rise only to cry out, "Flee!" and then he will fall headlong to the floor. This way is right. Thus far we are in perfect agreement, I hope. But perhaps you will observe that Desdemona (since she is, as I said, *the chief figure of the lyrical part of the piece*) should have four verses more than the others, especially since her first four verses do not lend themselves to being developed melodically by the music. In this case, here are the four verses that will conclude Desdemona's stanza, but in order to read them and also to transcribe them, I realize, the page must be turned.

> DESDEMONA
>
> . . . .
> . . . .
> . . . .
> . . . .
> . . . .
> . . . .
> . . . .
> . . . .
>
> Sun, serene and bright,
> That makes sky and sea happy,
> Dry the bitter drops
> That my sorrow sheds!

We had agreed that the lyrical part of the piece should have one meter and the dialogue part (including the chorus) a different meter. This is what I have done. The meter of the dialogue is an *endecasillabo* that can be split, or not, as you like, and if it is split it turns into so many *quinari* from beginning to end. So you can, as you choose, employ one of the two rhythms or the other. It was necessary for me to do this because an *endecasillabo*, prolonged beneath a lyrical movement, an *endecasillabo* all in one piece would perhaps have proved too heavy and the *quinario* too light. I didn't like the idea of mixing visibly the two meters, preferring the device that you see; for that matter, to me the effect seems effective.

Now I believe there is nothing left for me to say, except to thank you again for the lovely day at Sant'Agata, which will remain always in my memory and has reinforced, dear Maestro, my sincere fondness for you. Many greetings to Signora Giuseppina and the Sig.ra Sister-in-law. I leave again tomorrow for Monticello. Here is the address: Monticello via Monza. That's enough, if you write me your letter will reach me. But in a week's time I'll be back in Milan, and after that I'll go to Lake Como. Please don't spare me and do put me to work; when I work for you I am happy.

Yours most warmly,
A. Boito

⋙The "Sig.ra Sister-in-law" is Barberina Strepponi, Giuseppina Verdi's sister, a frequent visitor at Sant'Agata.

Boito, who was a creature of habit, every autumn paid a round of country-house visits, ending up at Lake Como in the villa of Donna Vittoria Cima, whose Milanese salon he—and other musicians and artists—frequented regularly during the season. In winter he usually sought out the milder climate of Nervi, near Genoa.

After Boito had left Milan, Verdi arrived there, to visit the exposition mentioned in Boito's letter no. 35 above.

The clever overlay of meters Boito mentions appears at the two dialogues in the third column of libretto text that Verdi quotes in letter no. 78 below (see the appendix for the original Italian texts). Through the skillful deployment of elisions and dactylic line endings Boito constructed a series of regular *endecasillabi:*

Una parola. E che? T'affretta! Rapido
Slancia la tua vendetta! Il tempo vola
that could also be divided as *quinari:*

> Una parola.
> E che? T'affretta!
> Rapido slancia
> La tua vendetta!
> Il tempo vola

etc., all the while maintaining, in either division, a complex pattern of rhymes. This technical tour de force continues until Jago's aside towards the end of the column.

Boito's suggested lines for the act 3 finale were adopted after some further minor changes.

[Milan, 27 August 1881]

38 Dear Boito,

I am in Milan, and your two letters were forwarded to me here from Busseto. Very, very good the finale. What a difference between this one and the first!

I will add the four verses for Rodrigo.

Perhaps the other four for Desdemona will not be needed.

It is so true that Otello mute is greater and more terrifying that I would be of a mind not to have him speak at all during the whole ensemble number. It seems to me that Jago alone can say, and more briefly, everything the spectator needs to know without Otello replying:

> JAGO Hurry! Time is flying! Turn your attention to the task! Only to the task! I will deal with Cassio... I will tear his vile wicked soul from him. I swear it. You will have news of him at midnight

(adjusting the verses, obviously).

After the ensemble and after the words "All flee Otello," it seems to me that Otello does not speak and shout enough. He is silent for four verses and it seems to me (from a theatrical viewpoint) that after "That robs him of all feeling" Otello should shout one or two verses... "Flee. I loathe you, myself, the whole world..."

And it also seems to me that some verses could be spared when Otello and Jago remain alone.

> [OTELLO] I alone am unable to escape myself... Ah the hydra! Lord,
> To see them clasped together. Ah cursed
> Thought... Blood, blood...

(a cry and The handkerchief.
he faints)

[JAGO]   My poison is working
[VOICES]   Long live the hero of Cyprus
[without]
[JAGO]   Who can forbid me to press this brow
           With my heel
[VOICES]   Glory
           To the Lion of Venice
[JAGO]   Here is the Lion!

A choked cry on the word "handkerchief" seems to me more terrible than a cry on a commonplace exclamation "Oh Satan." The words
"fainted," "immobile," "mute" arrest the action a bit. One thinks, one
reflects, whereas here the thing is to end rapidly. Tell me your opinion.

I haven't finished!! The chorus has little action, or rather none at all.
Couldn't a way be found to move it a bit? For ex., after the words "In
Cyprus he names a successor... Cassio!" chorus with four verses I won't
say of rebellion but of protest "No, no: We want Otello."

I know very well that you will promptly reply "Dear Sig.r Maestro,
don't you know that no one dared breathe a word after a decree of
the Most Serene Republic? And that sometimes the mere presence of
the Messer Grando was enough to disperse the crowd and put down
a riot?

I would dare counter-reply that the action takes place on Cyprus:
that the Most Serenes were far away, and hence perhaps the Cypriots
were more daring than the Venetians.

If you happen to come to Milan I hope to see you. I'm not sure, but
I believe you have all the poetry of the third act.

In haste. Be well.

G. Verdi
Hôtel Milan

◂◦While Verdi and Giuseppina were in Milan to visit the National Exposition, Boito returned to the city from Monticello and met the composer on 1 September. During his visit to the exposition, Verdi had
seen the stand of Cav. Giuseppe Pelitti, a well-known manufacturer of
brass instruments, who had supplied the special trumpets for *Aida*.
Impressed by what he saw, Verdi paid a visit on 30 August to Pelitti's
workshop in Milan, where, with the collaboration of some military
band players invited for the occasion, the composer was able to hear

and appreciate Pelitti's instruments. At Verdi's suggestion, Pelitti created a special bass trombone, which Verdi was able to hear on yet another visit two days later, this time in the company of Boito and Giulio Ricordi. The composer made careful note of the effect of combined trombones, recommending a quartet of them in three different extensions for future orchestral use.

The exposition had a musical section, held at the conservatory, where Verdi happened to encounter the pianist-composer Henri Herz (who was also a builder of pianos). Examining Herz's instruments, Verdi sat down at one of them and played Herz's Capriccio in A. Verdi mentioned that he had played the same composition many years previously during his examination for admission to the conservatory, whose rejection of him was by this time notorious. "I played it so well they would have nothing to do with me," Verdi is reported to have said [CVB, p. 310].

The Verdis returned to Sant'Agata on 2 September. There is now a silence of a year in the correspondence; it is unlikely that letters are missing. The fact is that Verdi exhibited no interest in composing. In October of 1881 he wrote his old friend Clara Maffei, "I concern myself with fields, buildings, land, and so I pass the day without doing anything perhaps useful" [CVB, p. 311].

Giulio Ricordi, naturally distressed by Verdi's musical inactivity, at Christmas sent him a *panettone*—traditional Italian Christmas cake— with a Moor on it made of chocolate. Early in January 1882 Giuseppina wrote the publisher: "As for cooking the chocolate [. . .] while there seems to me no scarcity of wood, the will to light the fire is wanting... and even if there were a scrap of will, it fades when certain remarks are read, for example, about agricultural occupations, about lawyers, about lawsuits over water rights, etc., etc. [. . .] who knows, perhaps one of these days, without any pressure, he may present the newborn infant" [Abbiati, 4:189–90].

Instead, as that spring approached, Verdi began contemplating another version of *Don Carlos*. In May of 1882 he went to Paris because of this project and, at the same time, to straighten out his affairs there, since his French publisher, Léon Escudier, had died the previous year.

That summer, Boito was making his usual round of visits; and from Donna Vittoria's villa on Lake Como, he broke the silence between himself and Verdi, using the future French translation of *Otello* as a pretext.

Villa d'Este (Lake Como)
10 August [1882]

39

Dear Maestro,

A good two months ago the Baron Blaze de Bury asked me a question, through his wife, whom I met in London. The question boils down to these terms, which I transcribe: "Un jour ou l'autre le *Jago* existera et par conséquent sera donné ici (in Paris) sur la scène de l'Opéra," etc... To be concrete, Blaze de Bury asked his wife, the baroness, to ask me to ask you, Maestro, to grant him for that "jour ou l'autre" the French translation rights to *Otello.*

"Vous trouverez je pense Verdi très favorable à cet arrangement dont Vous pourrez lui parler tout de suite" the lady goes on, but the "tout de suite" has been such that her letter was dated 22 June and I am carrying out the mission today (11 August).

For several reasons I was in no hurry to fulfill the request of Blaze de Bury: First of all, at that time I did not know, dear Maestro, where you were. I knew only that you were no longer in Genoa and you were not at Sant'Agata either, and I wrote this truth to the baroness to justify my delay. Another reason is that, however worthwhile the request of such a highly cultivated man, an artist in spirit, and a man I admire and consider the most authoritative critic in France, I thought that this proposal was ill-timed and hence I did not hurry to carry out my assignment. This consideration, however, I did not confide in the baroness because I did not feel I had the authority to decide for the lady whether the proposal was opportune or not. You, Maestro, are the judge of that. But another letter from la Blaze de Bury repeats the request, and this time... and this time, before I reply, I must go to the source and I could not say again that I do not know where Verdi is currently to be found.

So then, Maestro, please send me a line about this matter or, if you prefer, send it to Blaze de Bury himself, to his address in Paris, rue Oudinot 20. It is all the same for me, provided a word such as *yes,* or *no,* or *later,* or *perhaps* be said. I would not like that distinguished writer to think that in this matter I acted in bad faith, though to tell the truth I have, but not in the sense that he (whom I admire) might think, for I have shown *good faith* in not wanting to trouble you, Maestro, as I know from experience, when an opera is not yet finished, how tiresome every word is, and every deed, that seems meant only to press on that secret toil the mind that impels and regulates itself, as it alone knows its way and its goal. Yet from all these signs it is obvious what feverish expectation surrounds that opera in France; and if it is so great in France, which is the most vainglorious of nations and the least friendly to ours, imagine what it must be here and elsewhere. But enough of that; I have already said too much.

By the way, you were complaining of a verse that had the word "arce" [citadel], too farfetched. If my memory does not betray me, the verse said:

E l'*arce* ascesa alla breccia fatal
[And the *citadel* scaled at the fatal breach]

I have thought that it is easily corrected by changing the word "ascesa" [scaled] into a noun, e.g.:

E l'aspra ascesa e la breccia fatal
[And the harsh climb and the fatal breach]

See if in this way it would fit with the meaning of the preceding verse.

Giulio Ricordi is at Trescore to treat his hand, which is bothering him.

I will stay at Villa d'Este until the 28th of this month, then I will go to pay a visit to a Benedictine monk by the name of Guido d'Arezzo. I still do not know Tuscany (shameful, isn't it?) and this will be a good opportunity to make its acquaintance.

Many affectionate greetings to the Sant'Agata house and to its dear inhabitants.

Yours,
A. Boito

❧Blaze de Bury refers to the opera in gestation as *Jago,* the working title that Verdi and Boito at first used. Originally Verdi seemed reluctant to call the opera *Otello,* either out of deference to Rossini's opera of that title or perhaps out of awe of Shakespeare. But now that he has resumed work, he has apparently banished scruples, as the first sentence of the letter below indicates. Not *Jago.* From now on the new opera will be called *Otello.*

Boito had written the verses for an anthem set by Luigi Mancinelli in honor of the eleventh-century monk Guido d'Arezzo, whose anniversary—though his exact birth date is unknown—was being celebrated in Arezzo. Boito's verses for the occasion were an imitation of the Latin hymn "Ut queant laxis," from which Guido derived the syllables for solmization. The festivities also included the unveiling of a statue of Guido by the sculptor Salvino Salvini and a production of *Mefistofele.*

Busseto, 16 August 1882
Sant'Agata

Dear Boito,

40

"Un jour ou l'autre *Jago* (*Jago* no!) existera"... I am surprised by this confidence on the baron's part, because I... I personally do not know if "existera." I am also all the more surprised that a literary figure of the standing of Blaze de Bury, the most authoritative critic in France, as you most rightly say, would want to sentence himself to genuine penal servitude, translating an opera from Italian into French, an even more arduous job than from French into Italian. We have *verso sciolto,* but they, being constricted by rhyme, and by the masculine and feminine couplets one after the other, find it almost impossible to preserve the literal meaning, along with the phrasing and the musical accent. In this regard I said a few months ago to a translator of an opera of mine: "Why do you make rhymed verses in my recitatives, and in the dramatic dialogues?" But the nature of their poetry does not allow them, or at least no one dares, to write *le vers blanc.*

But, I repeat, why speak now of an opera that does not exist? Of an opera that will have Italian dimensions, and heaven only knows how many other (God save us!) Italian features?... Perhaps some melody (if any can be found)... And melody is always Italian, essentially Italian, and can only be Italian, wherever it may come from. And further, an opera that will not have *mise en scène!* And will not have a ballet! Imagine: an opera at the Opéra without ballet!!! I will add another opinion of mine, my personal opinion, and it is that I am convinced, absolutely convinced, that it is impossible in the present theater of the Opéra to have a real success with new music. The reason lies, according to me, in the acoustics, in the splendor, in the beauty of that monument. Am I mistaken? That is possible; but until I see a success I will not change my mind.

Meanwhile, write to the baron as you think best, and, happy at having received your news after such a long time, I am

always yours warmly,
G. Verdi

&sVerdi's *Othello* was not given at the Paris Opéra until 1894 (see letters no. 217 ff.), in a translation by Boito and Camille Du Locle, and with some ballet music Verdi had composed, reluctantly, to conform to the Opéra's tradition. This ballet music was the last Verdi would compose for the stage.

Villa d'Este
[after 16 August 1882]

41   Dear Maestro,

There are magnetic currents in the air. While your welcome letter was about to reach my hands, I was writing to my French translator the same remarks as yours on the prosody of those neighbors of ours, and almost with the same words, and I talked about *vers blanc* in the identical fashion and about masculine and feminine endings, expressing the same opinion.

I also experienced the same amazement you felt at the baron's proposal. I will answer him this very day, but without mentioning this amazement; I will limit my reply to a pure and simple sentence like an Order of the Day in our distinguished Parliament. And the sentence will be: "The Maestro is writing *Otello* (or *Jago,* as may be) especially with Italy in mind, as the story is so vigorously Italian"... No, here the sentence is spoiled. If I bring up Italy again, the good relations between the two countries could also be spoiled. I will simply say you do not believe the opera you are writing will ever have the requisite dimensions and form that are traditional at the Opéra. And that is enough.

Forgive the nuisance I have caused you. Guessing your feelings, I did everything to spare you, but in the end I was unable to. I console myself with the thought that you suffered this nuisance only once; three times I suffered it, thanks to the three letters that, including today's, I will have written to the baron's wife, certainly a most intelligent lady, but not beautiful or, still less, young. And writing letters is always for me a most tormenting vexation, except when I am writing to Sant'Agata... or to Palazzo d'Oria, or to my brother, or to some rare good and loyal friend; then the chattering of the pen would never stop and would flow easily, as now, and pleasantly.

Many, many greetings to Signora Giuseppina.

Yours most warmly,
A. Boito

⮑Boito's French translator was Paul Millet, whose version of *Mefistofele*—now entitled *Méphistophélès*—was first performed in Brussels, 19 January 1883. Boito was present on this occasion.

Since 1860 Verdi and Giuseppina had spent the most severe winter months in the mild climate of Genoa. After several changes of residence, they settled in a splendid apartment in the Palazzo Doria (which Boito here pedantically spells "d'Oria").

Now there is another long gap—eight months—in the correspondence. Verdi had put aside *Otello* to devote himself to *Don Carlos,* of which he was making a more manageable four-act version, with the assistance of his sometime French translator Nuitter (anagram pseudonym of Charles-Louis-Étienne Truinet, 1828–1899) and, through him, the surviving original librettist of *Don Carlos,* Camille Du Locle (1832–1903), with whom Verdi—who had unwisely lent Du Locle money—was not on speaking terms in this period.

5 April [1883]

Dear Maestro,

42

On the 22d of March [a slip of the pen; Boito means 22 May], anniversary of the death of Manzoni, Milan will inaugurate the monument in Piazza Manzoni, and that same evening at La Scala, if they can find worthy singers in time (and there is good reason to hope they will be found), the city administration of Milan would have in mind to organize a performance of the Mass of Verdi. Unless I am mistaken, Masini, Teodorini, and Nannetti have no engagements for the end of May; and with the powerful contribution of the orchestra and choruses of La Scala, the Mass would again have a perfect performance.

It is a solemn occasion.

The day of 22 May '83 will glorify the name of Alessandro Manzoni, and this glorification has to include the Mass you wrote for him; and to make sure that the nobility of the celebration is complete, you, Maestro, should *come and conduct it in person.* This is what the city administration thinks, and what I think. Nobody knows anything about this as yet; not even Giulio Ricordi knows I am writing you today. Our excellent Negri, city councillor (you know that Negri is one of the most worthy men of Milan), Negri, as I was saying, begged me to ask you this unofficially, to beseech you affably, and I obey wholeheartedly. If we find perfect performers, will you say yes? I await a line in reply.

I was so sorry to miss the feast of St. Joseph in your house. I was going to travel, but the snow frightened me and I stayed in Nervi an extra four or five days. I wanted almost to be *brazen* and turn up unannounced at Palazzo Doria, but then I lacked the *brass.* The next day I reached Milan where we have enjoyed Spring only for the past three days.

Yesterday I spent the whole evening with Edmondo De Amicis and we talked and talked about you and Signora Giuseppina, to whom you will kindly remember me affectionately.

And you, Maestro, even if I bother you from time to time, don't cease to show me your good friendship.

Yours,

A. Boito

❧Typically, the absent-minded Boito writes March for the death of Manzoni, when he means May.

For the Manzoni anniversary Ricordi—at the urging of Milan's mayor Negri—had originally asked Verdi to write "anything, a triumphal piece for orchestra and brass band, an anthem!... a chorus [CVB, p. 315]." Verdi, whose dislike of occasional music was notorious, apparently refused (no written reply seems to exist), so a performance of the *Requiem* was suggested.

The statue of Manzoni was by Francesco Barzaghi, sculptor of the Verdi statue in La Scala (see the note following letter no. 31 above).

The feast of St. Joseph, 19 March, was the name day of both Verdi and Giuseppina, and was traditionally celebrated in the Verdi household, often with a few intimate friends.

Edmondo De Amicis (1846–1908), Italian writer, was at this time known chiefly for his collection of sketches *La vita militare*. Three years later, he published his enduring, sentimental classic *Cuore*. He saw a good deal of the Verdis in Genoa and wrote a charming "portrait" of Giuseppina in his *Nuovi ritratti letterari ed artistici* (1908; reprinted in *Bollettino dell'Istituto di Studi Verdiani*, no. 2, pp. 779–84). Edmondo's cousin, the engineer Giuseppe DeAmicis, lived in Genoa and was a devoted, helpful friend of the Verdis, often running little errands for them when they were away from the city.

During this period, while Verdi seemed to give no thought to *Otello*, the opera was much in the mind of Boito and Ricordi, though—on 8 February 1882—Verdi had written the publisher sternly: "For God's sake let's leave the *chocolate* in peace, along with *Desdemona* and *Jago* [CVB, p. 311]." A year later, from Brussels, Boito wrote Ricordi: "I will surely see Verdi in Genoa and I will bring up that subject" [CVB, p. 314]. At this and subsequent meetings with Verdi, Boito may have mentioned *Otello*, but there is no evidence that Verdi responded to the hints.

Sant'Agata, 7 April 1883

43

Dear Boito,

I have received here your most dear letter forwarded from Genoa.
The occasion is certainly solemn, but... it would be an Encore. I
loathe Encores. You are an Artist and you will understand me.

At times it's a good idea to be a bit *brazen!* If I had been able to
imagine that on St. Joseph's day you were still at Nervi, I would have
come personally to drag you by the legs... Continue writing me with no
fear that your very dear letters bother me.

In all friendship,

your
G. Verdi

The *Requiem* was performed at La Scala on 22 May 1883, with a mediocre quartet of singers. Franco Faccio conducted.

On 10 January 1884 the revised, four-act *Don Carlo* was given its
premiere at La Scala, also under Faccio. The cast included Francesco
Tamagno (the future Otello) in the title role, Silvestri as Filippo, Paul
Lhérie as Rodrigo, Abigaille Bruschi-Chiatti as Elisabetta, and Giuseppina Pasqua (the future Mistress Quickly) as Eboli. The Verdis were
present. During their stay of several weeks in Milan, the composer
almost certainly met Boito.

Nervi
Hôtel Victoria
Monday [21 January 1884]

44

Dearest Maestro,

The ravioli of Genoa are excellent and I adore them and would
come to devour them at your board next Thursday. If I have chosen a
bad day you have time to answer me: no.

But I think that if there are ravioli on the table I will eat too many
of them, and you will eat some yourself, and it will cost us some effort
to digest them. I believe that whatever creates work for the stomach
does not create work for the brain, and I am reminded of the words you
said to me referring to the "Moor of Venice": "It's all a matter of the
stomach."

So then, *no ravioli;* we will dine together Thursday (it seems to me
that in Genoa you dine as usual at six), we will dine, but without the

temptation of the ravioli; we will have a sensible, healthy totally intellectual little meal.

So, if you consent (if you don't answer it will mean that you do consent), then good-bye until Thursday at six.

My best greetings to Signora Giuseppina. A warm handshake.

Yours,
A. Boito

❧In this letter Boito is obviously answering an invitation from Verdi, indicating that the two men met at least once during the winter of 1883–84, while the Verdis were in residence at Palazzo Doria and Boito spent some time, as usual, in nearby Nervi. Boito's correspondence with others also suggests that he saw Verdi fairly regularly until the end of February, when Boito left Nervi for a stay in Naples (see note to letter no. 45 below).

Genoa, 7 February 1884

45 Dear Boito,

How quickly you have worked! If only I could do the same. Very well. Until we meet.

Warmly,
G. Verdi

❧On 19 February 1884 Boito—who was about to go to Naples for the first rehearsals of his *Mefistofele*—wrote to Tornaghi at Casa Ricordi: "It seems to me that this time Verdi is seriously thinking of getting to work. I have made a few adjustments to a piece in the first act of the Moor" [CVB, p. 318].

Returning to Nervi for a short stay before a second trip to Naples, Boito wrote again to Tornaghi, on 28 February, of his plan to see Verdi that same day. Then, from Naples, on 20 March, Boito wrote an excited letter to Ricordi: "I have some good news for you, but for heaven's sake don't tell anyone, don't tell even your own family, don't tell even yourself; I'm afraid I am already being indiscreet: The Maestro is composing, indeed he has already written a good deal of the beginning of the first act and he seems enthusiastic. I will see him in a few days" [CVB, p. 318].

The machine was in motion again; but—because of something that happened during Boito's stay in Naples—it risked being stopped permanently.

Milan, Saturday [19? April 1884]

Dear Maestro, **46**

    I made a quick trip to Turin to see the Medieval Castle, a marvel; and I arrived back in Milan yesterday. For many reasons I am pleased to have made this excursion; in Turin I saw my brother and some good friends, including Giacosa, who acted as my guide, and Faccio, who was just then rehearsing his *Cantata,* which produced in me, especially in the beginning and the cadenza, the great effect I was expecting. But the chief reason why my excursion proved even more fortunate than I had anticipated, and unexpectedly opportune, came from some confidences of Faccio about a letter you had written him. If I hadn't gone to Turin, who knows how many months I would have had to wait to learn what you wanted my friend to tell me.

    I thank you with all my heart, my dear Maestro. I thank you, but it already seems too much for me to have to answer you seriously and say I do not accept. I do not accept your great, noble offer. These journalists must belong to a breed quite different from that of respectable people. I don't mean all of them, but the majority. This one has found a way to misunderstand my words so brutally that he turns them into a statement at the opposite pole from my meaning, and then he prints this statement and other journalists repeat it; and so, thanks to the work of obtuse fools, between you and me a situation is created that does me harm, a foolish and sensitive situation from which I find myself released only today. And I find myself released from this false position, Maestro, thanks only to you, and for that, more even than for your offer itself, I thank you fervidly because it gives me the opportunity to open my heart to you with complete confidence.

    I read that tasteless report in the *Roma,* a Neapolitan newspaper I had with me as I was traveling to Genoa. I cannot tell you how upset and outraged I was. All during the journey I pondered how to remedy the journalist's idiocy. My first impulse was to write myself to the *Roma*'s editor; then I felt a scruple at having to write about you without your consent and I decided to ask you to grant it. For this purpose, I rushed to Palazzo Doria the very morning of my arrival in Genoa. I decided to do this also because I had the excuse of delivering the Morelli photograph. But Signora Giuseppina immediately came into the room and then I hadn't the heart to trouble your wife with such an inane matter, a subject I couldn't have broached without showing my profound irritation. Several days went by and I calmed down. I began to consider that the *Roma* is a paper known only to the Neapolitan provinces and that no other newspaper would pick up the nonsense. I thought that rectifications and writing letters to editors are almost always an act of vanity and always useless. I soon regained my serenity, secure as I was in my own feelings. I thought the public would have read the *Roma* article with indifference, and that must be true. I hoped that you would never see it. But human foolishness has long legs. *Il piccolo* of Naples reproduced the report (and as I learned the day before yesterday in Turin), *Il pungolo* printed it also, and this surprises me because Fortis knows me too well to have believed what he printed, and as soon as I see him I will ask him privately if he had read the proofs of his paper that day; and he will tell me no. But the Italian public has scant faith in newspapers, and that allows me not to worry about the impression of the public. But I have to worry about the effect the news may have had on you, Maestro. This letter is growing long, forgive me, but now that I have begun, I must say everything. Here is the source of the misunderstanding. (Lucky you, who have so much glory and so much authority that you can refuse dinner invitations. I cannot allow myself this luxury, because I would only seem presumptuous.) At the dinner given for me by some colleagues after *Mefistofele* in Naples, a polite journalist, a cultivated and courteous man, Signor Martino Cafiero, made this remark to me point-blank: *Othello* would have also been a subject for you. (This proves how a well-meaning man can still say things that embarrass the hearer.) I replied denying the idea, I added that I had never thought of *Othello* for myself; but then, realizing that if I persisted in this denial without explanation it could be interpreted to mean I had little fondness for the subject Verdi was to set to music, so I explained my answer. I said I had never thought of it because I felt Shakespeare's masterpiece too passionately in its *tragic* form to be able to turn it into a *lyrical* expression (and this is partly true). I added that I would never have believed it possible to transform the Shakespeare tragedy into a good libretto until I actually did this job for you, Maestro, and with you (and this is true); and that now, only after many revisions, I saw, to my great contentment, that the work I had approached with much hesitation has proved to be endowed with eminently lyrical qualities and with forms perfectly suited to music, responding in every respect to the demands of opera. I said these words in a tone of profound conviction, and Signor Cafiero, who heard them properly, did not publish them because he is not the sort of man who publishes table conversation. Another man, to whom obviously I had not addressed these words, overheard them, got them all wrong, and published them in the *Roma* in his own version, perhaps without any malicious intention, but reversing the import and attributing to me a wish whose motive offends me and that is precisely the opposite of my great wish, which is to hear your music to a libretto I wrote only for the joy of seeing you pick up your pen again *through my efforts,* for the glory of being your working companion, for the ambition of hearing my name linked with yours, and our names with that of Shakespeare, and because that subject and my libretto are yours by sacred right of conquest. You alone can compose *Otello;* all the theater that you have given us affirms this truth. If I have been able to sense the powerful musical possibilities of the Shakespearian tragedy, which I did not feel before, and if I have been able to prove it in deed with my libretto, it is because I worked from the point of view of Verdian art; it is because, in writing those verses, I felt what you would have felt in illustrating them with that other language a thousand times more intimate and more powerful: sound. And if I have done that, it is because I wanted to seize an opportunity, in the maturity of my life, in that age when one's faith no longer changes, an opportunity to show you, better than with praises cast before you, how much I love and how much I feel the art that you have given us.

Now tell me if you believed true the report of the *Roma*'s editor that was reprinted by *Il piccolo* and by *Il pungolo.* I hope not. And yet the report existed; and since you read it, you felt the same need that I feel to clear up a snarled confusion, a delicate question, and you resolved it in the most exquisitely appropriate way possible. You turned in confidence to my most trusted friend so that he could speak to me, probe my heart, and if he had discovered even a remote germ of truth in the journalist's report then you were ready to give me *Otello* so that I could compose it myself.

For a moment, regarding me, you had the suspicion of the wise man who recognizes in human beings the weakness of Adam; but you resolved this suspicion with a benevolent and generous offer. Maestro, what you cannot suspect is the irony I felt in that offer, through no fault of yours. You see, for seven or eight years now perhaps I have been working on *Nerone* (put the "perhaps" where you like, next to the word "years" or the word "working"). I am oppressed by that incubus: on the days when I do not work I spend hours calling myself lazy; on the days when I do work I call myself an ass; and so my life flows on and I continue existing, slowly asphyxiated by an Ideal too lofty for me. To my misfortune I have studied my period too much (that is to say, the period of my story), and I am terribly enamored of it, and no other subject in the world, not even Shakespeare's *Othello,* could distract me from my theme: it suits in every respect my nature as an artist and the concept I have developed of the theater. I will finish *Nerone* or I will not finish it, but it is certain that I will never abandon it for another work; and if I do not have the strength to finish it I will not complain, and I will spend my life, neither sad nor happy, with that dream in my mind.

Now judge for yourself if, given this obstinacy, I could accept your offer. But for God's sake do not abandon *Otello;* do not abandon it, it is predestined for you. Do it; you had already begun working on it and I was so encouraged and was already hoping to see it finished, on some not-too-distant day.

You are healthier than I, stronger than I. We have pitted the strength of our arms against one another, and mine bent beneath yours. Your life is tranquil and serene; take up your pen again and write me soon; "Dear Boito, do me the favor of changing these verses," etc., etc., and I will change them at once, joyfully, and I will be able to work for you, I who am unable to work for myself, because you live in the true and real life of Art, and I in the world of hallucinations. But I must stop. Many greetings to Signora Giuseppina.

An affectionate handshake.

Yours,
A. Boito

ಈThis letter is crucial not only in the history of *Otello* but also in the development of the friendship between Boito and Verdi. Boito sums up the story, with his usual tact and his keen insight into the difficult, touchy side of Verdi's character. After having read the *Pungolo* version of the article in question, Verdi had written to Faccio on 27 March in these terms: "The worst of it is that Boito, *regretting* that he cannot set [the libretto] himself, naturally prompts the supposition that he has no hope of seeing it composed by me as he would like it. I admit this absolutely, I admit this completely, and therefore I am writing you, Boito's oldest and staunchest friend, so that on his return to Milan you may tell him in person, not in writing, that without the slightest resentment, without any bitterness, I will return his manuscript to him intact. Moreover, since that libretto is my property, I will make him a gift of it if he means to set it. If he accepts, I will be happy in the thought of having thus contributed to and enhanced the art we all love" [*Copialettere,* p. 324].

The actual words in the *Roma* (between some talk about *Nerone* and some dutiful praise of the Naples orchestra and chorus) report Boito as saying that "he had at first taken up the subject [*Jago*] reluctantly, but then, once the libretto was finished, he felt regret that he could not be the composer destined to set it to music."

The Medieval Castle, which still stands in the Valentino Park in Turin, was constructed for the National Exposition of 1884, originally proposed by the architect Alfredo D'Andrade and realized by a group of artists, writers, and historians. Boito's great friend, the playwright and future librettist Giuseppe Giacosa (1847–1906) was much interested in feudal Piedmont and later wrote a book on the castles of the Valle d'Aosta and the Canavese region. Camillo Boito (1836–1914), Arrigo's older brother, was a successful architect, who favored the Gothic revival style. A gifted writer and architectural historian, he was professor of architecture at the Brera Academy in Milan.

The Morelli photograph was of a painting by Verdi's old Neapolitan friend Domenico Morelli (1826–1901). Verdi owned a number of Morelli's works and followed his successful career with affectionate interest. They exchanged several interesting letters about the imagined physical appearances of Othello and Iago.

Martino Cafiero (1841–1884) was an outstanding Neapolitan journalist and editor. A notorious ladies' man, he had seduced and abandoned, about a decade earlier, the young actress Eleonora Duse, who was shortly to fall in love and have a serious affair with Boito.

Leone Fortis (1824–1898) was a kind of all-purpose writer (dramatist, librettist, columnist, critic, biographer), who founded *Il pungolo* in 1859 and was its editor for about thirty years. He was an early supporter and close friend of Giacosa.

Genoa, 26 April 1884

47

Dear Boito,

Since you will not accept, then the letter I wrote to Faccio has no further meaning or purpose.

I only skim the newspapers and never believe everything in them. If something strikes me, I stop, I reflect, and I try to get to the bottom of it, to see clearly. The question asked you point-blank and in that way at the Naples banquet was, at the very least... odd, and surely concealed other meanings that the words did not express. You perhaps could reply only as you did, I agree; but it is equally true that the sum of that conversation could prompt those comments I mentioned in my letter to Faccio.

But at this point it is useless to speak any more about this, since you absolutely will not accept the offer I made you, believe me, without any shadow of irony.

You say "I will finish *Nerone,* or I will not finish it"!!... I repeat your same words with regard to *Otello.* There has been too much talk about it! Too much time has gone by! The years of my age are too many! And too many my YEARS OF SERVICE!!!! I wouldn't want the public to have to say to me too obviously "*Enough!*"

In conclusion: All this has cast a chill over this *Otello* and has stiffened my hand, which had begun to write a few measures! What will happen next? I do not know! Meanwhile, I am very happy to have had this explanation between us, though it would have been better if it had happened the moment you got back from Naples. I shake your hand affectionately and greet you also in the name of Peppina.

> Yours,
> G. Verdi

⊷After Verdi's cautious forgiveness, Boito took another tack in the hope of getting the composer back to work. The stratagem of sending him some new text was successful, though not immediately.

[Milan, after 26 April 1884]

48 Dear Maestro,

Your letter, though wise and good, left me, I cannot say why, with a lingering uneasiness, and I could find no peace until I set myself to work for you. I remembered that you were not satisfied with a scene for Jago in the second act in double *quinari,* and that you wanted a more broken-up form, less lyrical. I suggested that I write for you a kind of *Villainous Credo,* and I have ventured to write it in a broken and non-symmetrical meter. Now we lack the connection between this passage and the recitative that comes before, but I don't have the manuscript at hand and therefore I could not attend to that; but the lacuna will consist of no more than two verses, three at most. If this attempt of mine is unsuccessful, blame my haste and my agitation, I will redo it better whenever you like. Meanwhile, if you do not find it absolutely wrong, please put this bit together with the other pages of *Otello.* I wrote this for my own consolation and for my personal satisfaction because I felt the need. Interpret this need as you like: as childishness, as sentimentality, as superstition; it doesn't matter. I beg you only not to answer me, not even with a "thanks" (which this page does not deserve), otherwise I will be uneasy all over again.

Here then I transcribe for you Jago's Credo.

JAGO

. . . .
— I believe in a cruel God, who created me
   In his own likeness, and whom I name in wrath.
   ~~And whom I name in wrath.~~
— From the wretchedness of a germ or an atom,
   Wretched I was born;
   I am a villain
   Because I am a man,
   And I feel the original mud within me.
— Yes! this is my faith!
— I believe with firm heart, just as
   The little widow in church believes,
   That the evil I conceive and that proceeds from me
   I carry out thanks to my destiny.
— I believe the just man is a mocking mummer
   Both in his face and in his heart.
   That all in him is a lie:
   Tear, kiss, gaze,
   Sacrifice, and honor.
— And I believe man the toy of wicked fate
   From the germ of the cradle
   To the worm of the grave.
— After so much mockery comes Death!
— And then? Death is Nothingness,
   And Heaven an old wives' tale.

See how many rascalities I've made him say.
An affectionate greeting to you and to Signora Giuseppina
from your
A. Boito

Genoa, 3 May 1884

49

Dear Boito,
Since you do not want me to, I will not say thanks; but I will say bravo.
This Credo is very beautiful: very powerful and Shakespearian in

every way. Naturally you will have to link it with some verses to the preceding scene between Cassio and Jago, but you will think about this later. For the present it is best to leave this *Otello* alone for a bit, for he is also nervous, as we are. You perhaps more than I.

If you come to Sant'Agata later on, as you have led me to hope, we can talk about it further, and then with the necessary calm.

A ban, therefore, on all uneasiness, and with greetings from Peppina I declare myself always

yours affectionately,
G. Verdi

P.S. I am late in answering you because I have been to Sant'Agata!

&sThe verses Boito sent Verdi in letter no. 48 ended up, exactly as proposed, in the final version of the opera.

Now the correspondence ceases for about four months. At the beginning of May the Verdis made their annual move from Genoa back to the villa at Sant'Agata; and at about the same time Boito met Eleonora Duse, who had recently created the role of Santuzza in his friend Giovanni Verga's drama *Cavalleria rusticana.* She was married to an actor in the same company; but they were soon to be separated, and for the next decade she was to occupy an important part in Boito's life. He went to great lengths to keep their liaison a secret, shared with only two or three friends, including Giacosa, but not Verdi.

In June the Verdis went to Turin to see the National Exposition. Boito, meanwhile, kept regularly in touch with Giacosa, and made his usual visit to Donna Vittoria Cima at Cernobbio that autumn.

Milan, 25 [September 1884]

50 Dear Maestro,

If you want us, Giacosa and I will arrive at Sant'Agata during the day of the 29th, that is to say, next Monday.

For three months now we have been planning this excursion, and finally we have both found, to our great joy, two days available to put it into effect.

Giacosa will arrive from Valle d'Aosta, where there is no cholera, and will meet me in Milan, where the public health is, thank heaven, excellent. So we will not bring with us the tiniest microbe. We will take the carriage at the most immaculate hotel in Piacenza and will arrive at your house completely pure.

If, however, this plan conflicts with your engagements and would be inopportune, please send me a telegram to Milan on the same day you receive this letter (I think you will receive it the day after tomorrow) so I can call off the trip, informing Giacosa.

Affectionate greetings to you and to Signora Giuseppina.

Yours,
A. Boito

⮜The cholera epidemic of the summer of 1884 had affected certain areas of northern Italy. Verdi mentions it in letters to other correspondents during this period.

As this was Boito's first encounter with Verdi since the Naples incident, he may have taken the amiable Giacosa with him to lighten the atmosphere.

[Telegram]

26 [Sep] 84

Arrigo Boito, Principe Amedeo 1, Milan
From Busseto
Do not take carriage at Piacenza. Come by direct train at 2 to Fioren- **51**
zuola, where you will find my carriage.

Verdi

Sant'Agata, 26 September 1884

Dear Boito, **52**

I certainly do want you here with Giacosa!

I sent you a telegram as soon as I received your letter, but I am also writing these few lines to make myself clearer.

It is pointless for you to take a carriage at Piacenza. You can leave Milan Monday morning at 11:40 and, without changing coaches at Piacenza, you arrive at 2:01 at Fiorenzuola, where you will find my carriage. My driver knows you. If Giacosa is coming from Piedmont he will arrive in Piacenza a few minutes after you. He can change coach and come with you to Fiorenzuola, I repeat, at 2:01.

We have no great fear of microbes here! You will not even be infested with chlorines or phenic acids.

Until Monday then, and farewell—or rather, without farewell.

Yours,
G. Verdi

◄▪Another silence follows the visit of Boito and Giacosa, which contributed to a final clearing of the air after the Naples incident. Verdi was in the right mood to resume work.

Giacosa was to meet Verdi on many future occasions. He published a charming account of life at Sant'Agata.

Genoa, 9 December 1884

53 Dear Boito,

In what part of the globe are you? This letter will reach you in any case, I hope.

It seems impossible, and yet it is true!!! Hmm!!!! I am keeping myself busy, and I am writing!! I am writing... to write, with no aim, with no concern, with no though of *afterwards*... indeed, with a decided aversion to *afterwards*.

So bear with me:

In the scene in the second act involving four characters, the dialogue between Jago and Emilia ends too quickly. The musical phrase is assigned to Desdemona; Otello declaims in the intervals; the others almost talk (one word per note); and since they end too quickly, as I said before, I would need four verses for each *aside*. Jago happy to have that handkerchief in his hands; and Emilia frightened because it is in his hands. The meter is *quinario*. I will transcribe the last strophe for you:

JAGO	Don't you fear me?
EMILIA	Cruel man
JAGO	Give me that...
EMILIA	What are you trying to do?
JAGO	Give me that veil!

That's all.

Peppina greets you and I shake your hand.

Yours,
G. Verdi

[after 9 December 1884]

54 My dear Maestro,

I possess not one sheet of writing paper and I am using the blank page of your letter to answer you. I have found, however, a nice little card, on which I have transcribed the verses you wish. I have added others, suspecting those might not suffice. I had to make an effort of memory to recall the construction of the strophes between Jago and Emilia, but I believe I've got it right. The addition I am sending can perhaps be of use to you because the *one word per note* ratio in a rapid meter like the *quinario* devours many verses. That addition also has this other good feature: for a few measures it introduces a new, almost joking, tone into the scene with the four characters, it suitably prepares the violent final action of Jago, and it allows a certain economy in the development of the effect. In short, see for yourself if it works or doesn't work.

Your letter was a joy, which I have kept all to myself; but it did not surprise me. There is no escaping one's own destiny, and, by a law of intellectual affinity, this tragedy of Shakespeare is predestined for you.

We will chat together within a few weeks. I will be in Nervi for the Christmas holidays or by the first of the year at the latest.

The good Giacosa had to undergo a rather serious surgical operation, the removal of a mucous membrane from the nose; now he is in Valle d'Aosta and is well. How often have I recalled the beautiful days at Sant'Agata!

Affectionate greetings to Signora Giuseppina and to you.

Yours,

A. Boito

If the verses do not fit, write me and I will do some others.

Here are the concluding verses you want:

. . . .
Give me that veil!

——————

JAGO (after having seized the handker-chief)	(Already my desire I conquer, and now On this weft Jago works!)
EMILIA	(~~His horrible, impure Hand won out God defend us From misfortune.~~) (The talons won, Grim and cowardly. God save us always From dangers.)
JAGO	(~~Already my agile thought Has found the noose.~~)
EMILIA	(~~Mute but vigilant Guard will I be.~~)

And if the verses are still not enough, here is an addition that can be placed *in the center of the aside* between Jago and Emilia, after the first time that Jago says "Give me that veil!"

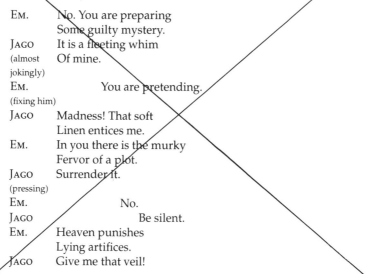

Em.	No. You are preparing
	Some guilty mystery.
Jago	It is a fleeting whim
(almost	Of mine.
jokingly)	
Em.	You are pretending.
(fixing him)	
Jago	Madness! That soft
	Linen entices me.
Em.	In you there is the murky
	Fervor of a plot.
Jago	Surrender it.
(pressing)	
Em.	No.
Jago	Be silent.
Em.	Heaven punishes
	Lying artifices.
Jago	Give me that veil!

The cancellations through the verses in this letter—preserved at Sant'Agata among the pages of the manuscript *Otello* libretto—are in pen on one side of the page and in brown pencil on the other side. The final version of the scene, in the second act of the opera, contains precisely those eight lines that escaped cancellation.

[Nervi] 7 Feb [1885]

55 Dear Maestro,

I will return to Genoa soon, but meanwhile, before I forget it, here is the verse that serves to obviate any misunderstanding of the words of Cassio by the audience.

Cassio	Here I thought to find Desdemona
Otello	(He named her)
Cassio	I want to speak to her again
	To learn if my pardon has been granted

The word "profferta" [granted] rhymes with "certa," [certain] I have noted.

Many greetings and I hope to see you soon.

> Yours most affectionately,
> A. Boito

&sSince Boito was in Nervi during the months of January and February, it is likely that Verdi expressed his reactions to these verses during meetings with the librettist.

Here Boito furnishes new words for act 3, scene 5 (the words survive in the definitive text).

Wednesday [Genoa, 18 February 1885]

56

Dear Boito,

If you don't mind, we'll postpone until Saturday our little dinner of tomorrow. Peppina is ill.

Be well.

> Yours,
> G. Verdi

Milan
Easter [5 April 1885]

57

Dear Maestro,

I put off my departure from Nervi one more day: instead of leaving Friday, I left Saturday. A few hours after my arrival I saw Giulio.

The impression he made on me was excellent. He didn't even seem to me to have lost weight, but this is a small consolation; he couldn't grow any thinner even if he wanted to. I'd been told he was much depressed in spirit, but I saw no sign of that. We spent the evening together at the Thomas Holden Marionettes and enjoyed ourselves immensely at that wonderful show.

When Holden comes to Genoa go and see him; he is the Liszt of marionettes, you cannot believe such perfection unless you see it. After the theater we went to the café and we separated at about midnight. Today Giulio is going out to spend the day at Villa d'Este. Tornaghi and other friends, from whom I had asked news of Giulio before seeing him, had mentioned with some uneasiness a repugnance towards work that he has shown since his illness, but then I received the explanation of this repugnance from Giulio himself, spontaneously. He is not yet perfectly well, he has to be very careful, about both his diet and his activity. He confessed to me that an attempt to write had immediately made his arm swell slightly. So it is natural that work repels him for the present, but the explanation for this repulsion is not to be found in any unhealthy spiritual or intellectual state but rather in his physical condition, not yet completely restored. I believe a good cure this summer, well advised and carefully followed, will heal him completely.

This is my impression and I believe I am not mistaken.

Most cordial greetings to Signora Giuseppina, and to you, Maestro, an affectionate handshake

from your
A. Boito

◄§Verdi left Genoa at the end of April 1885 for Milan, where he visited his doctor and an American dentist, who extracted five of his teeth. Verdi also had a visit from Amilcare Ponchielli, whom he liked. Ponchielli, in a letter to his wife, reported Verdi's favorable opinion of some (but by no means all) parts of *Mefistofele* and his conviction that *Nerone*'s completion was still in the distant future, as Boito had not yet finished setting the first act.

At an unspecified date (probably less than three weeks after his arrival in the city), Verdi left for Sant'Agata, where he spent most of the summer, as was his habit. Little is known on Boito's movements during these five months (presumably he made his usual summer visits), until he proposes himself as a guest at Sant'Agata in the following letter.

Milan, Wednesday [9 September 1885]

58 Dear Maestro,

My desire to see you again is great, but my fear of disturbing you is equally great. If you assure me that I will not be a nuisance I will descend on Sant'Agata next Sunday; but if my coming could disturb, even to the slightest degree, the beautiful tranquillity of your house or, what would be worse, the progress of your work, you should tell me openly with that frankness of yours I so like, and your frank words would make me as happy as would your courteous hospitality.

And I urge the same thing of Signora Giuseppina.

Most cordial greetings to you both

from your most affectionate
A. Boito

Sant'Agata, 10 September 1885

Dear Boito,

59

You could never disturb us! Come, and you will give both me and Peppina great pleasure. And have no fear of interrupting the progress of my work, as you put it! Alas, alas! Since I have been here (I blush to say it) I have done nothing! The country to some extent, the baths, the excessive heat, and... let me declare it openly, my inconceivable laziness have created obstacles.

Till Sunday, then. If you take the *direct* train from Milan at 11:40 A.M., get off at Fiorenzuola (I repeat *Fiorenzuola*) at two P.M. and you will find a bucephalus of mine that will bring you here.

So we will meet soon. Peppina greets you and I shake your hands. Be well.

Affectionately,
G. Verdi

◆◆Boito's visit to Sant'Agata apparently stimulated the composer, as the following letter suggests. The correspondence now becomes intense for several months, as work on *Otello* made real and rapid progress towards its conclusion.

Sant'Agata, 5 October 1885

Dear Boito,

60

I have finished the fourth act and I can breathe again! It was difficult for me to avoid too many recitatives and to find some type of rhythm, some phrases for all the fragmented *versi sciolti.* But in this way you have been able to say everything that had to be said, and I am now tranquil, and happy as a lark. In writing the music of this ultra-terrible scene I felt it necessary to cut a strophe that I myself had asked you to add, and to add here and there some verses, some half-verses, and especially a beautiful strophe that had been wrongly omitted. Consequently there are some disconnected verses, which you will easily *connect.* You have overcome far worse difficulties!

"And her eyes wept so much, so much,
    They would have moved stones to pity!"

This is more beautiful than the original. I will transcribe for you the whole scene as it has now been set to music.

Scene 3

. . . .
. . . . as it is as far as:

. . . .

                You love Cassio!

DESDEMONA	No! Upon my soul!!
OTELLO	That handkerchief
	I gave you, you gave him.
DES.	That's not true!
OT.	I saw it in his hand!
DES.	It was a trick!
OT.	Confess
DES.	I swear
OT.	Beware of perjury!
	Think: You are on your deathbed!
DES.	Not to die!
OT.	To die soon
DES.	Help!
	I do not love Cassio... Let him come here... let him speak...

OT.   You will see him no more...

DES.   What are you saying?... Dead?!

OT.   Dead!

> Revise this verse as you like but avoid a long sentence like the one we had before: "Closed is his mouth forever."

DES.   I am lost... he betrayed!

OT.   And you dare weep for him?

DES.   Otello, do not kill me

OT.   Down... fall

      Prostitute

> Keep if you can "Otello, do not kill me!" It is heartrending!

DES.   Mercy

OT.   Die

DES.   Let me live

      This night

OT.   No

DES.   One hour

OT.   No

DES.   One instant!

OT.   No!

DES.   Let me say only an Ave

OT.   It is late, it is late... (long pause)

      Calm... as the tomb

EMILIA knocks at the door   Open!

OT.   Emilia!!

EM. entering   ~~Open!...~~

    Horrible crime!... Cassio killed
    Rodrigo

> I would like Emilia to say again "Open! Oh, what a crime!"

Oт.	And Cassio?
Em.	He lives!
Oт.	Cassio lives?!
Des.	Unjustly killed... unjustly
Em.	Heaven, what a moan! Horror
[Des.]	I die innocent...
Em.	Who was it? Who was it?
[Des.]	No one... I myself... to my...

[Des.] Lord... commend me... Farewell!... dies

Oт. She lied! is a liar!
I killed her

Em. Murderer!

Oт. She was Cassio's
Whore! Ask Jago!...

Em. Jago?...

Oт. Jago!

Em. Succor... Help, help!... Seize the murderer!

Enter Lodovico, Cassio, Jago, and soldiers

All What cries... Heaven!... Desdemona killed!

Em. to Jago Jago, give the lie to that base murderer...
Do you believe the chaste
~~Did you believe~~ Desdemona faithless?

Jago So I believed her.

Em. You?

Jago Yes

Oт. interrupting That handkerchief
That I one day gave her she gave to Cassio.

Em. Oh divine powers!

Jago Be silent

Em. No
I will reveal all

Jago Be silent

Em. Accursed
By Heaven

Jago Be silent

Em. No

Jago Tremble

Em. He
Seized that handkerchief from my hand
By force!

Cassio And in my dwelling
I found that veil!

Montano entering, cries Rodrigo dying
Revealed the dreadful deeds of this
⌜villain

Perhaps it is too much to say "Cassio" three times, but that "Cassio lives" suits Otello so well.

I do not much like the word "chaste" in this place. Couldn't you say: "Did you believe," etc.?

This passage seems long, but set to music it turned out rapid, and more brief than if it were recited.

OT. to Jago   Ah! Exculpate yourself

JAGO with ~~contempt~~ a cry   No! and he flees

LOD.   Pursue him, and let him be
⌈taken

To prison!

OT. with a shout   And has Heaven no more thunderbolts?!

LOD. to Otello   You are my prisoner!

OT. long pause   All is finished!...

Glory is a flash, a lying dream!

approaches Desdemona

And you... how pale you are! And tired and mute and
⌈beautiful

Sainted creature born under an evil star

Cold, as your chaste life, and assumed into heaven!

Desdemona, Desdemona! Ah!... Dead, dead, dead!!

After a long pause he runs to the table where he had laid his sword...
forestalls him
Cassio ~~blocks him~~ and takes the sword. Then Otello takes out a dagger and says:
~~rapidly and kills himself~~

I have this dagger left! and he kills himself.

ALL   Ah wretch!

[OT.]   Before I killed you, etc., etc... as it stands...

· ·
_____

Amen, and a heartfelt greeting.

Affectionately,
G. Verdi

⮐The first lines that Verdi asks Boito to "connect" are from Desdemona's Willow Song early in act 4.

The "scene" is translated here as Verdi sent it to Boito with the above letter. When composer and librettist met at Sant'Agata less than two weeks later, they made a number of changes.

Villa d'Este
Lake Como
9 October [1885]

My dear Maestro,

61

First of all, *Hurrah* from the bottom of my heart. Next, I must confess to you that I have an irresistible desire to hear what you have written for that page so full of horrors, for what is the most anguished page ever conceived by the human mind.

I must add that I will not be able to do properly that brief job of connection that you are awaiting for that scene without first having heard the agogics and rhythms you have written. If they have captured all the awesome truth with the same power and simplicity as in the preceding scenes, the prospect of hearing them is frightening, and this is no doubt the case.

During these next few days I will have the opportunity to come to you. I have to be in Rome on the morning of the 19th of this month. On my way there or on my way back I can stop at Fiorenzuola and from there make a beeline for Sant'Agata. I will stay in Rome for about a week. If our interview were to be feasible for the trip down, I would leave Milan the morning of the 16th, I would stop over at Sant'Agata on the 17th, and leave again for Rome the morning of the 18th. If, on the contrary, we agree that it be for my return, our meeting would take place around the 25th or 26th; but then my friend Giacosa would be traveling with me, and I wouldn't have the heart to leave him by himself on the train so close to the threshold of the Shakespearian realm. You choose between these two possibilities.

But perhaps you will prefer to postpone our meeting to Milan if you will pass through again this year, stopping over for a few days before going on to Genoa. I will remain at Villa d'Este through the 14th, that is, through next Wednesday, then I go to Milan.

Is this all clear?

I repeat: In order to do well the little that remains for me to do, I must have the text of Shakespeare before my eyes and your music before my pen. I await an answer from you. Many cordial greetings to Signora Giuseppina. To you, Maestro, a handshake and once again: Hurrah!

Yours affectionately,
A. Boito

P.S. Unless you got the date wrong, I received your letter after a long delay.

◄§The postmarks on the envelopes of Verdi's and Boito's letters confirm the dates, so Verdi's cannot have taken long to arrive.

Boito's "hurrahs" may refer to Verdi's birthday (9 Oct.), but are more
likely prompted by the progress of *Otello.*

Sant'Agata, 11 October 1885

62 Dear Boito,

Fine, I will expect you on the 16th. It would be impossible later, also
because Peppina must go as usual to her sister. So you will find a bucephalus of mine at Fiorenzuola at 2 P.M. on the 16th. However, send
me a telegram the day before to confirm your coming.

Until then.

Yours,
G. Verdi

◄§Boito's trip to Rome was probably connected with the preparations
for an important international music conference to be held in Vienna.
Boito—now very much a pillar of the Italian cultural establishment—was to be a delegate.

Milan, 23 [October 1885]

63 Dear Maestro,

I can say with Aristophanes: "J'ai perdu ma fiole." On leaving
Sant'Agata I forgot the *Othello* volume, and I realize now, putting my
papers in order, I also forgot the copy that you made of the last scene,
which I received at Villa d'Este, the copy on which we worked together
these past days. I'm afraid that, coming across that manuscript, you
may tear it up and throw it into the trash basket. But I hope to reach
you in time to save it. It means a great deal to me. It is a memento of our
work, and attached to it is a letter from you to me; so I beg you not to
destroy it and to put it in the volume of our tragedy so it will not be
mislaid.

Giulio, who is well and whom I saw the other day, told me that the
payment on behalf of Signora Giuseppina has been made. All I can do
now is say good-bye to you and thank you again so much for the strong
and lofty intellectual emotions I savored at Sant'Agata, and for your
and Signora Giuseppina's kind and dear hospitality.

Yours affectionately,
A. Boito

P.S. There is no necessity for you to go to the trouble of sending me the volume and the manuscript, because we will surely meet again fairly soon in Milan.

◆s"J'ai perdu ma fiole" ("I have lost my phial") is a quotation from the French translation of Aristophanes' *The Frogs*.

Sant'Agata, 27 October 1885

Dear Boito,

64

I found your French Shakespeare, and the draft, etc... But what will you do with the latter? It seems to me it should be burned, and I would have burned it if you hadn't asked me for it. But we will perform this operation when I come, in 15 or 20 days, to Milan to *have my teeth trimmed.*

I am still at the fourth act, which I want to finish completely, including the orchestration, to seal it and not mention it again until... until...

Good-bye. Give me your news, and tell me if your poet has finished *Nerone...*

Yours,
G. Verdi

◆sThe Shakespeare volume was the French translation of *Othello* by François Victor Hugo (son of the famous writer), on which Boito relied heavily, his command of English being shaky. Verdi did not return his letter or the draft; they remain in the Sant'Agata archives.

A Boito letter written about this time has been lost, but Verdi's reply below survives. For some years there had been an international debate about establishing a standard concert pitch. In October Boito presumably attended a preliminary meeting in Rome to discuss Italy's position on the question before the opening of the conference in Vienna on 16 November 1885 (the 1881 Congress of Italian Musicians had adopted 432 Hz as the national standard). Boito was one of the two official Italian delegates (the other was a professor of physics from the University of Rome).

Sant'Agata, 8 November 1885

Dear Boito,

65

There is no doubt about it. The conclusion of your letter is perfect. Principal aim, *the standard of concert pitch.* Give in, if it cannot be avoided; but not without declaring openly, loudly, and publicly the error, from the scientific point of view, of the *870* vibrations. You are a clear and fluent speaker, and you will easily expound the truth.

With the authority of our conservatories, it could surely be declared that we maintain the concert pitch of 864 vibrations because it is more correct; but this firmness could seem mere pique, a childishness that could almost lend itself to ridicule, and it would immediately be taken up by your transalpine brothers.

Conclusion: *Give in,* I repeat, *if it cannot be avoided;* and the *standard,* etc.

Write me from Vienna the result of it all, and with Peppina's greetings I wish you a good journey and bid you farewell.

> Yours,
> G. Verdi

▪Instead of writing Verdi from Vienna, Boito met him in Milan, where the composer was spending a few days en route to his winter residence in Genoa. Though the Vienna congress passed a resolution establishing concert pitch at 870 half cycles per second (that is, 435 Hz, for the equivalent of concert a'), the problem was not entirely solved, and Verdi later instructed Ricordi to forbid performances of *Otello* in theaters where standard concert pitch was not respected.

The abrupt opening of Verdi's next letter, some weeks later, suggests that he and Boito had been in communication. The fact that Verdi is already thinking about possible interpreters indicates that work was well advanced.

Genoa, 11 January 1886

66 Dear Boito,

... *Montano* comes on stage in the first act to get himself duly stabbed; he returns in the last to accuse Jago; but why doesn't he appear in the third-act finale?... This is a very annoying question because if you found it cogent you would write me eight verses, and (now that the finale is done) it would cost me a lot of trouble to add another *independent* part in that number, as I would not like to double the part of another bass. So what do you think? Write the eight verses, or let Montano sleep? I would wish him pleasant dreams, and I would be happier than he.

And that's not all!

It seems impossible!... but in the passage that precedes the ensemble there are two verses that prolong, drag, and encumber!

Here they are:

> . . . .
> Honestly I could not. You yourself
> Study and judge his behavior
> With keen mind
>
> OTELLO   Here he is
> In his soul examine him

I would ask you to make only two verses out of these four. It would be easy to use the first and the third, but it is good for Otello to say "examine him" and it seems to me easy to fit it in there.

If you go to hear *Roberto,* tell me in absolute secrecy if a Desdemona could be found in either of those two young women (sopranos).

Pay attention to the quality of the voice, to the intonation, and, of course, *intelligence* and *feeling* above all. Even if they sing badly, no matter! On the contrary, so much the better. Then it will be easier for them to sing my way...

Good-bye.

Affectionately,
G. Verdi

⋖ Meyerbeer's *Robert le diable* (in Italian translation) opened at La Scala on 14 January 1885 and was a great success (it ran for twenty-two performances). The two young sopranos were Gemma Bellincioni (1864–1950) and Ernestina Bendazzi-Secchi (1864–1931). Boito's reply to the above letter does not survive; but—as we can infer from Verdi's next letter—the librettist expressed a negative opinion on Bendazzi-Secchi even before attending the Meyerbeer opera, in which she was well received. Barely twenty-one at this time, she had made her debut (in Trieste) in 1884. She married the tenor Alfonso Garulli in 1887; both he and she enjoyed long and successful careers. Like Bendazzi, Bellincioni did not sing Desdemona. Though she was soon to become a favorite interpreter of *verismo* operas (she created Santuzza in Mascagni's *Cavalleria rusticana*) her repertory also included *La traviata,* and Verdi much admired her Violetta.

Genoa, 14 January 1886

67   Dear Boito,

Thank you for the two verses:

[LODOVICO]	. . . . warrior
	. . . .
[JAGO]	He is what he is.
[LODOVICO]	Make your thought clear.
JAGO	On that better to keep the tongue dumb.
OTELLO	There he is. It is he. In his soul examine him.

Scene 8

Amen

I am happy, very happy that you have kept Montano in his bed because of the wound received. I had a hellish fear you would tell me it would be a good idea to see Montano also in the finale. I breathe easy! There are truly 11 independent parts, including the choruses, and sometimes 12! They would have become... with Montano! We'll say no more about la Bendazzi. You will tell me something about la Bellincioni!

Oh, you will surely not hear all of *Otello* a month from now! I have many things to retouch in the first act... Indeed, I will recast a large part of it!...

I am very sorry about Ponchielli! The moment I received your letter I telegraphed Giulio to telegraph me immediately with news of him, which I expect any moment. You too might be kind enough to drop into the letter box a few words on this matter.

Poor Ponchielli! He is still young and sturdy! Let's hope! But three doctors!!!! who will not have the courage to take from his veins a dozen of ounces of blood, which would relieve him at once, since it is a case of pneumonia!

Good-bye.

G. Verdi

☞The verses Verdi quotes here remain in the final libretto, act 3, scene 7. In discussing the number of independent parts, Verdi avoids writing the number 13, deferring to the popular superstition.

Ponchielli had fallen ill on 8 January; his condition was immediately recognized as serious, and Verdi, who admired him as a man and as a musician, telegraphed Milan several times to enquire about his condition.

Saturday evening [Milan, 16 January 1886]
7 o'clock

Poor Ponchielli has worsened again since this morning, and already **68** this morning the doctors feared he might die at any moment. If there is any improvement tomorrow I will write, but now only a genuine miracle of nature can save him!

Poor friend!

A. Boito

[Milan, 18 January 1886]

Dear Maestro, **69**

You already know that poor Ponchielli is dead; now, one way or another, he will find that peace he never had in life, thanks to the wicked egotism of his wife's family.

I know Giulio was with Corti in Genoa, and Giulio, whom I have just seen, has repeated to me some excerpts from the eloquent oratory of the impresario of La Scala. I admire Corti's command of words, but I did not admire the fact that, in the heat of inspiration, he used my name to invent foolishly a tale that hasn't even the shadow of a germ of a beginning of an embryo of a basis of truth. Corti told you I had announced to him *Otello* was finished and that I urged him to leave for Genoa. I said nothing of the sort, not to Corti or to Ricordi, or to anyone. I said not one word. What displeases me is that this invention fits with the last letter you wrote me and therefore could assume in your eyes an aspect of truth. Chance is sometimes a rogue and this is a rascality of Chance. But Corti is shameless and deserves to be corrected. Imagine: I haven't even seen him for many months, and when I see him on the street I always avoid speaking with him rather than undergo indiscreet questioning. Certainly I cannot be the one who sped him to Genoa to annoy you with pointless words and insistence that will have no power to advance even by one hour the conclusion of your work. To Gailhard, who also turned up in Genoa for *Otello,* I spoke in a discouraging way, because I knew you were not thinking of the Opéra for the first performance of your score. But now the *Otello* hunt is open and all try to snatch the prey. It's all very well for me to be silent or to say the most vague and most noncommittal words on this matter; my name is nonetheless involved, in your presence, in their greedy talk and this annoys me, it truly, truly annoys me. It annoys me so much that now I am annoying you with this letter. I can tell you nothing about la Bellincioni because I didn't attend the performance of *Roberto.* When it is given again I will go to hear it and will write you my impression. Cordial greetings to you, dear Maestro, and to Signora Giuseppina.

Yours affectionately,
A. Boito

◄▪Cesare Corti was impresario of La Scala. Considered one of the best theater managers of his time, he directed La Scala for many years. He had met Verdi and Ricordi on 17 January, in an attempt to secure the premiere of *Otello* for La Scala. Pierre Gailhard was director of the Opéra.

[Milan, 20 January 1886]

70   Dear Maestro,

Yesterday evening I saw her and I heard her. If I were ten years younger I would already have fallen in love with her. She is so pretty: she is tall, slim, young, elegant, dark, supple; and with blonde hair she would perhaps be even more beautiful, because there is much sweetness in that face and a whole aura of affection enfolds her. The public also feels this aura and enjoys applauding her and applauds her beyond what she deserves, because, in the final analysis, this charming girl is not yet an artist and I do not know if she ever will be.

The voice is charming and slim like her figure, but it is not a true theater voice. It has a thin timbre that cuts through the crowd without occupying any space. The quasi-pastoral part of Alice is fairly well suited to this young lady: some phrases here and there she says well and even with a certain vitality, or rather with a certain lucky boldness derived, I believe, from her confidence in her physical attractions. True dramatic feeling, true spontaneity and power of accentuation, I do not feel she possesses. Her gestures have obviously been taught by her professor of mime, and the phrasing of her singing must be the faithful imitation of what some sort of Lamperti taught her and this is transparently clear. Everything she does on the stage seems to me something borrowed from someone else.

She has two noticeably good qualities: she enunciates well (though not superbly) and she very seldom looks at the conductor. If I were Faccio I would protest against this latter good quality, but it is a sign that there is something musical in the girl. Something; but true artistic talent does not seem to me to be there.

I was in a box near the stage and thus in a position to judge rather optimistically the strength of her voice and the clarity of her phrasing. At the end of the evening I realized I had always *watched her sing;* that demonstrates the charm of her face and of her figure and the whiteness of her teeth and nothing more. Too bad! but I do not believe la Bellincioni was born to be strangled on the island of Cyprus. Too bad! The report is ended. Cordial greetings

from your most affectionate
A. Boito

◆❧Bellincioni, in fact, was not approached for Desdemona, though Boito's judgment, in the light of her subsequent career, seems harsh (except for his admiration of her looks). Ricordi sent Verdi a more positive report, and the composer made a special trip to Milan to hear her (see note following letter no. 72 below).

Francesco Lamperti (1813–1892) was a well-known voice teacher, a professor at the Milan Conservatory (1850–1876), and author of some technical works on singing published by Ricordi. Among the singers he worked with were Sophie Loewe, Maria Waldmann, Teresa Stolz, and Sophie Cruvelli—all Verdi interpreters of significance.

Genoa, 21 January 1886

71

Dear Boito,

Thank you for the news... though I would have preferred it to be more favorable.

Can you tell me now about la Teodorini? Do you remember her well? Tell me only about the voice: How are the middle notes, and how high do her top notes go?

The result of the long dialogue with Corti and Giulio is this: That I have not finished the opera, and I do not know *if I will finish it.* If I do, I will give it; always provided there are suitable performers. No formal commitment, absolutely none. Conversationally, I mentioned *Maurel, Tamagno, Teodorini.* But afterwards, thinking and looking over the score, I saw that while Tamagno would be excellent in many places, he would not succeed in the final duo of the first act, and still less at the end of the opera; and so two acts would end coldly (as I wrote to Giulio). You do not know the first duo, but you know the finale of the opera. I do not believe that he could express effectively that brief melody "And you, how pale you are" and still less "A kiss, another kiss..." especially since between this second kiss and the third there are 4 measures of orchestra alone, which must be filled with delicate, moving action that I imagined while writing the notes. Action very easy for a real actor, but hard for... someone else.

As you know, Gailhard came to see me, and I am surprised that he did not tell me he had first spoken with you. I said to him that the opera was not finished; that the opera was in Italian, written in good Italian, and for the first time it had to be performed in Italian.

They talk, and they write me always about *Jago!!!* It seems useless for me to keep replying *"Otello,* pas *Jago,* n'est pas fini!!" since they continue to say and to write to me *"Jago, Jago."* He is (this is true) the Demon who moves everything; but Otello is the one who acts: *He loves, is jealous, kills,* and *kills himself.* And for my part it would seem hypocrisy not to call it *Otello.* I prefer them to say "He chose to wrestle with the giant and was crushed" rather than "He wanted to hide behind the title of Jago." If you agree with me, let us then begin baptizing it *Otello,* and tell Giulio at once.

And the petition? It is a kind gesture... that commits me... and it is also "kind if you like," but a pressure as well. No, no: It does not commit me at all, because I will not give the opera unless I am convinced... and besides, I well know that all those who have signed, with a few exceptions, will be the first to cast stones, out of that spirit of demolition that characterizes our time, and to make up for the kindness shown me! Isn't this true? *Amen.*

Good-bye,
G. Verdi

⋙Elena Teodorini had sung in several productions of Boito's *Mefisto-fele.* She was also recommended by Ricordi.

Victor Maurel and Francesco Tamagno did, in fact, create the roles of Jago and Otello, and Maurel then created Falstaff. Verdi had known them from, among other things, the revised *Boccanegra* at La Scala.

The "giant" with whom Verdi imagined wrestling was probably Rossini, whose *Otello* (1816) had been popular for a half-century, though it had not been heard at La Scala since 1870. Verdi naturally was thoroughly familiar with the score.

The "petition" was addressed to Verdi by the box holders of La Scala and by the exclusive Club dell'Unione, asking him to give the premiere of *Otello* at La Scala.

PLATES

FIGURE 1. Verdi in the late 1880s. (Archivo Storico Ricordi, Milan)

FIGURE 2. Boito in the 1880s. (Fondazione "Giorgio Cini," Venice)

FIGURE 3. Giuseppina Strepponi in a rare photographic portrait from her late years. (Archivio Storico Ricordi, Milan)

FIGURE 4. Giulio Ricordi in the 1880s. (Archivio Storico Ricordi, Milan)

FIGURE 5. The last photograph taken of Franco Faccio. (Reproduced from De Rensis, ed., *Franco Faccio e Verdi*)

FIGURE 6. Romilda Pantaleoni as Desdemona. (Archivio Storico Ricordi, Milan)

FIGURE 7. Francesco Tamagno as Otello. (Archivio Storico Ricordi, Milan)

FIGURE 8. Victor Maurel as Falstaff. (Museo Teatrale alla Scala)

FIGURES 9 & 10. In the summer of 1892 Verdi was in Milan to discuss plans for the production of *Falstaff*. These images of the usually camera-shy Maestro are part of a series (published in an issue of *Illustrazione italiana* celebrating the opera's premiere) taken by hidden photographers in the garden behind Giulio Ricordi's Milan residence. In the first shot, an

amused Verdi—informed that the shots would be taken, but not where and when—speaks with Tito Ricordi; a self-satisfied Giulio, who had arranged the photographic session, stands to the right. Composer and librettist are together in the second image; Boito, according to the article, was aware of the scheme. (Archivio Storico Ricordi, Milan)

FIGURE 11. Verdi at his writing desk in the apartment he reserved at the Grand Hôtel Milan, and where he died a year after this portarit was taken. (Archivio Storico Ricordi, Milan)

FIGURE 12. Boito and Verdi on a terrace of the Casa di Riposo per Musicisti in Milan. (Archivio Storico Ricordi, Milan)

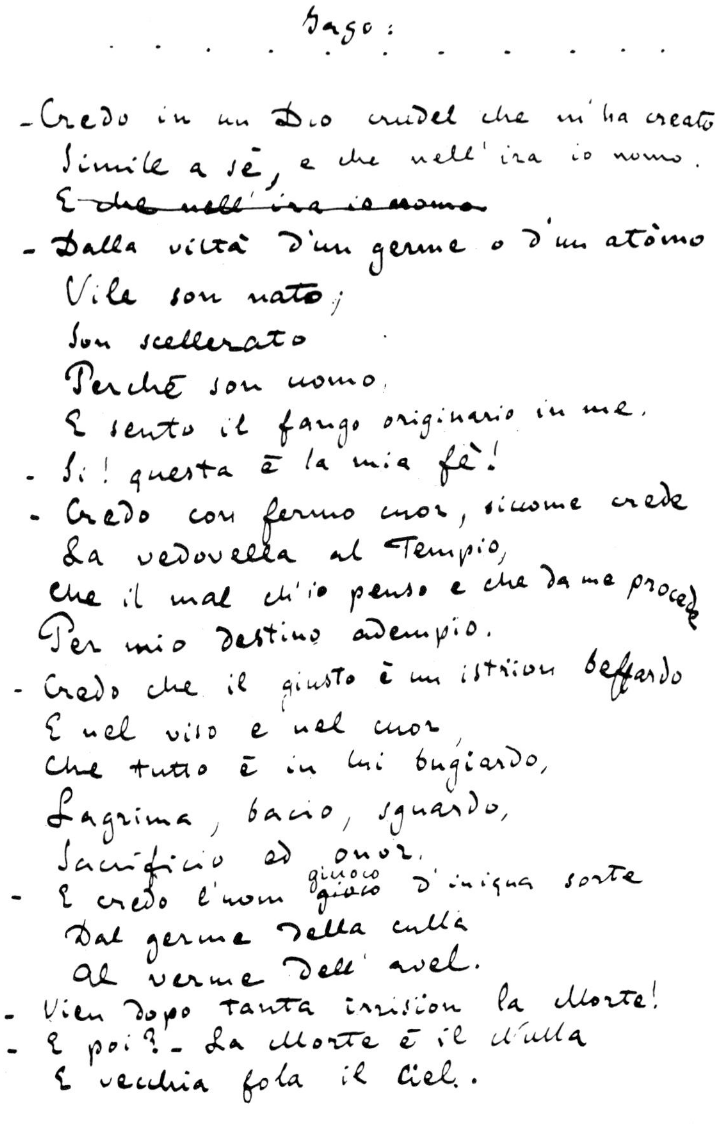

Jago:

— Credo in un Dio crudel che m'ha creato
Simile a sè, e che nell'ira io nomo.
~~E che nell'ira io nomo~~
— Dalla viltà d'un germe o d'un atòmo
Vile son nato;
Son scellerato
Perchè son uomo,
E sento il fango originario in me.
— Sì! questa è la mia fè!
— Credo con fermo cuor, siccome crede
La vedovella al Tempio,
Che il mal ch'io penso e che da me proced
Per mio destino adempio.
— Credo che il giusto è un istrion beffardo
E nel viso e nel cuor,
Che tutto è in lui bugiardo,
Lagrima, bacio, sguardo,
Sacrificio ed onor.
— E credo l'uom giuoco d'iniqua sorte
Dal germe della culla
Al verme dell'avel.
— Vien dopo tanta irrision la Morte!
— E poi? — La Morte è il nulla
E vecchia fola il Ciel.

FIGURE 13. Jago's Credo, as Boito transcribed it for Verdi in letter no. 48. (By kind permission of Alberto and Gabriella Carrara Verdi, Sant'Agata, Villa Verdi)

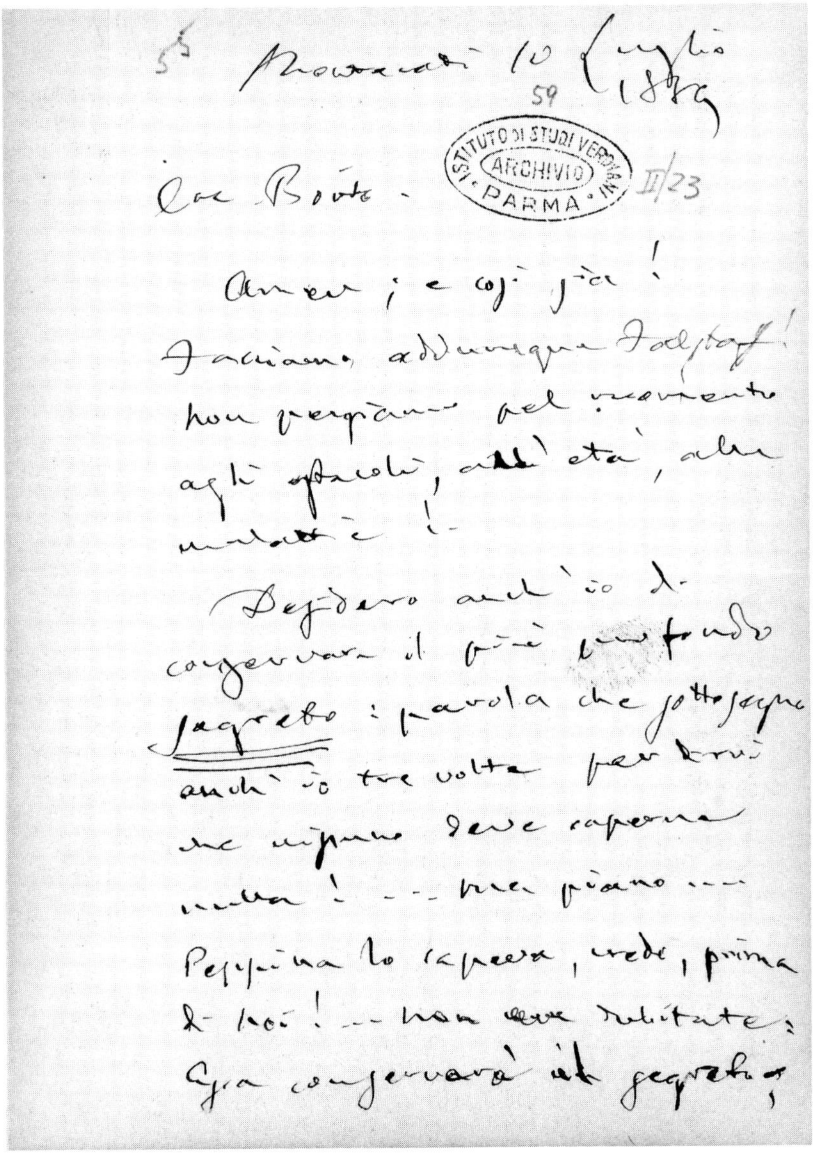

Montecatini 10 Luglio 1889

Car. Boito.

Amen; e così sia!

Facciamo adunque Falstaff! Non pensiamo pel momento agli ostacoli, all'età, alle malattie!

Desidero anch'io di conservare il più profondo segreto: parola che sottolineo anch'io tre volte per dirti che nessuno deve saperne nulla! ... ma piano ... Peppina lo sapeva, credo, prima di noi! ... Non dubitate: Essa conserverà il segreto;

FIGURE 14. Verdi's letter of 10 July 1889, finally accepting to undertake *Falstaff* (see no. 122). (Istituto Nazionale di Studi Verdiani, Parma)

[Milan, 23 January 1886]

72

Dear Maestro,

You ask me to tell you only about the voice, *the voice* of la Teodorini; I obey, but with this restriction the question proves rather dire. The voice was never that artist's chief gift, and for some time now people have been saying that her vocal powers have deteriorated and that the impresario Ferrari was not satisfied when he took her to America. If what they are saying is true, if that singer is losing the security and the timbre of those few effective notes she had *towards* the lower and *towards* the higher registers, the instrument will have become almost useless. The middle notes were weak even when I heard her in Madrid, and the highest notes had no ring, no phonic power. You ask me how high she can go: in the fourth act of *Mefistofele* there is a C that is not held long, in fact it is very brief, and that C did not ring out. Before that C there is a B♭ and it did not ring well. As I write this, I interrogate myself, to make quite sure that my memory is not failing me, but I dismiss this scruple when I think that a beautiful voice, a real voice, with beautiful and powerful high notes, once heard is never forgotten. If I were to speak of la Teodorini's other gifts, criticism could give way to praise, because she does possess theatrical, dramatic qualities, real ones, and I am indebted to her for many beautiful performances of my opera.

But here, to go into this new argument, I would have to begin another very long chat, so I remain faithful to my orders and stop.

In a month's time, dear Maestro, we will see each other, and then we will be able to talk at length and in breadth.

I knew nothing (I never see anyone) of the petition the Club dell'Unione and Milanese "society" sent to you. That is, the day I saw Gailhard I had heard that the box holders of La Scala and the gentlemen of the club, alarmed by the news of the visit of the director of the Opéra to Genoa, meant to send that petition to you, but I was unaware that it had been done. I realize that this gesture must not influence any decisions you may make, but undeniably it is a gesture of beautiful courtesy and noble reverence that does them honor.

Affectionate greetings to you and to Signora Giuseppina.

Yours,

A. Boito

◄§After this letter there is a pause of over three months in the correspondence, largely because Boito and Verdi had occasion to meet probably in Milan in late February and certainly in Genoa the month after. At the end of January Verdi officially granted the premiere of *Otello* to La Scala. The purpose of the February visit to Milan was to hear Gemma Bellincioni, Ricordi's candidate for Desdemona. Another candidate was Romilda Pantaleoni, whose lover was Faccio, future conductor of the opera. In late February Pantaleoni signed a contract with La Scala and was assured the part of Desdemona. Between March and April Verdi made a trip to Paris, to ascertain for himself the condition of Victor Maurel's voice, of which he had heard upsetting rumors. The rumors apparently proved unfounded, and Maurel was assigned, as he had expected, the part of Jago. During these months, when not traveling, Verdi worked on the orchestration of the score.

Quinto, 6 May [1886]

73 Dearest Maestro,

Yesterday I received a letter from Giulio telling me that Edel was leaving for Venice next Saturday, taking advantage of a few days he had free to begin his studies for the costumes, and he asked me for instructions. I replied that I could not give him the list of costumes for two reasons: first because this operation must be done in agreement with you, and also because I did not trust my memory and did not have the libretto before me.

All the same, I did not refuse to expound general instructions to him so he could base his preliminary studies on them. In these instructions there is a very important point that you, Maestro, must judge: *the choice of period.* See if my reasoning is right. If it does not seem right to you, we still have time to make it right with a telegram to Giulio or with a letter to Edel. What is the origin of the *Othello* of Shakespeare? A novella by Cinzio Giraldi in the *Hecatommithi.* What is the date of the *Hecatommithi?* The sack of Rome, 1527. What is the date of the novella in question? Giraldi himself tells us: a few years before the general date found in the proem to his novellas, therefore a period of time that cannot go beyond these limits: 1520–25. These dates for us have the value of history, and we could not find others, in my opinion, more probable. A conflict between Venetians and Turks in those years was quite possible: the Kingdom of Cyprus (namely, the heritage of Caterina Cornaro) had already passed under the dominion of the Venetian Republic. There is another observation to be made. Storytellers like Boccaccio, like Sacchetti, like Cinzio Giraldi take the subjects of their works from their imagination, or from history or current events, or from folk tales that are often based on history or current events. Therefore Giraldi took his subject, in the novella of "Otello," either from his own imagination or from reality. If we assume the first hypothesis, Giraldi's imagination is our law, because where greater laws are missing, lesser laws decide. If we assume the second hypothesis, the more we believe Giraldi's dates have a basis in the truth, the more we must remain faithful to them. My personal conviction is that the novella is based on reality, if not in every detail, surely in a general way. Numerous arguments could be adduced to support this conviction, but I know already that you must share my opinion.

But even if our theatrical action can be limited to one of the five years between 1520 and 1525, the pictorial representation of the *costumes* can have a much wider margin. Today if we go about the streets we find the *gommeux*

[A. Boito]

◆This letter is incomplete and remained unsent, but another of similar content was sent on 16 May (see no. 77 below).

Giovan Battista Giraldi Cinthio (or Cintio or Cinzio) was a sixteenth-century writer, philosopher, and dramatist. In 1528 he began preparing a collection of novellas, which he published in 1565 as the *Hecatommithi.* The collection comprises one hundred novellas in ten groups of ten. Novella no. 7 in the third group was the source of Shakespeare's *Othello.*

The painter Alfredo Edel (1859–1912) provided numerous covers for Ricordi scores; he had designed costumes for many productions at La Scala (including the *Boccanegra* of 1881 and the *Don Carlos* of 1884), before *Otello.* He worked also in London, Paris (for Sarah Bernhardt), and New York.

Gommeux is a French slang term meaning "fops."

Sant'Agata, 8 May 1886

74

Dear Boito,

For the three verses written recently I have consulted the original...

For,	sir,	were I	the Moor,	I	would not be	Iago
Perché	Signor	fossi io il	Moro	io	vorrei non	esser Jago

Hugo also says:

Si j'étais le More je ne voudrais pas être Jago
[If I were the Moor, I would not like to be Jago]

Also in the Maffei translation:

> ...Quand'io potessi
> Trasformarmi nel Moro essere un Jago
> Già non vorrei...
> [If I could transform myself into the Moor,
> I would surely not want to be a Jago...]

And so the Rusconi translation is not correct... all the same, I did not dislike it...

> Vedermi non vorrei d'attorno un Jago.
> [I would not like to see around me a Jago.]

Now then, what do you plan to do?
Do you want to let the three verses stand?
Do you want to redo them?
Do you want to cut them, leaving what was there before?
I go forward, very slowly, but I go.

Send a word in reply to Busseto, Sant'Agata, and greetings, greetings.

> Warmly,
> G. Verdi

The definitive libretto follows the Rusconi translation:

> *Così è pur certo che se il Moro io fossi*
> *Vedermi non vorrei d'attorno un Jago* (act 1, scene 1)
> [So it is sure that if I were the Moor
> I shouldn't want to see around me a Jago.]

Boito, in the next letter, rationalizes this choice.

Quinto, 10 May [1886]

75 Dear Maestro,

What I am about to write seems blasphemy: I prefer Rusconi's sentence. It expresses greater things than the text does. It reveals Jago's malice, Otello's good faith, and it announces to the listener a whole tragedy of snares. For us, who had to renounce the wonderful scenes that take place in Venice, where those feelings are depicted, Rusconi's sentence is very useful. My opinion is to retain it as the translator gives it to us. The fact remains that Rusconi was wrong to adulterate a thought of Shakespeare's. A translator's fidelity must be very scrupulous, but the fidelity of one who illustrates with his own art a work from a different art can be less scrupulous, in my view. The translator's duty is not to change the letter, the illustrator's mission is to interpret the spirit; the former is a slave, the latter is free. Rusconi's sentence is unfaithful, and this is wrong in a translator; but it enters quite well into the spirit of the tragedy and the illustrator must exploit this quality to his own advantage. Continuing this line of reasoning, we arrive at the following result: *In adopting Rusconi's wrong we are right.* I would suggest resolving in this way *the question of conscience* that you bring to my attention in your letter today.

I will stay at Quinto for all of May. At the very beginning of June I will be in Milan.

In Milan I will await word to come to Sant'Agata. In any case, when I am home again I will write you.

Many greetings to you and to Signora Giuseppina.

Yours most warmly,

A. Boito

Sant'Agata, 14 May 1886

76

Dear Boito,

Most happy that you have kept the three verses:

. . . . around me a Jago.

One more little thing and I have finished... Or rather, you have finished! You know that the storm (musically speaking) continues during the entrance of Otello, and through the chorus of *senari*. There are too many verses in the solo of Otello, and the storm is interrupted for too long. I believe the scene would lose nothing if it were shortened by 4 verses, and then I could write a phrase for Tamagno, perhaps a very effective one—in fact, it is already done... like this:

	etc., etc., etc.
[CHORUS]	To the oars
	To the shore!!
	Anchor the vessel
	Hurrah, hurrah!
OTELLO	having disembarked at the rear of the stage, upraised...
	Rejoice. The Moslem pride
	Is buried in the sea; ours and heaven's the glory
	After our arms, he was defeated by ...-cane (enters the castle)
ALL	Long live Otello! Victory victory!

Send a word in reply. Fond greetings from Peppina.

Yours,

G. Verdi

🙢 Verdi's proposals, above, are incorporated in the definitive version of the libretto. The final words of Otello's lines originally rhymed with part of the text Verdi deleted, so his "-cane" here suggests a rhyme with a new, surviving line. This suggestion would in fact lead to the choice of the word "hurricane," now in the libretto.

Quinto, 16 [May 1886]

77 Bravo!!! I approve most completely of that cut of four verses that allows shifting Otello's entrance to the other three verses that you quoted. Now the entrance we were seeking for the one that did not satisfy us is found, and is splendid. A mighty exclamation of victory that ends in a burst of hurricane and in a cry of the people—bravo, bravo! Excellent also the idea of having that sentence said from a high point of the stage!

Edel has decided for himself already to begin preparing the study of the costumes for *Otello*. He asked me for the list of the designs, but I would not give it to him because we must make this list together, you and I, at Sant'Agata. He asked me for some instructions as to the historical period and the painters he must study, and I thought it opportune to give him these instructions because I know that Edel is as lazy as he is good and he needs a long time to complete a job. Meanwhile he will prepare himself, doing research and making sketches and acquiring photographs. I hope to be able to bring this preparatory work of Edel to Sant'Agata, and with these materials before our eyes we will make a definitive choice of our costumes, and after that he will do the sketches.

The period (indeed, virtually the exact date) of our tragedy is offered by the text itself, with no need for us to rack our brains hunting for it. Cinzio Giraldi, who, as you know, is the source of Shakespeare's tragedy, gives us two time limits between which lies the date of the action of *Otello*. I have torn out a page from an ugly cheap edition of the *Hecatommithi* so it can serve you as documentation. It is a page of the proem. Cinzio Giraldi, imitating the *Decameron* also in this, sets the collection of his "hundred novellas" in a historical frame. He pretends that these novellas are told in a band of refugees from the sack of Rome in 1527, just as Boccaccio does in the proem of his stories, where he imagines them narrated by fugitives from the plague in Florence. So then, 1527: this is not so much a *date* as a *datum* that is useful to us. You have another datum at hand: open my volume of Shakespeare that has remained at Sant'Agata, look for the Giraldi novella that is translated there, and you will find in the first three lines how the bloody story of Otello and Desdemona took place *a short time before.* So our period then is set by Giraldi: *a short time before 1527.* I believe I was not mistaken in telling Edel the latest limit is the year 1525. A couple of years' margin between the event and the narration of the event does not seem too much to me. So, in my opinion, Edel must not go beyond 1525 in his studies, but before that last date he should have a broad range of years to consult. Dress changed then less rapidly than it does now. Today, wherever a number of people are found, we see perhaps thirty years of fashion illustrated; the Italian-style cape that you still wear is the proof of that, and the high collars of your shirts, another proof! Thirty years separate the latter from the former. I have advised our Edel to study the Venetian painters of the last years of the fifteenth century and the entire first quarter of the sixteenth century. Luckily for us the two great documents of that span of years are Carpaccio and Gentile Bellini! Their paintings will provide the dress of our characters.

Have I done the right thing? Or the wrong thing?

If I am wrong, we still have time to correct my mistake.

Cordial greetings to Signora Giuseppina.

A warm handshake to you.

> Yours,
> A. Boito

Sant'Agata, 17 July 1886

78

Dear Boito,

I too am a bit concerned about the printing of the third-act finale in the libretto, because I would really like the audience to be able to see and understand everything at a glance.

Turn this page over and you will see what I would propose. If something better can be found... so much the better. Obviously, the page where there are the three columns should be complete in the middle of the libretto, with the stitching where there are the margins.

It is all right for Desdemona's solo to be printed at the bottom of the preceding page; in this way the audience will not be distracted, and would concentrate all its attention on her. Then, turning the page, they would find the whole hullabaloo of the ensemble laid out.

Giulio must not make objections about whether the edition is then less beautiful. The important thing is to let them understand... if they will want to understand!

Tomorrow I hope to be of a mind to leaf through and revise what has been done.

Be well.

Yours,

G. Verdi

As it is, etc.

· · · · · · · · · · · · · · · · · ·

· · · · · · · · · · · · · · · · · ·

· · · · · · · · · · · · · · · · · ·

OTELLO We will set sail tomorrow. To the ground! and weep!

and he seizes Desdemona furiously and Desdemona falls. Emilia and Lodovico go to her and pityingly raise her. In his terrible action Otello will have thrown the parchment on the floor, and Jago will have picked it up and read it...

DESDEMONA

To the ground!... yes... in the livid
Mire... struck... I lie...
I weep... the shudder of my dying soul
Chills me.
One day in my smile
Hope blossomed, and a kiss,
And now... anguish in my face,
And agony in my heart.
That sun, serene and bright,
That gladdens sky and sea,
Cannot dry the bitter
Teardrops of my grief.

OT. A word

JAGO What?
          Hurry! Quickly

OT. Unleash your revenge! Time flies.

JAGO You say well
          Wrath is idle chatter. Bestir yourself!
          Turn your eyes to the task! To the task alone.
          I will deal with Cassio. He must expiate his plots
          The grave will swallow his infamous, guilty soul.

OT. Who will tear it from him?

JAGO   I!

OT.   You?

JAGO   I swore

OT.   So be it

JAGO You will have news of him tonight
          he leaves Otello and heads for Rodrigo
          Your dreams will be at sea tomorrow
          And you on the harsh land
                                   Alas, sad me!
                                         Ah, fool!

ROD. Fool! If you want, you can hope; grasp human
          Daring now, and hear me

JAGO   I am listening.

ROD. The vessel sails at first dawn. Now Cassio

JAGO Is the Commander. And yet if it happens that some
          Misfortune befalls him... Then Otello remains here
                                                          ⌈Lugubrious

ROD. Light of another lightning

JAGO   Hand on your sword!
          In deepest night I will follow his path
          And study the meeting place and time, the rest is up
                                                             ⌈to you

ROD. I will be your lookout. To the hunt, the hunt! Gird on
          Your bow
                       sold
                       Yes, I have given[?] you honor and fealty!

JAGO (Run to the mirage! Your fragile intelligence
aside A lying dream has already confounded.
          Follow my astute and agile direction,
          Deluded lover, I follow my thought)

ROD. The die is cast! Fearless, I await you,
          Final fate, my hidden destiny
          Love spurs me on, but an avid, terrible
          Star of death infects my path

CHORUS
*in groups, their dialogue proceeding at the
same time as the dialogues of Jago*

WOMEN
Have pity!

KNIGHTS
Mystery!

WOMEN
          Grim, mortal anxiety
Still encumbers spirits absorbed in long horror

KNIGHTS
That black man is sepulchral, and in him
There is a blind shadow of death and terror

LADIES
Cruel sight! He torments with his nails his
                                          ⌈horrid
Breast!

KNIGHTS
          He fixes his immobile gaze on
                                    ⌈the ground

Then defies Heaven with grim fist,
                              ⌈raising his rough
Face to the lofty shafts of the Sun

LADIES
He struck her! That sainted pale mild face
Bows and is silent and weeps and dies
Thus in Heaven the angels weep their tears
When lost the sinner lies.

EMILIA
That innocent one makes no gesture
Or shudder of hatred,
She checks the moan in her breast
With painful restraint.
Her tears start
Silently on her sad face.
No, whoever does not weep for her
Has no pity in his breast.

RODRIGO
(For me the world darkens,
My destiny is clouded,
The angel gentle and blonde
Vanishes from my path.)

CASSIO
(The hour is decisive. A thunderbolt
Indicates it on my path
My fate's climax already now
Is offered to my inert hand.
Drunken fortune accelerates
The race of life.
This which lifts me to heaven
Is the wave of a hurricane.

LODOVICO
He shakes his gloomy hand
Gasping with wrath.
She turns her ethereal face
Weeping, towards Heaven
Observing that weeping
Charity sighs
And a tender compassion
Melts the heart's chill

◄﹩This letter, apparently an answer to Boito, suggests that a letter of the librettist is missing. But since the two men had met in Milan a few days before, it is possible that Verdi is replying to some verbal question from Boito.

The composer's trip to the city from Montecatini had been prompted by the news that his old friend Clara Maffei was dying. He and Giuseppina rushed to her bedside. She died on 13 July 1886.

Verdi's concern about the clarity of the libretto's printing is a reminder that house lights were not dimmed in Italian opera houses until the very end of the nineteenth century (Toscanini introduced this practice—against much opposition—at La Scala). Thus the audience expected to be able to follow the text during the performance.

After some further, minor revisions, the libretto was printed in accordance with Verdi's wishes.

Villa d'Este, near Como
21 July [1886]

79

Dear Maestro,

While you thought about the typographical problems of the libretto and resolved them in the best possible way, I was pondering the observations you made to me about the inadequately prepared presence of Desdemona in the big ensemble scene.

That observation of yours at first seemed to me a bit finicky, then it seemed to me fair and worth examining. I have tried to correct that fault in the most concise and suitable way I could. Tell me if I have succeeded.

I suggest two additions: the first, of three verses, in the scene between Jago and Otello in act 3; the second, of two verses, in the scene after that.

JAGO	. . . . My Commander
(starts with Otello	I thank you. Here are the Ambassadors.
towards door at back.	Let us go to them. *But... I believe it best*
But suddenly he	*(Also to deflect suspicions or tedious enquiries)*
stops.)	*That Desdemona receive those Gentlemen.*
OTELLO	*Yes. Bring her here.*
(Jago exits rapidly	. . . .
through the door, left.	. . . .
Otello continues	. . . .
towards the rear	
to await the	
Ambassadors.)	
LODOVICO	My Lady,
(to Desdemona, who	Heaven hold you in its grace.
will have entered with	
Jago, followed at a	
short distance by	
Emilia)	
DESDEMONA	And may Heaven hear you.
EMILIA	*(How sad you are.*
(to Desde-	
mona aside)	
DESDEMONA	*Emilia! a great cloud*
(to Emilia aside)	*Troubles Otello's mind and my destiny.)*
	. . . .

The rest remains as in the manuscript.

The libretto copied out by Giulio is now in the hands of Tornaghi, who will give it to Edel to read. I would not want those pages to be read by other people. Giulio told me that you had already nearly completed the orchestration of the first act!! Take care not to overtire yourself. You do not lack for time. On occasion it is good to follow the advice of the lazy.

Many greetings to Signora Giuseppina and to you.

From the heart,

your

A. Boito

P.S. Write me just one line to let me know if this letter has reached you.

Thursday [Sant'Agata, 22 July 1886]

80 Dear Boito,

I have received your latest. Those verses are good, and I believe they will work well. They will be awkward for the composer, who will be forced to suspend or prolong that little concert of offstage trumpets, etc... But no matter. Thanks and be well. Peppina greets you.

Yours,

G. Verdi

25 July [1886]

81 Dear Maestro,

What follows is better, a verse is spared:

[JAGO]   Here are the Ambassadors.
Receive them. But to avoid suspicions,
Let Desdemona show herself to those Gentlemen.
OTELLO   Yes, bring her here.

This way, without the long parenthesis, the sentence can be said rapidly by Jago.

Yours,

A. Boito

[Verdi to Boito—before 6 September 1886]
Memorandum

82

1. In the brindisi of the first act what are the women to do? Are they to drink too?... And why not?

---

2. If you don't mind, in the scene in the third act between Otello and
   Desdemona I would restore four verses that were cut:

   . . . .

[OTELLO]	Yet here already nests the kindly demon of ill counsel,
	That lights the charming ivory of the little talon
	Languidly it poses in prayer and in pious fervor
[DESDEMONA]	And yet with this hand I gave you my heart

   To my Lord commend me... Emilia... Farewell

   [G. Verdi]

◦◦On 29 August Ricordi accompanied Romilda Pantaleoni to San-
t'Agata, and it is probable that Verdi gave his publisher the above
memorandum to deliver to Boito, who was at Villa d'Este, not far from
the Ricordi villa at Cernobbio.

The lines in Verdi's point 2 are, with minor changes, in the definitive
act 3, scene 2.

Desdemona's words at the end of the note have been slightly
changed from the version in letter no. 60; here they are definitive.

Villa d'Este [6 September 1886]

83

Dear Maestro,

Musical reasons must determine in my opinion, the answers to the
questions you submit to me.

Will the women's voices enhance the effect of the brindisi? Then let
us add them. They will repeat the men's words in the refrain. Are they
of no use? And would you add them merely because they should not
stand idle on the stage? This argument does not seem to me strong
enough to devote two staves of score to them, if these two staves are not
musically effective, and worse if that female timbre were to undermine
even minimally the virile assertiveness of that number. I repeat: if it is
only some staging concern that prompts you to add the women, don't
add them. They will not remain idle. There are forty-five women at La
Scala. After the "fire of joy" about twenty or more will gradually scatter, and we will divide those who remain into two parts: some go to the
rear of the stage to stroll or sit with their lovers, others can spread the
fishermen's nets on the rampart; the more beautiful and the less prim-
looking we will have sit at the table with the men, and these will be
perhaps ten or twelve, and they will think only of getting themselves
pinched and drinking and eating. Both these and the others who have

remained at the back, more than twenty in all, will cry out "Let us flee" the two indicated times and "They are killing each other" at the moment of the brawl, and if they are not enough to give the cry power, then the other twenty or more who had scattered into the wings can come running at the noise a few moments before and, seeing the drawn swords, they can cry "Let us flee" with the other women. This, more or less, is the staging for the chorus of women for the entire time between the "fire of joy" chorus and Otello's rebuke.

If the four verses previously cut from the scene between Otello and Desdemona in act 3 are helpful to you musically, use them. I have nothing against it; and who could be a better judge than you? The same applies to the monosyllable "Vien" [Come] instead of the disyllable "Andiam" [Let's go] at the end of the first act. In these matters I am *neutral*, like Switzerland.

If, while you are coloring your opera with various timbres, you have some doubt or some concern that requires my presence at Sant'Agata, write me and I will come running.

Affectionate greetings to you and to Signora Giuseppina.

Yours,
A. Boito

As for Desdemona's last words, again you are the sole arbiter and judge.

Thursday [9 September 1886]

84 Dear Boito,

All right then, *pinches* it is! In this way I can keep the women quiet during the brindisi (which they would have spoiled), and I will have them snicker a couple of times in F-sharp minor on their own initiative, or because of Cassio, or because of the pinches.

Tomorrow morning I will send to Casa Ricordi, completely finished, all the first act and all of scene 6 of the third; and so, with the fourth already sent, perhaps three-fifths of the Moor is ready. I breathe a little!

I thank you! I cannot say now if I will have to trouble you again (it will not be for anything serious) because I plan really to do nothing for 6 or 8 days. My eyes are a bit tired, thanks to that cursed paper with 32 staves.

I have gone through *one* by *one* the three leading parts to see if they were suitably garbed, without patches, if they stood up properly, and if they flowed well... *They flow!!* And, a curious thing! The part of Jago, except for some *éclats*, could all be sung in mezza voce!

But... all this is of no help, if the *notes* do not please the esteemed... Be well.

Until we meet again, I hope, soon.

Yours,

G. Verdi

⏺In the period between this letter and the next, over six weeks later, Verdi devoted himself to the final orchestration, the correction of the proofs, and the practical details of the production. These preparations required several trips to Milan, where Verdi met designers, painters, and technicians (he had a special run-through of the thunder and lightning for the opening scene).

In October Romilda Pantaleoni visited Sant'Agata for twelve days to go over her part with the composer. Verdi had some lingering misgivings about Pantaleoni, as he had about the tenor Tamagno, but they seemed the best interpreters available and the obvious choices.

Sant'Agata, 29 October 1886

85

Dear Boito,

The second-act ballet is excellently devised, and they will be pleased with it. It is understood that the *ballet* will serve only for the Opéra. For the other places *Otello* will remain as it is now, or rather, as it will be tomorrow or afterwards, when, I hope, the last note of the orchestration will be finished...

Now give some thought to the translation.

As you know, Sig.ra Pantaleoni was here, and she left yesterday. She knows all her part very well, and will produce excellent effects from it, I hope. Only in the scene of the first act something is wanting. It is not that she does not deliver her solos well, but she delivers them with too much emphasis, and too dramatically. We will have more rehearsals, however, and I will keep at her until she manages to find the right shading for the situation and the poetry.

Yesterday in the *Corriere* I read the description of the costumes of *Otello*, and I saw, to my surprise, that Desdemona keeps wearing a splendid dress throughout the first act; and Otello, the fierce, savage costume with his arms bare in the last act, like a *Cetywayo* without the belly. Take a careful look, for these seem to me big mistakes. And take a look also at the other costume that you yourself dubbed a *toreador's*.

Be well. With the greetings of Peppina, I affectionately shake your hand.

G. Verdi

◦⊸Cetywayo (ca. 1830–1884) was the warrior king of the Zulus and a well-known figure in the international press. He was defeated by the English in 1879 at Ulundi and deported to England. He was later sent back and encouraged to regain his throne, but rival tribes defeated him and he had to seek permanent refuge in British territory.

[1 November 1886]

86 Dear Boito,

It's finished!

Good health to us... (and also to *Him*!!)

Be well.

G. Verdi

◦⊸The original (and now missing) letter was undated, but 1 November appears on its transcription in Verdi's *Copialettere,* in which his correspondence was recorded. On the same day Verdi wrote Ricordi with the same information, and Giuseppina, on 5 November, wrote to their Neapolitan friend Giuseppe De Sanctis: "The last note of *Otello* was written on All Saints' Day" [CVB, p. 355].

[ca. 16–17 December 1886]

87 Dear Maestro,

Forgive the modesty of these scraps of paper. Haste is my excuse and I can find nothing else at hand. The page in pencil answers the letter you wrote to Giulio.

A variant occurs to me for the added verses of Jago:

Beauty and happiness agreeing in sweet song,
I will shatter your tender harmonies.

or else:

Beauty and Love agreeing in sweet song,
etc., etc.

With the translation we have arrived at Cassio's entrance in the third act. The translation of the third is better than that of the fourth but it is equally difficult. I have written to Du Locle and I have had Giulio rectify in the *Gazzetta musicale* an item in *Le figaro* that could have displeased Du Locle. The rectification will appear in the next number of the *Gazzetta*.

Cordial greetings.

Yours most affectionately,
A. Boito

◄ßThe "page in pencil" has not survived. It probably contained some last-minute changes in the part of Jago, which Verdi was then going over with Maurel. The lines Boito supplies in this letter refer to Jago's comment following the chorus in act 2, scene 3. The definitive version uses the alternative of the first line. During this period Verdi had made a trip to Milan and, from Sant'Agata, had been in regular correspondence with Ricordi about the final *Otello* matters before the opera actually went into rehearsal.

The French translation had been in progress for about a month. Boito had begun with the fourth act. Camille Du Locle, Verdi's longtime acquaintance and collaborator, was to work with Boito on the project, which was also the occasion of a quasi-reconciliation between the composer and the French writer. The rectification Boito refers to concerns an announcement that he was translating *Otello*, with no reference to Du Locle. Though Verdi was in a hurry to see the translation completed, *Otello* was to wait another eight years before being given at the Opéra, in 1894, after *Falstaff*.

Genoa, 18 December 1886

88

Dear Boito,

Thanks for the two verses. I have just handed Garignani the last acts of *Otello!*... Poor Otello! He won't come back here again!!!

If you go to hear Emanuel tonight, write me a line tomorrow and tell me if I am very far off the mark!...

Be well.

G. Verdi

◄ßGarignani (or Garegnani, the spelling is uncertain) was Ricordi's chief copyist.

Giovanni Emanuel (1848–1902) was at that time performing the title role in an Italian translation of Shakespeare's *Othello* in Milan. He was a controversial actor, considered particularly "modern," as opposed to the older, more traditional Ernesto Rossi and Tommaso Salvini (see Boito's response below). Giulio Ricordi found Emanuel's performances of the Shakespeare tragedy not only an excellent advertisement for the opera but also worthwhile in their own right. Boito, however, was distressed at the thought that the Scala singers would see an "ugly" interpretation of the tragedy. Verdi, an admirer of Salvini, agreed with Boito [see CVB, p. 358].

[Milan, 21 December 1886]

89 My dear Maestro,

The Moor will not come again to knock at the door of Palazzo Doria, but you will go to call on the Moor at La Scala.

Otello is. The great dream has become reality. What a shame! And yet, despite the sadness that follows completion of the work, I wish that the French translation would also become reality soon. We work a great deal and, if I am not mistaken, well. In a week's time the terzetto will be finished. Then I will probably leave for Nervi, where I will confer with Du Locle and will see what he has done, and he what I have done. If Du Locle works well, by mid-February or the end of February at the latest the translation can be finished.

Meanwhile, Ricordi will be able to engrave the fourth act and then very soon the third, which is already, as I told you, well along, and the first of Du Locle. The second will arrive last.

I did not go to see Emanuel. He is a most mediocre actor, cold, monotonous, disagreeable. If from a hen's egg an eagle cannot be hatched, so from Emanuel's head no kind of interpretation of Othello can come. Rossi and Salvini, now there are the two giants! From them Tamagno might have been able to learn something; but from Emanuel he can have learned nothing at all, and I wish he had not attended that performance. I know that the other actors were even worse than Emanuel!

At this point Shakespeare's *Othello* possesses its commentary *and you have made it,* and that's that, and there is no need to go begging effects from others.

I wrote my last letter in such haste that, when it had already dropped into the post box, I realized I had forgotten to stick a stamp on it. I was afraid you might not receive it. The budget of the State will have earned the fine of ten centesimi.

Cordial greetings to you and Signora Peppina.

Yours most affectionately,

A. Boito

❧*"Otello* is." Boito echoes the Moor's line at the conclusion of the opera: "Otello fu" ("Otello is no more").

Verdi arrived in Milan on 4 January 1887 to supervise the rehearsals and preparation of *Otello*. He stayed in the city about two months. Full rehearsals of the opera began on 27 January; the dress rehearsal took place on 3 February.

Two nights later, 5 February 1887, *Otello* had its premiere, with Pantaleoni, Tamagno, and Maurel in the principal parts, Franco Faccio conducting. Alfredo Edel was responsible for the costumes, Carlo Ferrario for the sets. There were twenty-four performances of the work over the period from its premiere to the end of April.

At the gala opening, in addition to critics from all over the world, there were numerous composers, including Jules Massenet, Ernest Reyer, Filippo Marchetti, and Paolo Tosti, and several writers headed by Boito's close friend Giuseppe Giacosa. Prior to the premiere, Giacosa informed Boito that Eleonora Duse, who was appearing in Milan, had tried in vain to get a seat. Boito apparently found her one, and a few nights later Boito invited the Verdis to see the actress in Goldoni's *Pamela*. At about this time the forty-five-year-old Boito and the twenty-eight-year-old Duse became lovers. The affair, which for various reasons was more epistolary than physical, continued for almost a decade.

[Telegram]

14 April 87

Arrigo Boito, Nervi
From Genoa
Was expecting you yesterday. Today will not be in Genoa. Come tomorrow if you can.

90

Verdi

❧The silence of almost four months in the correspondence, broken by this telegram, is easily explained. Verdi spent almost two months—January and February—in Milan, where he saw Boito frequently. Afterwards, when Verdi was in Genoa, Boito was in nearby Nervi, working with Du Locle on the French translation of *Otello*.

[Telegram]

17 April 87

Arrigo Boito, Eden Hotel, Nervi
From Genoa
91 Whenever for you and two.
Verdi

    ◖Verdi was still at his winter residence, and Boito at Nervi. The enig-
matic message, presumably a reply to a lost communication, probably
refers to one of Verdi's regular invitations to Boito to visit him at
Palazzo Doria.

[Telegram]

22 April 87

Arrigo Boito, Eden Hotel, Nervi
From Genoa
92 A thousand thanks. Peppina better and better. Greetings.
Verdi

    ◖Giuseppina Verdi had undergone a delicate operation in mid-April.

Genoa, Tuesday [26 April 1887]

93 Dear Boito,
    I read it yesterday in the papers, and today I have received a letter
that confirms the excellent success of your *Mefistofele* in Nantes.
    Splendid.
    Accept the sincere congratulations of your
G. Verdi

Peppina steadily improving.

    ◖The Nantes production, on 23 April, was the premiere of *Méphis-
tophélès* in France.

Sant'Agata, 24 May 1887

94 Dear Boito,
    Du Locle has accepted his half (5000 fr.) of the sum I offered you
and him *sur vos droits d'auteur* for the translation of *Otello*. If you accept

the other half as I offered you then, I would be very happy and, as I said before, I would be *more serene!*... Write me then a *yes* and I will have you paid your 5000 lire!

Peppina improves constantly, indeed, she can be said to be cured. I get along, going back and forth in the fields, cursing this horrible weather... but finally, after four months of... I am at ease and I can breathe.

I clasp your hands and say farewell.

Yours,
G. Verdi

⊸Boito, always afraid of seeming to exploit Verdi, was reluctant to receive his payment for the French translation, which actually was not an outright payment, but simply an advance against the librettist's and cotranslator's royalties from future French performances. See letter no. 96 below.

Verdi's enigmatic phrase "four months of..." may refer to Giuseppina's period of poor health, or he could mean the prolonged difficulties in finding a Desdemona for Rome and for subsequent productions of *Otello.*

Milan, 26 May [1887]

95

Dear Maestro,

Since you wish it and since Du Locle has accepted, I reply: *Amen* and I thank you.

If I did not answer like this it would seem that I were acting arrogantly towards you (which is not possible) and also towards my collaborator. So I accept the kind and cordial offer you make me. I appreciate the scruples of your goodness, but I declare them scruples. I accept on the conditions set on the page you wrote in Genoa.

In all things therefore let your will be done.

I am delighted at the good news of Signora Giuseppina, who does not believe in my visit to Sant'Agata, but I will amaze her incredulity before the summer is over.

For the present the summer is represented by rain and cold.

So Otello triumphs also in his adoptive country, before the real lion of St. Mark's. And he will continue his great flight in space and time,

Beyond what the human mind can foresee.

My dear Maestro, be well and strong and happy, and continue to think a bit fondly of me.

Yours most affectionately,
A. Boito

Cordial greetings to Signora Peppina.

Yesterday I dined with Morelli, great artist and likeable man, and the subject of discussion was one alone. Morelli will stay on in Milan for several days; he is here because he is a member of the committee for the facade of the Duomo.

> ◄With the line "Beyond what the human mind can foresee," Boito adapts a familiar quotation from Dante's *Divina commedia* (*Inferno*, canto 7, verse 81).
>
> For the Venice performances Boito mentions, the conductor was Faccio, and the male principals were Tamagno and Maurel. The Desdemona was Adalgisa Gabbi, who had already sung the role in Rome. Verdi considered her much inferior to Romilda Pantaleoni, even though he had some reservations about the role's creator. Pantaleoni had been unwell during the Scala run, and Verdi—who liked her personally—felt she should rest her voice for a while. In any case, he thought her best suited to a more dramatic repertory.
>
> The building of the Duomo of Milan, begun in the latter part of the fourteenth century, continued, with interruptions, until the late nineteenth century. The facade was finished between 1805 and 1813, but the turrets and the ornamentation were still being built—and debated—in 1887. As a leading Italian artist, Domenico Morelli (see note following letter no. 46), Verdi's Neapolitan friend of many years, would inevitably be asked to sit on one of the constant committees named by the Italian government (Boito himself was an assiduous committee man). "To take as long as the Duomo of Milan" is a common Italian expression meaning "to take forever."

Sant'Agata, 27 May 1887

96 Dear Boito,

Ricordi will pay you, for me, fr. *5000.* I repeat, *francs;* in other words, the equivalent of *250* gold napoleons.

You need do nothing but declare to the agent for your *droits d'auteur* in Paris (I imagine it is Roger) that when *Otello* is performed in France, your *droits d'auteur* for the translation belong to me up to the sum of *5000* fr. Amen.

When we have reached the end of summer I will be able to tell you if you are a man of your word. Give many, many greetings to Morelli, truly a great artist.

Oh, if he...!

Oh, if you...!

Be well. Greetings from Pep. I shake your hands.

Sant'Agata! You arrive at Fiorenzuola at two; at four at Sant'Agata!

G. Verdi

•◦Roger was the agent of the Société des Auteurs et Compositeurs Dramatiques in Paris.

Though Verdi and Morelli corresponded sporadically, they saw each other rarely; and as Verdi indicates, he would have welcomed a visit from the artist, or one from Boito.

30 May [1887]
Milan

97

Dear Maestro,

Now you can sleep easy. Today Tornaghi gave me the 250 twenty-franc pieces. If you, kind and dear Maestro, had them all weighing on your digestion, and Du Locle's as well, I assure you it was quite a weight. A weight that breaks the pockets, I mean to say literally, and not after a manner of speaking.

Thanks again with all my heart. But now this *Otello* really must go to France, otherwise I will be your debtor for all eternity for those five thousand lire and the weight on the digestion would pass to me. I have begun tempting Morelli towards Sant'Agata, but so far he has resisted, suffering like his own St. Anthony.

I will keep tempting him.

I enclose a copy of the letter I wrote about the *droits d'auteur*. I know that Maestro Muzio is in Milan, and I told Tornaghi to ask him to deliver personally that letter to the right person.

Affectionate greetings to you and to Signora Giuseppina.

Yours,
A. Boito

•◦A copy of Boito's letter to Roger, in French, is attached to the back of the sheet.

The Italian expression "to break the pockets" is a euphemistic version of another expression meaning to be profoundly irritating.

Morelli's *The Temptations of St. Anthony* was one of his most admired paintings. It is now in the Galleria d'Arte Moderna, Rome.

Emanuele Muzio (1821–1890) was a native of Busseto who, thanks to the encouragement of Verdi's great patron Antonio Barezzi, became in the mid-1840s Verdi's pupil and amanuensis and friend. Though he never had any great success as a composer, Muzio had a respectable career as a conductor in Europe and America; and he often conducted local premieres of Verdi's works.

9 June [1887]

98 Dear Maestro,

Here is a letter from our fine English translator, Signor Hueffer, the editor of the *Times* whom you know. He suggests using the Latin text for the first part of Desdemona's *Ave Maria*, where the words are murmured over the repeated ⟨musical notation⟩ Afterwards he would begin the English version, when the prayer takes on a character of totally personal religious effusion. I like the idea. See if you like it, and please let me know your view so that I can send it on to the translator.

The shift from Latin to English, it seems to me, would help underline the dramatic and musical concept of that episode.

I have heard with pleasure that Jago's Credo will not be part of the soirée at the Opéra. That would have been a great mistake.

Most cordial greetings to the inhabitants of Sant'Agata, among whom I will also be for a few days in the near future. An affectionate handshake.

from your
A. Boito

The German-born Francis Hueffer (1843–1889) studied music in London, where he eventually settled and became a distinguished music critic (for the last decade of his life he was the critic for the *Times*). He wrote an early biography of Wagner, translated the Wagner-Liszt correspondence, and published various studies of nineteenth-century music. He was also the author of two opera librettos for Alexander MacKenzie. He married the daughter of the painter Ford Madox Brown; their son became the novelist Ford Madox Ford.

Hueffer's long and interesting letter to Boito was published in the English edition of *Otello* as a preface. Dated July 1887, it says in part:

"Those who know Shakespeare without knowing music will say that I have taken all manner of liberties with the sacred original; and those who know music without knowing Shakespeare will be staggered at a style of diction so entirely different from that of the ordinary libretto. The only person whom I have a faint hope, and at the same time the greatest desire to satisfy, is yourself." Hueffer omitted much of the rhyme in the Italian and restored a certain amount of Shakespeare's original text. He concluded: "The trouble and anxiety, which this translation has cost me, are more than amply repaid by the consciousness of being connected in ever so humble a way, with a work which, in my opinion, marks an epoch in the development of Italian opera."

Hueffer's suggestion of using Latin words in the *Ave Maria* of the last act was apparently rejected; in the printed text the entire passage is in English.

After the destruction of the Salle Favart (the home of the Opéra-Comique) by a fire on 25 May 1887, a benefit concert for the victims was organized in which Victor Maurel planned to sing (in Italian) Jago's Credo. Verdi was firmly opposed and, while reluctantly giving his personal consent, he adroitly left it to Giulio Ricordi to refuse to cede the rights.

Sunday [Sant'Agata, 12 June 1887]

99

Dear Boito,

I am expecting you. Write me or telegraph me when you will arrive at Fiorenzuola (day and hour) so I can send a bucephalus of mine to bring you to Sant'Agata.

Be well.

Yours,
G. Verdi

⤜Boito visited Verdi around the middle of June for a few days, then slipped away to Palermo, where he met Duse, engaged in a Sicilian tour. They traveled to Reggio Calabria together, then to Messina. At the tour's end, in August, they spent a week in a mountain locality, San Giovanni Bianco, north of Bergamo. There, in a little rented house, they read Dante and Shakespeare together, and conceived the idea of a Boito translation of *Anthony and Cleopatra*, which would become a reality (and a fiasco) some time later.

Except for a trip to Milan and his usual stay in Montecatini, Verdi spent the summer at Sant'Agata. Among his other concerns was the *disposizione scenica* or production book of *Otello,* which Ricordi was about to print, for the guidance of impresarios preparing Verdi's new work.

Sant'Agata, 16 September 1887

100 Dear Boito,

On my return from Milan I find your letter.

You and Giacosa will always be welcome, whenever you want to make a dash to Sant'Agata. Just tell me the hour and day.

So far so good; but now I am very worried about being asked for the French manuscript of the third act of *Otello*. I don't remember this manuscript at all! I don't have it here. It could perhaps be in Genoa, but who knows? Perhaps it no longer exists! I have to tell you that in my bedroom in Genoa there was a near-flood. A pipe of the big Nicolai reservoir burst, ruining carpets, walls, and furniture, including a cabinet with a writing desk under it, both of them very beautiful and antique. In this furniture there were a number of papers, and when I went to Genoa and tried to open the drawers with the keys, everything fell to pieces: the intarsia, the gum or the glue, the soaked papers all had become no more than one stinking mess. It could be, but I don't think so, that among those papers there was also the French manuscript! I don't think so because in those drawers there should have been only papers dating back a long time! Do you know what you must do? Think no more about that translation, which will surely be fine as it is. Don't waste your time on such tasks; and don't waste time looking for the impossible in Caccini and Peri, etc., etc. You have more important things to do!

Oh, forgive me, forgive me... I realize I have given you some advice... I, who loathe advice, and advisers!...

Forgive the long speech. Greetings; hoping to see you soon.

Yours,

G. Verdi

≈Boito's letter to Verdi is missing. In his scrupulous way, he obviously wanted to retouch the French translation of *Otello* (its third act was, for that matter, largely the work of Du Locle). The translation had evidently been discussed during Boito's visit to Sant'Agata in June.

The "return from Milan" refers to a brief visit made by the Verdis there from 12 to 14 September.

Verdi's reference to Caccini and Peri is connected with one of Boito's numerous official tasks—this time, as adviser to the minister of education about the teaching of music (see the following letter).

Cernobbio, Villa d'Este
Lake Como
4 October [1887]

Dear Maestro,

101

First of all I thank you for the beautiful and intellectually stimulating days I spent at Sant'Agata. Then I must ask you a favor; and do not scold me for having accepted yet another assignment—it will be the last. The minister of education wants to confer with me about the music institutions of the kingdom. We know that currently in Italy music is studied badly, the minister's invitation is a good opportunity to try to orient properly the study of music in our state schools, and therefore I have ceded to the wish of the man in charge of them. This means a trip to Rome and a couple of days spent there (perhaps not in vain), after which I will return to my work. I do not mean to advise the minister to reform the statutes of the music schools, or even to make their various constitutions uniform. These questions are as huge as they are futile and difficult. Let them keep the statutes they have, since good or bad students are not produced by statutes. The student's natural talent draws supreme benefit from good studies and can be misdirected by bad studies. The point is this: *the direction of those studies.*

This is an opportunity to put into practice that advice that you were able to sum up in four words, with clarity and wisdom and truly age-old concision: *Return to the past.*

So let us return to the past, but let us also make our schools return there. Unless they are made to do it, they never will. In the state syllabuses of the middle and high schools it is compulsory to study Virgil, Horace, Lucretius, Cicero. So I believe that in our conservatories it too should be *compulsory* to study Palestrina and the other Italian master musicians of the sixteenth, seventeenth, and eighteenth centuries. That is the right path, that is what must be studied in the schools and in vocal training. The art of singing must be uplifted, it must be steeped in the full sound that is in the writing of Palestrina. *Make* young students who, still in the cradle, prattle abstruse nonsense, make them bathe in that stream, be washed in that purity. Composers would have a change of heart; singers would also benefit. Composers and singers, this is where the rot lies in today's studies, and this is what should be remedied. We have the instrumentalists, they develop on their own. Good, cultivated pianists abound. Naples has produced some excellent ones in these past years, Milan as well. Bologna continues to turn out good string players, and Naples good brass. But it is the study of composition that is sunk into putrescence. Young composition students are full of conceit and ignorance.

They must be educated through the great music of Italy's great centuries. When they are educated they will be less vainglorious and will see their art more clearly. They must also be compelled to study a bit of history from texts written simply and well, so as to learn at the same time the great struggles of mankind and the beautiful style of the language. They must be compelled to study a bit of prosody and declamation so as to learn to stress dialogue naturally, as Truth demands, for music is nothing other than the sound of feeling and of passion. I learned all these things from you, who have put them into practice. You must tell me yourself if I have learned them well. I too would like to be able to put them into practice in my work, and to suggest them to those in charge of education in order to offer students the possibility of studying well.

Now here is the favor I would ask of you:

Please give me a brief list, a list of six names, no more: six names of masters you believe most suited to be studied by the young.

These six names, beginning with Palestrina, should represent the six most radiant points of the *vocal art* of the sixteenth, seventeenth, and eighteenth centuries. I would like this favor from you because I trust your judgment as I trust no one else's. No one better than you can compile this list, which will serve as a program of study.

&sThe letter ends without closing or signature, perhaps through Boito's distraction, or perhaps because a closing page is missing. Boito was, as usual in September, visiting his friend Donna Vittoria Cima at Lake Como.

Sant'Agata, 5 October 1887

102 Dear Boito,

If you promise to give me neither the credit nor the blame for it, I will give you some names, the first that come to my mind. They are more than six, but there are so many good ones in that period that there is no knowing which to choose.

1500
- ⊕ Palestrina (*in primis et ante omnia*)

  Victoria

  Luca Marenzio (a most pure writer)

  Allegri (who wrote the *Miserere*)

and so many other good composers of that century, except Monteverdi, whose voice leading is poor

Early 1600s
- ⊕ Carissimi

  Cavalli

Later
- Lotti

  ⊕ Scarlatti Alessandro (who boasts harmonic treasures as well)

  ⊕ Marcello

  Leo

Early 1700s
- ⊕ Pergolesi
  Jacomelli

Later ⊕ Piccinni (the first, I believe, to write quintets and sextets, etc.; composer of the first true opera buffa, *Cecchina*)

If you really do want only six, I believe the preferable ones are those marked with ⊕.

Later on we have Paisiello
Cimarosa
Guglielmi Pietro
etc., etc...
then   Cherubini, etc.

I wish you success. If you do succeed you will have performed a sacred task, because (I do not speak of schools, which can all be good) the young study obliquely, or rather, they are already on the wrong track; and if music is—and it is—as you describe it, then it is really necessary to know a bit of prosody and declamation, and to have sufficient culture to understand what must be understood. When you understand well what you have to set to music, and you have to shape a character or depict an emotion, it is less easy to let yourself be misled by eccentricities and outlandishness of any kind, vocal or instrumental.

Give me news of yourself and of what you do and achieve.

In haste, I shake your hands and greet you for Peppina.

Yours,

G. Verdi

🖛Encouraged by Verdi's letter, Boito went to Rome in October, and on his return he sent a brief report to the composer.

Villa d'Este

31 October [1887]

103 Dear Maestro,

Here is what happened. The teaching texts (sixteenth, seventeenth, eighteenth centuries) were approved unanimously by the heads of the leading conservatories of the Kingdom. We will see what happens next. After this voting I departed from Rome, leaving those gentlemen to come to an agreement to harmonize their statutes (there are no two that resemble each other) and their rules. Obviously, as you wished, I did not make use of your letter, although I had it with me in my pocket, and I was tempted more than once to exploit it. In a few days' time I will be in Nervi, and if you are in Genoa I will come, as usual, to Palazzo Doria and spend an hour with you.

Affectionate greetings to you and to Signora Giuseppina.

Yours,

A. Boito

🖛There is now a silence of about two months in the correspondence. In November Verdi accompanied Giuseppina to Genoa and settled her in their apartment, while he continued making brief business trips to Milan and to Busseto (where he was involved in constructing a hospital at his expense, near Sant'Agata, for the local population).

Meanwhile, Boito went to Turin at the end of November. There, largely to please him, Duse was staging a new production of Giacosa's *Tristi amori,* which had been a failure earlier that year, given for the first time by another company in Rome. In Turin it was a triumph both for the author and for the actress. Giacosa was one of the very few friends aware of Boito's love affair with the young star.

[Telegram]

5 Jan 88

Arrigo Boito, Eden Hotel, Nervi
From Genoa
Thanks for the most welcome news. Sending telegram to Giacosa.
                     Verdi

104

     The "welcome news" refers to *Tristi amori,* which had repeated its success in Milan a few days before. Though not informed of the Boito-Duse relationship, Verdi may have guessed at it. Boito had taken the composer to see Duse perform (see note following letter no. 89 above), and when the librettist visited Sant'Agata she wrote him there frequently.

[Telegram]

3 March 88

Arrigo Boito, Eden Hotel, Nervi
From Genoa
Please please please. Tomorrow at six.
                     Verdi

105

     This cryptic telegram, without documented context, presumably refers to a meeting between Boito and Verdi, while they were both on the Ligurian coast.

Sunday [Milan, 8 April 1888]

106

Dear Boito,
    I am in Milan for a few days.
    Today I am going to the concert by the Swiss, and will not be at home this evening.
    I will see you later; either I will come to you, or you to me.
                     G. Verdi

     The Zurich *Männerchor* was performing at La Scala. Verdi and Giuseppina attended one of the concerts.
    Tito Ricordi, Giulio's father, died in Milan on 7 September, after a long illness.
    During the silence between this letter and the next, Boito and Verdi had had occasion to meet both in Milan and in Genoa (and it is also

possible that they wrote letters now lost). Neither man was devoting much time to composing. Boito was, as usual, involved in official matters (an international music exposition in Bologna) and in brief, furtive meetings with Duse. Verdi was chiefly concerned with family questions and with Giuseppina's troublesome health.

(Ivrea) San Giuseppe
9 October [1888]

107 Dear Maestro,

The lovely plan has gone up in smoke, and I have also gone up, back to these mountains. The lovely plan was to come to Sant'Agata with the Ricordis, but Giulio's illness prevented its realization. We will do it next year, but before then, of course, we will see each other either in Milan or in Genoa.

The cold will not drive me from the place where I am now writing you until November at the earliest. Meanwhile, dear Maestro, I have read your writing again on the little note that Sig. Mariotti brought me. I could not accept his kind offer, flattering and most honorable on his part, and I know that you had foreseen my refusal.

If I were one of those most enviable and privileged individuals who can perform several tasks at the same time, I would perhaps have accepted.

But to make myself work a little, I have had to isolate myself up here. If you could see this place you would admire it and would enjoy its peace. Yet as I write you a hellish wind is blowing, whistling through the windows, and I feel as if I were lodged in the pipe of a piccolo during an orchestral *forte*.

I have such a desire to see you again and to converse with you that, even in writing, I let myself chatter on and on. Enough. I would like that time to return when our every letter had as its subject the study of a great work of art.

Mariotti gave me excellent news of your health and I was relieved.

Please greet Signora Giuseppina for me. A heartfelt embrace

from your
A. Boito

⊷Giacosa, who came from Piedmont, had suggested to Boito, some years previously, the abandoned convent of San Giuseppe above Ivrea in the Canavese region, an ideally remote and beautiful place to work in peace and, now, far from indiscreet eyes, to bring Duse when she was free. The two had been there in early July, remaining until the end of August. After this stay, and after some trips here and there, Boito returned to the convent in early October, the period of this letter.

For the reference to Mariotti, see the note following letter no. 108 below.

Sant'Agata, 14 October 1888

108

Dearest Boito,

No, no! Your excuse is flimsy!

The Ricordis came and left... but since you are enjoying yourself in the midst of that orchestra of piccolos in the mountains of the Canavese, all right—we will do it next year!

Sig. Mariotti, who came to see you in vain, afterwards went to London to Bottesini, and it seems with good results. Now Mariotti is very busy taking care of the rest. I suggested some names, among others la Mariani, a good musician and among the finest artists. She would do well.

Be well. Nothing new here, or beautiful. After two splendid days, today we have rain, rain, rain!

I greet you for Peppina, and if you *work*, I absolve you of all your sins and I shake your hands.

Affectionately,
G. Verdi

❧Giovanni Mariotti (1850–1935) was a historian and politician from Parma. He had arranged for Parma's school of music to be raised to the status of conservatory and wanted its first director to be an eminent musician. On Verdi's suggestion, he approached Boito. After Boito's refusal, he turned to Giovanni Bottesini (1821–1889), composer, internationally celebrated contrabass player, and conductor. Bottesini had conducted the premiere of *Aida* in Cairo in 1871, and he had set Boito's libretto *Ero e Leandro* in 1879. He accepted the Parma appointment, but died barely six months later.

Maddalena Mariani-Masi (1850–1916), soprano, had created the title role of Ponchielli's *La Gioconda* and was a frequent Margherita in Boito's *Mefistofele*. If Mariotti offered her a teaching post in Parma, she did not accept it. She retired from the stage around 1890 and took private pupils, among them Lina Cavalieri.

[Telegram]

3 Nov 88

Arrigo Boito, Principe Amedeo 1, Milan
From Busseto
109 Very well and bravo.

Verdi

☙The letter to which this telegram is a reply has not survived.

Milan, 6 December [1888]
110 Dearest Maestro,

I was so sorry to have missed your greeting that I cannot refrain from telling you so. I thought you had already left on Monday, and yesterday a thousand concerns required me to be out of the house all day.

When I came back I found your kind note.

I hope to see you often in Genoa in January.

Many warm greetings to you and to Signora Giuseppina from me and from my brother.

Yours most affectionately,
A. Boito

☙Though the date of this letter is incomplete, there is convincing reason for assigning it to the year 1888. Verdi made two short visits to Milan in that period to deal with the purchase of the plot where the future home for retired musicians, the Casa di Riposo per Musicisti (now known simply as Casa Verdi), was to be erected. Boito's brother, Camillo, was to be its architect.

Genoa, 17 February 1889
111 Dear Boito,

I am guessing at your present address, but am sure this letter will reach you.

I am sorry to distract you, even for a few minutes, from your work, but I feel the need to talk with you about that... jubilee, which I find futile, with no hope of producing any good result.

We'll set aside my *ego*, my reserve, my pride, and all the rest... Just let me ask you:

What will all of you do on that evening of 17 Nov.? A concert with various excerpts from operas?

Good Lord! how pathetic!

Or performances of some operas?

In that case, to give these performances any meaning, three or four should be presented. The *first*, the *last*, and another somewhere between these two. For the latter two the execution would not be difficult, but the first would be difficult and expensive. It would require four prominent artists (who also know how to sing), a *mise en scène*, and all the rehearsals as if for a new opera.

And the result?

Try to imagine whether our audience, with tastes so different from those of fifty years ago, would have the patience to listen to the two long acts of *Oberto!* Either they would be bored in polite silence (always humiliating), or they would demonstrate their disapproval. In this case it would no longer be a celebration, it would be a scandal.

For the other plan, to found an institution *in perpetuum* with a national subscription, again let me ask:

What sum could be collected? A small sum would serve only to award one of those usual competition prizes that are of no help to art or to the winner. A truly useful sum, difficult to collect in these critical times, would have to be substantial, very substantial, in order to constitute a capital whose interest would be enough to underwrite a young composer's debut in the theater.

And here, how many difficulties crop up!

1. The impresario would have to be guaranteed as to the work's value.
2. The conductor would have to guarantee a good performance.

To succeed in this, the only (and for that matter, anything but certain) course would be to name a committee... or rather, two. One to examine the poem, the other to examine the music. It would be easy to find the first, and I would immediately suggest: *Boito* and two others. The second is more difficult: again *Boito*... and?

Furthermore, these committees should assume the thankless and difficult task of keeping a severe eye on the *mise en scène* and on the musical and dramatic performance, to prevent the impresario from putting on the opera as a *pis-aller* with the sole purpose of pocketing some money.

And here another question arises: Where will the opera be given? In Milan? But if it is a national subscription, why couldn't the Romans, for ex., claim it for Rome? The Neapolitans for Naples?... and so on and on...

How many difficulties!

I finish (take a breath) and conclude by saying what I said to Giulio at the beginning of last Nov.: this jubilee, besides being extremely disagreeable for me, is neither useful nor practical. If you share my opinion, at the first meeting that is held, you, with greater authority than the others as composer and as poet, must see that everything is calmly laid to rest, leaving no loophole by which it could be brought up again, and you will be doing an excellent thing.

Obviously this letter is private. There is nothing in it I could not say openly; but it is useless for me to make myself heard again on this subject.

I have made you lose a bit of time and I am sorry. Forgive me!

Be well. With Peppina's greetings, I heartily shake your hands and declare myself

affectionately yours,
G. Verdi

☙The year 1889 marked the fiftieth anniversary of Verdi's operatic debut, with *Oberto, conte di San Bonifacio* at La Scala (17 November 1839). The idea of a formal celebration had been suggested in the newspapers as early as November of the previous year, apparently inspired by Giulio Ricordi and by Boito (who in the following letter pretends to Verdi to have been drafted by the committee).

San Remo
20 February [1889]
Wednesday

112 Dear Maestro,

I have just this moment received your letter.

As soon as I read in the papers that I was part of the committee for the jubilee, I wrote Giacosa to advise me when the first meeting would be held. I want very much to be present precisely to block the approval of any proposals that you might not like. You see, dear Maestro, that even before I received your letter I was preparing to act as if I had already read it. Trust Giacosa, Negri, and me. I cannot promise you to scotch the jubilee: the country wants it.

But I assure you that we will do everything to avoid provoking criticism from you or from any such wise judge.

If a telegram from Giacosa does not call me to Milan before Sunday, I will be in Genoa Sunday and I will come, if you permit, to collaborate in the destruction of your dinner.

Affectionate greetings to you and to Signora Giuseppina.

Till we meet again soon.

Yours,

A. Boito

Genoa, 21 February 1889

113

Dear Boito,

Alas! Alas!

I was hoping for a different reply from you! I have nothing more to add, after what I have written repeatedly to Giulio and to you; I will only say again that I was, am, and always will be against the celebration of this jubilee.

Until Sunday, then, when you will take your soup with us.

Sans adieu.

Affectionately,

G. Verdi

◄ɛDespite the fact that Boito was the source of the original proposal to celebrate Verdi's jubilee, he apparently felt it more important to respect the composer's wishes and sincerely attempt to block the project. If this is the case, he was successful, for there was no official celebration at La Scala.

At the end of February, Verdi made a very brief trip to Milan, probably to complete the acquisition of the land for the future Casa di Riposo. He and Boito possibly met at that time, and discussed a curious music scale published several months before in Ricordi's *Gazzetta musicale di Milano.* The scale was presented in these terms: "From Bologna we have received the following SCALE—which, according to its inventor, is not without effect when properly harmonized. We leave this operation to musicians, who delight in harmonic investigations."

Verdi's curiosity was aroused by the puzzle, to which some solutions were published in a later issue of the *Gazzetta,* including that of its inventor, Adolfo Crescentini (1854–1921), a professor at the *liceo musicale* in Bologna.

Genoa, 6 March 1889

114 Dear Boito,

As I was leaving Milan I threw some papers in the fire, among them also that awkward scale. I remember the first part of this scale, but in the second, jotted down then and there, I have forgotten the modulations and the voice leading, especially for these three notes:

If you have not burned it, send me the chords for the A-sharp and the G-sharp.

You will say that it is not worth concerning oneself with such trivialities, and you are quite right. But what do you expect? When one is old one becomes a child, they say. These trivialities remind me of when I was eighteen and my maestro amused himself by battering my brain with similar bass lines.

What's more, I believe that a piece with words could be made with this scale, for ex., an *Ave Maria,* adding however the same scale beginning a fourth above the tonic, with different modulations and voice leading, for the tenor or the soprano part. It would, however, be difficult to get back to the tonic with ease. Another *Ave Maria!* It would be the fourth! In this way I could hope, after my death, to be beatified.

Yours always,
G. Verdi

◄Referring to his teacher, Verdi means either Ferdinando Provesi (1770–1883), who taught him music in Busseto, or Vincenzo Lavigna (1776–1836), his teacher in Milan. Both men were experienced composers, severe and conservative in their didactic method.

Verdi counts the prayer "Salve Maria" in *I lombardi alla prima crociata* (1843) as his first *Ave Maria.* The second is a setting of the alleged Dante text in vernacular, for soprano and strings (1880), and the third is Desdemona's prayer in the last act of *Otello* (1887). This fourth setting—the first to use the Latin words—was to become one of the *Quattro pezzi sacri,* published only in 1898.

Milan, Thursday [7 March 1889]

115

Dear Maestro,

It was a good thing I copied out those two little pages with the battered scale steps, which you ran up and down with such facility.

Every difficulty overcome without effort is a grace.

In those contrapuntal pieces they sing there is a sad charm that suggests vespers. Welcome to this fourth *Ave Maria.*

I won't tell anyone about it, trust me. It will take many *Ave Maria*s before you can be pardoned by His Holiness for Jago's Credo. Saturday evening I plan to go and hear *Otello.* I will give you news of it.

Played at the keyboard, those two little pages delight me even more than when I heard them with the ear of memory.

Affectionate greetings

from your
A. Boito

P.S. The mayor passed my letter on to Cambiasi, but after having read it, he hid it and keeps it a secret and has not communicated it to the committee. I have asked Aldo Noseda to demand a reading of it at the next meeting.

>Two years after the premiere, *Otello* was revived at La Scala. Maurel was again Jago, but the tenor and soprano had been changed, not for the better (see Boito's report to Verdi in letter no. 117 below).

The letter mentioned in the postscript probably refers to the jubilee. Pompeo Cambiasi (1849–1908), theatrical historian, brother-in-law of the librettist Felice Romani, was an official of the municipal government of Milan. No doubt he was on the committee, as was Aldo Noseda (1852–1916), music critic of the *Corriere della sera.*

Genoa, 11 March 1889

116

Dear Boito,

Indeed, I thank you for having prepared the way for me with Sig. Edwards. It will thus be easier for me to give a negative answer.

In Shakespeare's homeland they will reproach us for having omitted the first act; but they will not criticize you for Jago's Credo. And by the way: You are the one, you are the chief culprit who should seek forgiveness for that Credo! Now you cannot help but set a four-part Catholic Credo in the style of Palestrina—naturally only after having finished that... whose name I dare not utter.

As for me, I hope I have settled my concerns well with His Holiness. The *Ave Maria*s have become five instead of four.

How?

That scale was not enough for the whole prayer; and so I thought to add the same scale at a fourth above the tonic for the soprano... but it is impossible afterwards (yet it seems so easy) to return to the tonic with grace and naturalness. So then I added another scale on C for the alto, and another on F for the tenor: and thus I made the two *Ave Maria*s. Odd that with that rickety scale the modulations and voice leading work out so well!!

I was not a close friend of Paolo Ferrari, but I learned with profound sadness of the loss of this playwright of ours, who really was the best.

Be well. With Peppina's greetings I cordially shake your hands.

Yours,

G. Verdi

◄Obviously, an earlier letter from Boito is missing, with a first reference to Henry Sutherland Edwards (1829–1906), English journalist and music critic, who—in the imminence of the British premiere of *Otello*, in Italian—was urging Boito and Verdi to attend.

In referring to the newly completed *Ave Maria* on the enigmatic scale, Verdi refers to it as "two," because to achieve the conclusion with the desired "grace and naturalness," he decided to repeat the entire text. Thus it is set first with bass, then alto scales beginning on C; and afterward tenor, then soprano scales beginning on F.

The "name I dare not utter" is, of course, *Nerone*, title of Boito's eternally unfinished opera. Consciously or unconsciously, Verdi was quoting Bellini's *Norma* ("che nominar non oso"), act 2, scene 3.

Paolo Ferrari (1822–1889) was a Risorgimento figure who, among many other activities, was for a time on the board of directors of La Scala. He wrote a number of popular plays, of which the most successful was *Goldoni e le sue sedici commedie nuove* (1851), still occasionally revived in Italy.

Wednesday [Milan, 13 March 1889]

117 Dear Maestro,

I will not go back again. That opera, where every note has an intellectual weight, cannot be performed by idiots. It's enough to make you leave the theater with a bilious attack. That tenor is a rabid dog. I have never seen a more beastly scoundrel on the stage. And the jackass has a good voice, but what a jackass! The woman is a nonentity, well nourished and round, a zero.

But when Maurel appeared I recognized the great artistic impression, full and profound, of two years ago. He seemed to me even more controlled than he was then and more perfect, and equally powerful.

His voice seemed to me also sturdier. That man will keep on singing for another fifteen years.

The theater was so crowded that I had to ask for hospitality in the boxes. The public swallows complacently both the tenor and the woman, and its attention is not distracted by them.

So much the better. We are more demanding, and we want the artistic impression to be exquisite; this is our wrong and our punishment. Patience.

I have a great wish to see the fifth *Ave Maria*. The next time we meet I will ask you to indulge me. Thinking back to the outline you gave me in your letter, I suspected that the rickety scale, transferred to the soprano and the other voices, would not sing naturally. But then, thinking it over and looking at the two little pages that remained with me, I understood that the harmony surrounding it and tempering it and governing it transforms that scrawl into a line that truly sings and easily plays a pivotal role in the modulation of the whole. And so one learns something every day.

I have heard nothing more from my Englishmen; they came back to see me for a new onslaught. They are full of good and serious intentions and they are not cheap speculators. But their insistence knows no limit. After having said no twenty times, in order to rid myself of them I had to say that if I have time I will go to London!

But I added that very probably I would not have time. And with this ghost of a promise that is the equivalent of a no, I freed myself.

Another four lines and I have finished.

The end of the second act of *Otello* is much more clear and effective now than it was before, so it seems to me, though I have not forgotten the strong artistic impression I had of that finale when I saw it in the first sketch.

Many warm greetings to Signora Giuseppina and to you.

> Yours most affectionately,
> A. Boito

⋼The tenor Francesco Giannini had replaced, after an unfortunate opening night, Giuseppe Oxilia as Otello. Amelia Cataneo was

Desdemona. The opera had thirteen performances. The second-act changes to which Boito refers concern not the music but the staging, particularly of the homage to Desdemona at the rear of the stage.

In April of 1889 Verdi had occasion to visit Milan, and he and Boito met more than once. In late June, on his way to Montecatini, the composer again stopped off in Milan and met Boito; and it was at this time that the *Falstaff* project came into existence. The official announcement of the work in progress was made more than a year later by Giulio Ricordi in an article in the *Gazzetta musicale di Milano* (30 November 1890). It says, in part: "For many years, on various occasions, the Maestro had expressed to some intimate friends his wish to write a comic opera; but he considered almost insuperable the difficulty of finding a subject [. . .] When Verdi was in Milan last summer speaking with Arrigo Boito, in fact, about comic opera, the latter caught the ball on the bounce and suggested a subject to Verdi; and not only did he suggest it, but also with marvelous speed, virtually in a few hours, he sketched it out and handed the composer an outline: *Falstaff*, creating this individual character from the various plays in which Shakespeare presented him."

Actually, the subject of *Falstaff* had been in Verdi's mind for many years. If he was unfamiliar with the Salieri opera on the subject (1799), he can hardly have been unaware of the Italian version of Nicolai's *Die lustigen Weiber von Windsor* (Merry Wives of Windsor, 1849). In 1868 a Milanese paper had published the news that Verdi was writing an opera on the subject, libretto by Ghislanzoni. Both Verdi and Ghislanzoni denied the story, but it may well have reflected some vague discussion.

Montecatini, 6 July 1889

118 Dear Boito,

Excellent! Excellent!

Before reading your sketch I chose to reread the *Merry Wives*, the two parts of *Henry IV*, and *Henry V*; and I can only repeat *excellent*, for it would be impossible to do better than you have done.

Too bad that the interest (it is not your fault) does not grow all the way to the end. The climax is the finale of the second act. The appearance of Falstaff's mug amid the laundry, etc., is a genuine comic invention.

I fear also that the last act, despite its fantastic element, could seem weak, with all those little numbers, songs, ariettas, etc., etc. You bring back *Bardolfo!* Then why not bring back *Pistola* too, and have both commit some little, or big, rascality?

You have only two weddings! All the better, since they have little connection with the main plot.

The two trials by water and by fire suffice to punish Falstaff suitably; though I would have liked also to see him soundly thrashed.

I am just talking... and pay no attention to my talk. Now we have quite different things to communicate to each other, about this *Falstaff* or *Wives*, which two days ago was in the world of dreams, and now is taking shape and can become a reality! When? How?... Who knows!! I'll write you about it tomorrow or after.

Greetings from Peppina. Be well.

Affectionately,

G. Verdi

Montecatini, 7 July 1889

119

I told you yesterday that I would write you today, and I am keeping my word even at the cost of annoying you.

As long as we roam in the world of ideas, everything smiles on us; but once we come to earth, and face practical questions, doubts and discouragement arise.

In outlining *Falstaff*, have you ever thought of the enormous number of my years? I know well how you will reply, exaggerating the state of my health, good, excellent, sturdy... And let's assume that is so; nevertheless, you must agree with me that I could be accused of great temerity in taking on such a task! And what if the effort were too much for me?! And what if I did not manage to finish the music?

Then you would have spent time and labor in vain! For all the gold in the world I would not want that. This thought is intolerable to me; and all the more intolerable if, in writing *Falstaff*, you were to—I will not say abandon, but even to distract your thoughts from *Nerone*, or delay the time of its production. I would be blamed for this delay, and the thunderbolts of public malice would fall on my shoulders.

Now how to overcome these obstacles?... Can you offer good answers to my objections? I wish you could, but I don't believe it possible. Still, let us think it over (and take care to do nothing that might harm your career), and if you were to find *one* argument on your side, and I the way to remove, say, ten years from my shoulders, then... What joy! To be able to say to the Public:

We're back again!!

Here's to us!!

Be well.

Affectionately,

G. Verdi

120 first letter   7 July [1889]

Dear Maestro,

No doubt about it: the third act is the coldest. And this, in the theater, means trouble. Unfortunately, this is a law common to all the comic theater. The tragic has the opposite law. The approach of the catastrophe in a tragedy (whether foreseen as in *Othello,* or unexpected as in *Hamlet*) increases the interest prodigiously because its end is terrible. So the last acts of tragedies are always the most beautiful.

In comedy, when the knot is about to be unraveled, interest always dwindles because the end is happy.

You have recently reread Goldoni and you will recall how in the last scenes, though the whole marvelous context of dialogue and characters remains admirable, the action declines almost always and with it the interest. In the *Merry Wives,* even Shakespeare, with all his skill, could not escape this general law. And likewise Molière, and likewise Beaumarchais, and likewise Rossini. The last scene of the *Barbiere* has always seemed to me less wonderful than the rest. If I am wrong, correct me.

In comedy there is a moment when the audience says *"It's finished,"* and instead on the stage it is not yet finished.

A knot cannot be unraveled without being loosened first, and when it is loose, the solution can be foreseen and the interest is gone before the knot is.

Comedy unravels the knot; tragedy breaks it or severs it. So the third act of *Falstaff* is indeed the coldest. But since it is so because of a universal law, the trouble is less serious than might be believed. And a way will be found to warm it up and to make it more brisk and less fragmented. First, the advantages of the last scene must be exploited to the fullest degree. The fantastic atmosphere, which has never been exploited in the rest of the opera, can help: it is a fresh note, light and new. Besides, we have three quite good comic moments: (1) Falstaff's monologue with him wearing his horns; (2) the interrogation (we will have Bardolfo and Pistola do it to the sound of sticks striking Falstaff's paunch as he lies flat on the ground, and at each blow he confesses a sin); (3) the benediction of the two weddings, in mask.

We will shift the duet of Fentone and Nannetta to the first part of the same act, as evening is falling.

This little love story between Nannetta and Fentone must appear in very frequent bursts; in all the scenes where they appear they will kiss secretly in corners, cleverly, boldly, taking care not to be noticed, with fresh little phrases and brief, very rapid and sly little dialogues from the beginning to the end of the comedy. It will be a very lighthearted love, constantly disturbed and interrupted and always ready to begin again. We must not forget this color, which seems good to me. To be sure, Fenton's song is pasted in there to give the tenor a solo, and this is too bad. Shall we cut it?

The correspondence resumes. I await the letter you have announced to me.

Many affectionate greetings to Signora Peppina and to you, dear Maestro—and enjoy your cure.

Yours,
A. Boito

⌘This letter was obviously written immediately after Boito received Verdi's letter of 6 July and before receiving the announced letter of the following day. Hence Boito's heading "first letter." Verdi's pensive letter of 7 July must have arrived soon after this reply to the first was written; the second reply was then written, and both letters were sent together.

second letter   9 July [1889]

121

Dear Maestro,

You see here two letters. I did not give the first to the post because I thought I should wait for the one you announced to me. Then I thought to wait some more in order to reply to your doubts. After 24 hours I am answering you; my thoughts have ripened. The fact is that I never think of your age either when I speak with you, or when I write to you, or when I work for you.

The fault is yours.

I know that *Otello* is just over two years old, and that as I write you it is being presented as it should be to Shakespeare's compatriots. But there is a stronger reason than that of age, and it is this: It was said of you after *Otello*: "*It is impossible to finish better!*"

This is a great truth that contains great and very rare praise. This is the only serious argument. Serious for our contemporaries, not for History, which chooses to judge above all the essential value of men. And yet it is extremely rare to see the life of an artist conclude with a worldwide victory. *Otello* is this victory. All the other objections—*age, strength, your labor, my labor,* etc., etc.—do not matter and are not obstacles to a new work. Since you oblige me to speak of myself, I will tell you that despite the commitment I would assume with *Falstaff* I will be able to conclude my own work by the promised date. I am sure of that. Let us go on to the other doubts.

I do not believe writing a comic opera would fatigue you.

Tragedy makes the person writing it actually *suffer:* his mind is subjected to a painful influence that morbidly excites the nerves.

But the joking and laughter of comedy exhilarate mind and body.

A smile adds a thread
to the fabric of life.

I do not know if this is the exact wording of Foscolo, but it is certainly a truth.

You have a great desire to work, this is an indubitable proof of health and strength. *Ave Maria*s are not enough; it takes more.

All your life you have wanted a good subject for a comic opera. This is a sign that the nobly merry vein of art exists potentially in your brain; instinct is a good counsellor. There is only one way to end better than with *Otello,* and that is to end victoriously with *Falstaff.* After having made all the cries and lamentation of the human heart resound, to end with an immense outburst of hilarity! It's dazzling!

So, dear Maestro, give some more thought to the subject I have sketched for you, see if you sense the germ of the new masterpiece in it. If that germ is there, the miracle is done. And meanwhile let us promise each other the most scrupulous secrecy.

I have told *no one.* If we work in secret we will work in peace. I await your decision, which, as is your custom, will be free and resolute. I must not influence it. Your decision will in any event be wise and strong whether you say *Enough,* or you say *Again.*

Yours affectionately,
A. Boito

⌐sOn 5 July 1889 *Otello,* conducted by Faccio, had opened (in Italian) at the Lyceum Theatre in London, with Tamagno, Maurel, and Amelia Cataneo.

The quotation from Ugo Foscolo is from the preface to his 1825 translation of Sterne's *A Sentimental Journey*. Writing under the pseudonym of Didimo Chierico, Foscolo said, attributing the sentiment to Sterne himself: "A smile can add a thread to the very brief fabric of life."

In the last paragraph, Boito underlines "no one" three times, well aware of Verdi's passion for secrecy, confirmed in the letter below.

Montecatini, 10 July 1889

122

Dear Boito,

Amen; and so be it!

Let us do *Falstaff* then! We will not think for the moment about the obstacles, age, illnesses!

I too desire to maintain the deepest *secrecy*—a word that I too underline three times to say to you that no one must know anything about it!... But wait a minute... Peppina knew it, I believe, before us!... Never fear: she will keep the secret. When women have this quality, they have it to a greater degree than we do.

I will bear in mind your words, "*despite the commitment I would assume with* Falstaff *I will be able to conclude my own work by the promised date.*"

And now a last word. A very prosaic word, but, especially for me, necessary and due. But no, no... Today I have *Falstaff* too much in my mind and could not speak to you of anything else. I will talk to you about the *anything else* tomorrow.

Meanwhile, if the spirit moves you, go ahead and start writing. In the first two acts there is nothing to change except, perhaps, the monologue of the jealous husband, which would go better at the end of the first part than at the beginning of the second. It would have more warmth and effectiveness.

Till tomorrow. With Peppina's greetings I say to you

Be well.

Affectionately,

G. Verdi

◆In the definitive version Ford's jealous monologue "È sogno? o realtà?" appears towards the end of act 2, part 1.

11 July [1889]

123 Dear Maestro,

Hurrah!!!

Soon it will be done. I will certainly bring you at least the first two acts in October to Sant'Agata.

I need the rest of July to clear up some details in my own work.

At the very beginning of August I will begin ours. Signora Giuseppina knew it before us! This is the miracle of female intuition.

Now, dear Maestro, the other miracle is up to you!

Many greetings to Signora Giuseppina the prophetess.

An embrace

from your
affectionate
A. Boito

Montecatini, 11 July 1889

124 Dear Boito,

... To continue yesterday's letter: When your work is finished, you would cede the rights to me for the sum of... (to be established). And if, whether because of age or ailments or any other reason, I were not able to finish the music, you would recover your *Falstaff*, property that I myself offer you as a memento, and which you will use as you see fit.

I am in perfect agreement with you as to the demands and the nature of tragedy and comedy; and the examples you cite confirm what you say. But if in comedy (as you say) there is a point when the audience says *"It's finished!"* and on the stage it is not yet *finished,* then something must be found that can firmly fix their attention either on the comic side or on the musical side.

You have already improved this third act:
the Fenton-Nannetta duet in the first part is better;
the fantastic part with the Song of the Fairies is good; Falstaff's monologue is good, and so is the interrogation to the sound of thrashing, etc... But afterwards the weddings distract the attention that should be all addressed to Falstaff, and the action cools. At this point there would be a musical number ready-made in Shakespeare:

MRS. PAGE   Hold up the jest no higher.
FALSTAFF   And these are not fairies?

MRS. FORD	Do you think, though we would have given ourselves without scruple to hell, that ever the devil could have made you our delight?!
FORD	A whale!
FALS.	Good!...
ANOTHER	A hodge-pudding!
FALS.	Good!
ANOTHER	Old, withered
FALS.	Very good
ANOTHER	Slanderous as Satan
FALS.	Still good
OTHERS	Poor as Job
[FALS.]	Very good
ALL	And given to fornications, and to taverns, and sack, and wine, and metheglins, and to drinkings and swearings and starings...
FALS.	Amen... and so be it
MRS. [PAGE]	Now, Sir John, how like you Windsor wives?
FALS.	I do begin to perceive I am an ass
ALL	Bravo! Well said! Well said! Hurrah Hurrah Hurrah!... *They clap their hands and the curtain falls.*

But what do we do with the weddings, you will ask? I don't know! But you, who have been so clever in the *invention* in the second act with the appearance of Falstaff's mug amid the laundry, will surely find some other devilment.

Good-bye for now.

Affectionately,
G. Verdi

◄As he had done so often in the past with other librettists, Verdi firmly points out the way for Boito, taking the final scene of *The Merry Wives of Windsor* (in the Rusconi translation) and rearranging and compressing it. Boito then compressed it still further.

12 July [1889]

125

Dear Maestro,

Everything you think is good. I thank you with all my heart and our pact is sealed. In about two weeks I will set to work on our comedy. The fragment of dialogue you quote had already been marked down to be inserted. But the nuptials are necessary; without weddings there's no happiness (don't tell Signora Giuseppina or she would start talking to me about marriage again!), and Fenton and Nannetta must marry.

I like that love of theirs, it serves to make the whole comedy more fresh and more solid. That love must enliven all of it throughout and to such a degree that I would almost like to eliminate the duet of the two lovers.

In every ensemble scene this love is somehow present:
it is present in the second part of the first act;
in the second part of the second act;
in the first and second parts of the third.

So it is pointless to have them sing a genuine duet together by themselves. Their part, even without the duet, will be very effective; indeed, it will be more effective without. I don't quite know how to explain myself: I would like to sprinkle the whole comedy with that lighthearted love, like powdered sugar on a cake, without collecting it in one point.

Affectionate greetings to you and to Signora Giuseppina.

Yours,
A. Boito

&sIn late July Boito went back to the former convent at San Giuseppe, where Duse joined him for three weeks. There Boito began working on the libretto for *Falstaff,* while the actress rested after an exhausting season that had included the fiasco of Boito's *Anthony and Cleopatra* adaptation. Boito stayed on at San Giuseppe until it was time for his annual visit to Donna Vittoria Cima at Lake Como.

San Giuseppe via Ivrea
1 August [1889]

126   Dear Maestro,

Here I am, ready. Please send me back the outline of *Falstaff*: reading it and thinking about it again, I will work more easily.

Affectionate greetings

from your
A. Boito

Sant'Agata, 2 August 1889

127   Dear Boito,

Bravo, bravo, thrice bravo! How exact you have been!!!

Here is the sketch of... and to work... Hurrah! It seems a dream to me!

Be well.

Yours,

G. Verdi

◄§Having promised (see letter no. 123) to start work "at the very beginning of August," Boito was faithful to his word. Hence Verdi's congratulations on his collaborator's precision.

Sant'Agata, 18 August 1889

128

Dear Boito,

Help me do a good deed. As you know, the post of director of the Parma Conservatory is open. I have thought of Faccio. He would receive a salary of 6000 lire as well as 1000 lire for lodging (in Parma he would spend half that for suitable lodging). In addition, the city would be prepared to allot 4000 lire for the conductor of the performances in the theater. And even if it did not suit the city administration to put on a season or two, the stipend would be paid all the same. Since the conservatory is now state-governed, he would be entitled to a pension, and they would also count the years of service at the Milan Conservatory. I wrote to Faccio that in his place I would have accepted even *before having finished reading my letter,* for the offers he might receive elsewhere are precarious, his position itself at La Scala is precarious, etc., etc...

Suppose that in the musical upheavals that go on the impresario of La Scala were to become some *Piontelli* or other; the conductor would be a Cimino. Further, Faccio should understand that the atmosphere surrounding him in Milan is not as limpid as it was ten years ago! A misfortune for him also is *I maestri cantori* [*Die Meistersinger*]. If it goes well they will give him very little credit; if it goes badly the fault will be his. Faccio trusts Giulio, and this is fine; but Giulio has his own interests, and must account for his actions to his stockholders, whose interests could conflict with those of Faccio. He wants to have a talk with me! But I have nothing further to say to him. He is hesitating as usual, and as usual he will do something foolish!

You, his oldest and dearest friend, write him if you are of my opinion, tell him to accept: and if you do not want to write him, write me a fairly strong letter and I will show it to him, and who knows?!... Amen, amen.

You are working, I hope? The strangest thing is that I too am work-ing!... I am amusing myself by writing fugues!... Yes, sir: a fugue... and a *comic fugue*... which might fit nicely into *Falstaff!*... But what do I mean by a comic fugue? Why comic? you will ask... I do not know *how*, or *why*, but it is a *comic fugue!* I will tell you in another letter how the idea was born!

Meanwhile, greetings and a heartfelt farewell.

Affectionately,

G. Verdi

❧Bottesini, the director of the Parma Conservatory (see letter no. 108 above), had died on 7 July 1889. For the past two years, Faccio's health had been declining. The symptoms of his nervous disorder were be-coming alarmingly evident, and at the same time his position at La Scala was in jeopardy. The ups and downs of Romilda Pantaleoni's career also disturbed him. He was driving himself relentlessly, prepar-ing the Italian premiere of *Die Meistersinger* (given in translation, it opened the 1889–1890 season with great success and ran for sixteen performances), which was to be his last appearance in the house.

The Piontelli to whom Verdi makes such a contemptuous reference is Luigi Piontelli (died 1908), who had been impresario of the Teatro Carlo Felice in Genoa the previous season, producing both *Otello* and *Mefistofele*. Later he moved to the Teatro Regio in Turin, where he played an important role in Toscanini's early career, and in 1892–93 he was at La Scala, when *Falstaff* had its premiere. Gaetano Cimini (1852–1907), while not a conductor of the absolutely first rank, en-joyed success in most leading Italian opera houses—excepting La Scala—and in a number of foreign theaters.

It is a likely hypothesis that Verdi's comic fugue mentioned here was to become the finale of *Falstaff:* "Tutto nel mondo è burla."

San Giuseppe (Ivrea)
20 August [1889]

129 Dear Maestro,

I have read your letter and I am answering immediately.

I too, if I were in Faccio's place, would accept without hesitation the position being offered him in Parma.

But Faccio will hesitate. The sentimental nature of his spirit leads him to hesitate whenever, if he would improve the conditions of his life, he would be forced to leave Milan. And after having hesitated, he refuses.

If today this deadly sentimentality were to be reawakened in him, I would see no more security or peace for our friend. After thirty years of work (or little less) he finds himself today with much praise and scant savings, in a position that is not enviable but much envied, illustrious, yes, but also precarious. In that city that he loves, the war waged against him is constant and is animated by disloyalty and envy. That post he occupies today, unsure that he will occupy it much longer, has always been beset by furies; nobody has remained there as long or been as solidly established as he, but this solidity already shows signs of tottering. And it would be a great stroke of luck for him if he could make up his mind to abandon that position in time, to accept the other one offered him, so honorable and secure and tranquil and proficuous.

You write me that the directorship of the Parma Conservatory is paid 6000 lire, plus 1000 for lodging; 7000 lire in Parma is the equivalent of 12,000 in Milan—without considering the theater, which would add 4000 to the salary, and without considering that in the months of vacation Faccio could accept other important engagements. I am convinced that Faccio would prove an excellent conservatory director.

He knows most profoundly, both in theory and in practice, everything a conservatory director must know. And he keeps his hesitation to himself, for his private affairs, like a fine pearl, but does not transmit it to others. Hence it follows that he knows how to command large groups, even rowdy and rough, and he knows how to make them obey him, because he has a very clear sense of order and equity. So he will quite easily be able to make himself obeyed by the students of a conservatory that has just been organized, that has no moldy traditions or inveterate ills like the conservatories of Naples, Florence, or Palermo. Parma will be his peace and his good fortune, provided he goes there alone, without family and without troubles at home.

Dear Maestro, you should insist in encouraging our friend, and if you think my words can have any influence on him I beg you to let him read this letter, which is the frank expression of my thought.

Many affectionate greetings to you and to Signora Giuseppina.

> Yours,
> A. Boito

And this page, dear Maestro, is for you.

A playful fugue is what is needed; there will be no lack of a place for it.

The games of art are made for jocose art.

I live with the immense *Sir John,* the big paunch, the bed-destroyer, the stool-smasher, the mule-masher, with that besotted bag of sweet wine, that living heap of butter, amid the barrels of sherry and the merriment of that warm kitchen at the Garter Inn.

In the month of October you too will live there.

At first I was in despair at the thought of sketching the characters with a few lines, moving the plot, extracting all the juice from that enormous Shakespearian pomegranate, allowing no useless seeds to slip into the glass. I wanted to write colorfully and clearly and concisely to outline the musical plan of the scene so that an organic unit results that is a *piece of music* and at the same time is not; I wanted to make the merry comedy come to life from beginning to end, to make it live in a natural and communicative merriment. All this is difficult, difficult, difficult, but it must seem easy, easy, easy.

Onward, with courage.

I am still on the first act. In September, the second. In October, the third.

This is the program. Onward.

Again, a good and strong handshake to muster courage.

Yours,
A. Boito

Wednesday, 30 [October 1889]
Milan

130   Dear Maestro,

I will arrive next Monday (4 November), and if the second act is not yet finished I will finish it during the week I will stay at Sant'Agata.

That act is possessed of a devil and if you touch it you burn your fingers.

The content of Alice's scene as we decided it in Milan no longer satisfies me. It has a defect, and it is this: If Alice expounds the details of the joke, the joke then loses interest.

I have drafted the hamper scene and it seems promising to me.

But there is still much to do.

So till we meet again Monday. I will get off at Fiorenzuola at the hour of the usual train.

Many warm greetings to Signora Giuseppina and to you.
Cordial greetings to Maestro Muzio.
Till we meet.

Yours most affectionately,
A. Boito

◄ƨFor several years, from 1844, Muzio (see note following letter no. 97 above) lived with Verdi as his pupil, assistant, and companion. He remained a devoted friend and, like Verdi's other friends, was happy to run errands and serve as the composer's extra eyes and ears.

Monday [Sant'Agata, 11 November 1889]

131

Yesterday evening a letter arrived here for you. I forwarded it at once to Milan; but I fear I got the address wrong... Principe *Umberto* instead of Amedeo.

The letter will reach you in any case... but I thought it best to warn you.

GV

◄ƨThe letter, which arrived shortly after Boito had left Sant'Agata, was from Duse. Describing the envelope to her, Boito wrote that "a strong hand that knows how to command obedience from the pen" had scratched out Sant'Agata and added the Milan address. Later Boito said that the two handwritings suggested "a lion's paw on a swallow's wing."

Tuesday [Milan, 12 November 1889]

132

Dear Maestro,

Thank you. I received in good order the letter you kindly forwarded to me.

The address was correct.

The election, which made me leave the agreeable life at Sant'Agata, seems to hold good promise for the moderates. Tomorrow we will have the definitive news.

I have resumed work.

I have seen no one, except Giacosa, therefore no one has spoken to me about the piece in *Le figaro*.

I beg you, dear Maestro, to greet Signora Giuseppina warmly for me.

Till we meet again in Milan, soon.

A warm handshake from your
                              most affectionate
                              A. Boito

◄⅊The elections were for the Milan city council. After his rebellious youth, Boito was now a moderate, or even in some respects a conservative.

The reference to an article in *Le figaro* is unexplained.

Verdi spent the last week of November and the first days of December in Milan. Having succeeded in scotching the projected jubilee at La Scala, he had been unable to block a more modest celebration in Genoa, so the visit to Milan was, as he described it, an escape. During his Milanese stay, he and Boito obviously met. Boito later went to Genoa, where he spent New Year's Day with the Verdis. He remained in nearby Nervi until mid-March, so they certainly had other meetings.

Genoa, 6 January 1890

133 Dearest Boito,

My manservant has been discharged. Another has presented himself, one *Vittorio Falsetti* (nasty word! as Ford would say), who was for many years in the service of Marquis Gropallo. If the marquis were kind enough to tell you in confidence something about him... and especially if he was discharged for some rather abrupt reason, he would be doing me a real favor. Falsetti also knows D. Marco Sala. You follow me? I await therefore a reply from you; and I would have to have it by Wednesday morning.

Forgive me.

Our affectionate greetings.

                              G. Verdi

◄⅊Ford's "nasty word" (*Falstaff,* act 2, part 1) refers to "le corna" ("the cuckold's horns").

Marco Sala (1842–1901), known to his friends as "Don Marco," was a well-to-do dilettante violinist and composer. A friend of Boito's, he had also befriended the young Puccini (whose *Le willis,* later entitled

Le villi, was given a first piano reading in Sala's salon, after which the host, Boito, and others underwrote a staged performance in 1884).

Saturday [Genoa, 15 February 1890]

134

Dear Boito,

Do you have private news of Faccio? Look at this article in *Il pungolo!*

What are we to read between those few lines?

There is surely something I do not want to identify.

Be well. Till we meet.

Yours,
G. Verdi

◄Faccio's health was deteriorating rapidly, after the overwork on *Die Meistersinger.* The *Pungolo* article, which Verdi included with his letter, announced that Faccio had asked for two weeks' leave from La Scala. There was talk of his being replaced as artistic director of the theater (one paper actually reported Puccini as a possible successor). The same *Pungolo* article also mentioned Faccio's acceptance of the Parma positions for the following year.

1 March [1890]

135

Dear Maestro,

Here is the latest news of Faccio. It is good and I hasten to communicate it to you.

The letter from our good Fortis reached me at this very moment.

In three or four days at the latest I will have finished *Falstaff.* The third act proves shorter than I had hoped, but it is the most varied of all.

Many affectionate greetings to Signora Peppina and to you.

Till we meet Tuesday or Wednesday.

Yours affectionately,
Arrigo

◄The letter of the journalist Leone Fortis (1824–1898), obviously included with this letter to Verdi and probably describing Faccio's improved health, is not with Boito's letter in the Sant'Agata archive.

This is the first of only a few rare occasions when Boito signed a letter to Verdi simply with his first name.

Genoa, 2 March 1890

136   Dear Boito,

Thank you for the better news you have given me about the poor man's health. I will be happy when I know that he has completely recovered, as I wish with all my heart.

Big Belly then is almost finished! Hurrah!... I have no fears about the length because I am sure there will be nothing superfluous in it.

You say you will be in Genoa Wednesday. Wait a few days. I am leaving tomorrow morning for Sant'Agata and will not be back until Saturday. As soon as I arrive I will telegraph you.

Greetings from Peppina. I shake your hands.

Affectionately,
G. Verdi

[Telegram]

9 March 90

Arrigo Boito, Eden Hotel, Nervi
From Genoa
137   Am back. Greetings.

Verdi

☙This telegram was obviously sent before the following letter. The date of the telegram probably refers to its arrival.

Genoa, 8 March 1890

138   Dear Boito,

Accept this... not as payment, but as a sign of gratitude for having written this stupendous *Falstaff* for me.

If I were not to finish the music, the poetry of *Falstaff* will remain your property.

I shake your hands.

Thank you again. Be well.

Affectionately,
G. Verdi

☙It is likely that, on returning to Genoa, Verdi found the completed third act of *Falstaff,* which Boito had sent in his absence; and with his usual scrupulousness about money, he sent Boito's payment at once. All in all, the work on Verdi's last opera went much more smoothly and rapidly than it had done on *Otello.* Though there were, of course, revisions to be made, everything was painless, also because of Verdi's largely serene humor and his now closer, almost paternal relationship with Boito.

9 March, 1890
Genoa

139

Dear Maestro,

Thank you with all my heart and with total gratitude. The payment you give me is too much. To be able to accept it and to feel I deserve it, I must remember that I worked for you impelled only by the affection I bear you, and that the splendid reward you give me comes from your having recognized this affection.

Now, Maestro, again in the name of Shakespeare, give Art and our country another, new victory.

An embrace.

Yours,
A. Boito

◆This letter was delivered by hand. The closing ("An embrace") is unique in the correspondence and seems to confirm Boito's profound emotion.

Thursday, Milan [13 March 1890]

140

Dear Maestro,

I have not yet been able to see Faccio. I have been twice to his house and twice the concierge would not admit me. The doctor's orders are that he see no one, to spare him the effort of conversation and to spare him any emotion. I insisted a bit, trying to circumvent the orders, but then I realized the prohibition was very strict and so I confined myself to writing my name on the list of visitors.

For that matter the news from the concierge's quarters is good: our friend is improving, but his mind needs absolute rest. Dr. Levis continues to hope. So let us hope with him.

Remember, dear Maestro, that whenever you find in the libretto of *Falstaff* something to change or to revise, I am always completely ready to hear you and to make the variant at once. I am very slow in writing, but very swift in revising what is already written. When a work of art is good on the whole, improving the details is very easy.

I have not yet seen Giulio.

Most affectionate greetings.

Yours,
A. Boito

Many cordial greetings to Signora Giuseppina.

Sunday [Milan, 16 March 1890]

141   Dear Maestro,

I have seen F. twice. I left him half an hour ago in the home of a woman friend, where we had arranged to take him so as to be able to talk with him calmly about his affairs, without the presence of that brother-in-law of his.

I found F. much better than I had expected, indeed, much better than when I saw him four months ago. The treatment he has undertaken is helping him.

One of the causes of his illness is a blood infection, which is treated with mercury injections. There is reason to hope that, once this infection is overcome, his health can improve very much or he may recover it completely. He no longer regrets having accepted the Parma offer, and when he does try to regret it, it is more out of an old emotional habit than because of any painful notion. In fact, today, making fun of these attempts of his at whining, I made him laugh with such enthusiasm that a healthy man could not have laughed more heartily and better than he.

And yet he has difficulty speaking (for that matter he always has had): I mean, in conversing, he searches a bit for the word, but he finds it with precision; I never heard him mistake one word for another.

The inflection and tone of voice are his natural ones. His eyes are fine and observe keenly. In short, I have hope. He will soon go to Graz, where there is a very effective treatment for this sort of illness. He will go there with his brother-in-law.

As I was informed of this, before letting him leave I wanted to be reassured regarding the security of his savings.

His savings are quite secure: they are deposited in the Cassa di Risparmio in the form of personal bonds, in the keeping of an employee of the institution itself, a man of absolute probity who has kept them for him for many years. Some personal securities are safeguarded in themselves, so there is no fear that they will be taken away from him. If the illness, instead of improving, should worsen and the savings of F. should somehow be threatened through an interdict made by someone with a legal right to demand it, then I would consult my lawyer Dina and ask advice. But I hope, I believe that by the grace of God we will not come to these extremes.

For the rest, that poor friend has gone through some horrible bitter experiences that are repugnant to recall.

Affectionate greetings to you, dear Maestro, and to Signora Giuseppina.

> Yours most affectionately,
> A. Boito

◄§Although Faccio had been persuaded to accept the Parma post, he was unable to fulfill his obligations there (until Faccio's death Boito acted as his substitute; see letter no. 153 below).

Alessandro Dina, Milan's most prominent lawyer, was the legal consultant also for Casa Ricordi.

Genoa, 17 March 1890

142

Dear Boito,

Let us hope then... but that strict confinement alarms me! When I was in Milan I went to the house, but found he was not in, and a few days later he accompanied la Pantaleoni to the train. And now... We must hope, hope. Let me know something, when you can.

The first act is finished without any change in the poetry, exactly as you gave it to me. I believe the same thing will happen with the second act, except for some cuts in the ensemble piece as you mentioned yourself. We will not talk now about the third; but I believe there will not be much to do in that either.

And you?... I say this in a whisper: "*Work.*" And I say it not only in the interest of Art, but also to some extent in my own interest, because when, sooner or later, it becomes known that you have written *Falstaff* for me, they will turn on me furiously because I have made you lose time. Naturally, we will let them yell, but if you *seize them by the gullet* (as Otello might say) and stifle the cries, it will be better.

Do you want the accent in the word *Falstaff* on the first syllable or the second? For the verse it makes no difference; but which is better?

I greet you for Peppina and I shake your hands.

> Affectionately,
> G. Verdi

◄§Verdi's injunction to Boito—"*Work*"—refers not to *Falstaff* but to *Nerone*, which Boito had promised to La Scala (see following letter).

Thursday, Milan [20 March 1890]

143   Dear Maestro,

I let the feast of St. Joseph go by without writing you, so as not to add yet another letter to the hundred or so you must have had to read yesterday. Now I answer you.

First of all, a first *Hurrah* for the news you give me, that you have completed the first act of *Fàlstaff.*

Fàlstaff, like all English disyllabic names, is accented on the first syllable. Ask Signora Giuseppina if I am right or wrong. In my memory I cannot find any English surname that has more than one syllable and is accented on the last. Only the French, who incorrigibly distort foreign surnames, pronounce it Falstàff.

I too believe it will be necessary to shorten the episode of the hamper and of the screen. I cede to you, dear Maestro, the scissors. Cut wherever you like. I was deliberately abundant so that in that mass of material you could tailor the piece in your own way and with greater ease. In the development of ensembles it is impossible to foresee the needs of the music, so it is better for the verses to abound.

Don't worry about me. I am working. Today the Cortis came to see me and I repeated to them the promise I made last summer, certain I will keep it.

They controlled their curiosity and asked me no indiscreet questions about the work at Palazzo Doria.

Yesterday I saw Faccio again. In his house, and in his presence, I had an appointment with his accountant, who is a most estimable person. Our friend's money is safe and sound. I know you must have received a letter from him for the feast of St. Joseph, and this fact also pleased me. I repeat my impression: His is a tired mind, but not a mind on its way to extinction. Rest will make him healthier than ever.

Remember me cordially to Signora Giuseppina.

An affectionate greeting

from your
A. Boito

✯Cesare Corti and his brother Enrico were leading Italian impresarios and for some years managed La Scala. In 1891–92 they were replaced by Piontelli.

Boito's promise refers to *Nerone.*

25 March [1890]

Dear Maestro,

144

Our poor friend left yesterday evening for Graz. I had a hard time making him postpone his departure for a couple of days. It would have been impossible to prevent it altogether, not because of the inevitable objections of the brother-in-law, but because of the desperate emotion I would have aroused in the sick man himself, worsening his illness. F. has a boundless faith in the Graz cure and he is rushing there with the impatience of someone sure of finding recovery.

I forced him to postpone the departure because I wanted Todeschini to examine him, and he did. I arranged a gathering of physicians on my own and it took place yesterday.

Before allowing him to leave, I wanted a very clear idea of my friend's physical condition. Our Todeschini demonstrated on this occasion once again how the nobility of his heart is equal to his talent. The meeting took place yesterday in his home, with me present, after he had examined the patient the day before with tireless affection. Present were Todeschini, Levis, who is his usual doctor, and De Vincenti, a specialist in diseases of the brain.

The outcome is this: *There are serious reasons to suspect a cerebral paralysis.*

It is best for the public not to know the name of the threatening disease.

If, in four or five months, our friend can observe a constant improvement from the Graz cure, he is saved: if not, he is worse than dead. Until this time has gone by, I will find a way to temporize with Parma; the doctors themselves have advised me to do this.

A thread of hope exists, but very slender.

The doctors bade me good-bye with these words: *Let us hope;* but the tone was not that of true hope. Todeschini and Levis have a bit more confidence than De Vincenti, who has very little confidence. But the fact remains that in the whole world there is no cure more suited than the one at Graz.

De Vincenti, who knows that institution because he has visited and studied it, spoke with genuine enthusiasm of Dr. Krafft-Ebing, who directs it, and he has no hesitation in declaring this scientist the emulator of Charcot.

Dr. De Vincenti himself promised me that he will write to Krafft-Ebing, whom he knows personally, in order to receive frequent news of our friend.

There are several ways of keeping an eye on the situation, between

Milan and Trieste, Milan and Graz. La Pantaleoni's brother has a friend who goes to Graz every month, and he will take care of any pressing matters. I too, when it is necessary, can take a trip up there.

Sad days, dear Maestro. My first impressions of the sick man were good, because on those days I saw him always in the afternoon hours. But then when I saw him in the morning hours and in the evening I was aghast. I could never have imagined such a change.

Yesterday was the last evening. I found at his house only two friends: Orsi and Alcèo Pantaleoni, who always came twice a day. On the other days I found Countess Dandolo and a close woman friend of la Pantaleoni, I am sorry not to remember her name. I did not accompany him to the station, to spare him any stronger emotion. I said good-bye to him an hour before his departure, at ten in the evening, yesterday.

He was so good and so straightforward and honest.

We had studied together.

Dear Maestro.

A handshake.

Yours,
A. Boito

◄§Dr. Baron Richard von Krafft-Ebing (1840–1902), now best known as the author of *Psychopathia Sexualis* (1886), was professor of psychiatry at Graz, where he had a private sanatorium. Jean Martin Charcot (1825–1893), the pioneering French physician of La Salpêtrière, was the leader of the earlier generation of students of nervous disorders.

Alceo Pantaleoni (1839–1923), brother of Romilda, was a conductor. His sister wrote him frequently at this time, and her letters, which survive, represent a valuable documentation of Faccio's last days.

The Orsi referred to was probably Romeo Orsi (1843–1918), clarinettist and instrument maker. He devised a bass clarinet in A for *Otello*.

Countess Ermellina Dandolo was a friend of Boito, who frequented her salon in Milan.

Genoa, 31 March 1890

145 Dear Boito,

Thank you for the news you give me about the health of our poor friend! It is not the news I would have wished, but I know that, unfortunately, it tells the truth! Naturally I have never been as close to him as you are, and yet I am profoundly grieved by the misfortune of this Artist so gifted, of this man so honest! Rare qualities! and they will learn this at La Scala with time.

Let us hope, let us hope; and be kind enough to send me a word about him from time to time.

You mentioned Parma! If you have already written, no harm done; but not to write is perhaps better. When la Pantaleoni expressed the same idea, I said to her that she, better than we, could write in a friendly way either to Count Sanvitale or to the mayor. I believe she has done this.

I greet you in the name of Peppina, and I shake your hands affectionately.

Yours,
G. Verdi

➷Count Sanvitale, an aristocratic music-lover, was head of the board of the Teatro Regio in Parma. The mayor of Parma was now Giovanni Mariotti; see note following letter no. 108 above.

Monday [7 April 1890]
Milan

146

Dear Maestro,

I would have many things to say to you, but time is pressing and the letter will be brief. Poor Faccio returns to Milan tomorrow. The doctor in Graz would not admit him to his institution and advised taking him back to Milan and putting him in an asylum. These last days he has grown worse.

Here I am once again making the via crucis of doctors and lawyers for him. And yet I am glad he is coming back in our midst.

It is not at all true that his sister came to Milan. At Faccio's house they assured me that she has not been seen, not even for an hour. The house today is exactly as it was when he left. So much the better. Our suspicions were exaggerated. Dina, to whom I spoke yesterday, offers me his full support. As far as material interests are concerned there is no longer anything to fear.

Let us change the subject. Yesterday evening I heard *Don Pasquale*. It went well. I think I have found a good Ford, and a good merry wife in the singer who played the part of Norina. The bass's voice is beautiful, suitable and healthy and young. The person seems to me intelligent. He will have to rid himself of the old traditions of the Italian *buffi*, which are all right for Don Pasquale but for Ford would be blasphemy.

And now I ask you a favor: Today or tomorrow a certain Signor Rouillé Destranges will arrive in Genoa. He is a Frenchman but one of the good ones, who showed me the most unselfish cordiality when *Mefistofele* was given in Nantes. I do not know him personally but only through letters, and from his letters I became aware of the man's goodness. This gentleman wishes most ardently to meet you, that is, to be admitted for a few minutes into the drawing room of Palazzo Doria.

By now at least a hundred people must have asked this same favor of me; I have denied it to all of them. But I haven't the heart to deny it to this good Frenchman. He has nothing to ask of you; he wants only to pay his respects. I do not know if he is a musician, but I know that he has a profound and vast knowledge of artistic matters. I beg you to tell me either with a telegram or with a note if you will allow me to announce to Signor Rouillé Destranges that the favor he asks is granted. In this case I would telegraph the good news to the Hôtel de la Ville (where he will be staying from today or tomorrow). I believe he is staying in Genoa for a few days.

Many warm greetings to Signora Giuseppina.

An affectionate handshake.

A. Boito

⊷Donizetti's *Don Pasquale* was given at the Teatro Manzoni in Milan in early April. The cast included Cuttica-Tancioni (soprano), Mandolini, Majocchi, and the comic bass Galletti-Gianoli. None of them sang in the premiere of *Falstaff*.

Louis Rouillé Destranges (1863–1915) was a music critic. He later published an account of his visit to Verdi, including several controversial comments by the composer, in *Monde artiste* (Paris).

Genoa, 8 March 1889
[but actually 8 April 1890]

147 Dear Boito,

Unfortunately, my presentiments did not deceive me! The rejection at Graz, it seems to me, is serious! It is a death sentence!...

Poor friend! So honest and gifted!...

Go ahead and send the Frenchman when you like.

Be well.

Affectionately,
G. Verdi

[Telegram]

10 April 90

Arrigo Boito, Principe Amedeo 1, Milan
From Genoa
Think it best to advise you that Saturday I leave for Sant'Agata for three
or four days.

148

Verdi

[Milan] 15 April [1890]

149

Dear Maestro,

Our poor friend is doomed. There is no hope of saving him now.

It is better to die.

I will spare you the details of his condition rather than renew grief in speaking of it.

The newspapers, in their impatient impudence, have told the whole sad story though I begged them to remain silent.

In a few days we will take him to a house in the country, very well chosen, near Monza, isolated and peaceful. Let us hope he stays there until the end and that the end comes quickly. He will be very well cared for by his good and intelligent maid, by a good man who takes excellent care of him already, and by an honest and very skilled male nurse.

Yesterday the governor of the Parma Conservatory came to the sick man's house to speak to me. I did not hide the truth from him. Meanwhile his salary is accumulating in Parma and, for him to benefit from it, he must sign a paper. I don't know if he will be capable of signing it. I am awaiting the return of my lawyer Dina, who is out of town, to assemble a family council and proceed to a declaration, at this point inevitable, of incompetence, and to select a guardian.

Our poor friend has two hundred thousand lire of his own soundly invested, the sacrosanct fruit of the tireless work of a whole life and of virtuous saving! The irony of human foresight!

I thank you, dear Maestro, for having sent me the telegram that announced your departure for Sant'Agata. I believe this letter will find you back in Genoa. I also thank you for having courteously received the person I recommended.

Many affectionate greetings to you and to the good Signora Giuseppina.

Yours affectionately,
A. Boito

⚯Faccio was taken to the Villa dei Boschetti, a private asylum in Monza, about half an hour by train from Milan. His father, who was also suffering from syphilitic dementia, was already confined there. He survived his son.

Thursday [Genoa, 17 April 1890]

150 Dear Boito,

On arriving yesterday evening I found your letter.

Unfortunately, any word is now useless.

Better to die!

About the Parma matter, it seems to me there is something that should be said. It is a very delicate question. We will talk about it when I come to Milan in the near future.

Be well. I greet you for Pepp. and I shake your hands.

Affectionately,
G. Verdi

Friday [Milan, 18 April 1890]

151 Dear Maestro,

In the name of Faccio and for Faccio I accepted from the governor of the Parma Conservatory only the part of his check that represented the salary from the ministry, and I rejected the part representing the stipend from the city of Parma. I did this after having repeatedly asked for assurance that the money I was accepting for my friend was his by right, and I was pressed to accept it by the insistence of the governor of the conservatory himself. It is the salary for a trimester, namely, one and a half thousand lire, which from the ministry's treasury has accumulated in the treasury of the conservatory.

Did I do the right thing or not? If not, tell me; there is still time to remedy the situation.

Affectionate greetings

from your
affectionate
Arrigo

P.S. I know that *La Lombardia* has reprinted from a Parma newspaper a reply of mine to the governor of the conservatory, in which there is a word of hope for our friend's health. I must tell you that this answer of mine was in an official letter, and therefore I did not think it correct to make the whole truth public.

I told the entire truth to the same governor when I saw him, and I urged him also to go to Dr. De Vincenti, so that he might obtain more exact information on Faccio's illness by consulting the doctor who is taking care of him.

Yours most affectionately,
Arrigo

Genoa, 20 April 1890

152

Dear Boito,

This is a personal opinion of mine! Nothing more... It seems to me that poor Faccio is no longer entitled to the Parma salary. Before the doctors had pronounced the dreadful sentence, as he was the appointed though not yet functioning director, he could *demand*; but now, I think not. I am not talking about rights: it is a delicate question. In any case, I repeat, this is only my opinion.

I have seen your letter! But, my dear Boito, in the future speak in your own name, and omit his family, the principal, if not the only, cause of the great misfortune.

I went yesterday evening to *Orfeo*. La Har—— (Orfeo) has talent: disjointed voice with twenty registers and without *charme*. The second act is truly beautiful. Hearing it, I could only confirm my feeling that the Germans must remain Germans, and the Italians, Italians. Even then, a period when only melody existed in the theater, or, more precisely, melodic phrases, the German was more successful with the instrumental part, despite the limited possibilities of the orchestra at that time. In this same second act the Choruses of the Demons and the dances are powerful; but the notes that Orfeo sings, accompanying himself on the lyre, are missing something. He could never find a calm, broad melody, with suitable feeling. Instead, phrases tormented by modulations (the modulations of that time), and cold.

We'll meet soon in Milan, and greetings from us.

Be well.
G. Verdi

I haven't finished.

I told you of the conversation I had with Maurel. Well, he's wasted no time: he has turned to Coquelin, who has immediately sent him a sketch for a work drawn from... *Shakespeare!* When I read that name in the letter I had an attack of the shudders! Luckily it was not *Falstaff*... The very extended sketch is taken from *The Taming of the Shrew*. It is not badly done: they have cut the prologue and have given important parts to Katharina and Petruchio, namely, to the tamed Shrew and the Tamer. It's not up to *Falstaff*—not on your life.

Forgive the long letter.

&sGluck's *Orfeo ed Euridice* was given eight performances in the spring of 1890 at the Teatro Carlo Felice in Genoa. The Orfeo was Elena Harstreiter.

Maurel had apparently suggested to the French actor Constant-Benoît Coquelin (1841–1909) that he adapt a Shakespearian comedy. Clearly, Verdi was worried that a successful production of a play involving Falstaff might somehow lessen the impact of his own *Falstaff*. When Coquelin brought his *Taming of the Shrew* to Milan in February of 1892, Boito sent his impressions to Verdi (see letter no. 189 below).

[Milan] 21 May [1890]

153 Dear Maestro,

The day before yesterday, all of a sudden, came a bolt from the blue: a letter from Commendatore Mariotti announcing my appointment (already signed by the king) as honorary director of the Parma Conservatory. Who could have expected such a thing? I had to bow my head beneath the blow. He who bows his head is saying yes. I have accepted. In his letter Mariotti explains to me how the thing went. That worthy and most affable Mariotti is a force of nature, not a man; his vigor sweeps all before it. So then, the sudden event came about like this:

It seems there was a renewed pressure to appoint in Parma that certain Neapolitan musician that you know. At the first hint of this threat Mariotti left for Rome, persuaded the minister to add an article to the statutes of the Parma Conservatory allowing for an honorary director, mentioned my name, had the decrees drafted, and informed me when all was done. For that matter, I had already arranged to pay a thorough visit to that institution; but I realize this appointment will now oblige me to make more than one and thus to substitute somehow, from time to time, for poor Faccio, whose salary (and also on this point the good Mariotti was vigorous and unyielding) will continue to be paid. Meanwhile the threat of the Neapolitan musician has been deferred.

I will be in Parma on Monday, and before the following week (next week, that is) ends I will come and spend a day at Sant'Agata on my return from the conservatory visit.

So then, dear Maestro, before we meet again soon, prepare some new bit from Big Belly for me to hear!

By the way, the variant necessary for the final fugue is still lacking. See if what I transcribe for you on the back of this letter will do.

Everything in the world is jest
Man is born a jester.
In his brain his reason
Is always reeling.
All mocked! All mortals
Taunt one another,
But he laughs well who has
The last laugh.

Affectionate greetings to Signora Giuseppina and to you. Till we meet. I will wire you the day of my arrival. Where shall I get off: Fiorenzuola? Alseno?

> Yours affectionately,
> A. Boito

P.S. Look at the nonsense in the papers: *La tribuna* in Rome says that *you* had repeatedly offered me the directorship of the Parma Conservatory and that I had refused.

Those reporters are unable to write anything correct.

But *La perseveranza* is a proper paper: they have just sent me (at this very moment) the article, already prepared, taken from *La tribuna,* so that I can look it over, and I have cut the error from the proofs. Again

> yours affectionately,
> A. Boito

❧The Neapolitan composer was Paolo Serrao (1830–1907), professor of composition at the Naples Conservatory, where his pupils included Cilea, Leoncavallo, Giordano, Martucci, and Mugnone. Boito considered him a "threat" only to Faccio's position (and much-needed salary).

Boito's variant of the final fugue underwent further revision. See letter no. 202 below.

Sant'Agata, 23 May 1890

154

Dear Boito,

You did exactly the right thing! You will be helping both Art and the poor sick man, and you have saved the institution from harm. As for your earlier refusal, let the papers talk all the nonsense they like. That's their business, and anyway it's a matter of no importance.

As for Big Belly, alas, alas! I have done nothing!!... *"Man is born lazy"*... except for an occasional detail added or changed in what was already done. But we will talk about all of this at Sant'Agata.

The most convenient train from Parma is the one that leaves at *12* and arrives at Alseno at 12:56. The train trip is a bit longer, but you save almost half an hour of carriage. Write me or wire me from Parma the day before you come to Sant'Agata, and you will find the carriage at *1:56* at the Alseno station.

Be well. No, no, *sans adieu.*

Till we meet!

Affectionately,
G. Verdi

Peppina has just come into my room and she wants me to greet you.
Amen.

    ◀sProbably written in haste, Verdi's letter contains an obvious slip of the pen: it is unlikely that he would have made Boito wait an hour in the Alseno station before the arrival of his carriage.

After this visit, there is a long silence in the correspondence. Boito was concerned with Faccio's illness and, at the same time, with his own love affair with Duse (they again spent part of that summer together at San Giuseppe). Verdi stopped in Milan on his way to and from Montecatini in late June and mid-July, so it is possible that he and Boito met then.

"Man is born lazy" is a quotation, slightly altered, from *Falstaff.* Instead of "L'uom è nato burlone" ("Man is born a jester"), Verdi writes "L'uom è nato poltrone."

3 October [1890]
Milan

155   Dear Maestro,

It's been a century since I had news of you or of Signora Giuseppina, and since I had news of Big Belly.

I will come and collect the news personally in a couple of weeks. I will be at Sant'Agata on the 18th of this month; I will be coming from Parma on the train that arrives at Alseno at 1:59, as I did last time.

I am now staying in Milan a couple of days because of poor Faccio, who grows progressively worse. The day after tomorrow I will return to Ivrea (San Giuseppe), where I will remain until the 12th of this month. Then I must go to Parma, and from Parma, as I said, I will stop off at Sant'Agata to breathe in a bit of peaceful air and art.

This world is a mass of sorrows: the condition of our friend becomes increasingly dire, his aged father threatens to pass away, he is very ill...

We must see to it that we remain healthy, dear Maestro, as long as we can, and that, in working, we forget about life.

We'll meet then on the 18th.

I will wire you confirmation from Parma.

Affectionate greetings to Signora Giuseppina and to you.

> Yours affectionately,
> A. Boito

᎙Visits to Faccio were severely limited, but at one point that summer, Romilda Pantaleoni managed to elude the doctors and guards and visit him with a woman friend. She sent an account to her mother: "We waited in the driveway where he customarily takes his walk, and I met him!... *Everyone* claims he no longer remembers anyone. That may be so, but he recognized me *at once,* and was moved; and he held me tight when it was time for me to leave and he wouldn't let go of me... not until I promised I would visit him again soon! I will never forget his deep, impassioned gaze as he looked at me! And as we walked a little way together, he talked to me, calling me the sweetest names! [. . .] I shall never, never be reconciled to not having the right to care for him and console him in these last months left of his life... for they say he has *only months* still in this world..." [CVB, p. 402].

Sant'Agata, 6 October 1890

156

Dear Boito,

Divinely good! We will see each other then on the 18th, and we will talk about many things!

I have worked little, but I have done something.

I was being tortured by the sonnet in the third act; and to rid myself of this nagging, I set the second act aside and, beginning with that sonnet, I went on, one note after the other, until I reached the end.

It's only a draft! And who knows how much will have to be redone! We will see later.

Thieving world. Rascally world
Evil world!... He says!

I know, and, alas, I knew it thirty years before you.

That poor Faccio! It was less than a year ago that he came here and, strolling in the garden late, I spoke to him frankly, sincerely, also perhaps a bit harshly, and now I reproach myself for those words...

Thieving world!...

Till we meet again soon.
I greet you for Peppina and I affectionately shake your hands.

Yours,
G. Verdi

✒The quotation is from the beginning of act 3 of *Falstaff*.

After the October visit to Sant'Agata, Boito and Verdi probably met in Milan the following month, as Verdi spend several days there on his way to Genoa. It was a sad time for the composer: on 14 November his lifelong friend and regular correspondent Giuseppe Piroli died in Rome; and on 27 November Emanuele Muzio died in Paris. Like Piroli, he was a native of Busseto.

In late November the composition of *Falstaff* was publicly revealed in the *Corriere della sera* and then confirmed by Ricordi's *Gazzetta musicale di Milano,* causing the predictable stir.

Tuesday, Milan [9 December 1890]

157 Dear Maestro,

I recognize that name. It is my Lily, my old Lily, whom I too thought to be a man the first time she wrote me, ten years ago, to ask me for a seat at the premiere of *Nerone!!!*

That English name, appropriate for a lapdog, has remained in my memory. Lily, correspondent of the *Daily News,* daughter of a wolf of the breed of Israel, lived in Naples even then.

I replied to *Monsieur Lily* (!) agreeing to give him the seat requested in such haste. Then Lily wrote me a second time to thank me and to reveal to me her sex and her age (mature) and her status. It seemed she wanted to initiate a lifelong correspondence with me.

I said *Enough,* and didn't reply afterwards.

The best thing is not to reply.

They write to you, dear Maestro, and they make use of your name to create their own *réclame* and the *réclame* of the paper they write for.

Thieving world! Evil world!

I return Lily's letter to you.

I will delay my trip to Nervi, I will postpone it until towards the middle of January. For that period I promise myself a great treat, which will be to hear the entire first part of the second act of Big Belly.

Affectionate greetings to Signora Giuseppina and to you.

Yours,
A. Boito

᳁Lily Wolffsohn ("daughter of a wolf," Boito calls her) had written Verdi asking for an advance look at the libretto of *Falstaff,* with the purpose of publishing a pre-performance summary of it in the *Daily News.* Verdi evidently sent her letter to Boito with a request for further information in a letter now lost.

[Milan] 31 December 1890

158

Dear Maestro,

You should begin the year smiling, and this is why I send you a letter from the good Zorzi of Vicenza, received this morning, informing me that the historic cane is already in order.

Good and happy wishes to you and to Signora Giuseppina.

Yours most affectionately,
A. Boito

᳁Member of an ancient Venetian family, Count Andrea Zorzi was an admirer of Verdi from the early days. He had a cane with a silver handle, on which—beginning with *Ernani,* the premiere of which he attended in Venice in 1843—he had engraved the titles of Verdi's new works as he heard them. The handle gradually had to be lengthened. Verdi was fond of this noble eccentric.

Genoa, 1 January 1891

159

Dearest Boito,

Let's laugh then!

That poor Zorzi is definitely mad! And he considers Big Belly as something finished, to be put on that curious cane of his, which by now must be completely termite-infested!

To you, too (also from Peppina), good and happy wishes, and I will add just one word...

Finish!

Big Belly does not proceed. I am troubled and distracted... The very sad past months, the present cold, the holidays, etc., etc., have put me off.

Yours affectionately,
G. Verdi

🖙Verdi's peremptory "Finish!" refers to Boito's *Nerone.*

[Milan] 19 March [1891]

160   Dear Signora Giuseppina,

My best wishes on this day to you and to the Maestro, to the Maestro and to you, distributed in strictly equal portions.

I had news of you from the Ricordis and I learned that on arriving in Genoa you would not allow yourself to be carried in a palanquin, and this news did not surprise me. I know that your aversion to doctors prevented you from consulting one, and this news too did not surprise me.

Today I am writing you for two reasons: first of all because I enjoy writing to you, and second so as not to burden the Maestro with yet another letter. But I beg you, I beg you seriously not to answer me, otherwise my precaution would provoke another error, that of making you bear the burden.

I have seen the watercolor, which by now will have arrived in Genoa. It seemed to me masterfully done. The characterization of Falstaff approaches closely what I had imagined, except that I would like him to be even heavier and with hair and beard less white. I don't know if the Maestro is of the same opinion. Please greet him fondly, as I greet you, with all my heart.

Your most devoted
A. Boito

🖙Boito's "best wishes" refer to the feast of St. Joseph, 19 March (see note following letter no. 42). The Verdis had previously been in Milan for almost a month, from early February to early March, while the ailing Giuseppina was treated by Dr. Todeschini. Hence the silence in the correspondence.

The watercolor was by Adolph Hohenstein (1854–1928), a Russian-born painter who had settled in Milan in the 1880s. He soon became artistic director of the poster department of Casa Ricordi. He was to design sets and costumes for *Falstaff*, and he did a famous, harrowing series of deathbed drawings of Verdi.

Genoa, 21 March 1891

161

Dear Boito,

Thank you for the good wishes, and I thank you also for Peppina in case she hasn't answered you: you gave her your permission.

I have received Falstaff (the watercolor). It is handsome, distinctive, but you are right to say he should be a little fatter (not much) and his beard and hair should be less white. I would add then that with those sleepy eyes, he has the appearance of a man dead drunk. Falstaff should not be obese, not a drunkard, since he always has so much wit. Further, the waistcoat and the trousers in that style are not three hundred years old; they are too modern. But these observations are pointless at present, we will have plenty of time to talk about this. Unfortunately, we will have time! How much time I have lost! I still haven't been able to warm up the engine!

Tell me meanwhile if you want the word "Windsor" accented on the first or on the second syllable!

For ex., in the verse:

C'è a Vindsor una donna...
[In Windsor there's a woman...]

the accent seems to be on the first.

In this other verse:

Gaje comari di Vindsor! È l'ora!
[Merry wives of Windsor! Now's the time!]

the accent seems to be on the second; unless you want an *endecasillabo* with the accent on the seventh.

Decide as you like.

Be well. Always your

affectionate
G. Verdi

The first verse quoted by Verdi ("C'è a Vindsor...") is sung by Ford in act 2, part 1 of *Falstaff*. The other verse ("Gaje comari...") is sung by Alice in act 2, part 2.

Sunday [Milan, 22 or 29 March 1891]

162   Dear Maestro,

     Wìndsor. Like this:

Gàje comàri di Wìndsor è l'ora, etc.

It is exactly what you say, an *endecasillabo* with the accent on the seventh, and the word Wìndsor in this way is correctly accented. I don't believe that in the whole English language there is a word that is accented on the last syllable. Ask Signora Giuseppina if this rule can be established. I haven't seen it in any grammar book, but I believe it is correct.

And here I must confess that once, in your libretto, I have broken this rule, just once, and it is in a verse not very far from the one mentioned, and it is where Falstaff says:

Quand'ero paggio
Del Duca di Norfolk ero sottile, ecc., ecc.
[When I was page
To the Duke of Norfolk I was slim, etc., etc.]

The nature of this verse would put the accent on the sixth, whereas the word Nòrfolk is accented on the first syllable like Wìndsor and Fàlstaff, etc.

I have tried several times to correct this verse; but if I fixed the accent I spoiled the verse, and I preferred, between the two evils, to falsify the accent of the word.

Meanwhile I note that you have already arrived with the music at the verse "Merry wives of Windsor, now's the time," and this consoles me with the thought that the engine is already beginning to warm up; a few pages further and you will see the engine is already boiling and then: Forward! *à toute vapeur!* and then the four months lost will be recovered in a week. I am quite sure of this.

Your remarks about the watercolor are in total agreement with mine.

Most cordial greetings to Signora Giuseppina. I hope that rest is the best treatment for her knees.

    To you, dear Maestro, a warm handshake

from your
A. Boito

P.S. Here we have had a ruckus because of Chiarina Faccio, who wanted to take her father to Trieste. We have prevented it.

⸗Chiarina Faccio, the conductor's younger sister, was married to a man named Piero Fabricci from Trieste. They were much resented by Boito, Romilda Pantaleoni, and Faccio's other friends.

Saturday, Milan [25 April 1891]

Dear Maestro,

163

If, on your way back to Sant'Agata, you were to stop for a day in Milan, on that day the conductor of the orchestra of La Scala would be born and our beautiful theater would be saved. I would bring our friend Bazzini to the Hôtel Milan, and the three of us, conversing in perfect accord, would resolve the question that is so pressing and is the most important in everything that concerns the reorganization of La Scala.

The municipal committee is so convinced of the supreme importance of this problem that they would like to see it resolved in the best possible way.

The best possible way is this one I am proposing to you: a conscientious conversation among you, Bazzini, and me.

Negri, who is the good man you know him to be, has insisted very much that I should write you these things.

Any other arrangement would be defective.

If a public competition were announced, only the mediocre would compete.

If the choice of the conductor were left to the management, it would be an imprudent move, worse than imprudent.

The theater committee does not have the artistic competence necessary to decide on such a serious question.

The city administration is in the same position. Publishers must not participate. So who should then?

So here I am, required to write you this letter.

Warmest greetings to you and many good wishes to Signora Giuseppina.

Yours most affectionately,
A. Boito

⸗The enforced absence of Faccio from La Scala and the arrival of a new impresario there meant that a chief conductor had to be appointed urgently. The city had authorized Boito to get in touch with Verdi and to draft the composer Antonio Bazzini (1818–1897), director of the Milan Conservatory (his pupils had included Catalani and Puccini), to arrive at the best choice. The prospect of the *Falstaff* premiere made the decision all the more vital.

Genoa, 26 April 1891

164 Dear Boito,

I have to go immediately to Sant'Agata for business of mine, and I could not come now to Milan. The suitcases are being packed; and tomorrow morning the servants will leave, and the next day at 7 in the morning we will set off, arriving at Sant'Agata around 3 P.M.

For that matter, I could not be very useful to you in the choice of a conductor of the orchestra of La Scala. Since I go infrequently to the theater, I don't know the best conductors... neither the two Mancinellis nor Mascheroni. In any case, I would never be of the opinion to have a competition. A conductor is judged on the *podium*.

I will write you again tomorrow if I have a bit of time, or else as soon as I arrive at Sant'Agata.

I greet you for Peppina and affectionately shake your hands. Be well.

Affectionately,
G. Verdi

Luigi Mancinelli (1848–1921) and Marino Mancinelli (1842–1894) were both composers and conductors. Marino had conducted, among other important works, the Italian premiere (in translation) of Wagner's *Der fliegende Holländer* (Bologna, 1877); he committed suicide in Rio de Janeiro, after a theatrical venture had gone bankrupt. Luigi's compositions include a setting of Boito's *Ero e Leandro* (also set by Bottesini). He was conductor at the Teatro Comunale in Bologna from 1879 to 1886, as well as founder of the local Società del Quartetto. It is likely that Verdi is being disingenuous in saying he was unfamiliar with his work; Luigi had conducted a memorable *Aida* in 1879 and had received the composer's congratulations.

Edoardo Mascheroni (1859–1941) was also a composer as well as conductor. He had conducted several of Verdi's works and the Italian premiere of Beethoven's *Fidelio* (1886). Largely thanks to Verdi's influence (see the letter below), he was appointed to the post at La Scala and thus conducted the first *Falstaff*.

[Genoa] 27 April 1891

165

... So, as I wrote you yesterday, since I don't know the best conductors, I can't talk about them. The biggest reputations are the two Mancinellis and Mascheroni.

I believe there would be no hope of getting Luigi... Between the other two I would choose Mascheroni, whose qualities, I am told, include that of being a great worker (an indispensable quality at La Scala), a conscientious man without special likes and, better still, without dislikes.

The conductor must be made entirely independent of the management and he must be given complete musical responsibility, regardless of the committee, the management, and the public. He should choose the chorus master, to whom not only the music instruction should be entrusted, but also the stage instruction. The chorus master, or his assistant, should further be obliged to dress in costume during the performances and sing with the choruses.

La Scala absolutely needs a stage director of great ability. There has never been one in that theater, but the demands of today's productions require one urgently.

Finally, the program of productions must be clear and precise, and the operas should not be chosen at random as they have been these last few years, nor should the management engage the first singers who come along. Either choose the singers for the operas, or the operas for the singers. Companies should be complete and engaged for the whole season; and two operas should be staged for the opening, etc. In this way the ill humor of the public would be avoided: ill humor that then lasts throughout the whole season.

Everything would go well, but... there is always a *but*... everything lies in finding the MAN!

Don't pay too much attention to what I have said, because I have said it privately to you.

Write me at Sant'Agata, where I will arrive tomorrow at three.

Be well.

Affectionately,
G. Verdi

29 April [1891]
Milan

166

Dear Maestro,

Since you cannot be a part of that committee that will select the conductor of the Scala orchestra, we will have to compensate in numbers for the authority lacking because of your absence.

The committee will consist of five composers: Bazzini, Martucci, Catalani, Gomes, and me.

I will do all I can to have Mascheroni named, but I cannot guarantee (one against four, if the other four do not agree with me), I cannot guarantee the result of the election.

You would have to authorize me to read to the committee the following words of your letter: "I would choose Mascheroni, whose qualities, I am told, include that of being a great worker (an indispensable quality at La Scala), a conscientious man without special likes and, better still, without dislikes."

These words, which I have copied from your letter, if read at the appropriate moment, could tip the scales in Mascheroni's favor.

But if you do not authorize me to say them, I will not say them; but then I will be lacking a very powerful weapon for victory.

I want Big Belly to find La Scala organized in the best possible way.

The reorganization committee has done a good job, and our work is in full agreement with the ideas of your letter.

The elimination of the fifth row of boxes is an excellent decision. It frees the theater of a part of the audience that by age-old tradition was distracted, bored, and unruly, and puts in its place a great gallery of middle-class spectators who will pay very little and, once the opportunity arises, will enjoy themselves very much.

The gallery public is today the best audience at La Scala, and this audience, should we destroy the fifth row of boxes, will be doubled from now on. I await a further word from you.

I am thinking that in the peace of the country Big Belly must put on a lot of weight. Affectionate greetings.

Yours,

A. Boito

◄For Bazzini, see note to letter no. 163.

Giuseppe Martucci (1856–1909), conductor, pianist, composer, conducted the Italian premiere of *Tristan* at the Teatro Comunale in Bologna (1888), where he was also director of the *liceo musicale.* In 1902 he became director of the Naples Conservatory.

Alfredo Catalani (1854–1893) studied first in his native Lucca with Fortunato Magi, uncle and also first teacher of Giacomo Puccini. In Milan, Catalani studied with Bazzini. His graduation piece was the one-act opera *La falce,* libretto by Boito (1875). He was a close friend of Toscanini, who conducted the premiere of *La Wally* (1892), Catalani's most successful work. At the time of this letter he was professor of composition at the Milan Conservatory.

Carlos Gomes (1836–1896) was Brazilian, but studied in Milan and wrote his most successful works there, notably *Il Guarany* (1870) and *Salvator Rosa* (1874), for Italian theaters.

Sant'Agata, 1 May 1891

167

Dear Boito,

There is no harm in reading those few lines of mine to the committee, advising them, however, that I do not know those conductors except personally and by name, nor do I mean therefore to express an opinion. I repeat that, since we are unable to have Luigi Mancinelli, between the other two, the better, especially for La Scala, is Mascheroni.

Excellent the decision to do away with the fifth tier. The gallery public, namely the public that allows itself to be moved, and manifests its impressions sincerely, is the true public. The other, posing as *blasé,* acting the *savant,* passes judgment, and talks about the Future, modernity, idealism, *verismo,* the classic, etc., etc... God help us! And now also program music?!... But all music must have a program: that is, it must produce sensations in the people who listen to it, according to age, period, and nationality (and herein lies the true power of music).

Music that does not have this program is bad; but music that *imposes* a program is even worse! Oh, how I am running on!!

Big Belly? Poor thing! After that illness of four months he is skinny, so skinny! Let's hope to find some fat capon to swell his belly again!... Everything depends on the doctor!... Who knows?... Who knows? Greetings and more greetings.

Affectionately,
G. Verdi

[Milan] 2 May [1891]

168

Dear Maestro,

Thank you for your authorization; I will put it to the most opportune use and it will help.

And to reply to what you say, continuing your letter, I will add that those who impose a program on music deny the divine essence of that art.

Around the middle of this month I will go to Parma; then, as usual, I will stop over at Sant'Agata, and that will be around the twentieth or, more probably, it will be the twenty-first.

If the weather is fine and if you feel like it, we will make an excursion to that handsome ancient cloister Mariotti told me about.

Till we meet again soon, then, and many warm greetings to Signora Giuseppina and an affectionate handshake to you.

Yours affectionately,
A. Boito

☙Performing his duties as honorary—or acting—director of the conservatory, Boito went to Parma in mid-May to see how suitably prepared the students were for the forthcoming examinations.

The cloister Boito mentions is probably the Abbey of Fontevivo; whether or not he and Verdi visited it is not known.

Sant'Agata, 5 May 1891

169 Dear Boito,

Very good! We'll meet on the 21st then. You will tell me later whether I should send a carriage to meet you at *Borgo,* or at *Alseno,* or at *Fiorenzuola.*

Greetings from Peppina and a handshake from your
affectionate
G. Verdi

☙Boito spent two days at Sant'Agata, during which visit he read Verdi the libretto of *Nerone.* Verdi, writing to Ricordi, defined it as "splendid" and "theatrical," in the good sense [CVB, p. 409].

[Milan] 28 May [1891]

170 Dear Maestro,

I have visited the "terryble" Mr. Terry, who has promised me to dedicate all the learning of his most delicate hands to Signora Giuseppina and to you. I warn you, however, that bookings for the treatments of the eminent odontologist are made several days in advance; I, for example, had to reserve yesterday for next Tuesday, as if for a Rubinstein concert.

The impresario of La Scala is Piontelli; I would have preferred the Cortis.

The conductor of the orchestra will be Mascheroni, engaged for a year; if, as is hoped, he works out well, the contract will be extended.

I have no other news to give you.

I hope the devil is riding at Sant'Agata on the bow of a violin, and that you, dear Maestro, are very busy with the laundry hamper.

Finally today the sun promises to last, making me hope that Signora Barberina can regain her health and go down into the garden. I beg you to give her my friendly greeting and to greet warmly Signora Giuseppina.

To you, dear Maestro, a warm handshake, in the hope of meeting again soon.

Yours most affectionately,
A. Boito

&s Despite her perennial ailments, the "Signora Barberina" (actually signorina), Giuseppina's valetudinarian sister Barberina Strepponi, survived both Verdis.

"The devil is riding [. . .] on the bow of a violin" is a reference to *Falstaff*, act 2, part 2 ("Il diavolo cavalca / Sull'arco di un violino!!"). The laundry hamper refers to the conclusion of the same act.

[Milan] 29 May [1891]

171

Dear Maestro,

Today I write you to tell you I have received from the good Vellani a letter full of warm gratitude for the autograph you have given the library of the *liceo musicale* of Bologna. Vellani, who is an innocent and very simple soul, lacks the courage to thank you directly, he is afraid of annoying you by obligating you to read the expression of his gratitude; so he charges me to act in his stead, which I do with the greatest pleasure. But to Vellani's thanks I add also my own, because you were so prompt to grant my plea that I cannot help but thank you.

I wrote you also yesterday a letter that, like this one today, expects no answer.

You must not waste time uselessly with correspondence. You have to deal with the laundry.

Dear Maestro, I hope to see you again soon, and affectionate greetings to all.

Yours,
A. Boito

&s Federico Vellani was secretary of the *liceo musicale* of Bologna and largely responsible for the reorganization and cataloguing of its important library. Like others, he made use of Boito as a go-between—in requesting an autograph for the *liceo* collection—with the notoriously intransigent Verdi.

[Milan] 9 June [1891]

172   Dear Maestro,

Yesterday evening I heard a true alto voice at the Dal Verme in *La Cenerentola*, a certain Guerrina Fabbri, pupil of la Galletti. An ample voice, secure pitch, resonant without forcing, and in the middle notes so beautiful that it recalls that of la Alboni.

A fair *comédienne* and, when necessary, lively; fair musical delivery; fair pronunciation. This singer should not be judged in *La Cenerentola* because she seems unaware, completely unaware, of Rossinian style. But I believe she could become a very good Quickly. When you come to Milan you will hear and judge, and perhaps you will find in that Dal Verme company some other performer worth consideration.

Giulio showed me yesterday a passage in a letter of yours, and it gave me the keenest joy. When I have your approval, dear Maestro, in matters of art and in those of life, I am sure of not erring and I ask no other reward.

Camillo left for Rome before I had time to read him the libretto because I wanted to read it to him all neatly copied out and with those two cuts that you advise. The cut in the second act works well; it has been done and is very helpful. I am abbreviating the fourth a little.

Giulio tells me that Signora Barberina still has a bit of fever and this news saddens me. I beg you to greet her warmly for me.

Many affectionate greetings to you, dear Maestro, and to Signora Giuseppina.

Yours most affectionately,
A. Boito

◄sGuerrina Fabbri (1868–1946) did not create the role of Quickly, but she later sang it with great success at La Scala in 1906 (under Mugnone) and in 1913 (under Toscanini).

Isabella Galletti Gianoli (1835–1901), mezzosoprano. Her career was cut short by a throat ailment, but she had a long and successful second career as a teacher.

Marietta Alboni (1826–1894), celebrated contralto, a favorite of Rossini. Her range was so exceptional that, on one occasion, she sang the baritone role in Verdi's *Ernani*.

The letter Giulio showed Boito is the one mentioned above (see note following letter no. 169) concerning the libretto of *Nerone.*

Constructed on the site of an earlier theater, the Teatro Dal Verme in this period was the most modern in Milan. Both plays and operas were given there. Puccini's *Le willis* (later *Le villi*) had its premiere there in 1884, and Leoncavallo's *Pagliacci* in 1892, conducted by Toscanini, starring Maurel.

Sant'Agata, 12 June 1891

173

Dear Boito,

If you have discovered a good Quickly I am the happiest man on earth. I have devoted much thought to that part, for besides the dramatic interest, the music has a very low tessitura. I could not do otherwise. Since there are four women's parts, at least one has to be low.

Big Belly is on the road that leads to madness. There are days when he doesn't move, sleeps, and is ill-tempered; at other times he shouts, runs, leaps, makes a great rumpus... I let him frisk a bit, but if he persists, I will put a muzzle on him and a straitjacket.

Barberina is better, she is getting up, and has been dining with us for three or four days.

Peppina greets you and I shake your hand affectionately.

Yours,

G. Verdi

[Milan] 14 June [1891]

174

Dear Maestro,

Hurrah! Give him free rein, let him run; he will break all the window panes and all the furniture of your room, no matter, you will buy others; he will smash the piano, no matter, you will buy another—let everything be turned topsy-turvy! but the *great scene* will be done! Hurrah!

Harder! Harder! Harder! Harder!
What pandemonium!!!

But a pandemonium clear as the sun and dizzying as a house full of lunatics!!

I know already what you will do. Hurrah!

I guarantee Quickly. Down to *low G* the voice is excellent, and the *middle* is beautiful.

I am very, very pleased to hear that Signora Barberina is better. Greet her warmly for me, along with Signora Giuseppina.

A warm handshake

from your most affectionate
A. Boito

❧In mid-June, Verdi and Giuseppina stopped in Milan for about two weeks before continuing on to Montecatini. In an interview Verdi granted to Ricordi for the *Gazzetta musicale di Milano* the official announcement of the construction of the Casa di Riposo per Musicisti was made. Verdi also said that, although he was working on *Falstaff,* he had not yet finished it, and had no definite plans about its premiere.

The apparent quotation from *Falstaff* is not to be found in the actual libretto.

Montecatini, 5 July 1891

175   Dear Boito,

I return *Le rêve* and I thank you. There are some good intentions... but with good intentions, they say, Hell is paved!

In this opera there are no spoken recitatives, no word repetitions, no *couplets,* no motivic reprises, nor many other formulas so much in use especially at the Opéra-Comique! All this is fine; but less fine is the fact that all the action is contained and strangled in the circle of three or four—I won't call them motives, but orchestral phrases that keep recirculating throughout the opera, without the relief of a little vocal melody. And yet in the drama, though it was not entirely suitable for music, there was no lack of moments to create this. On page 28 there are six verses delivered by the Bishop: "Heureuse heureuse enfant," etc., etc., and later a scene between the Bishop and Angélique... and another between the Bishop and his son, and still others, where some heartfelt, dramatic, simple music could have been written, without so many orchestral curlicues that are not beautiful and, worse, are useless. There is also throughout the opera a constant use of slurred notes, with an effect that must be quite monotonous. Further, a frightful abuse of dissonances that make you want to shout, like Falstaff, *"a brief respite"* of a simple triad! What a lot of blather!

Here all goes well. Yesterday's *orage* has cooled the air, and today we get along nicely...

Peppina greets you and I shake your hand.

Affectionately,
G. Verdi

◄§Boito may have given Verdi the score of Alfred Bruneau's opera *Le rêve* (Opéra-Comique, 18 June 1891) in Milan. Bruneau (1857–1934) was also a distinguished critic and an admirer of Verdi.

Sant'Agata, 23 July 1891

176

Dear Boito,

He too is gone! Poor Faccio!

Yesterday, on arriving at Sant'Agata, we were all saddened by the news we found in the *Corriere!*

Though his artistic intelligence was gone and, with it, the other qualities of that good spirit, I can imagine the heartache you must have felt at this loss!

Poor Faccio was your schoolmate, companion and friend in the stormy and happy times of your youth... (And he loved you so much!) In the great misfortune that struck him, you rushed to him, giving him solemn, wondrous proof of your valid friendship. You should be content with yourself, as you have merited all praise from honest people!

Poor Faccio, so unfortunate! So talented! So good!

Farewell.

> Affectionately,
> G. Verdi

◄§Faccio died on 21 July in the asylum in Monza. Boito, returning from Venice the next morning, learned the news from Faccio's brother-in-law, whom he encountered in the station. With Faccio's sister and her husband and daughter, Boito immediately took the train for Monza.

24 July [1891]
Milan

177

Dear Maestro,

It's all over. Our friend rests in peace and has reentered the eternal normality of souls and substances. Only death could heal him, and death has truly healed him. On that face, when life had ended, the noble expression of human reason reappeared.

I telegraphed the grievous news to you at Montecatini the morning of the 22d, but from the telegraph office there in the evening I received a notice that you had left.

Today your letter, so kind, arrives to console me; thank you, dear

Maestro, thank you. And today I repeat to you what I wrote you in the spring of last year: *Better thus.*

Again many thanks, and my affectionate greetings to Signora Giuseppina.

To you a grateful handshake from your

most affectionate
A. Boito

 ◆sFaccio's death did not liberate Boito immediately from his duties at the Parma Conservatory. He was promptly offered the position of director, but he rejected it and—with Verdi—successfully urged the candidacy of Giuseppe Gallignani, then music director of the Milan Cathedral.

Giuseppe Gallignani (1851–1923) composed seven operas, of which five were performed, but his greatest achievement was in the field of sacred music. He ended his tenure as director of the Parma Conservatory in 1897 to become head of the Milan Conservatory. In 1923, unwilling to join the Fascist Party and refusing to resign his post, he was unjustly accused of embezzlement and committed suicide.

3 September [1891]
Milan

178   Dear Maestro,

It's been a century since I had the pleasure of writing you.

Now Gallignani offers me the opportunity: he wants to be escorted to Sant'Agata by a letter of mine. Here it is. Mariotti, a month ago, offered me the directorship of the Parma Conservatory; I didn't accept, but he wouldn't take no for an answer.

He returned ten or twelve days ago to repeat the invitation; I didn't accept, but Mariotti wouldn't take no for an answer. He went off to Rome, with a plan that Maestro Gallignani will tell you about, and he wouldn't take no for an answer.

Meanwhile, this unwillingness of Mariotti to resign himself to my refusal can facilitate the activity of other influences much feared by the same Mariotti, and this would be a disaster. To prevent this disaster, Maestro Gallignani must be helped to become director of the Parma Conservatory.

Gallignani will ask you, dear Maestro, for a letter to Commendatore Mariotti, I will write him another, in which I will repeat with a final and firm stroke my refusal; thus Maestro Gallignani, we hope, will be named director.

Many, many greetings to Signora Giuseppina and to you, dear Maestro, and till we meet again in October.

Yours most affectionately,
A. Boito

Sant'Agata, 5 September 1891

179

Dear Boito,

Gallignani, as you now know, did not find Mariotti in Parma. He was unable to discover where he is. He left my letter to be given to him when he returns.

Now Gallignani wants a letter of mine for the minister. This, in my opinion, would be a misstep! In this way Mariotti would be passed by; and that would be wrong. Moreover, I am convinced that when Mariotti manages to convince himself that you will not accept that position as director, he will not oppose what we (you and I) have suggested on the matter. And finally Mariotti will write me, and we will see.

From the letter Gallignani wrote me yesterday evening I see that he is very upset and nervous. Try to calm him, and tell him there is nothing to be alarmed about in this matter so far.

Many greetings from Peppina and from me. Until later... and then till we see each other in October.

Affectionately,
G. Verdi

8 September [1891]
Milan

180

Dear Maestro,

What agitated and impetuous people! Mariotti is a cyclone, and Gallignani an earthquake. I find myself between these two unleashed furies of nature, and I don't know how to save myself.

I decided to read to the earthquake the letter you wrote me, and he promised to calm down and to wait quietly for events to develop. In the event of extreme danger you will be asked to write to the minister, but only in the event of extreme danger.

Nobody knows where Mariotti has got to; Gallignani is in the presbytery of the Duomo waiting *quietly*, with feverish expectation, for news from Rome to arrive at any moment.

We shall see.

Meanwhile I have heard it said that *Falstaff* is finished. Hurrah! I can't wait till October to gorge myself.

Until we meet, then, in not too many days.

Many greetings to Signora Giuseppina and to Signora Barberina. An affectionate handshake.

Yours,
A. Boito

☙Boito had apparently seen a newspaper article announcing the completion of *Falstaff*. Ricordi published a formal denial on 20 September in the *Gazzetta musicale di Milano.*

Sant'Agata, 10 September 1891

181 My dearest Boito,

Just one word:

Correction:

It's not true that I have finished *Falstaff*. I am at work filling out the full score with everything I have done so far because I am afraid of forgetting some passages and instrumental textures. Afterwards I will do the first part of the third act... and then Amen! This part is shorter, and less difficult than the others... However, Falstaff's first recitative must be done carefully, as well as the part where the wives exit... Here what is needed is... I have to say a *motive,* which diminishes, fading into a *pianissimo,* perhaps with a solo violin in the catwalks over the stage. Why not? If now they put orchestras in the cellar, why couldn't we put a violin in the attic!!?... If I were a prophet my apostles would say... *"Oh, what a sublime idea!"... Ha ha ha ha!* What a beautiful world this is!!

Peppina and Barberina thank you, and greet you. I

[G. Verdi]

☙Only the first page of this letter survives, thus it ends in midsentence and without closing or signature.

"They put orchestras in the cellar" is a reference to Wagner's concealing the orchestra at Bayreuth—a reform of which, for that matter, Verdi elsewhere expressed his approval.

Sant'Agata, Tuesday [15 September 1891]

182 Dear Boito,

Here is Mariotti's letter, which you will return to me after having read it to *earthquake.*

You already know that Giuditta, Giulio, Tito Ricordi are here. Giulio asked me to let him read the libretto of *Falstaff*. I handed it to him, and in his room I believe all three of them have read it... No harm done. The impression was very good...

... Till we meet again.

Yours,
G. Verdi

❧"Earthquake" is Gallignani (see letter no. 180 above). Mariotti's letter to Verdi assured him that Gallignani would be appointed to the Parma post "as quickly as possible." The formal appointment came on 10 October 1891.

Tito Ricordi II (1865–1933), Giulio's son, succeeded his father in 1912 as head of the firm, but resigned in 1919.

16 September [1891]
Milan

183

Dear Maestro,

I have already taken Mariotti's letter to Gallignani. Gallignani has read it and is calm now and asks me to give you his most heartfelt thanks.

I knew the Ricordi family was at Sant'Agata and I imagined they would ask to read the libretto of *Falstaff*. I am glad their reading produced a good impression.

I am here, still enslaved by the matters poor Faccio left in my hands.

In a few days' time a new family council must be formed for the guardianship of his father; then they will have to proceed to a new inventory and other legal formalities.

Thanks to these matters, this year I have been unable to go to the country; and if I succeed (as I hope, desire, and believe I will) in taking refuge at Sant'Agata, it will not be for a long stay as I had planned. But in any case, I will arrange things so that at the very beginning of October I will be able to enjoy a bit of freedom. As soon as I am able to set the date of my arrival I will wire you.

At this point I have become more expert in courts, magistrates, and legal paper than in violins, clarinets, and trumpets.

Many warm greetings to all the inhabitants of Sant'Agata.

A warm handshake

from your most affectionate
A. Boito

3 October [1891]
Roma

184 Dear Maestro,

Gallignani, at last, has been appointed director of the Parma Conservatory. It wasn't easy!

The minister called a meeting of the music board to deliberate this and other questions, and that's why I am here, flung all the way to Rome by the earthquake Gallignani.

But finally it's finished!

I hope to be able to leave tomorrow, when we will have resolved the other questions that Villari has submitted to us. I will tell you everything later.

Meanwhile, I enjoyed myself yesterday watching the highly comical hunt for pilgrims.

Today the whole city is calm and it is raining.

For the present I will return to Milan, where the interests of Faccio's father summon me. I hope to be free soon of that nuisance as well and then, God willing, I will come to spend and enjoy several days, with our friend Falstaff, at Sant'Agata.

I will inform you of my arrival from Milan.

Many warm greetings to you, dear Maestro, and to Signora Giuseppina.

Yours most affectionately,
A. Boito

P.S. The board appointed Gallignani *unanimously* without even discussing the candidate, casting their votes on the *sole* basis of the letter that you, Maestro, wrote to Mariotti. So they should have done. Maestro Marchetti (who is a man of intelligence) took the floor first and directed the voting in this way.

    Pasquale Villari (1826–1917), the distinguished Neapolitan historian, was minister of education from February 1891 to May 1892.

    The "hunt for pilgrims" refers to a group of French tourists who defaced the tomb of Victor Emanuel II, in the Pantheon, with offensive graffiti.

    Filippo Marchetti (1831–1902) was the composer of the successful opera *Ruy Blas* (1869). From 1886 to 1901 he was director of the *liceo musicale* of the Accademia di Santa Cecilia, in Rome.

    The following silence in the correspondence may be explained by a possible visit of Boito to Sant'Agata in October, and by the fact that the Verdis spent nearly a month in Milan, from 10 November to 8 December, before settling in Genoa for the winter. Boito in this period was still occupied with the Faccio family's difficulties and with his far from easy relationship with Duse.

1 January 1892

185

Dear Maestro,

I want these first words that I write today to be addressed to you, dear Maestro, with affectionate wishes of all good things for you and for Signora Giuseppina.

Good health and best wishes for your work.

Yours most affectionately,
A. Boito

Till we meet again in February.

Genoa, 2 January 1892

186

Dear Boito,

Thank you for your kind words.

We are a bit *marotti* (as they say in Genoa). Peppina is in bed with catarrh and nausea; I am tormented by a heavy cough that racks my stomach. Let's hope things improve soon!

If you have begun the year well, continue so to its end. I wish you that with all my heart, together with Peppina.

Affectionately,
G. Verdi

❧*Marotto* is Genoese dialect for "malato" (ill).

Genoa, 23 January 1892

187

So you were ill too! Ah, this cursed influenza! Giulio, however, tells me you are better, and only a slight cough remains. But take care: these raging dry coughs last a long time. We know this from experience. Since the last days of December we have been confined indoors, almost always in bed. Peppina has been up and about for only two or three days; and I first went out in the carriage only three or four days ago! So take great, great care of the cough!

But what a grim year! How badly it has begun! Almost two months of time lost! And when I think that in Milan I worked willingly and profitably! I was hoping to continue here, too!... But no!!

Get well soon, then, and change air as soon as you can.

Be well.

Affectionately,
G. Verdi

[Milan, 23 January 1892]

188 Dear Maestro,

Good news of Signora Giuseppina is beginning to arrive and I am glad, and I hope the news gets better all the time.

I know that you, dear Maestro, have been on your feet for some days and can go out of the house.

The storm is past. I have also been ill with influenza. A week in bed and a week stuck in the house. Camillo was worse than I, but he is already perfectly recovered and also goes out. I have been going out now for three days, and I feel so well on my feet that in a couple of hours I will leave for Turin to hear *La Valchiria.*

I am curious as to what impression it will make on me and to what extent a staging can correct an artistic monstrosity by a man of great talent or make it seem beautiful. We shall see. In a fortnight I will go to Nervi and will turn up in Genoa, and we will have a long chat.

My warmest greetings to Signora Giuseppina and to you.

Yours most affectionately,
A. Boito

❧Wagner's *Die Walküre* was given its first performance in Italian at the Teatro Regio in Turin on 22 December 1891, conducted by Vittorio Maria Vanzo (1862–1945), a young musician who became something of a Wagner specialist. *Die Walküre* had been heard in Turin in German, in 1883, given by a touring company under Anton Seidl.

Wednesday [Milan, 10 February 1892]

189 Dear Maestro,

Your last note to Giulio says nothing regarding health; I choose to take this as a good sign, meaning that every trace of that most irksome *influenza* has disappeared from your house and that Signora Giuseppina is no longer suffering from seasickness, which is the worst sickness of all.

I have put off my arrival on the riviera because I could not avoid (despite all my parrying) a mission assigned me by Villari to inspect the Palermo Conservatory. So I will arrange for my trip to Sicily to follow my stay on the riviera in March. But before then, dear Maestro, it seems we are to see each other in Milan: all the better.

Yesterday evening while I was present at the *Mégère apprivoisée* I ran into Maurel. He has put on weight. Excellent! And they tell me he has never been in better voice than he is this year. I said I was present at the *Mégère apprivoisée;* I will add that I enjoyed myself very much, though in that Parisian botch the lighthearted picture created by Shakespeare has been repainted coyly and stupidly by a highly mannered *boulevardier* artist. In the first act the speeches from the original text (I counted them) are *six;* all the rest is by the adapter. Six speeches are few, and yet they suffice to create that wonderful character of Petruchio, splendidly interpreted by Coquelin.

In the following acts the share of the original text is greater, and the infelicitous additions by the French adapter do not succeed in spoiling it. All in all, the adaptation is well paced, and if the adapter had respected the dialogue there would have been little to criticize.

Many, many greetings to Signora Giuseppina, of whom I hope to hear that she is completely recovered.

Until we meet, soon.

> Yours most affectionately,
> A. Boito

📌This *Mégère apprivoisée* was the adaptation of *The Taming of the Shrew* made for Coquelin; see letter no. 152 above.

Genoa, 12 February 1892

190

Dear Boito,

Giulio wrote me deeply distressed by the sudden death of Dina! To be sure, Giulio has lost a friend, an intelligent man, and a man of honor. I myself required his advice on several occasions, and I know how capable and dependable he was. Poor Dina!

We have talked no more, true, of *influenza,* but we still feel its effect: I, in a very great weakness that prevents me from doing any work for more than half an hour; and Peppina, in a total loss of appetite. I can't wait to change air, even for a more severe climate, provided I am freed from this wretched wind that splits my brain and puts thorns in my throat.

So you found *Mégère* rather well paced? In the *brouillon* they sent me the defect of the dialogue was less obvious. But in this respect I know what the French usually do. *In diebus illis* I attended in Paris 8 or 10 of Shakespeare's most powerful dramas. All frightfully altered. And as for the dialogue, I thought I was hearing a conversation either on the *boulevards* or in the *passage* of the old Opéra. This is true even of the adaptation of *Hamlet* made by Dumas *père!* Need I say more?

For the French, beauty exists only in their own works:

Cela ne va pas...

Ce n'est pas pour nous...

Ce n'est pas de bon goût.

These are their sacramental phrases. And with this *bon goût* they allow themselves to change everything, and to remove the character and originality from the productions of other countries!

So you are going to Palermo? Do some good if you can...

I hope to see you soon. Peppina sends greetings and thanks you for your concern. I shake your hands.

Be well.

> Affectionately,
> G. Verdi

◄In the third week of February 1892 Verdi and Giuseppina went to Milan, where they remained until their departure for Genoa on 21 March. Presumably during this stay Giuseppina went to Boito's dentist as arranged. From Genoa, on 7 April, Verdi returned to Milan, having agreed—after much resistance—to conduct on the following evening the Prayer from Rossini's *Mosè* at La Scala, to celebrate the centenary of the composer's birth.

On that same 7 April, in Hamburg, the conductor Hans von Bülow wrote a curious letter to Verdi, apologizing for a hostile article he had written almost twenty years earlier, and begging forgiveness, especially since, after becoming familiar with *Aida, Otello,* and the *Requiem,* the German musician had come to realize the Italian's worth. He concluded by saying: "Long live VERDI, the Wagner of our dear allies!" Verdi's reply—not without a certain wry humor—was written in Genoa on 14 April. Four months later Ricordi published both letters in the *Gazzetta musicale di Milano.*

For Alessandro Dina, see note following letter no. 141 above.

Genoa, 15 April 1892

Dear Boito,

191

I have replied to Bülow... and today I sent Bülow's letter back to Giulio with a copy of my reply, for, in the event that Bülow were to publish those letters in German, Giulio would then do well to publish the two original Italian letters.

I too have written to Roger.

I am a bit embarrassed by these singer-celebrities! For Nannetti there would be only the part of Bardolfo, which may even be a bit low for him. But this isn't the trouble... When we are in rehearsal what will he say when he hears that almost all the others have better parts? Thence ill humor, and so on and so forth... We shall see!...

And now before I lock up the first act completely orchestrated, tell me if these two verses are final:

Fine benefit! Can one who is dead feel honor?
No. Does it live only with the living? Not even, because wrongly

etc...

I greet you for Peppina, and affectionately shake your hands.

Yours,
G. Verdi

◆For Roger, see note following letter no. 96. Verdi is probably referring to a matter he and Boito had discussed during his recent trip to Milan for the Rossini centenary concert (see note following letter no. 190).

As *Falstaff* was close to completion and newspaper speculation about its production was growing, singers naturally began to approach Verdi, through Ricordi or Boito, about taking part. Romano Nannetti (1845 ca.–1910) was a bass who had appeared in a number of Verdian roles and often as Boito's Mefistofele. Instead of Bardolfo (a tenor role), Verdi almost certainly meant Pistola. Nannetti did not sing it, in any case.

Easter [17 April 1892]

Dear Maestro,

192

Bel costrutto! L'onore lo può sentir chi è morto?
No. Vive sol coi vivi? Neppure, perché a torto

Lo lodan le lusinghe, *lo* corrompe l'orgoglio,
Lo ammorban le calunnie. E per me non ne voglio!!
[Fine benefit! Can one who is dead feel honor?
No. Does it live only with the living? Not even, because wrongly
Flattery praises *it*, pride corrupts *it*,
Slanders infect *it*. And I want none of it!]

It seems to me better like this and more faithful to the original. I have changed the articles from feminine to masculine because the subject has become masculine. In this way, by not prolonging the image that originated with the word "aria" [air], we return to the word "onore" [honor] and the conclusion is more straightforward and stronger. I found myself than required to alter a word in the penultimate verse, and I have put:

                    a torto
        Lo *lodan* le lusinghe.
                    [wrongly
        Flattery *praises* it.]

You can lock away the first act and turn your hand to the second. I have read the reply to Bülow: Giulio showed it to me. Bravo, Maestro. It is very noble and beautiful.

You have the secret of *the right note at the right moment*, which is the great secret of art and of life.

Warm regards to Signora Giuseppina.

> Yours most affectionately,
> A. Boito

◄The libretto quotation refers to Falstaff's monologue at the end of act 1, part 1. Eventually "lodan" was also changed, becoming "gonfian" (swells).

9 May [1892]

193 Dear Maestro,

When Giulio went to Genoa he was to carry out an assignment I gave him for Signora Giuseppina. I don't know if he carried it out or not: he was to say that the price of the *Dictionary of Ancient and Modern Terms of Medical Science* is thirty lire. If he failed to say it, then I have said it now.

The painter Hohenstein is working on the costume and set designs for *Falstaff*. I have given him what information I had, but it would be well for him to have the scene descriptions as they are in the libretto. You might therefore take the trouble to write them out, because I don't have a copy of my manuscript.

A number of engravings illustrating the character of Falstaff were sent from London. Some of these can help, others not. It is absolutely necessary for you to see them. When Giulio comes back to Milan, I'll have him send them to you. In the costumes of our characters we must avoid the *too beautiful*, because the *too beautiful* is so rarely associated with the *picturesque*. Pistola and Bardolfo must wear clothing that seems threadbare: we want to see finally on the stage something that they never dare show, namely, *real rags*, pictorial rags in tone and cut, which will make Pistola and Bardolfo seem two figures straight from a painting. If Murillo could lend us his, that would be ideal!

The women's costumes, simply but very elegantly cut, will perhaps be found in the engravings sent from London.

It is good that the painter is at work: this way there will be more time to revise and ponder and do things well.

Many greetings to Signora Giuseppina, and to you, dear Maestro, best wishes for your work and a warm handshake.

> Yours most affectionately,
> A. Boito

Sant'Agata, 11 May 1892

194

Dear Boito,

We have been here for almost a week, still half-ill because of the terrible journey from Genoa. Imagine! A wait of almost 3 hours (that's THREE HOURS!!) at Voghera!

With that cold!

With that wind!

And in that station!!

Giulio told Peppina the price of the dictionary and she thanks you.

Too soon, it's too soon to think about the costumes and sets for *Falstaff*. First of all:

Will it be given?

Where will it be given?

Who will the singers be?

Which theater?

What impresario?

And besides... Will I finish what I have left to do?... Right now I feel so tired, so listless, that it seems impossible that I will succeed in finishing the work that remains to be done! When Giulio is back we will talk about it then!...

So! A bit of rest for the present, then we shall see—

Peppina greets you and I shake your hand.

Affectionately,
G. Verdi

Verdi's exclamations about the cold, the wind, and the station echo lines from *Falstaff*, act 3, part 1: "Con quel tufo! E quel caldo!" ("With that stench! And that heat!").

This letter is followed by a silence of three months, but—as on previous occasions—Verdi visited Milan several times during this period. In late July Verdi heard the soprano Emma Zilli, a candidate for the part of Alice (which she duly sang at the premiere).

Since early June Verdi had been seriously thinking of presenting the opera at La Scala in the coming season; and while he apparently wrote nothing to Boito in this period, he sent Ricordi numerous letters about the choice of theater, impresario, production, and cast. During his July visit to Milan, the choice of La Scala and of the coming season became final.

Sant'Agata, 6 August 1892

195   Dear Boito,

I don't believe I have ever been one of those most indiscreet people who speak to you too often about *Nerone*.

But after the article in the *Secolo XIX* of Genoa, which I am sending you, I believe it my duty, because of the friendship and esteem I have for you, to tell you that now you must no longer hesitate. You must work day and night if necessary, and see that *Nerone* is ready by next year. Indeed, at this moment you should have the news published: "This year at La Scala, *Falstaff*; next year, *Nerone*"...

To you this will seem a reply to the impertinences quoted by the Genoa newspaper. True! But there is no help for it and, in my view, nothing else to done.

If I have spoken out of turn, if I have said too much... consider it all unsaid!... You know that the aged are *bavards* and grumblers.

Be well.

Affectionately,
G. Verdi

◄sThe article in the *Secolo XIX* was an account of a musical dinner, at which Pietro Mascagni and Alberto Franchetti were present. The young, but already successful composers discussed their works in progress and their future plans; and Mascagni announced that he was thinking of a *Nerone*. Since Boito's long-cherished project was well known, the guests reacted with surprise, to which Mascagni replied: "Yes, *Nerone,* since the distinguished Maestro Boito allows me still plenty of time!"

Tuesday [9 August 1892]
Milan

196

My dear Maestro,

I assure you that the article in the *Secolo XIX* had no effect on me whatsoever, and that, by itself, it could not make me hasten the completion of the opera by even one day; but the good and strong letter that accompanies the article has so stirred me that if I don't start running now I will never run again.

I promise you, with all my great affection for you, that I will bend every effort to finish the work in time for it to be staged the year after *Falstaff.* I will make every effort, I promise you; a promise made to you, I know, is valid. What is said is said.

If I succeed, I will owe this great benefaction to you. Your letter was like a firm hand that has pulled me back on my feet; it reached me in a very painful moment of my life. Enough. Man to man, no more is said.

I thank you with the deepest affection.

Many warm greetings to Signora Giuseppina.

An embrace

from your
A. Boito

◄sThe "very painful moment" in Boito's life was probably connected with the affair with Duse, which had virtually run its course. That summer Boito and the actress did not meet, as before, at San Giuseppe. Duse was in Venice; Boito remained in Milan. It is also possible that Boito's distress was connected with the mysterious "Fanny," the woman in his life before Duse, who—perennially ill—was now dying, or had actually died. Her illness and the fact that she was married are all that is known about her.

Sant'Agata, 22 August 1892

197   Dear Boito,

In conversation in Milan you said you would come here in August... August is almost over... but no matter! Come when you like and you will always be welcome!

I write and work like a dog, but I never finish it...

Greetings from Peppina.

Until we meet.

Affectionately,
G. Verdi

23 August [1892]
Milan

198   Dear Maestro,

The work schedule to which I have subjected myself would make me a most tedious guest: that's why I have had to forgo, for now, the pleasure of coming to Sant'Agata. If by September I have succeeded in making my contrary brain produce the amount that I have set for myself, I will come to your house, dear Maestro, to rest for a week.

Milan in this season is very propitious for work, everyone is on vacation, the building where I live is completely empty, I can play, sing, and dance without bothering anyone and turn night into day and ignore the conventional hours for sleeping and for eating. All these advantages keep me in the city. If only five or six hours of work would suffice for me I would come at once to Sant'Agata, but you impelled me (it was you) to this accelerated dash and the best I can do is adhere for now to the conditions in which I am living.

I imagine that the orchestration of *Falstaff,* if not finished, has reached the last drops of ink.

Lucky you! I greet you affectionately along with Signora Giuseppina.

Yours,
A. Boito

P.S. If you need some verses or some retouching, the kind of thing that is noticed only when the work is finished, write me and in a wink it will be done. For you I can work fast. In any case, I still hope to see you in September.

11 September [1892]
Milan

199

Dear Maestro,

Yesterday I received from Rome a letter for you and I sent it on.

The letter is from that person who wanted to come to Sant'Agata, sent by the officials of the Columbian Exposition in Chicago. I saved you from the visit but I couldn't save you from the letter.

Maurel is still in Milan to complete the details of his contract. Let's hope that this business is quickly concluded and doesn't have to be mentioned again.

I have nothing else to tell you today except to send you and Signora Giuseppina my affectionate greetings.

Yours,
A. Boito

ക Victor Maurel, despite his difficult character, was Verdi's first choice for the role of Falstaff. Aware of his value, the baritone tried to extort an excessive fee from Ricordi. He called in his wife to act as go-between, alarming Verdi, who insisted that Giulio stand fast. Maurel finally accepted the proposed conditions.

Sant'Agata, 20 September 1892

200

Dear Boito,

Imagine! As long ago as last Thursday Tito Ricordi gave me a packet containing 25 lire from your brother for the rent of the plot... and I haven't written or sent a receipt!... How horrible!!

I have given Tito the third act of *Falstaff*. Yesterday I sent back the libretto and the piano reduction of the first act with a few unimportant observations on the *mise en scène* and the reduction.

I am now examining in detail the second act, but though I pay close attention some wrong notes always elude me, many ♯ and ♯♭♭. The person doing the vocal score and Giulio will deal with them...

Good-bye then and till we meet, who knows when. Greetings from Peppina.

Affectionately,
G. Verdi

ക The rent of the plot probably refers to the land where the Casa di Riposo per Musicisti was to be erected.

Sunday [25 September 1892]
Milan

201 Dear Maestro,

When will we see each other? In eight or ten days at most. We will descend upon Sant'Agata, Giulio and I, with the stage model in our overnight bag, to show you all the maquettes of *Falstaff*, with all the partial drops and practicable structures in order. In this way we will be able to see and judge precisely every slightest detail of the staging, and thus we will have no unpleasant surprises at the stage rehearsals.

Today I will see the proofs of the third act (libretto) and we will send them to you after I've corrected them.

Many warm greetings to Signora Giuseppina, to Signora Barberina, and to you.

Until we meet soon.

Yours most affectionately,
A. Boito

☙There is no documentation of this projected visit to Sant'Agata. If it did not take place, then Verdi probably saw the model of the stage and drops when he was in Milan from 13 to 16 October.

27 September [1892]
Milan

202 Dear Maestro,

I suggest the following variants for act 3: Instead of having Meg say:

Ho nascosto i folletti *dietro al* fosso
[I've hidden the sprites *behind* the ditch]

have her say:

Ho nascosto i folletti *lungo il* fosso
[I've hidden the sprites *along* the ditch]

—————————

Instead of having Falstaff say:

Sono le Fate. Chi le *guarda* è morto
[It's the Fairies. Whoever *looks at* them, dies]

have him say:

Sono le Fate. Chi le *guarda* è morto
[It's the Fairies. Whoever *looks at* them, dies]

After the verse:

L'arguzia mia crea l'arguzia degli altri
[My cleverness creates the cleverness of others]

all exclaim "Mò bravo!" ["Why, good for you!"]. That "mò" is a dialectal form and I don't like it. I suggest replacing it with the two words: "Ben detto!" ["Well said!"].

And finally, I suggest that the third and fourth verses of the fugue be changed in this way:

Tutto nel mondo è burla.
L'uom è nato burlone;
La fè nel cor gli ciurla,
Ciurla la sua ragione.

[Everything in the world is jest.
Man is born a jester;
Faith reels in his heart,
His reason reels.]

Or else:

La fede in cor gli ciurla,
Gli ciurla la ragione.

Take a look and decide for yourself.
The original verses are:

Nel suo cervello ciurla
Sempre la sua ragione.
[In his brain reels
Forever his reason.]

The musical accents would not, I believe, be upset if this version were adopted:

La fede in cor gli ciurla,
Ciurla la sua ragione.

and the two verses would, I believe, turn out better.

I await your opinion and I greet you affectionately, promising myself to see you again soon at Sant'Agata.

Many greetings to Signora Giuseppina.
Yours,
A. Boito

⮆Verdi accepted Boito's first proposed variant. In the printed libretto, the word is "lungo."

"It's the Fairies", etc.: an obvious slip of Boito's pen. Originally, the verse probably read "Chi le vede" ("Whoever sees them"). The final version reads "Chi le guarda."

Verdi apparently agreed that the dialectal "mò" was an unhappy choice; but instead of accepting Boito's suggested "Ben detto," the composer settled on the "Ma bravo" now printed in the score and libretto.

For the final suggested changes, the original verses remained in the autograph score and were adopted for the vocal score; Boito's second proposed version was printed in the libretto.

Six months were to go by before the next letter: a period of intense activity and frequent meetings between Boito and Verdi. Verdi moved to Genoa on 24 October; Boito arrived in Nervi soon afterwards. During the next few weeks Boito and the Verdis saw each other daily.

Boito then moved to a more isolated house in Pegli, where he was supposed to work on *Nerone*. But Ricordi, who was eager to have the French translation of *Falstaff* ready, pressed Boito repeatedly to begin work on it, and even tried (unsuccessfully) to enlist Verdi's support in this matter. Ricordi may have had less faith than Verdi in the probable completion of Boito's opera. In any case, Boito did begin work on the translation.

Finally, on 2 January 1893, after Verdi had corrected the proofs of the vocal score and worked with the singers in Genoa, he and Giuseppina arrived in Milan, with Boito. The rehearsals at La Scala began two days later, and Verdi took charge, working six to eight hours a day.

On 7 February the dress rehearsal took place, and on 9 February the premiere, with Maurel in the title role, Antonio Pini-Corsi (Ford), Edoardo Garbin (Fenton), Giovanni Paroli (Cajus), P. Pelagalli-Rossetti (Bardolfo), Vittorio Arimondi (Pistola), Emma Zilli (Alice), Adelina Stehle (Nannetta), Giuseppina Pasqua (Quickly), Virginia Guerrini (Meg), and Edoardo Mascheroni conducting.

The first-night audience included government officials, writers, painters (among them Giovanni Boldini, who painted the most famous portrait of Verdi), publishers, numerous Italian and foreign music critics, and younger composers, headed by Puccini and Mascagni. Count Zorzi was naturally there with his famous cane (see letter no. 158 above). The performance was a total triumph: Verdi was called before the curtain many times, often sharing his bows with Boito. The crowd acclaimed Verdi again at the stage door, and under the balcony of his hotel room. The Scala orchestra had gathered there, too, with their instruments, but were persuaded—in Verdi's name—not to play a serenade.

The Verdis stayed on in Milan until 2 March, when they returned to Genoa. Boito wrote them there for their name day, 19 March, the feast of St. Joseph.

[Milan] 19 March [1893]

203

Dear Maestro,

All best wishes to you and to Signora Giuseppina, to Signora Giuseppina and to you.

Our good Milanese by now have all become citizens of Windsor and spend their life at the Garter Inn and in Ford's house and in the Park. I cannot remember, and believe there has never been, an opera as capable as this one of penetrating the spirit and the blood of a people. This transfusion of joy, strength, truth, light, and intellectual health will produce a great benefit for art and for the public.

This regenerative therapy must be extended to other places as well, and in particular it must be spread among those most degenerate Romans of Rome. Giulio and I are convinced that this time your presence in the capital is, for many reasons, highly opportune. Giulio asks me to convey this opinion of ours to you, and he doesn't have to ask me twice; so I am conveying it. A very new form of art, like the art of this *Falstaff*, must not be abandoned by its author after a first test, however wonderful the results it produced. You today are not only the Maestro: you are the Physician (don't tell Signora Peppina this), the Physician of Art. Today Milan is entirely purged of any ultramontane fog.

But after the healing of Milan we must proceed to the healing of the capital, and if the remedy is to work perfectly the presence of the doctor is indispensable.

Falstaff will be presented in Rome in a new situation, with a new orchestra, and with two very important variants to deal with.

Believe me, Maestro, your presence is necessary.

I didn't say this for *Otello*, but I say it now because the significance of *Falstaff* is still, and very much, greater than that of *Otello;* it is a true revelation, and the Roman audience must not be left on its own in the face of such a profoundly novel work of art. And further, many other expedient considerations lead me to wish ardently for your presence in the capital: considerations I won't go into now, though in my mind I sense their eloquent truth.

So ends my chatter.

The translation proceeds well, much better than in the first act.

My affectionate greetings to you and to Signora Giuseppina.

Yours,

A. Boito

Giuseppina's aversion to doctors was a familiar private joke (see letter no. 160 above), so in referring to Verdi as a physician, Boito has to ward off her possible remonstrances. The "ultramontane fog" may refer to the performances of *Der fliegende Holländer* (in Italian), which had alternated with those of *Falstaff* at La Scala during late February and early March.

Before its important Roman premiere, *Falstaff* was given four times between 6 and 11 April at the Teatro Carlo Felice in Genoa, with the orchestra and chorus of La Scala and the original cast, Mascheroni again conducting. On 15 April the opera was presented in Rome, once more with the original cast and Mascheroni, but with the orchestra and chorus of the Teatro Costanzi. Reluctantly, Verdi allowed himself to be persuaded to attend, with Giuseppina and Boito. Their stay in Rome of just under a week was a succession of celebrations: Verdi was received by the king and queen, was awarded honorary citizenship of the capital, and was serenaded by the Costanzi orchestra. A plaque on the facade of the Albergo Quirinale commemorates the visit.

The two variants mentioned by Boito, first introduced in the score used for the Rome performances, involve the concertato at the end of act 2 and the end of the first part of act 3.

4 September [1893]

Milan

204 Dear Maestro,

We must think of another work to do together, because otherwise we, who do not like pointless letters, will end up writing each other once in a blue moon.

Meanwhile, the French translation has reached its last page; only fourteen verses are missing, and they will be done in two evenings of work.

I will arrive at Sant'Agata with the completed translation this *Saturday*, I will take the usual train that stops at Fiorenzuola at the usual hour.

We will work together revising the translation, then I will return to Milan and deliver everything to Giulio. But in October, my favorite month, I will return to Sant'Agata for a longer stay.

Cordial greetings to Signora Giuseppina and to you.

Yours most affectionately,

A. Boito

P.S. The editor Gilder of New York wrote me to get you to write something on Palestrina, or at least to allow a conversation with you on the subject to be *stenographed!!* I answered him that I thought it unlikely that this could be arranged.

Till we meet Saturday.

⏦This letter comes after a silence of nearly six months in the correspondence, but, as in other cases, the two men had ample occasion to meet during this period: in Milan, in Rome, in Genoa. In June Boito had gone to Cambridge to receive an honorary doctorate in music, along with Max Bruch, Tchaikovsky, and Saint-Saëns.

Boito had been working on the French translation of *Falstaff* in collaboration with the French writer and journalist Paul Solanges (1846–1914), who lived in Milan and wrote for various French papers. Solanges had translated *Mefistofele, La Gioconda,* and *Cavalleria rusticana,* as well as the texts of many salon songs. Their translation underwent a further revision by Boito's friend Camille Bellaigue (1858–1930), the esteemed, if conservative, French music critic and biographer, a regular contributor to *La revue des deux mondes.* He was a strong supporter of Verdi, with whom he corresponded.

Richard Watson Gilder (1844–1909) was editor of *The Century Magazine,* New York, and an important figure in the American cultural world of the time. His wife Helena was Duse's close friend and the sister of the famous Mrs. Bronson, who lived in Venice and befriended Browning, Henry James, and other literary lions. The occasion of Gilder's request was the approaching tercentenary, in February 1894, of Palestrina's death.

[Telegram]

6 [Sep] 93

Arrigo Boito, Principe Amedeo 1, Milan
From Busseto

205   Agreed. Saturday you will find carriage at Fiorenzuola after three o'clock.

Verdi

Sant'Agata, 15 September 1893

206   Dear Boito,

I hope that you arrived safe and sound in Milan;
that you have now recovered from the giddy whirl of Sant'Agata;
that you delivered the beautiful translation to Giulio;
and that you have given my watch to the watchmaker... which is very important for me!

Peppina beats her breast because of a word that escaped her, quite against her wishes, at the moment of your leaving!... "*Let that word be considered unsaid.*" This is what she has told me to write you.

I greet you for her, and for myself I shake your hands.

Yours,
G. Verdi

Barberina has left!

➳Giuseppina's imprudent remark probably concerned either the un-mentionable *Nerone* or Boito's bachelor state.

The exclamation mark after Verdi's postscript suggests that his sis-ter-in-law's regular visits were something of a trial to the less-than-patient Verdi.

Sunday [17 September 1893]
Milan

207   Dear Maestro,

The watch is in the hands of Signor Milani, watchmaker of the Brera Observatory, where (not at the observatory but at the watchmaker's) I was told that in a couple of weeks (or slightly longer) the watch will be returned to me in perfect condition and I myself will bring it back to Sant'Agata at the beginning of October, and this is to demonstrate that I myself, before you in your scrupulous kindness informed me, had in-terpreted as involuntary the farewell of Signora Giuseppina, and if I lie *may my belt break.* And that is the longest sentence I have written since I came into this world.

So I thank you very much, dear Maestro, for your good letter; and Signora Peppina must not beat her breast. We were born, the three of us, to understand one another very well even when our words are unfaithful to our thoughts.

Till we meet in October.

My affectionate greetings to you and to Signora Peppina.

Yours,

A. Boito

❧"If I lie may my belt break" echoes a line from *Falstaff,* act 3, part 2: "E se mentisco / Voglio che mi si spacchi il cinturone!"

1 November [1893]

Milan

208

Dear Maestro,

Camillo hasn't come back yet and I don't know where he is, the people who could have given me detailed information about hospices are still in the country, and this is the reason for my delay in writing you. But here is a card that is worth more than any verbal information: it is the financial report of the Luogo Pio Trivulzio, where the aged poor are housed, and of two other charitable institutions. The average for each resident at the Luogo Pio Trivulzio is, I believe, much the same as that of the Albergo dei Poveri, which comes to 345 lire annually for each resident in good health.

Warmest regards to Signora Giuseppina and to yourself.

I hope Signora Maria continues to improve.

Giulio has left for Paris.

Till we meet again soon.

Yours most affectionately,

A. Boito

❧Both the Luogo Pio Trivulzio in Milan and the Albergo dei Poveri in Genoa are still in existence. Verdi was obviously investigating the future requirements of the Casa di Riposo per Musicisti he was planning to build in Milan.

"Signora Maria" was Verdi's young second cousin Filomena Maria Verdi (often mistakenly called his "niece"), whom he and Giuseppina took in as a child. She looked after the Verdis in their old age, even after her marriage to Alberto Carrara in 1878. Her descendants still live in the Villa Sant'Agata.

Sant'Agata, 3 November 1893

209 Dear Boito,

A thousand thanks! Don't bother to collect further information. What I have is enough; we will have time later to talk about it.

Maria is getting steadily better...

We will soon leave Sant'Agata...

Greetings from Peppina and from me.

Till we meet again.

Affectionately,
G. Verdi

◆◦The Verdis traveled to Milan in mid-November and spent about three weeks there before moving on to Genoa for the rest of the winter.

Shortly after their departure, Boito was involved in a curious incident, which was reported in the newspapers and prompted Verdi to send the telegram (now lost) referred to in Boito's next letter. The story is complicated and, at the distance of a century, slightly ridiculous. Briefly, what happened was this: An opera by the English composer Sir Frederick Cowen (1852–1935) was produced in Milan under the auspices of the publisher-impresario Edoardo Sonzogno, bitter rival of Boito's friends the Ricordis. Sonzogno reneged on certain commitments to Cowen, who complained to Boito of Sonzogno's treatment and, after his return to England, wrote Boito, with whom he had remained on friendly terms. Boito's reply, half in jest, urged Cowen not to judge all Italians by Sonzogno, whose "good faith" he questioned. Boito's letter was, of course, private; but Cowen published it, without the writer's permission, in a London newspaper. Infuriated, Sonzogno publicly called Boito a "vigliacco" (coward); Boito challenged him to a duel, and promptly left Milan for Naples, where Sonzogno was managing the Teatro Mercadante. On arriving, Boito named seconds, but Sonzogno's seconds "for their own particular reasons" refused to meet them. Both sides named new seconds, who met and, playing down the gravity of Boito's behavior and justifying Sonzogno's reaction, agreed that the duel would not take place.

Dissatisfied with the solution, Boito was enraged and desperate. On his return journey north, Verdi met him at the Genoa station and tried to persuade him to stay over and talk about the question. But Boito refused and continued his journey to Milan. Hence Verdi's telegram urging him to be calm.

[arrival postmark: Genoa, 22 December 1893]

210

Dear Maestro,

I received the telegram. Thank you.

Yes, *calm and more calm.* I have regained it.

I have to revise my fine plan to spend a day in Genoa: that day will not be Christmas Eve, but will be instead the last day of the year.

So till we meet then on 31 December.

Yesterday evening I learned from Origoni that, having been informed I don't know by whom (I had authorized no one to do this) of my passing through Genoa and of my intention to dine at your house, you had gone to the station the day before and had to delay the dinner hour at your house. I am very sorry that this misunderstanding took place; it must be the last curse of Maestro Cowen. My intention was to surprise you, not to inform you of my passing through, especially since the day of my departure was not certain.

Many warm greetings to you and Signora Giuseppina.

Yours most affectionately,

A. Boito

◄§Luigi Origoni was Giulio Ricordi's son-in-law.

[Milan] 31 December 1893

211

Dear Maestro,

The conductor of the Turin orchestra for *La Valchiria* was Vanzo; now he is conducting in Trieste.

The Milanese press has attacked Mascheroni like a mad dog and has made him answerable for the infinite boredom produced by the opera, and this is unjust.

The first reason why the opera failed to please must be sought in the opera itself and in the system employed by Wagner. Another reason is the vastness of the stage, which makes the entire structure of the drama seem petty. An insipid action that proceeds more slowly than a milk train, stopping at every station, moving through an endless series of duets, during which the stage remains miserably empty and the characters stupidly immobilized. None of this is made to cause pleasure.

The ride of the Valkyries and their imploration, two scenes that made a great impression on me in Turin, left me cold at La Scala. And this is easily explained: our vast theater would require not nine Valkyries but thirty, and then the effect obtained in Turin would be achieved.

I gave the letter to S. Campes, who was moved by it and thanks you with all his heart.

All best wishes to you, dear Maestro, and to Signora Giuseppina. And a warm handshake

> from your most affectionate
> A. Boito

➳After the *Walküre* performance in Italian in Turin (see letter no. 188 above), Vanzo was conducting the opera in Trieste, where it had opened on Christmas day. The same opera had opened at La Scala on 26 December, under Edoardo Mascheroni, conductor of the first *Falstaff.*

For some years the Opéra had been eager to stage *Otello.* Their first thought was to give the work in Italian with Tamagno and Maurel from the original cast; but Verdi was against this idea, since it broke a long-standing tradition that, at the Opéra, all works were given in French.

Dissatisfied, at least on some points, with the Boito-Du Locle translation, Gailhard, director of the Opéra, had had a new version made, apparently based on the existing translation sanctioned by Verdi. Since Verdi was in Genoa, Du Locle on Capri, and Boito in Milan, there were some difficulties in communication, as Boito indicates in the letter below. Verdi thought it best to avoid becoming involved and tried to make Ricordi answer all letters from the Opéra. Another year was to pass before the premiere of the French *Otello.*

The "S. Campes" who received Verdi's moving letter is a mystery; he does not appear elsewhere in the Verdi literature.

Milan [18 January 1894]

212 Dear Maestro,

The question of the translation of *Otello* was threatening to go on forever and was becoming extremely complicated, so I thought it best to make things simpler by writing yesterday a letter to Gailhard. I made a copy and transcribe it for you herewith:

"Cher Monsieur. Je n'ai eu connaissance de votre à Verdi qu'avant-hier par Mr Ricordi; ceci vous explique le retard de ma reponse. Les pourparlers sur la traduction d'*Otello* ne doivent-pas, à mon avis, se prolonger davantage. Si toutes les personnes interessées dans cette affaire devaient se consulter à tout propos il faudrait établir un réseau télefonique entre Paris, Gênes, l'île de Capri, et Milan. Pour mon compte je profitte d'une circonstance qui me permet de simplifier la question. Le passage incriminé (recit et chanson du saule) se trouve dans mons domaine, le 3ᵉᵐᵉ et le 4ᵉᵐᵉ acte etant traduit par moi; je puis donc sans envahir l'oeuvre de mon collaborateur Mʳ Du Locle et sans froisser les convenances faire bon marché de ce fragment. Je viens de le relire, il est détéstable. Je serais désireux de le refaire, mais puisque vous paraissez satisfait de celui que vous lui avez substitué je Vous autorise à le presenter au Maître, son approbation sera la mienne.

"Recevez, cher Monsieur, l'expression de mes condoléances pour l'incendie des magazins de l'Opéra. Agrééz," etc., etc., etc., etc.

So then, as far as the most incriminated passage is concerned, the concession has been made; other little details of lesser importance will remain, but it will be easy to agree on them. Gailhard's letter to me speaks of "legères critiques," so it is not a matter of a new translation of the whole opera.

Gailhard's motives are, I believe, sincere.

The recitative and the Willow Song really are *detestable* (they were the first verses, the first attempts at collaboration with Solanges) and they must be redone; I want to be fair. The good of the work of art must come first. If the variant offered by Gailhard proves to be good, so much the better; if it is bad, Solanges and I will make another and we will still say: *So much the better.*

I have just received a letter from Du Locle in which he asks me if he must write to Nuitter for information. I would answer him telling him to do so; thus we will know every particular. I am convinced that in all these dealings there is no threat to our personal interests and that the directors of the Opéra are acting in complete good faith.

I add a little page on which I have transcribed the new entrance of the Fairies in act 3 of *Falstaff.*

Affectionate greetings to you and to Signora Giuseppina.

Yours,
A. Boito

◆Given Verdi's knowledge of French, Boito did not think of translating his letter to Gailhard, which says:

"Dear Sir, I learned of your letter to Verdi only the day before yesterday through M. Ricordi; this explains the delay of my answer. The discussions concerning the translation of *Otello* should not, in my opinion, be further protracted. If all the people involved in the matter had to consult one another on every question, a telephone network would have to be set up between Paris, Genoa, the island of Capri, and Milan. For my part, I would exploit a circumstance that allows me to simplify the question. The incriminated passage (recitative and Willow Song) lies in my domain, since acts 3 and 4 were translated by me; I can then deal summarily with that bit without intruding on my collaborator M. Du Locle's work and without overstepping the bounds of courtesy. I have just reread it, it is dreadful. I would like to redo it, but since you seem satisfied with your replacement of it, I authorize you to present it to the Maestro; his approval will be mine.

"Accept, dear Sir, my condolences for the fire of the Opéra's warehouse. And believe me your," etc.

Note: Boito's French has been retained, above, complete with its several small errors, due probably to his haste in transcribing it (and perhaps also to his continuing agitation after the Cowen-Sonzogno incident).

For the French version of *Falstaff,* Verdi decided to add text in the twelve bars originally for solo orchestra before Nannetta's aria (as Queen of the Fairies) in the last act. Boito sent them in French (on a page now lost), then he translated them into Italian as they now appear in the definitive printed score and libretto.

Genoa, 19 January 1894

213 Dear Boito,

Allow me to say that you were too conciliatory and too optimistic in the reply you sent to Gailhard! I believe there was no need to tell him you translated the third and fourth acts, and Du Locle the rest. Further, I wouldn't have given anyone the right to change a single word; and on this point, indeed, I declare that I will never assume the responsibility of approving those changes before anyone else! Those changes must be handed to me by the translators I recognize: *Boito* and *Du Locle*... and by nobody else!.

Besides, I am also less optimistic than you... *"convinced,"* you say, *"that in all these dealings there is no threat to our personal interests"*...

I know nothing about this!! but I ask myself: Why did they take it upon themselves to make a translation without asking your permission?...

It seems to me that those few verses in French will do very well. Translate them now into Italian, naturally without adding anything, etc., etc.

Many greetings also from Peppina, and believe me always your
G. Verdi

◆The Verdis spent some time in Milan in February and early March, probably seeing a good deal of Boito, who showed the composer Bellaigue's revisions of the French translation of *Falstaff.*

Genoa, 14 March 1894

Dear Boito,

214

Should I write to you? Or should I not? Yes or no?... No or yes?

Read this if you have time; otherwise throw it into the wastepaper basket, for I have no great important things to say to you.

Tomorrow evening they are giving Franchetti's opera. In Milan I heard the libretto spoken of so harshly that, on reading it, I found it less bad than I had been told. To be sure, the subject is very simple-minded; the verses are what they are; but despite all this, some good music could be written to it, and I wouldn't be surprised if Franchetti, momentarily abandoning his bloated and heavy style, *did* find something good. If you go to the theater, send me a word or two. I trust you; and never fear that the situation with that Englishman of yours will be repeated, may God preserve his talent, and his tact!

I am well; and I am bored. I do nothing; and I am tired... Or rather, these past few days I have worked for the three *Big Bellies* in *Lisbon, Berlin,* and *Naples!*... Fine things, but also a bit boring! But even among these nuisances, there was one merry note. After the Berlin premiere I received, as you know, a telegram from the director of the theater, and I was a bit surprised to see it, three hours later, printed in the *Corriere!* Scant harm done! But my surprise was greater when I read the next day, again in the *Corriere:* "Falstaff in Berlin!" What the devil! What's this? I read on, and when I reach the end I find more or less these words: "It is a pleasure to announce a genuine success of *Falstaff* without the encore of 'Quand'ero paggio'... Misovulgo." Ha! ha! ha! ha! Then I burst out laughing for five minutes... *Voilà le fin mot!* All this in order to say he doesn't like that piece... Once that initial moment of hilarity had passed, however, I thought to myself: "What do they want, these *avveniristi,* these id——" And why, in a comic opera, can't there be something light and brilliant? How does that little piece offend the aesthetic sense? I'll skip the musical motive, though it's apt to the situation. Falstaff, mocked because of his big belly, says "When I was a page I was slender"... It's written well for the voice; it's lightly orchestrated; it allows all the words to be heard undisturbed by the usual (*impolite*) orchestral counterpoints that interrupt the main discourse; correctly harmonized... Where is the harm then if it has proved popular?!!... And this is how criticism is written! It matters little to me, as I've finished, and besides I pay no attention, as I have never paid attention. But it is harmful for the young, who could easily be led to do what they don't really feel like doing. In fact, all the music that is written now, whether in our country or in all other countries, lacks naturalness and isn't sincere...

Oh, my God, what a long letter! What the devil have I done! Forgive me, forgive me!

Greetings. Be well.

Affectionately,

G. Verdi

&s;Alberto Franchetti (1860–1942) had already enjoyed some success with his *Asrael* (1888). Verdi had heard, without enthusiasm, his *Cristoforo Colombo* (1892), written for the Columbian celebrations. On 15 March 1894, La Scala gave the premiere of his *Fior d'Alpe*. A decent success, it had seven performances.

"That Englishman of yours" was Sir Frederick Cowen (see the note following letter no. 209 above).

In Lisbon *Falstaff* had been given on 27 February 1894; in Berlin on 6 March, in German translation (previously, on 1 June 1893, it had been heard in Italian); in Naples on 19 February 1894, at the Teatro San Carlo.

"Misovulgo" was the pen name of Aldo Noseda.

Maurel encored "Quand'ero paggio" (*Falstaff*, act 2) regularly. On his Fonotipia recording (1907), he sings it three times.

[Milan] 16 March [1894]

215   Dear Maestro,

Yesterday evening the audience was divided into three factions: those who were bored and kept quiet, those who were bored and applauded, those who were bored and hissed. I was bored and kept quiet. Boredom is an opinion, and it was mine last night.

This *Fior d'Alpe* proved to be a rambling piece of nonsense, and it isn't worth wasting the ink to write about it at length. Franchetti, who navigated well with Christopher Columbus, has drowned in a teacup, or rather he wanted to make a storm in a teacup and he was shipwrecked.

Many are similarly shipwrecked in their fury to *overdo* and to seek in their own subjects what isn't there and cannot be there: *Midi à quatorze heures* as the French say, the French whom we will *all* go to visit in about ten days—*all of us, I say,* and that means you, Signora Peppina, Giulio, and me. It is of prime necessity that you come.

I know (I was told by Solanges, who heard it from those present at the rehearsals), I know that the preparation of *Falstaff* proceeds very well from the musical, purely musical point of view, but the interpretation of the comedy is completely absent. And obviously it can only be thus.

That theater has academic traditions, quite proper and elegant and deeply felt, that no one dares breach. William Shakespeare among those Gentlemen must produce the effect of a lion turned loose in a shop of Saxe figurines. *Save the china!* this must be the instinctive feeling of those Gentlemen; and to save it, they will be obliged to render our lion impotent.

They will temper everything—accents, inflections, gestures, movements, words, kisses, blows, laughter, gaiety, vivacity, strength, power, youthfulness, folly, the effervescence of the whole opera—and the audience will witness a performance very different from what Shakespeare conceived, from what you created, from what all of us want.

Shakespeare is still waiting to be introduced to the French: he is waiting for a powerful hand that has the strength and the confidence to signal him out and to show him as he is.

This hand, Maestro, can only be yours; the mission is very noble and worthy of you. So then, "no more words, for here we are wasting the light of the sun."

The best thing would be for all of us to leave together on the 28th. We can meet in Turin. Giulio will take care of everything: he will take care to find us a *coupé salon,* he will arrange for us to sleep during the journey as comfortably as if we were in our own homes, he will make sure that we eat and drink. We will chat, we will laugh, and it will be a most delightful excursion. *It is said.* But time is pressing and we must agree so as to telegraph the *hôtel.*

Regards to Signora Peppina.
Affectionate greetings

from your
Arrigo

We'll see each other then when we are en route, all of us.

◦With "no more words, for here we are wasting the light of the sun," Boito again quotes *Falstaff* ("Non più parole / Che qui sciupiamo la luce del sole"; act 1, part 2).

After having said no more than once, Verdi allowed himself to be convinced that the journey to Paris was necessary. But the Italian contingent did not travel together. Boito left about 22 or 23 March, followed by Ricordi on 27 March. The Verdis—experiencing a wagon-lit for the first time—left from Genoa on 4 April.

The French premiere of *Falstaff* took place on 18 April at the Opéra-Comique, with Maurel in the title role. The cast also included Grandjean (Alice), Soulacroix (Ford), Marie Delna (Quickly), Landouzy (Nannetta), Chevalier (Meg), and Edmond Clément (Fenton). The reception by the French press was good; Verdi was less satisfied with the Italian reviews.

The Verdis returned to Genoa after the third performance, while Ricordi and Boito and stayed on in Paris. Duse arrived for a few days just before Boito was to leave. He was busy with Du Locle and Ricordi, resolving the final problems of the French *Otello*. He and Duse met briefly, then she went on to London and he returned to Italy. In London, a short time later, Duse saw *Falstaff*. "Arrigo, forgive me," she wrote, "but it seemed so melancholy, that *Falstaff*" [cf. R. Raul, ed., *Eleonora Duse-Arrigo Boito: Lettere d'amore* (Milan: Il Saggiatore, 1979)].

On his return to Milan, Boito wrote Verdi (the letter is lost) proposing a visit to Sant'Agata with the revised French *Otello*. But Verdi was still recovering from the Paris journey.

[Telegram]

8 May 94

Arrigo Boito, Principe Amedeo 1, Milan
From Busseto

216 Have a very bad cold and cannot talk. Delay your arrival few days. Will wire.

Verdi

11 May [1894]
Milan

217

Dear Maestro,

Yesterday I read in *Le figaro* that the *one-thousandth performance* of *Mignon* will take place at the *matinée* on Sunday, the day after tomorrow. Imagining that you might be unaware of this event, I thought to tell you in case a telegram should be sent from Sant'Agata addressed to the Paris Conservatory.

And now, with regard to Paris, this is the situation: Gailhard and Bertrand have an immense desire to give *Othello* at the Opéra. Their desire is so ardent that they would like to mount the opera *in the month of October* to enable them to give a great number of performances of it during the whole theatrical year.

To achieve this result it is necessary to begin quickly the study of the opera, and to begin this study the following things are indispensable:

1. that you approve the idea of staging *Othello* in October rather than in April
2. that you look over the translation as it now stands
3. that you agree to hear Mme Caron, who would come to Italy with the specific purpose of having you hear her in the fourth act.

I stayed over in Paris an extra day (after having made the changes in the translation) to hear la Caron, her voice restored, in *Salammbô,* and I liked her enormously.

I am making a clean copy of the translation. When you and I have analyzed it together, I will send it to Du Locle, he will make his comments from the literary point of view and will fill in some gaps in the first and second acts, that I left deliberately in order to give him some problems to solve. I will write him that this revision of the translation, which will be a great help to the work as a whole, will not in the least affect (and this is true) our literary rights. For that matter, all the lyrical part, with a very few exceptions, has remained as it was.

I hope, dear Maestro, that your cold is passing. Now you know everything I wanted to tell you. When you are perfectly recovered I will arrive with the copied translation, we will look at it together carefully.

Many warm greetings to you and to Signora Giuseppina.

Yours most affectionately,
A. Boito

⋦Ambroise Thomas (1811–1896), composer of *Mignon* (1866) and other operas, was professor at the Paris Conservatory from 1852 and its director from 1871. Verdi was on cordial terms with Thomas, who, at the time of the French *Falstaff* premiere, had received him and Giuseppina at the conservatory with full honors.

Boito had heard the soprano Rose-Lucille Caron (1857–1930) in the title role of Ernest Reyer's *Salammbô* (1890) during his Paris stay. She was, in fact, Verdi's first French Desdemona.

Sant'Agata, 12 May 1894

218 Dear Boito,

My voice has come back to me a bit, but the whole city of Paris still weighs on my stomach and my legs.

Come then when you like.

Mind you, the *direct train* that stops at Fiorenzuola leaves Milan at 13:30 and arrives at 15:27.

Till we meet. Greetings to all.

> Affectionately,
> G. Verdi

Monday, 14 May [1894]
Milan

219 Dear Maestro,

I will arrive at Sant'Agata on *Thursday,* I will be at Fiorenzuola on the train you spoke of. I hope that by Thursday you will be able not only to speak but also to sing, and I hope to be able to sing and speak myself, as I too have been ill for three days with a cold in the head and throat and chest.

Until Thursday then.

To be on the safe side, I will confirm my arrival with a telegram the day before.

Many warm regards

> from your affectionate
> A. Boito

Sant'Agata, 16 May 1894

220 Dear Boito,

I left the libretto of *Othello* in Genoa, the very one with the handwritten changes in the third finale. If you come tomorrow, as I will learn from the telegram I will receive later, then bring an Italian libretto of *Otello* with you.

Until we meet.

Be well.
G. Verdi

⚓Boito's telegram of confirmation has not survived, but the visit did take place. It was probably on this occasion that Verdi gave Boito a handwritten memorandum with some instructions to guide him in dealing with the directors of the Opéra.

Verdi was not pleased with the Opéra's idea of moving the *Othello* opening from April 1895 to October 1894, which meant canceling an announced production of *Tristan*. He also felt the premiere of his earlier opera would come too soon after the presentation of *Falstaff*. Further, Maurel would be free in April, but his availability in October seemed uncertain. And the composer also wanted more time in order to compose the required ballet music to add to his score. Verdi also made it clear that he wanted to hear Caron, though—out of respect for her dignity—he did not want to seem to demand her coming to Milan, as if to be auditioned. See letters nos. 221 and 222 below.

Sant'Agata, 25 May [1894]

221

Dear Boito,

I have just this minute answered the directors of the Opéra by telegram... "Vous pouvez engager Maurel pour la première d'*Othello* en octobre... Si Madame Caron est encore dans l'intention de venir en Italie je dois aller lundi ou mardi à Milan Hôtel Milan ou nous pourrions nous rencontrer"... etc., etc. And in this matter I need your help, and you should telegraph Paris at once. The question is very delicate, to tell the truth, and if I were Mme Caron I would not come to Milan to have myself judged... On the other hand, I want to be almost certain about la Caron's voice. All in all, the matter is more serious than it seems. If la Caron is in good voice, everything proceeds *comme sur des roulettes,* but if she proves not to be... then some serious troubles would arise for me... So let us avoid these scandals and telegraph Paris to fix everything...

Be well. In haste.

Affectionately,
G. Verdi

&sAs usual, Verdi relied on Boito's knowledge of French and so did not translate his telegram, which reads: "You can engage Maurel for the premiere of *Othello* in October... If Madame Caron still plans to come to Italy, I must go to Milan Monday or Tuesday. We could meet at the Hôtel Milan."

Saturday [Sant'Agata, 26 May 1894]

222 Dear Boito,

I have received your telegram. No indeed, no *entrusting the solution to the course of events!!* No! It would be an act of cowardice on my part, especially after Gailhard himself had suggested having la Caron come to Italy. I have wired the directors on the subject... I fear the question is becoming complicated. Du Locle is ill. We will fix or ruin everything in a few days' time in Milan.

Be well.

G. Verdi

&sBoito's telegram, to which this letter is a reply, is now lost.

Sant'Agata, 12 June 1894

223 Dear Boito,

I hope this letter reaches you before your departure...

It is well for you to know that in the past the theater of the Opéra specially paid foreign authors some so-called *primes* to reimburse them for travel and lodging. Rossini received them; I believe Meyerbeer, too; and I myself for all my operas except for *Aida,* when, like a GRAND SEIG-NEUR, I rejected them.

In the case of *Othello* it's not a question of *primes,* but of guaranteeing all our rights, and especially of preventing the opera from being tampered with and mutilated according to the whim of an artist, as now happens to *Falstaff* with Maurel (I am very irritated by this action... also with Giulio, who hasn't made his authority felt).

I add further that besides the *droits d'auteur* established by law, there are also the so-called *billets d'auteur* that have to be reckoned.

Roger will be able to give you all the instructions necessary to guarantee:

1. Our *droits d'auteur*
2. *Billets d'auteur*

3. *Intact performance* of the opera
Ask him also in my name; and I hope he will be willing to take care of this matter that is important for us.

Have a good journey and a good time.

Greetings from Peppina and from me.

Affectionately,
G. Verdi

P.S. Will you again go to the Grand Hôtel Capucines?

❧Bellaigue had written Verdi from Paris, informing him that, in later performances of *Falstaff*, Maurel had taken the liberty of making some cuts (and not always the same ones, as if testing various passages of the work). Maurel, who blackmailed the management by threatening to walk out, even wanted the chorus omitted: "Cela la fatiguait de voir tournoyer autour de lui" ("It tired him to see them moving around him"), Ricordi's correspondent wrote [CVB, p. 452].

Boito was, in any case, on his way to Paris to discuss *Othello* with the Opéra directors. Verdi wrote Ricordi to tell Boito to protest and convey Verdi's threat to withdraw the score of *Falstaff*. While in Paris, Boito also had one of his brief encounters with Duse, though their affair was virtually over.

Wednesday [13 June 1894]
Milan

224

Dear Maestro,

I will leave tomorrow morning. I will say to Roger everything you tell me to say to him.

I have prepared to the best of my ability the work I will have to do with Gailhard.

I don't yet know at which hotel I will stay. Not at the Grand Hôtel. I will write you from Paris.

I'm afraid I will find the hotels very full because of the *grand prix,* which takes place Sunday, but I'll find some cubbyhole or other. I'm sorry not to see Bellaigue in Paris; he has already left for Switzerland.

In the last letter he wrote me (ever more enthusiastic about *Falstaff*) he gave me warmest greetings for you and for Signora Peppina, and to those greetings I add my own, most affectionately.

Yours,
A. Boito

Sant'Agata, 23 June 1894

225   Dear Boito,

As I don't have your address, I am asking Giulio to send you these few lines.

If you have finished your work with Gailhard, come quickly to Milan. I will go there tomorrow and will stay there until it is time for me to go to Montecatini, until the evening of 1 July. If you could be in Milan around 27 June, we would have time to examine the notes on the translation and everything would be finished.

Greetings, greetings.

Affectionately,

G. Verdi

If you come across some Cypro-Greek dance... investigate!

✑A three-month silence follows this letter. Meanwhile, Verdi consented to the October date for the French premiere of *Othello*. Coming from Sant'Agata, the Verdis arrived in Milan on 24 June and stayed a week; it is uncertain whether Boito returned from Paris in time to meet the composer, who from Milan went to Montecatini. There he began to think seriously about the *Othello* ballet music (Ricordi sent him some Greek songs, which he found useless), and he revised the third-act finale, giving the character of Jago more prominence and dramatic coherence. He also made other cuts and additions. He continued searching for dances suitable for *Othello,* and on 12 July, from Montecatini, he wrote Ricordi: "Something Turkish! Something Cypro-Greek! Something Venetian! [. . .] Help me find something!"

Boito, meanwhile, was at Aix-les-Bains with an old friend, the *scapigliato* writer Luigi Gualdo (died 1898), who had been stricken by paralysis. At Aix *Falstaff* was given its local premiere in French at this time.

On 21 August Verdi completed the ballet music, making up, on his own, a "Greek" song and a *Muranese;* he wrote the good news to Ricordi at once. "This very day I am sending, special delivery, the package with the ballet for the Paris *Othello*. Your doctors of music could find nothing for me... but I found a Greek song of 5000 B.C.!... If the world didn't yet exist then, it's the world's tough luck! Then I found a *Muranese,* composed 2000 years ago for a war between Venice and Murano, which the Muranese won. No matter if Venice didn't yet exist, with this *find* I composed my fine ballet, imagining how it must be performed, and I have drafted the outline, which you will find attached to the score" [CVB, p. 456].

Also on 21 August Ricordi reported that Boito had returned to Milan, after some Alpine excursions; he immediately set about making the final (if dangerously tardy) revisions of the *Othello* libretto.

Once again, Verdi at first declared firmly that he would not go to Paris, but then the fear that the French would not do things properly made him change his mind, as the following telegram indicates. It is the reply to a telegram from Boito that has not survived.

[Telegram]

19 Sep 94

Arrigo Boito, Principe Amedeo 1, Milan
From Genoa
I do not understand clearly what is meant by preliminary studies completed. When I come to Paris I want to make some changes in phrasing and dynamics, adjust the serenade, and other things. That can be done only with keyboard rehearsals more or less as we did at the Opéra-Comique. If the rehearsals are too far advanced and do not allow this there is no point in my coming to Paris. Wire me about this in the event I could not be in Paris before Tuesday or Wednesday.

226

Verdi

On 26 September the Verdis arrived in Paris, and Verdi supervised rehearsals at the Opéra for two weeks. On 12 October, the premiere of the French *Othello* was conducted by Paul Taffanel (1844–1908), famous flutist and conductor, and director of the Société des Concerts du Conservatoire. The Othello was Albert Saléza, with Maurel and Caron. The president of the French Republic was in the audience; in the first-act intermission he conferred on Verdi the Grand Cross of the Legion of Honor. At the same time, the Opéra-Comique revived *Falstaff*, with a new baritone in the title role: Lucien Fugère (1848–1935), whom Boito had heard in the part in Aix-les Bains.

On 17 October Verdi, accompanied by Ambroise Thomas, attended the ceremony commemorating the death of Gounod at the Madeleine.

On 22 October the Verdis left for Italy. Paris was where they had first lived together, where the composer had known—and Giuseppina had shared—triumphs and fiascos. They had seen the city for the last time.

2 Nov [actually 2 December 1894]
Milan

227 Dear Maestro,

When I think about Paris it seems to me that an infinity has gone by since those happy days! I had your news from Giulio. When you passed through Milan we didn't see each other because you thought I was still at Lake Como, where I spent a week, and I, who had already returned, was unaware of your presence.

I hope your winter visit with us will not be too long in coming, and then I will make it up to myself for our failure to meet.

I finally went to Parma, where I heard some excellent performances of Palestrina: the *Missa Papae Marcelli* and some madrigals; but until I hear a completely ideal performance of that music—where through a perfect blending of the parts, one or another more sweetly singing voice comes lightly to the fore, first here, then there—I will prefer to enjoy those sounds in my mind and follow them in the score with my eyes.

A truly complete and profound artistic impression was afforded me this time in Parma by Correggio. One evening in the Church of San Giovanni they showed me the cupola illuminated by electric light. The naves were plunged in darkness—in the church there were three of us: Mariotti, Corrado Ricci, and I—and all of a sudden the painting on the inside of the cupola was lighted by the glow of a hundred Edison bulbs hidden in the cornice, and that sublime masterpiece appeared as if illuminated by the sun. A real miracle. Never has painting produced a greater emotion in me, not even Velasquez. Then I understood the admiration you feel for Correggio. It is absolutely necessary for you to see that cupola with that illumination. Soon they will also light the cupola of the duomo, even more marvelous. We will all go; I want Camillo to come too.

I saw the sweet Massenet, who spoke to me of his visit to Palazzo Doria. I don't know how *Werther* went last night; I didn't attend the performance.

Warmest regards to Signora Giuseppina and to you and to Signor De Amicis. I hope to see you again soon.

Yours most affectionately,
A. Boito

≈Corrado Ricci (1858–1934) was a great friend of Boito's. Writer, art historian, and critic, he was at this time the director of the Parma Royal

Gallery of Art. Among his many books is a volume on Correggio. His interest in archeology led Boito to consult him about details of ancient Rome for *Nerone*.

Massenet's *Werther* was given its Italian premiere at the Teatro Lirico in Milan on 1 December 1894. On his way through Genoa, Massenet stopped to visit Verdi at Palazzo Doria, a visit described (though probably erroneously dated) in the French composer's volume *Mes souvenirs* (1912).

Genoa, 3 December 1894

228

Dear Boito,

Lucky you, to have heard a bit of Palestrina. I can easily understand that the performance did not achieve your ideal, but all the same I wish that in every city there were such ceremonies, if for no other reason than to adjust a bit our poor ears, lacerated by the excess of dissonance! The trouble is that these inventions involving dissonance and orchestration are applied almost always illogically.

And *Correggio?!?!*

Marvelous and seductive painter! So beautiful, simple, natural, that when I see him, I imagine that he had no teachers. At times as grand as Michelangelo, but with the difference that I love Correggio's prophets and apostles, while those of Michelangelo frighten me!

And now an act of charity! (See the Calabrian earthquake *special publication*.)

Revise and rewrite for me, please, two verses:

Pietà Signor della miseria mia!
Ci salva tu . . . . e ria!
[Have mercy, Lord, on my wretchedness!
Save us . . . . -ness!]

I have written a phrase to these words, so I need those accents; and also in the second verse, the accent on the second syllable. If you don't want to rhyme the second verse it doesn't matter, provided that the verse is accented on the penultimate syllable...

Thanks from Peppina, who sends her warm regards.

Be well. Till we meet, let's hope soon.

Affectionately,
G. Verdi

◆The periodical *Fata Morgana* was to issue a special number in 1894 for the benefit of the victims of an earthquake in Calabria and Sicily that had occurred on 16 November. Verdi was invited to contribute to the publication, and on 30 November he sent a little prayer, "Pietà Signor," consisting of a few measures of music. Apparently he then had second thoughts and decided to extend those measures, for which he sought Boito's help with the text while asking the promoter of the special publication to return the music he had sent. He and Boito then exchanged several letters about the text, which became a kind of paraphrase of the Miserere and the Agnus Dei. The final product was thereafter submitted for publication as promised.

Tuesday [Milan, 4 December 1894]

229   Dear Maestro,

Here you are; see if this fits with the musical phrase. The first verse is yours and the second is by Dante Alighieri:

> di me
> Pietà ~~pietà,~~ della miseria mia
> Agnèl di Dio che le peccata levi.
> [Have mercy on me, on my wretchedness
> Lamb of god, who taketh away sins.]

Purg., Canto 16

And all together it is a paraphrase of the Agnus Dei.

Or else, if you prefer the effect of rhyme, here are two other verses:

> Pietà di noi, del nostro duol profondo.
> O Agnèl di Dio che levi il mal dal mondo.
> [Have mercy on us, on our profound sorrow,
> O Lamb of God who taketh away the world's evil.]

The paraphrase of this second verse is more complete:

> Agnus Dei qui tollis peccata mundi.

The first verse of this second version might be even better like this:

> Pietà di noi, del nostro *error* profondo.

You choose, and if it won't do, write me and I'll try to find something better.

Yesterday a piece of red ribbon came to me, sent from Paris. You must know something about it—indeed, I have a strong suspicion, indeed I firmly believe, that the leader of the conspiracy was you. Oh Maestro!

In any case I thank you.
Affectionate greetings

from your
A. Boito

↩Boito had been made Knight of the Legion of Honor.

Genoa, 5 December 1894

230

Dear Boito,

How beautiful would be the two verses:

Pietà di Noi, del nostro error profondo
O Agnèl di Dio che levi il mal dal mondo

but the word "Agnèl" sounds wrong on the notes written... and furthermore, I have a rest in the second verse after the 4th syllable.

I will transcribe the phrase for you to make myself clearer, putting in the words that would suit my situation... obviously you will adjust them in the best possible way.

Answer me quickly because in Rome they are waiting.

The Guilty Party is *Ressmann.*

Be well.

Affectionately,

G. Verdi

☙Baron Costantino Ressmann (1832–1899), a Triestine diplomat, was at that time Italian ambassador to Paris.

The text above the staff in Verdi's transcription is in Boito's hand.

[Milan] 6 December [1894]

231 Dear Maestro,

Pietà Signor del nostro error profondo
Tu solo puoi levare il Mal dal mondo.
[Have mercy, Lord, on our profound error.
Thou alone canst take away the world's Evil.]

This way it seems to me it should fit the beautiful notes fairly well. A few words will have to be repeated, as they are repeated in the first verse: no harm done in a piece with the tone of a supplication. Affectionate greetings.

A. Boito

☙The correspondence has another of its silences at this point: a period of six months. But, as usual, even though they were no longer actively collaborating, the two men had occasion to meet. The Verdis spent some time in Milan, from 28 January 1895 to early March; there, in the presence of his lawyer and Ricordi, Verdi read the provisions in his will, now including the Casa di Riposo, whose preliminary designs Camillo Boito later showed him. After another month spent in Genoa, by early May the Verdis were back at Sant'Agata.

During the weeks in Milan Verdi wrote a letter to Gallignani in Parma, asking him to copy out the chants of the "Te Deum," first indication that he was thinking about another sacred composition.

Boito's movements during this period are not recorded. He almost certainly did not see Duse (who just at this time met D'Annunzio and soon began a clamorous romance, as public as her relationship with Boito had been secret). Boito was involved in official matters concerning the reorganization of the Italian Society of Authors. In early June, he probably accompanied Camille Bellaigue and his wife when they went to visit Sant'Agata. The following letter of Verdi would then have been written immediately afterwards.

Sant'Agata, 9 June 1895

232

Dear Boito,
    You left here:
    4 handkerchiefs
    1 vest
    1 small case
    1 button
The manservant has given them to me and I have them all in my room. Do you want me to send them to you? Or do you want me to bring them to you in 7 or 8 days' time?

Be well,
G. Verdi

12 June [1895]
Milan

233

Dear Maestro,
    I must say that I was still half-asleep the other morning when I was packing to leave.

I laughed as I read the list of the objects forgotten at Sant'Agata. Don't go to the trouble of sending them to me, or of bringing them to me; I will come in person to collect them next autumn.

Many, many greetings to you, to Signora Giuseppina, to Signora Barberina.

Till we meet, a few days from now.

Yours most affectionately,
A. Boito

❧On 21 or 22 June the Verdis went to Milan for a few days before continuing their journey to Montecatini, where they stayed until 22 July. During Verdi's Milanese sojourn, his *Ave Maria* on the enigmatic scale was performed at the Parma Conservatory for a small, private audience by a choir of a dozen students. Some time earlier, Verdi had sent the holograph of the piece to the conservatory's director, Giuseppe Gallignani, who evidently had a copy made before returning it to the composer. From this copy he had the parts extracted for the performance, which he conducted (after first delivering an expository lecture). The version heard on this occasion differs somewhat from the final version, which Verdi allowed to be published only two years later, after repeated urgings from Giulio Ricordi, who learned of the piece and its performance from the Parma correspondent of his *Gazzetta musicale di Milano*.

9 October [1895]
Milan

234 Dear Maestro,

A wish: That you be always well and content. Another wish: That we have occasion to work together again.

I will leave for Vezia the 14th, the 15th I will travel with the heart of Kosciuszko, and the 17th I will be back in Milan—whence I will inform you about my arrival at Sant'Agata, which will be, I presume, no later than the 20th.

Camillo and Madonnina remember still the days spent with you and Signora Giuseppina.

I have had news of the new Yvette, whose acquaintance I will make with pleasure, not having been able to know the other one of the *Folies Bergères.*

So then, dear Maestro, we will see each other soon; it seems a century to me since I last saw you.

Many warm greetings to Signora Giuseppina.

Yours most affectionately,
A. Boito

❧Boito's "wish" was probably connected with the date of his letter; Verdi always celebrated his birthday on 9 October, though it is often given by biographers as 10 October. See note following letter no. 285 below.

Vezia is in the Tessin, the Italian-speaking canton of Switzerland. It was the summer refuge of Verdi's old friend Countess Giuseppina Negroni Prati Morosini, also a friend of Boito. In the Morosini chapel at Vezia, the heart of the Polish patriot Kosciuszko (1746–1817) was pre-served, a cherished family relic. Apparently thanks to Verdi's discreet intervention, on 17 October the relic was solemnly consigned to delegates of the Polish nation. Boito, whose mother was Polish, was present.

Camillo Boito and his second wife, Madonnina Malaspina, had visited Sant'Agata in late September with the revised plans for the Casa di Riposo.

Yvette was Verdi's new dog, a German shepherd.

Boito did not visit Sant'Agata until late October, after the Verdis had made a short visit to Milan.

Friday [Milan, 8 November 1895]

235

Dear Maestro,

As soon as I returned to Milan I went to see Giulio; I found him very calm and more resolved than ever in his decision. He will sell the printing plant and will print in the provinces. Already some publisher-printers in the small neighboring cities have made him some very advantageous offers. A bit of patience will be necessary for the first month, but then, when the new service has been well launched, the firm will enjoy the benefits of this new arrangement.

I am quite convinced that, in taking this step, Giulio is not deceiving himself. His associates are all in agreement with him and give him their full approval. I repeat, he is profoundly calm and at ease.

I have hastened to give you this news because I know it will please you. Giulio greets you affectionately.

Here I found the house still empty. No one has come back yet.

In my spirit I still feel the great and dear peace of Sant'Agata.

I hope that Signora Peppina will soon be well again. If she is still taking creosote, I advise her to take it with water; by itself it is a bit irritating. Greet her again for me warmly, and to you, dear Maestro, many affectionate regards.

Yours,
A. Boito

🙚In a period of national economic crisis and unrest, Casa Ricordi had been affected by a surprise strike of some of its workers. Ricordi then suspended publication of the *Gazzetta musicale di Milano* and decided to close his printing establishment and have the work done by others in the provinces.

236 Dear Maestro,

Yesterday I attended the dress rehearsal of a truly new opera, the newest of all operas, and I was delighted throughout the evening, apart from a few curses I silently hurled from the back of the house because of the singers. They are all dogs, but it doesn't matter; everything goes very well.

Maestro Mugnone has grasped the whole score with great power of penetration and the orchestra has grasped his concept; he has understood and has made himself understood.

The score saves everything and it is a rare example (fairly rare even for you, Maestro) of an opera production where the music by itself saves itself.

Another who did his job well is our Tito Ricordi, creating the movements of the staging.

This *Falstaff* will once again be the joy of the Milanese.

Christmas is approaching and I have an idea. If there is an extra place at your table, and if you want me, I would come and spend Christmas Eve in Genoa. Christmas Eve is Tuesday. Please let me know if this idea is practicable, and if it isn't, I send you my affectionate best wishes now, for you and for Signora Peppina.

Yours,
Boito

    ◕sLa Scala was now under the management of Ricordi's great rival, Edoardo Sonzogno (who only put on those operas issued or overseen by his publishing firm), so this revival of *Falstaff* was given at the Teatro Dal Verme. It opened on 21 December, with Arturo Pessina in the title role, and a few survivors from the original cast (Garbin, Stehle, Guerrini).

    The conductor Leopoldo Mugnone (1858–1941) enjoyed Verdi's esteem. He had conducted the world premiere of Mascagni's *Cavalleria rusticana* (1890) and, a few years later, would conduct that of Puccini's *Tosca* (1900).

Genoa, 21 December 1895

237 Dearest Boito,

Among your many good ideas, this one is very, very good. We will see you on Christmas Eve then, and Christmas too if you like, and for as long as you like. We will be alone with De Amicis.

I also received two telegrams about the *Falstaff* rehearsal. But if the singers are as you say the effect will change at the performance. When the theater is almost empty, the few present are chiefly impressed by the orchestra, by the music, by details, etc., etc. All this disappears with the large audience, whose attention is directed almost wholly at those who act!... and so?

What will be will be! Good Heavens! How many operas at La Scala! And are all of them good?

It seems that here the Carlo Felice will also open; but everyone is angry with Casa Ricordi because it has refused permission to perform *Lohengrin* and *Ugonotti,* since *Ratcliff* is being given. But in God's name, what harm could be done to Casa Ricordi and to the reputation of those operas even by a huge fiasco? With this petty, disagreeable refusal, the firm does not win friends.

Greetings, greetings, greetings. Till we meet.

Affectionately,

G. Verdi

◀In taking over the rival firm of Lucca in 1888, Ricordi acquired the Italian rights to the operas of Wagner, Meyerbeer, Halévy, and other foreign composers.

Meanwhile, Sonzogno had become the Italian representative of the younger French composers. At La Scala, between December 1894 and March 1896, Sonzogno presented Reyer's *Sigurd;* Bizet's *Les pêcheurs de perles;* Massenet's *Manon, Werther,* and *La Navarraise;* Saint-Saëns' *Samson et Dalila* and *Henry VIII;* and Paladilhe's *Patrie* (all in Italian translation). The Italian composers were Leoncavallo (*I Medici*), Mascagni (*Guglielmo Ratcliff, Zanetto,* and *Silvano*), and Giordano, whose *Andrea Chénier* was given its world premiere on 28 March 1896, the last opera of that season.

After Boito's Christmas visit to Genoa, the Verdis traveled to Milan in mid-January 1896, remaining there until mid-February. Much of that time was taken up by questions concerning the Casa di Riposo project.

Genoa, 18 February 1896

238

Dear Boito,

Eureka!

I've found a *Te Deum!* No less!... The author is Father Vallotti, for whom

I have the greatest respect, as you know. I have written to Tebaldini asking him to have a copy made for me.

I am telling you all this so that you will remember that on the 14th of February 1896 you saw a *Te Deum* of mine, in the event that they were to accuse me of... No, no, there's no danger, because I won't publish it.

I know Gallignani is in Milan; greet him for me.

Here we are much the same.

L'éclair asks me to express an opinion on poor Thomas... I am not going to answer at all... and you must not answer this letter.

Be well.

G. Verdi

⌐Francesco Antonio Vallotti (1697–1780), a Franciscan monk, composed a great deal of sacred music and for fifty years was music director of the basilica of Padua.

Giovanni Tebaldini (1864–1952) was a musicologist, composer, and editor of ancient music. He was music director in the basilicas of Venice and Padua then—succeeding Gallignani—director of the Parma Conservatory from 1897 to 1902. He and Verdi exchanged a number of letters at this time about some of the interpretations composers had previously given of the liturgical hymn "Te Deum." He later published various articles of memoirs concerning Verdi. Verdi's reference to 14 February 1896 is puzzling, since he supposedly left Milan on 13 February for Genoa. In all likelihood, the composer simply made a mistake.

Ambroise Thomas had died in Paris on 12 February. Verdi wrote to the widow, referring to his "old and loyal friend, whom I admired as an artist, and I loved as a man" [Abbiati, 4:591].

19 Feb [1896] Milan

239 Dear Maestro,

I am curious to know whether in Vallotti's *Te Deum* you will happen to find the same musical interpretation that you set forth in the last verses, the only interpretation that is truly natural and right. For that matter, you have no need to be reassured by examples from the past to sanction your own concept, which is so logical and clear. Anyone able to read and understand what he is reading will approve it.

I saw Gallignani, who has already left again for Parma, where he has finally been able to settle all the affairs of the conservatory in his own way and it is satisfied and at ease and asks nothing further.

I will not answer the request of *L'éclair* either.

I will be in Genoa for the inauguration of the Galliera monument and thus to refresh or revive Monteverde's memory.

Affectionate greetings to you and to signora Peppina.

Yours,
A. Boito

&s During the previous year, Gallignani—installed as director of the Parma Conservatory—had trouble getting along with his titular superior, the governor of the institution. On Gallignani's insistence, the office of governor was abolished.

Raffaele De Ferrari, duke of Galliera (1803–1876), was a Genoese businessman and industrialist, and as a senator (from 1858) was particularly active in encouraging the extension of Italian railways and the founding of shipping lines. In 1874 he contributed a huge sum to the construction of a new pier for the port of Genoa, which now bears his name (a central square in the city is also named after him). The sculptor Giulio Monteverde (1837–1917) was responsible for the monument, which is now in Via Fanti d'Italia. It is an allegorical group, featuring Commerce, Navigation, and Charity. Monteverde was on friendly terms with Boito and Verdi.

Genoa, 6 April 1896

240

Dear Boito,

Inauguration 12 April at 2 P.M.
Well?

Till we meet.

Affectionately,
G. Verdi

&s The Galliera monument was officially unveiled on 12 April. Verdi had returned to Genoa on 28 March after a quick trip to Milan regarding the Casa di Riposo. Boito and Verdi met on the occasion of the inauguration.

9 June [1896]
Milan

241 Dear Maestro,

We all rejoiced on hearing from Giulio that, on returning to Sant'A-gata, you found Signora Giuseppina on her feet and in good spirits. Let us hope that the improvement continues and will allow her to take her usual cure at Montecatini.

Tebaldini announces to me that he has discovered a *Te Deum* by Victoria, two alternating choruses with organ: it exists in the library of the *liceo* in Bologna.

Tebaldini offers to find a copyist in Bologna who will make a copy for you if you wish.

Another *Te Deum* exists, by Purcell, and it is easily accessible to anyone who wants it because it is published in the great edition by Novello of London, who also sells the volumes separately. But Tebaldini ends his letter by expressing his wish to perform the *Ave Maria*s of Verdi in November in Padua, to inaugurate the concert hall with them.

For this purpose he seeks an intercessor and this intercessor would be me, though with scant hope of obtaining the favor because I know how you feel about that piece being performed.

Warmest greetings to Signora Giuseppina and to you, dear Maestro. I will see you at Sant'Agata, but before then, I hope, in Milan.

Yours most affectionately,
A. Boito

⋙The Verdis had been at Sant'Agata since early May. Giuseppina's health was failing, and so at the end of that month, when Verdi had to go to Milan on business, he went alone. The business again concerned the Casa di Riposo: he deposited the entire sum necessary for its construction (which had already begun) in a Milanese bank.

Sant'Agata, 11 June 1896

242 Dear Boito,

Peppina is out of bed and isn't ill, but she doesn't eat, so she is regaining her strength with great difficulty.

As for Montecatini, it's out of the question for the present; but if we are able to make that journey, I will see you first in Milan.

Thank Tebaldini very much for the trouble he has taken over the

"Te Deum": but at this point what's done is done, nor could I give any other interpretation to that chant, even if a reading of the *Te Deum*s of Purcell and Victoria were to show me that I have got it wrong. Once I have finished (and only a few bits of orchestration are wanting), I will add it to the *Ave Maria*s and they will sleep together, never seeing the light of day... *Amen.*

Will we see each other then?

When?

Perhaps in Milan!... but certainly at Sant'Agata.

I thank you for Peppina and greet you. I affectionately shake your hand.

Yours,
G. Verdi

  In the period of nearly four months between this letter and the next, the Verdis spent a few days in Milan in July inspecting the Casa di Riposo, whose construction was progressing satisfactorily. On 15 July they traveled to Montecatini (Giuseppina's health had delayed this annual visit), and about a fortnight later they were again at Sant'Agata. The composer made another brief trip to Milan around the first of September on Casa di Riposo business.

At that time he may have seen Boito, who had spent the month of August in the Dandolo family villa in the province of Como to work on *Nerone.* In any case, Boito seems to have promised Verdi an October visit to Sant'Agata. The letter that arrived for him there (mentioned in Verdi's letter below) could have been from Duse, in Rome at that time.

Sant'Agata, 9 October [1896]   **243**

Dear Boito,

A letter for you arrived here two days ago. As you haven't appeared, I believe it's best to send it on to you in Milan.

Well? What are you doing?

I must advise you, by the way, that the day after tomorrow, *Sunday,* there will be no one left at Sant'Agata, as Peppina will go and visit her sister and will stay in Cremona until sometime around the fifteenth...

Plan accordingly then, and be well.

Affectionately,
G. Verdi

Sant'Agata, 11 October 1896

244   Dear Boito,

I have received yours of the 9th, and I realize that you haven't received mine written on the 8th!

In it I told you that around the *eleventh* there would be no one left at Sant'Agata, and that Peppina would be going to Cremona on the 14th to spend two or three days with her sister.

Now you tell me that on that day (14) you will come to Sant'Agata!! I will be going that very day with Peppina to Cremona, but will return that evening to Sant'Agata. So if, instead of coming to Fiorenzuola, you would be willing to travel to Cremona, we could come home together.

You could arrive at Cremona at about 1 P.M., and we could leave for Sant'Agata at 3 P.M.

If this arrangement doesn't suit you, then come via Fiorenzuola, but not on Wednesday, rather on *Thursday,* and I will send the carriage.

Write me at once about this.

Be well.

Affectionately,
G. Verdi

P.S. I must advise you that in Cremona the Albergo del Cappello no longer exists. Take the omnibus of the *Albergo d'Italia,* where you will find me.

&s Verdi's letter "written on the 8th" was actually written on 9 October (it is no. 243 above). Boito's "of the 9th" seems not to survive, nor does his reply to no. 244. In any case, Boito did indeed come to Sant'Agata (we do not know by what route), and remained over two weeks. During this visit, as the letter below suggests, he and Verdi discussed Bach.

9 November [1896]
Milan

245   Dear Maestro,

As soon as I arrived in Milan I set about putting my books in order, and in such good order that I could not find the score of Bach's *Mass in B Minor* until today. Now at last I have found it and I have also found the *problem* exactly as it is in the piano transcription: the two flutes play: the first an A♯ and the second an F♮, while the bass has a D♮; but this is a sweet problem, because the A♯ resolves properly to the B. The real problem lies in the chord that follows:

The crux of the problem lies in the alto part: F♮–D♯. If this spasm is deliberate (as I have no doubt) it is truly a spasm, but if it were not, he couldn't have wanted it; the ear can endure it—indeed, it must endure it—but our mind can approve. And now to move on to a more peaceful subject, I will copy out for you those stanzas of the *joyous Stabat Mater*, which like the other one is by Jacopone da Todi, but this one is very little known and perhaps more beautiful than the first:

Stabat Mater speciosa
Juxta foenum gaudiosa,
Dum jacebat parvulus.

Quae gaudebat et ridebat
Exultabat cum videbat
Nati partum inclyti.

Fac me vere congaudere,
Jesulino cohaerere
Donec ego vixero.

That "Jesulino" has the grace of a Perugino.

In Sabatier's book on St. Francis, from which I have made this copy, the other stanzas are missing, but they can be found in volume 5 of the works of Ozanam. If this little sample kindles your interest, tell me and I will find them for you.

P.S. Camillo must have written to you today. Many warm greetings, and thanks for the hospitality of Sant'Agata, to you, dear Maestro, and to dear Signora Peppina.

Yours most affectionately,
A. Boito

Boito uses the word "chiodo." Here translated as "problem," it literally means "nail," and is a deliberate reference to Bach's word painting in this Crucifixus.

The *Life of Saint Francis of Assisi* by Paul Sabatier (1858–1928), which appeared in 1893, was a "modern" view of the saint; the volume was an international success (Boito and Duse both admired it) and in 1894 was put on the Index Librorum Prohibitorum by the Vatican. A French Calvinist pastor, theologian, and historian, Sabatier founded in 1902 the Société Internationale des Études Franciscaines. Antoine-Fréderic Ozanam (1813–1853) was a Catholic historian and philologist, who taught foreign literatures at the Sorbonne. His most important work, to which Boito refers, was *Les poètes franciscains en Italie au XIIe siècle* (1852).

Boito's letter suggests that in the late autumn of 1896 Verdi was working on his *Stabat Mater* for four-part chorus, later one of the *Quattro pezzi sacri*.

Giuseppina's declining health made Verdi cancel a projected trip to Milan (to inspect the progress of the Casa di Riposo under construction) and postpone the move to Genoa until after 15 November.

Camillo and Madonnina Boito had visited Sant'Agata at the end of September.

Genoa, 6 January 1897

Dear Boito,

246

I won't answer!
I congratulate you...
Greetings.

G. Verdi

~At least one letter from Boito must be missing, and so this reply to it remains cryptic. It is possible that Verdi is sending congratulations after a highly successful performance of the *Mefistofele* prologue during a concert on 3 January at the Opéra in Paris.

As Giuseppina's health worsened, Verdi's papers became less orderly; consequently, there are more frequent lacunae in the correspondence with Boito. For the whole year of 1897 only some Verdi letters survive (scrupulously saved by Boito), but none written by Boito.

A few days after writing the above note to Boito, Verdi had an "attack" of some kind, involving temporary paralysis, a prelude of the fatal stroke four years later.

When Verdi was himself again, a period of improved health on Giuseppina's part allowed him to make a visit to Milan (22 February–16 March). In addition to inspecting the Casa di Riposo, he also went over the part of Desdemona with Rose Caron, temporarily in Milan, for she was to sing it in Italian at the Opéra.

Genoa, 15 April 1897

Dear Boito,

247

Well?
Let us rejoice and
Amen.

I have received this letter from Roger, which you will send back to me.

This is something new for me, because I never knew that Ricordi demanded *droits d'auteur!* Who granted them? In any case, talk with Giulio about it and decide between yourselves what you want to do, and answer Roger together...

Ah, these blessed *droits d'auteur.*
Be well.

Affectionately,
G. Verdi

Roger's letter has not survived in the Sant'Agata archives. It must have been connected with Verdi's and Boito's royalties from the performance of *Otello* at the Opéra on 13 April. Since this was a benefit performance for the Ligue Fraternelle des Enfants de France, Verdi waived royalties, and presumably Boito did the same. The cryptic first lines of Verdi's letter probably refer to the success of the performance.

Genoa, 17 April 1897

248 Dear Boito,

Very well, appoint Roger as arbiter in the matter. I will answer Roger today that you and Giulio will write to him about the question.

I haven't given any more thought to the *Stabat,* for which the orchestration is *in statu quo.* I haven't thought about it, nor am I thinking about it! And if I do think about it, I am repelled at exposing myself again to the public. In fact, why should I face opinions, pointless chatter, criticism, praise, hates, loves in which I don't believe?... At this moment I myself couldn't say what I want to do! Everything I might do seems futile to me! Now I am unable to make up my mind about anything! In the event that I complete the orchestration I will write and tell you!

Thank you for everything and be well.

Affectionately,
G. Verdi

Another six months of silence follow this letter. The Verdis, however, stopped off in Milan for ten days or so in early May, between Genoa and Sant'Agata. Verdi and Boito quite probably met, and the composer inspected the Casa di Riposo, its construction now well advanced.

During the early summer Verdi worked on revising the "enigmatic" *Ave Maria.* Boito paid a visit to Sant'Agata in late May-early June, already conspiring to arrange a performance of Verdi's latest sacred works, the eventual *Quattro pezzi sacri.*

On 1 July the Verdis began a week's visit to Milan—including another inspection of the Casa di Riposo (documented by a series of photographs)—then proceeded to Montecatini. By 22 July they were back at Sant'Agata, where Verdi set to work on the final revision of the *Pezzi sacri.*

Sant'Agata, 10 October 1897

249

Dear Boito,

You have the habit of coming to Sant'Agata when no one else is here! Now we are alone; and if you come, you will find Sant'Agata even more boring than usual.

Peppina was ill for a few weeks and sentenced to stay in bed. Now her cough has almost disappeared, but she takes no nourishment and is extremely weak; she is not happy, speaks very little, and seems almost irritated at hearing others speak. Though I myself am not particularly ill, I have a thousand ailments. My legs have trouble carrying me and I can hardly walk any more; my eyesight is weakened and I can't read at any length; furthermore, I am even a bit deaf. A thousand ailments, in other words! So you will understand that if Sant'Agata was boring in the past, now it is very sad! If you come and have the courage to face so many ailments, you will always be welcome, and you will perform a work of mercy...

            6. *Visit the sick.*

       Good-bye.

          Yours affectionately,

          G. Verdi

In the event that you do come you must let me know ahead of time, because Peppina, again this year, wants to drag herself to Cremona to spend 24 or 48 hours with her sister.

    Verdi's complaints about his own health are belied by his frequent short trips at this time and by his work. Giuseppina's health, on the other hand, was cause for genuine alarm, though she did "drag herself to Cremona" for the ritual visit to Barberina.

[Telegram]

13 Oct 97

Arrigo Boito, Principe Amedeo 1, Milan

From Busseto

Agreed then that Saturday at the usual hour you will find my carriage   **250** at Fiorenzuola. Peppina goes to Cremona tomorrow but will return Sunday or Monday.

                Verdi

    Boito visited Sant'Agata as arranged, presumably also to discuss with Verdi a performance of the *Pezzi sacri* planned (by Boito) for Paris. After this visit, Boito traveled to Paris to work out personally the details with the conductor Paul Taffanel.

On 11 November 1897, a few weeks after her return from Cremona, Giuseppina Verdi suffered a violent attack of pneumonia. She died on the afternoon of 14 November. In deference to her written wish, her funeral was extremely simple and, "at the first light of dawn" [Abbiati, 4: 618], then the remains were taken by rail from Fiorenzuola to Milan and interred temporarily at the Cimitero Monumentale, until she could be buried at the Casa di Riposo, in whose chapel Verdi had arranged a crypt for them both.

Boito received the news of her death while still in Paris. He immediately rushed back to Milan, arriving in time to be at the station to receive the coffin and accompany it to the cemetery. Verdi had remained at Sant'Agata, where Giuditta Ricordi and Teresa Stolz had gone at once on learning of Giuseppina's death.

Boito's letter referred to below has not survived.

Sant'Agata, 6 December 1897

251 Dear Boito,

My hand trembles, and I write you as best I can to thank you again and again for your very dear and kind letter. What you say is all very well... but I, who am half-deaf, half-blind, who speak with difficulty, unable to attend to things in any way. Plus other difficulties that you know about. Nothing is yet decided for Milan, and I am unable to decide!...

Greet Giulio, and your brother and Sig.ra Madonnina. And I greet you also on behalf of Sig.ra Stolz, Maria, and Peppina, very sad not to see you still here... And I, more than they!

I shake your hand with a thousand heartfelt thoughts, and I know I am shaking the hand of a fine man in every sense of the word.

Yours,
G. Verdi

ᛋRicordi, Boito, and other friends were insisting that Verdi should move to Milan, though the Carrara family at Sant'Agata took devoted care of him (the "Peppina" referred to in the letter is Maria Carrara Verdi's oldest daughter, named after Giuseppina Strepponi). Teresa Stolz (1834–1902), a great performer of Verdi's works and his longtime friend—and, years before, perhaps more than friend—was very close

to him in the last few years of his life. During this stay, or shortly afterwards, the composer gave her the autograph score of the *Messa da
requiem* (she had been the soprano of the first performances), which
she later donated to the Casa di Riposo; it is now in the Museo Teatrale
alla Scala.

Sant'Agata, Saturday, [18 December 1897]

252

Dear Boito,

Bravo!

I expect you then, and at 3:37 P.M. on Christmas Eve you will find
my carriage at Fiorenzuola.

Thank you, thank you, and greetings to all.

Affectionately,
G. Verdi

◄s Verdi evidently had decided not to spend the holidays in Genoa as
in the past. He did not give up the apartment in Palazzo Doria altogether, but his stays in Genoa became briefer as those in Milan became
longer.

[Telegram]

24 Dec 97

Arrigo Boito, Principe Amedeo 1, Milan
From Busseto
Agreed. You will find carriage at Fiorenzuola at 2:37.

253

Verdi

◄s The original of this telegram (and all others in this correspondence) does not survive, except in the transcription by Nardi, who
seems to have copied the hour incorrectly. In the previous letter it is
clearly 3:37.

[Milan, January 1898]

I was awaiting Taffanel's reply to a letter I wrote him, in which I asked

254

when Casa Ricordi would have to send to Paris the solo parts, the choruses, then the orchestral parts.

He should also be told that the pieces to be performed are no longer
four, but three:

A *Stabat Mater* for four-part chorus and large orchestra:

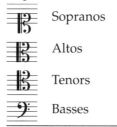

	Sopranos
	Altos
	Tenors
	Basses

A prayer in *Italian* on the first strophes of the last canto of Dante's *Paradiso* for four treble voices:

> Soprano
> Second soprano
> Alto
> Another alto

A *Te Deum* for two choruses and large orchestra. Assuming the chorus numbers, for ex., one hundred persons, it should be divided into fifty on one side, and fifty on the other.

The division within each chorus:

> 12 Sopranos
> 12 Altos
> 12 Tenors
> 14 Basses

> Total   50

The same for the other chorus.

For the prayer four women *soloists* would be needed, though the piece is short and without *solos.* At the Opéra it will not be hard to find the artists I want: my *rêve* would be, for ex.:

> First soprano   Caron
> Second soprano   ———
> First alto   ———
> Other alto   Eglon

The duration of the pieces:

> *Te Deum*   less than 12 minutes
> *Stabat Mater*   less than 10
> Prayer   less than 5

The Concert Society could perform in the first part of the program two or three orchestral pieces.

In the second part:

    1 *Stabat*

    2 Prayer for solo voices

    3 *Te Deum*

Will you come and eat some *gruel* here at 6?

                  G.V.

•sThis letter is on letterhead of the Grand Hôtel de Milan; it was delivered by hand and is undated, but it was almost certainly written in the last week of January 1898 in Milan, where Verdi had arrived on 6 January. A surviving letter to Taffanel (to which Verdi refers here) is dated 24 January.

Boito had been to Sant'Agata for Christmas and stayed until New Year's Day. In a letter to Bellaigue on 29 December he reported optimistically on Verdi's regained strength, and indicated that the composer would be coming to Milan [CVB, p. 482].

Preparations were under way for the public premiere of three of the eventual *Quattro pezzi sacri.* They were to be heard, under Taffanel, at a Concert Spirituel in Paris on 7 or 8 April. Originally all four pieces were to be given, but at about this time Verdi decided to omit the "enigmatic" *Ave Maria.* The "prayer in Italian" is the *Laudi alla Vergine Maria.*

Caron did not sing in the event; the soprano was Grandjean. By "Eglon" Verdi presumably meant Héglon.

Verdi stayed in Milan until 15 March, surrounded by the attentions of his Milanese friends, including, of course, Boito and Ricordi. In a letter of 4 February to Barberina Strepponi [CVB, p. 483], he complained of lack of appetite and of sleeping badly, but his health was generally good, and the *Gazzetta musicale di Milano,* announcing on 3 March the forthcoming concert, indicated that the composer would probably travel to the French capital for the occasion.

But on 20 March Verdi wrote Ricordi from Genoa that his physician had strongly advised against the trip to Paris [CVB, p. 484]. Boito promptly volunteered to make the trip in Verdi's stead and keep an eye (and an ear) on the rehearsals, after Verdi had gone over the pieces with him.

So on 27 March Boito went to Genoa and they looked at the three works together. Verdi made some changes, which he then sent on to Ricordi. On the morning of 29 March Boito left for Paris, arriving there early the following day. He had hardly left Genoa before Verdi was writing him with last-minute instructions. This was one of the rare occasions when Verdi was not present at a first performance of his work.

Genoa, 29 March 1898

255   Dear Boito,

By now you will have been in the capital for some hours, and perhaps you will already have been in touch with Taffanel and Gailhard and you will tell me what you have decided.

You have showed such intelligent and affectionate concern for those poor three pieces of music that I have nothing more to say to you, only to repeat that the parts that require the greatest refinement are:

In the *Stabat* towards the end, when the 4 horns in D play  etc., and the chorus has "Quando corpus morietur" *extremely piano,* so as to reach the entrance of the harps *morendo* and *piano,* etc., etc...

In the *Laudi* from Dante, there is only to observe the dynamics and phrasing, as, for ex., at measure 31 on the word "pace" and others as well, etc... And the phrase in *3ds* and *4ths* should be very sweet and *cantabile* on the words "La tua benignitade."

In the *Te Deum,* the main points are:

The beginning of the hymn as far as the "Sanctus" of the sopranos, who fade away in a *morendo,* ending with the *harmonics* in the violins.

Another thing is to broaden the movement a little on the phrase of the trumpets:

sounding pitches

but in such a way that no change of tempo is perceptible.

Return to the first tempo on "Salvum fac," etc., with full force.

Even more important is the unison on "Dignare Domine," which must be very expressive, pathetic, and without accents, and must end *pianissimo.*

Also important is the *pianissimo* of the sopranos:

mi - se - re - re

More important is the *pianissimo* on "Fiat misericordia," even though it is with full chorus.

Make sure the trumpet rings out right from the first two measures, so that it isn't thought to be the sound of an English horn, clarinet, etc., and the trumpet's note must last for two measures as written.

I urge you to pay attention also to the placing of the choruses and the orchestra. The violins must not be constricted by the choruses and the orchestra, and the choruses must be clearly set off from the orchestra and the two choruses distinctly divided. It would be an error and a horror if the choruses were to remain seated while singing.

Sincere greetings to Gailhard and to Taffanel and *à la grace de Dieu.*
My health remains the same.
Everyone here in the house greets you with very great fondness.
Be well.

G. Verdi

Friday [Genoa, 1 April 1898]

256

Dear Boito,

In the scale  the C really should be natural, but I prefer the C♭ because it has greater expression, can be more easily sung, and better prepares the resolution to G♭. In any case it will be another liberty taken, as in the penultimate measure of the *Stabat* where the F in the orchestra should be ♯ and I have written *F-natural!*

I am very happy to hear the news; and please thank Taffanel very much, but insist with him that the chorus sing standing.

I couldn't ask for anyone better than the four artists who will sing in Italian the *Laudi* from Dante. Pay them my respects and thank them profoundly.

—————————————

As for my health, the doctor says not bad, but I feel that I am not well... For that matter, as someone has sung, "The pitying lie is granted to doctors..."

I will not say a word to you, for the gratitude I feel is too great... Write me often.

Be well.

Affectionately,
G. Verdi

P.S. Affectionate greetings from my niece and her daughter, and Sig.ra Stolz.

Again, good-bye.

☙The scale Verdi cites here occurs in the *Te Deum,* five measures before "Patrem immensae majestatis."

"The pitying lie" is a quotation from act 3, scene 2 of *La traviata* ("Oh la bugia pietosa / A' medici è concessa...").

[Telegram]

2 April 98

Arrigo Boito, Grand Hotel, Paris
From Genoa

257   My opinion E pedal bass in octaves not too loud but long. If you find something else all the better. Writing.

Verdi

☙This telegram is explained in the following letter (no. 258).

Genoa, 2 April 1898

258   Dear Boito,

Everyone spoke so highly of those performances at the Opéra that I was hoping for some effect from those two pieces of mine; now I have little hope! But it's too late to back out now...

As I said in my telegram, I would give the pitch with the organ for

the "Te Deum" with a pedal in this range 𝄢 with bass *ripieno,*

holding the note quite a long time so that it will penetrate the ear thoroughly; and at the beginning of the *Te Deum* I would put only eight good voices for each chorus (but steady voices, in tune) up to "Sanctus," when they would all enter with the great *forte* with the orchestra.

I was hoping that this beginning up to the harmonics of the violins could make a certain effect; but I see that with those voices we will not achieve it.

Other important points besides the liturgical chant in the *forte*

are in the unison "Dignare Domine," etc., accompanied without chords, with a mourning expression, with the voice covered and without phrasing. The simple note precisely, strictly performed should suffice.

Further, pay close attention to the *solo voice* that follows. What is wanted is a distinct voice that would emerge from the mass of the soprano voices of the choruses, but the person should not be seen. A solo voice, not one from the choruses. La Grandjean, who is a good musician, and at the Opéra-Comique was *bon enfant*, might be appropriate. If so, then she should be placed hidden among the sopranos and as far as possible from the audience. But alas, if the choruses are not good, what will happen in the *Stabat?* Even more difficult because of the exposed ensemble passages.

At the beginning, on the first phrase, "Stabat Mater," etc., I would like from all a *mezzoforte* voice, sorrowful, hollow, detached... But if the intonation is unsure then let's have them at full voice, provided only they finish the phrase *diminuendo morendo,* and here they can even be off pitch.

In the cantabile of the baritones ♪ etc.,

even just six voices would be enough, but secure ones... Here also I had hoped for an effect by means of a mass of about *24* or *30* voices with that high lament of the violins... which will not happen...

And it will be even worse with the quartet of unaccompanied voices, so comfortable and easy for the voices!!!! Perhaps the altos' phrase will go better... but then afterwards? That ensemble?...

Again I urge you to devote your attention to the end, beginning

with that note of the four horns, F-sharp ♪ with

the *pianissimo* of the basses, then the quartet of voices, etc., etc.

À la grace de Dieu.

I will not add a word about you, though I know how attentively you will concern yourself with it all.

―――――――

As for the journey to Paris, tell everyone how happy I would be if I could make it. But I can only repeat to you what I wrote you in my last letter.

Good-bye. Thank you. Keep writing me, even if briefly. Keep well.

Affectionately,

G. Verdi

I return to the beginning of the *Te Deum.* Your idea of a reinforcement is quite right and necessary. Everything possible must be done to have it. Even if only for the "Te Deum," even only for the first measures...

Good-bye.

Write me.

And you may keep your idea of having just one E of the organ heard if necessary: not high, but long.

This is the right range:

Pedal:

In a letter that is missing but is quoted by Verdi in writing to Ricordi, Boito had told Verdi that the Paris choruses were disappointing. Only part of the chorus of the Opéra was participating in the concert, and it had been strengthened—at least in number—by aged members of the Société chorus. Verdi was immediately on his guard. The four women soloists, on the other hand, met with Boito's approval, and so Verdi was not worried about the *Laudi.*

Grandjean had sung the part of Alice in the 1894 premiere of *Falstaff* at the Opéra-Comique.

In the published score of the *Stabat Mater,* the cantabile of the baritones reads thus:

Sunday [Genoa, 3 April 1898]
8 A.M.

259   To give the pitch for the beginning of the *Te Deum,* Gailhard's idea is perhaps better.

A prolonged *E pedal* would reveal too clearly to the public any faulty intonation.

Instead, a prelude with full organ, *forte,* seems something attached to the piece. A prelude of *12* or *16* measures, based on *tonic* and *dominant* pedals to fix well in the choristers the key of *E minor.*

I will send this off to the post, as it is 8 o'clock.

Be well,
G. Verdi

Palm Sunday [Genoa, 3 April 1898]

260

Dear Boito,

I wrote you this morning at 8; I am writing you again at 5 about the beginning of the *Te Deum*. I am still of the opinion that, as the choristers need support, the lesser evil is a definite organ prelude *a tutto ripieno*. Further, also have the organ anticipate the first notes of the liturgical chant, like this:

Then continue the prelude for *8* or *10* measures, always based on the *tonic* and *dominant*, and end like this:

also in order to have the *fourth* scale degree heard.

Be well,

G. Verdi

Genoa, 4 April 1898

261

Dear Boito,

Much better! In this way all my observations prove unnecessary. Better, much better! But still I urge you to keep watch over the execution of the music and draw from it the effects that can be there, and that I have mentioned to you.

In the *Te Deum:*

1. The whole beginning to the emergence of the violin harmonics

2. In the liturgical chant ⟨music⟩ etc.

3. In the *fortissimo* passage for unaccompanied voices in E♭

3. In the unison "Dignare Domine"
4. And in the trumpets with the *E* and the *solo* voice

In the *Stabat:*
1. The beginning through the entire solo for the baritones
2. The chorus quartet, unaccompanied voices
3. The cantabile for the altos
4. Especially the *fortissimo* entry of the 4 horns (*F*♯) until the end

Not undemanding, our composer! I know... but those effects should come out.

I leave you, but continue to send me good news. I am neither better nor worse, therefore not very well.

Many, many regards to the distinguished director of the conservatory, and thank him for his courteous words.

Thanks to Taffanel and to all.

Remember me fondly to the most kind and dear Sig.ra Gabriella, and to her husband.

Good-bye, my dear Boito, and thanks to you more than to anyone else.

Be well,
G. Verdi

◄sProbably writing in haste, Verdi misnumbers the points in the first part of the letter.

The director of the Paris Conservatory, successor to Ambroise Thomas, was Théodore Dubois (1837–1924), composer and organist. He had to be thanked for lending the choruses of the conservatory for the concert.

Signora Gabriella was Gabrielle Bellaigue, wife of Camille.

[Telegram]

5 April 98

Arrigo Boito, Grand Hôtel Capucines, Paris
From Genoa

262 Letters and telegram received. Thanks for everything. Will send portraits a bit late because I have none with me. Regards to all.

Verdi

Genoa, 6 April 1898

Dear Boito,

263

We are almost there!

Tomorrow evening, the fateful evening! From your own letters I understand (I, who am suspicious) that many effects will not come off! And I'm not speaking only about the beginning of the *Te Deum.*

Taffanel writes that the choruses are difficult!! Except for a few passages, they are not at all difficult, but they are very demanding. Naturally, inasmuch as there are no *solo* main parts, it is necessary for someone to enunciate the words well. We could close an ear to the bad choruses of the Opéra for *Othello* because there were three colossuses who acted and declaimed splendidly the words of the drama. But in a psalm for choruses, the choruses are protagonist.

What will be, will be... I repeat, but it is painful to realize and to know there are passages that could produce an effect... but will not. I cite one (and not one of the best, all modesty aside): the "Salvum fac" in E♭ in the *Te Deum,* so well prepared, so centrally situated and resonant for all the parts, should produce in those 16 measures a sure effect, even winning applause. Similarly at other points. But whatever happens, I will always be grateful for the immense testimony of friendship you have given me in going to Paris. And I am also grateful to all those who have touchingly lent themselves to the performance of these pieces. It is no one's fault if the main part, the chorus, is not adequate.

I will write no more letters, only a telegram or two. You, however, will write, I hope, and wire and say when you will be here.

Cordial greetings to all. Tito is going to Paris!!! Why?

My health is not bad but it could be better.

Maria, Peppina, Sig.ra Stolz greet you fondly.

Be well.

G. Verdi

⮜"Peppina" is Giuseppina Carrara, daughter of Maria.

Genoa, 7 April 1898

Dear Boito,

264

Your telegram contradicts my forecasts and all my fears; and you can well imagine how happy I am to have been mistaken. So let us hope!

Tomorrow, through Casa Ricordi, I will send the four portraits for the devoted performers of the *Laudi.* Greet and congratulate all. I congratulate chiefly you, and I thank you very, very much!

I expect you Sunday then. Be well.

Affectionately,
G. Verdi

⊷The three *Pezzi sacri* (*Stabat Mater, Laudi alla Vergine Maria,* and *Te Deum*) were performed at the Opéra on 7 April 1898, conducted by Taffanel. The enthusiastic audience demanded an encore of the *Laudi,* whose soloists were sopranos Ackté and Grandjean and mezzosopranos Héglon and Delna (this last had also participated in the first French *Falstaff*). A second performance was given the following evening.

Genoa, 8 April 1898

265 Dear Boito,

In going to Paris in my stead, you did me a service for which I will always be grateful to you. But if, in rejecting any gesture of gratitude on my part, you are acting chivalrously, then I remain crushed by a weight that I cannot and must not bear.

Come now, dear Boito, let us speak frankly, without reticence, without veils, like true friends, as I am for you, and you for me:

To show you my gratitude, I could give you some object... but what would be the sense of it? It would be embarrassing for me, and useless for you.

Therefore allow me now, when you have returned from Paris, to shake your hand... and for this handshake you will not utter a word, nor will you say *thanks*. Further, absolute silence about this letter.

Amen... So be it.

Affectionately,
G. Verdi

⊷Typically, Verdi was worried about how properly to compensate Boito for his time and trouble. Writing to Ricordi on 3 April, the composer said: "He must be recompensed amply, but without seeming to pay him. *How much?* and, in your opinion, *Where?* and *How?"* [CVB, p. 487].

Genoa, 14 April 1898

Dear Arrigo,

266

Unfortunately I was aware of the condition of poor Madonnina!

I didn't want to speak about it here, so as not to inform you in advance of an inevitable sorrow!

I can imagine the grief of poor Camillo!... indeed I can imagine it!!

And you!... poor Arrigo!!! I can say only a useless word to you... *Courage!*

If I can do anything, I am at your disposal... Good-bye...

Affectionately,

G. Verdi

◆Camillo's beloved second wife, Madonnia Malaspina Boito, whom he had married in 1887, was mortally ill.

During that spring of 1898 the city of Turin—with the aid of several of Boito's friends, including Giacosa—was involved in preparing a great exposition to celebrate the fiftieth anniversary of the Statuto (the progenitor of the Italian constitution). The enterprising impresario of the Teatro Regio, Giuseppe Depanis, was planning a rich series of concerts in conjunction with the exposition and with the special show of sacred art. The conductor was to be the young but already well-known Arturo Toscanini. Having received Verdi's permission to schedule the three *Pezzi sacri,* Depanis went with Toscanini and the chorus master Aristide Venturi to visit the composer in Genoa in the latter part of April. Depanis later wrote that the eighty-five-year-old Verdi and the thirty-one-year-old conductor worked together at the piano, and the two understood each other at once.

The concert took place on 26 May 1898 in the new concert hall built for the exposition; it was repeated on 28 and 30 May. At all three hearings the *Laudi* had to be repeated. Its sopranos were Fausta Labia and Maria Pozzi; the mezzo-sopranos, Tina Alasia and Guerrina Fabbri. Boito had hoped to persuade Verdi to visit Turin for a rehearsal, but the composer would not be moved; and even later, when he could have heard the pieces in Milan, he did not take advantage of the opportunity. Boito, in a letter to Toscanini, suggested that the old man was afraid of an excessively "strong emotion" [CVB, p. 491]

Verdi had moved from Genoa to Milan on 26 April, and so he was there during the terrible days of early May, when the city—and much of Italy—seemed on the brink of chaos. Unemployment and poverty, exacerbated by a sudden, considerable increase in the price of bread, had provoked demonstrations all over the country. Between 7 and 9 May there were barricades in the streets of Milan, and the authorities panicked. King Umberto I sent General Fiorenzo Bava-Beccaris (1831– 1924) to the city, with cannon and cavalry. Mistaking a peaceful hunger march for an uprising, the general ordered fire; and eighty unarmed people were killed and four hundred and fifty wounded. Catholic and socialist leaders were arrested and given stiff prison sentences. Foreign journalists were expelled, many newspapers were banned. King Umberto named Bava-Beccaris to the Italian senate and made him a marquis.

Boito, once a young rebel and now a staunch conservative, wrote on 19 May to Bellaigue, reassuring his friend about his own and Verdi's health, and insisting that nobody in Milan was really hungry and the troublemakers were all safely in jail.

Meanwhile Bellaigue had written a review of the *Pezzi sacri* in *La revue des deux mondes*. Boito sent it on to the composer, who had returned to Sant'Agata at the end of May.

Sant'Agata, 10 June 1898

267 Dear Boito,

I would like to have heard better news of the poor sick woman, for this insistent aversion to food worries and saddens you and everyone... In the midst of so much sadness, if she is not *suffering* and *has hope,* this is still a consolation.

I have received the *Revue* and have read the kind article. I will keep the book and give it back to you at Sant'Agata.

I have given your greetings to Maria, Peppina, and Barberina, who are here and thank you and return theirs.

Good-bye, my dear Boito.

Affectionately,
G. Verdi

Sant'Agata, 24 June 1898

268 Dear Boito,

It's quite a while since I had your news! A word, even if not happy... but a word!

I am as I was in Milan 15 or 20 days ago. Here I am very bored and I live!

Regards to all, and affectionate good wishes for the poor sick woman!

Be well.

Affectionately,

G. Verdi

Madonnina Boito, after supporting her illness bravely, died on 24 June 1898. Camillo and Arrigo were alone once again in the big apartment at Via Principe Amedeo.

Sant'Agata, 24 June 1898

269

Dear Boito,

I have just this moment read the terrible news! I mourn with Camillo and with you your dreadful loss! If my poor house at Sant'Agata could be any comfort for you both, come. I await you with open arms.

Be well,

G. Verdi

P.S. La Stolz has just now arrived from Salso.

"Salso" is Salsomaggiore, a spa not far from Sant'Agata. Verdi also went there on occasion.

Sant'Agata, 2 August 1898

270

Dearest Boito,

I returned at six this morning from Montecatini. Sig.ra Stolz came with me to Sant'Agata, and will return to Milan the day after tomorrow, Thursday.

If you and your brother are still willing to face the boredom of Sant'Agata, you could take advantage of the carriage that will take Sig.ra Stolz to Fiorenzuola. In this case you should be at Fiorenzuola at 3:37 P.M. on Thursday.

Otherwise, later, as you choose.

My health is as usual. I hope to see you soon. Be well.

Affectionately,

G. Verdi

In early July Verdi had made his usual trip to Milan, en route to Montecatini, where he arrived 11 July. Camillo Boito had gone off to the Dolomites (he was a dedicated walker).

Sant'Agata, 4 August 1898

271 Dearest Boito,

You will both always be welcome at Sant'Agata, at any time!

I am very pleased that your brother can keep busy! Work, study, the fatigue of travel will be a sure solace for him.

Of myself I can tell you only that I am much as I was before going to Montecatini. But now, for about a year, I have felt the weight of age!

Life is going away!

Good night.

> Be well.
> Affectionately,
> G. Verdi

Sant'Agata, 10 August 1898

272 Dear Boito,

Everything you say is fine, for now and for later.

I see that Camillo hasn't the courage to face the boredom of Sant'Agata and the bad dinners of my murderer of a cook. A real murderer, despite your indulgence and that of la Stolz, Giuditta, and others, etc...

Now I am here alone with my sister-in-law, and my niece often comes to dinner with Peppina.

Until Sunday then.

You will find my carriage at Fiorenzuola at the usual time.

Be well.

> Affectionately,
> G. Verdi

&sBoito arrived at Sant'Agata on 14 August. Teresa Stolz also visited Sant'Agata at this period, before proceeding to Salsomaggiore at the beginning of September. Boito returned to Milan at that time. Around 7 September Verdi went to Genoa, but he was in Milan on 12 September and back at Sant'Agata three days later.

Sant'Agata, 29 (Thursday, I believe) September 1898

273 Dearest Boito,

Despite the *false*, all is well, very well, Oh what bores! They always invent something new! Never a bit of peace!

All is well, too, for your coming (with your brother) to Sant'Agata...

but why around mid-October? Why not immediately after the 9th?

Then there will be few of us... Perhaps Giuditta will come for a little while and Giulio will come for her a few days later.

Till we meet. Bring some work with you. Greet your brother, and an embrace to you.

Affectionately,
G. Verdi

↩The first paragraph of this letter remains cryptic, as Boito's relevant letter is missing. In fact, the following letter from Boito is the first to have survived after a lacuna dating back to early January of the previous year.

9 October [1898]
Milan

274

Dear Maestro,

Good health to you! I will arrive at Sant'Agata Saturday, no earlier, because on Thursday I have to attend a meeting about La Scala—it's indispensable—and on Fridays (as you well know) it's bad luck to travel; so Saturday then, at the usual time, I will get off at Fiorenzuola. A telegram will confirm my arrival.

Please give my greetings to the whole Carrara family. I have heard about the dire event! I was aghast and distressed, thinking of good Angiolino's desperation and everyone's terror. We are all at the mercy of fate!

We will see each other soon, and to you, on this day as always, good health, good health!

Yours most affectionately,
A. Boito

Camillo is well and asks to be remembered to you. He is leaving soon for Rome; on his return we will see him at Sant'Agata.

↩This letter was written on Verdi's presumed birthday. See note to letter no. 285 below.

The event Boito refers to above was a tragic accident that occurred at the Villa Sant'Agata. Maria Carrara Verdi's seventeen-year-old son Angiolino, having returned from a quail-hunting expedition, was cleaning his gun in the presence of his mother, Barberina Strepponi, and Teresa Stolz. The gun, mistakenly believed not loaded, went off and killed a maid who had come in to serve coffee.

Chiefly because of financial difficulties, La Scala had been closed for a full year, this for the first time in its history. Now some leading citizens of Milan had formed a company (Verdi was a stockholder) to run the house. Giulio Gatti-Casazza was named general manager and Arturo Toscanini chief conductor.

Sant'Agata, 12 October 1898

275 Dear Boito,

Good health! And so be it, inasmuch as we have to live.

Greet your brother, who will always be welcome at Sant'Agata, whenever he feels like coming!

Even without your wiring me, I will send the carriage to Fiorenzuola for you *Saturday* at *3:37* P.M. You will find la Stolz here for two days still, and my niece and her daughter. That's all!

Courage!

Till we meet. Be well.

Affectionately,
G. Verdi

⟞Boito spent the latter half of October at Sant'Agata, and at the beginning of November he was back in Milan. Verdi came to Milan probably in the first days of December. Meanwhile, the *Quattro pezzi sacri* (now including the "enigmatic" *Ave Maria*) had been performed on 13 November in Vienna, conducted by Richard von Perger, and apparently Boito suggested the works be included in the 1898–99 season of La Scala.

Milan, 15 December 1898

276 Dear Boito,

In the meeting you will have at La Scala today there will be a request from Giulio to prevent the performance of my sacred pieces.

Please plead my cause, and see to it that they leave those poor pieces alone.

Why? you will ask.

1. Because I don't believe those pieces would be effective at La Scala in view of the performance requirements and the present circumstances.

2. Because my name is too old and annoying. I even annoy myself when I say my own name.

Add to this the observations of the critics! It's true that I could avoid reading them...

I urge you to do this, and be well.

Affectionately,
G. Verdi

❧Verdi was unable to prevent the eventual performance of the *Pezzi sacri* at La Scala, though only the usual three were heard (*Stabat Mater, Laudi alla Vergine, Te Deum*). See note following letter no. 281 below.

Verdi left Milan around 10 February for Genoa. Boito, in a letter to Bellaigue at this time, described the composer's condition: "Verdi is splendid: he plays the piano, he sings, he eats what he likes, he goes for walks, he converses with youthful vivacity" [CVB, p. 496].

Genoa, 14 February 1899

277

Dear Boito,

I am writing not to disturb you but to enquire about your health, and to tell you:

1. That we had a good journey
2. That we are well...
3. That the season is mild!
4. That I am happy at the result of the *Ugonotti*; and that I beg you to urge strongly your brother to insist and obtain this wretched transfer for Prof. Pietro Dotti. We will be doing a good deed for the prof. and an act of mercy for his father-in-law, who is over 80 years old and blind, and wants him near.

And rather than bother you further, good-bye; and send me your news.

Affectionately,
G. Verdi

❧Meyerbeer's *Les Huguenots* had been given in Italian at La Scala beginning 9 February under Toscanini, with a cast including Hariclea Darclée (Puccini's first Tosca the following year), Emilio De Marchi (the first Cavaradossi), and Francesco Navarrini (the Lodovico of the first *Otello* and an admired Verdi interpreter). Until the very end of his life, Verdi maintained a keen interest in the events of the operatic world.

Pietro Dotti (1833–1911) came from Busseto. He was a teacher of art and literature. Camillo Boito, in his position as a professor at the Brera Academy, could help facilitate his transfer.

Genoa, 12 March 1899

278 Dear Boito,

Thank you for the telegram, and I congratulate the fine interpreters.

If you come the day after tomorrow, Tuesday, I will expect you without any further notice at 6:45 at the Doria. If you should change schedule or day, let me know. Greetings.

Affectionately,
G. Verdi

&sOn 11 March *Falstaff* had been revived at La Scala under Toscanini, with Antonio Scotti in the title role. From the original cast there were Edoardo Garbin, Gaetano Pini-Corsi, and Adelina Stehle.

Boito was about to leave Milan for a stay at Nervi, hence the arrangements to see Verdi in Genoa.

[Telegram]

19 March 99

Arrigo Boito, Pension Anglais, Nervi
From Genoa

279 Sorry not to see you here today. But even sorrier to learn you are ill. Hope for quick recovery. Today can't come, but will be with you tomorrow.

Verdi

[Telegram]

23 March 99

Arrigo Boito, Pension Anglais, Nervi
From Genoa

280 Had just this moment instructed Giuseppe to go to Nervi and receive the welcome telegram that says "Have recovered." It makes me very happy, see you soon, and protect yourself against this horrible weather. Warm regards.

Verdi

&s"Giuseppe" is probably Verdi's trusted manservant Giuseppe Gaiani. Boito had been suffering from influenza.

[Genoa] Thursday [13 April] 1899

281

Dear Boito,

Hurrah then!

From you, from others, even from the newspapers I have learned of Tamagno's great success in *Guglielmo Tell.*

I am delighted for the good name of the theater.

And now? There is only one sensible thing to be done:

Close the theater at once!

That would be a success, too.

Be well,

G. Verdi

◦ᴤRossini's *Guillaume Tell* (in Italian translation) had opened at La Scala on 10 April under Toscanini with Verdi's Otello, Francesco Tamagno, as Arnoldo, and his Nannetta, Adelina Stehle, as Matilde. The title role was sung by Edoardo Camera.

Verdi was urging the closing of the theater in jest, as if to forestall the announced performance of the three *Pezzi sacri.* They were duly performed at La Scala on Sunday 16 April, Toscanini conducting. No program was printed, but the *Gazzetta musicale di Milano* lists the soloists for the *Laudi:* Adelina Stehle, Angelica Pandolfini, Elisa Bruno, and Giulia Varesi-Tacconi.

[Milan] 19 April [1899]

282

Dear Maestro,

During these "end-of-season" days when all the skeletons come out of their closets, I have had so many trials that it was impossible for me to steal a quarter-hour to converse with you.

I confirm the news in my telegram, and I can compare the success of the *Pezzi sacri* as obtained in Paris, Turin, and Milan. The most sensational was, without doubt, that in Turin; I attribute this difference to the atmosphere of a concert hall, far more suitable to sacred music for a large ensemble, *where there are no soloists who shine,* far more suitable than the atmosphere of a theater that regularly presents staged works. The subscribers to the concerts of the Paris Conservatory are all of this opinion, and they deplore the enforced transfer of those concerts to the Opéra. The immense success achieved by your *Pezzi sacri* in Germany by the choral societies in the great concert halls is shining proof that confirms this truth. Conclusion: We were wrong to include them in the program of a theater season, and you were right when you advised against performing them. But after all, to tell the whole truth, what was the result of this performance? An *encore,* warmly, insistently demanded, of the *Laudi,* which were sung far better than in Turin.

Between the *Stabat* and the *Te Deum,* the palm went to the *Te Deum* (whereas in Paris it was the opposite; and in fact Stanford, who was present, wanted the concert in London then to end with the *Stabat*); here the audience would not stop applauding until it had made Maestro Venturi come out and take a bow with Toscanini, and until the choruses rose on their feet in response to the total and solemn applause. The *Stabat* was also applauded, but with less enthusiasm; and it was the first of the three pieces, and the *Te Deum* the last.

The press proved to have felt all the immense greatness and idealism of those three pieces, which for me are three cupolas by Correggio and so they will remain in history. But what about the public of La Scala? Did they or didn't they comprehend this most lofty idealism? For the *Laudi,* yes; for the other two pieces, in spite of the applause, no. And I, who was expecting for the *Stabat* and for the *Te Deum two irrepressible explosions of enthusiasm,* remained saddened. Perhaps the Scala audience, besides the reasons already mentioned, had raved too much over Tamagno's *high B*s and was tired.

The execution under Toscanini and Venturi, who learned the interpretation from you and who produced in Turin such an overwhelming impression, could only be excellent, *and excellent it was and wondrously expressive;* but our choristers (especially the sopranos and altos), tired after the long labor of the season, seemed weak at certain points, notwithstanding the addition of an extra fifty choristers, who were little help.

These are the facts and the things I wanted to say to you, so that you would know.

Affectionate regards to all. I hope to see you again soon in Milan.

Yours,

A. Boito

Plans for next year:

—*Aida* with la Darclée and De Marchi, favorites with the public

—*Otello* with Tamagno, Menotti

—*Tristano ed Isotta*

—*Mefistofele*

—and a new opera

➳Of the operas Boito announces, only *Otello* was performed the following season, the last complete season in Verdi's lifetime. The other works were *Siegfried* and *Lohengrin* (in Italian), and a new opera, *Anton*, by Cesare Galeotti; the season ended with Puccini's *Tosca* (fresh from its premiere in Rome) and Tchaikovsky's *Onegin* (another Milan premiere).

Sir Charles Villiers Stanford (1852–1924), British composer, conductor, and teacher, friend of Brahms, Saint-Saëns, and other leading figures in the European musical world. He wrote an essay on *Falstaff* for the *Fortnightly Review* in 1894.

For Correggio, see letter no. 227 above.

Genoa, 20 April 1899

283

Dear Boito,

I thank you, dearest Boito, for your good and friendly letter, whose reasoning I accept to a great extent, along with its judgments. As for myself, I believe and have always believed "that when the public does not rush to a new production, it is already a failure!" A bit of charitable applause, a few indulgent reviews as a solace to the *Grand Old Man* cannot move me. No, no: neither indulgence, nor pity.

Better the boos!
In about 10 or 12 days I will be passing through Milan, and then we will be able to chat a bit, even without talking of music.

Greetings and be well.
Yours,
G. Verdi

Regards to your brother.

> ◆In mid-May Verdi left Genoa for Milan, where he inspected the nearly completed Casa di Riposo, spent time with the Boitos, and heard news of a successful performance of the three *Pezzi sacri* conducted by Pietro Mascagni in Pesaro. In early June he traveled to Sant'Agata, and a month later he went straight to Montecatini, accompanied by Teresa Stolz. The famous photos of Verdi in Montecatini, at table or with Tamagno, were taken at this time. In early August the composer returned to Sant'Agata. Boito was then at Lavarone, in the mountains near Trento.

Sant'Agata, 7 August 1899

284

Dear Boito,

I received at the same time your two letters, and I repeat your phrase:

al Dia- vo- lo i sec- ca- to - ri

I have been back here for three or four days. I would even be in fairly good health if I were not crushed, stifled by the heat and nuisances; and also by the sadness at no longer seeing here that poor Peppina, a maid so good and clever, and so quiet! She died at the Cremona Hospital after an operation on the uterus, etc., etc.

Yesterday there was the marriage of Peppinetta, your pupil at billiards. They left immediately for Genoa.

Since you are so highly placed, be so kind as to climb a little higher and give my cordial greetings to the Director of the world of the Moon, asking him to send me the tune of a folk song... one assumes that they sing there, too.

Until we meet then in Sept., or in Oct., or in Nov., when you like, and whenever you come, yours will be a welcome visit for me and for all who will be here.

Farewell. A handshake.

Yours,
G. Verdi

Peppinetta was the oldest daughter of Maria Carrara Verdi; see note following letter no. 251 above. Her husband was Italo Ricci.

Milan, 8 October [1899]

285
You are forbidden to answer.

Best wishes for the ninth or the tenth of October:

Good health, good humor, good appetite, good digestion, good reading, good conversations, good drink, good massage, and good legs. For this last wish I would have a proposal to make to you for which, at this moment, I feel a great need. The proposal is this: You lend me your head and I will make you a present of my legs. But I believe that the legs of your horses are already serving you very well in your morning excursions.

I will arrive at Sant'Agata around the twentieth of this month.

I will inform you of my arrival a couple of days before, and we will enjoy ourselves.

Many greetings to Signora Stolz, to Signora Maria, and to the whole Carrara family. Camillo joins me in affectionate best wishes.

Yours,
A. Boito

    The date of Verdi's birth was and remains a matter of controversy. For a long time he thought he was born in 1814 (as his mother had told him), but he learned in 1876 from the records that it was 1813. As to the day, he always celebrated it on 9 October, though the birth certificate gives 10 October.

[Sant'Agata] 11 October 1899

286

Dear Arrigo,
> Your letter received.
> Very well.
> See you here!

G. Verdi

Thank your brother for his best wishes, and ask him if I can hope to see him here before the year ends.

G.V.

    Here Verdi addresses Boito as Arrigo, a rare occurrence and a convincing indication of his quasi-paternal affection. Boito, as planned, visited Sant'Agata around 20 October and stayed at least until 11 November. Young Tito Ricordi and his wife also came to Sant'Agata that autumn, as did Giulio and Giuditta. On 3 December Verdi moved to Milan. The Casa di Riposo was finished, and not long after his arrival, Verdi officially made the property over to the foundation that would be in charge of it.

[Milan] 2 February 1900

287

I rejoice with you and with your brother at your improvement: so I have been told at this very moment (11 o'clock) by Dr. Caporali. Terrible doctor who makes prisoners of us all, you because of influenza and I because of the bad weather! And for how long?

I too was greatly pleased by Giacosa's success, and I can imagine your joy!

Complete and rapid recovery to you and your brother, and greetings.

Affectionately,
G. Verdi

☙On 31 January 1900 Giacosa's play *Come le foglie,* arguably his finest work, was given with success at the Teatro Manzoni in Milan, starring the popular Tina Di Lorenzo and Flavio Andò (sometime leading man and, briefly, lover of Duse).

Verdi stayed in Milan until 1 March, when he went to Genoa.

Genoa, 30 March 1900

288 Dearest Boito,

I am glad you found the letter to Baccelli simple and without anything *surplus!* That is no small thing in these times, when everything is excessive and without common sense! Is it possible to imagine and believe what is now happening in the Chamber?!... And D'Annunzio?

I am sure you have worked, quite sure; and so I will see you here at Easter.

There is no need for the feast of St. Joseph for me to know you are a friend.

You will tell me now or later if before the end of April you will be back in Milan, where I would see you as I return to Sant'Agata.

And now: *Work, be well,* and good-bye.

Affectionately,
G. Verdi

☙Boito's letter to which this is obviously a reply is missing.

On 1 October 1899, after there had been some mention in the papers of a possible imminent honor (perhaps, as once before, he was threatened with being made a marquis), Verdi had written to the minister of education, Guido Baccelli (1830–1916). His letter—which probably came to Boito's attention through its publication in some newspaper—was meant partly to ward off the empty honor, but more importantly, to ask Baccelli's intervention in a question regarding his burial. Special permission was required for private entombment, and Verdi asked Baccelli to secure such permission for him and Giuseppina to be buried in the chapel of the Casa di Riposo. Their remains are in fact there, along with a memorial tablet to Verdi's first wife, Margherita Barezzi, who had died in 1840.

Gabriele D'Annunzio (1863–1938), by now a famous poet and novelist, had been elected to the Italian Parliament in 1897. On 24 March 1900, with a grand gesture, he had moved his seat—and his political stand—from the extreme right to the extreme left. He was moving, he declared, "towards life."

Boito disliked D'Annunzio intensely, and not only because the poet had replaced him as Duse's lover and mentor.

[Milan, between 10 and 19 October 1900]

289

Dear Maestro,

I am working desperately because I have been seized by the fear of time pressing, and the days go by and I have not yet found that day on which to inform you of my arrival at Sant'Agata; I no longer know the dates of the month and the weeks, but I know that at this time I should be with you, I say *should be* but what I mean is *would like to be*, because I would always like it and I have to struggle between this great desire and my work, which keeps me tied here because I fear that if I were to leave I would interrupt my now-acquired habit of working without any rest.

But I hear from Giulio that you will soon make a dash to Milan, and so this is what we will do: I will press onward, far enough so that I will be able to accompany you on your return to Sant'Agata, where I will take along something to do and will stay a bit less than in past years. Dear Maestro, it was better when we worked together, you and old Shakespeare and me; the two of us, or rather the three of us, got along so well! Much, much better than I now, alone, get along with myself!

So I will wait for you in Milan with the hope of being able to accompany you home and stay with you a while.

Fondest greetings

from your
A. Boito

Many warm greetings to Signora Stolz, to Sig.ra Maria and family.

◆This letter follows a six-month silence in the correspondence. Some letters may have been lost; in any case the two men had several opportunities to meet: in Genoa, where Boito spent Easter with the Maestro; and in Milan, where Verdi spent the period between 5 and 22 May, and where he returned briefly in July.

Boito was, once again, at work on *Nerone.* In 1901 he finally published the libretto, implying that the text, even without the music, was a work of literature.

Sant'Agata, 20 October 1900

290 Dear Boito,

I will be brief because writing tires me; and, be it said once and for all, whenever you like and your commitments allow you to come to Sant'Agata, your visit will always be a gift for me and for all of us.

I am as God wills! I am not really ill, but my legs hardly carry me any more, and my strength diminishes with every passing day! The doctor comes for the massage twice a day, but I feel no improvement.

I don't know when I'll be able to come to Milan. I need Winderlingh, but I don't yet know if he is staying long in Milan.

We are agreed then; and with a warm handshake I say good-bye.

Affectionately,
G. Verdi

◆Winderlingh was Verdi's dentist.

This is the last dated letter of the correspondence. On 4 December, after having arranged to collect and burn his early compositions, Verdi left Sant'Agata for Milan, where he took up his usual residence at the Grand Hôtel Milan.

Verdi arrived in Milan accompanied by Maria Carrara Verdi. He spent Christmas with a few friends, including Boito, and New Year's Eve again with Boito, the poet Cesare Pascarella, the painter Carlo Mancini, and some others. All commented on his vigor and his excellent health.

On the morning of 21 January, Verdi's physician, Dr. Caporali, made his regular visit to the composer and pronounced him fit to go out that day in his carriage. But about an hour after the doctor's visit, when Verdi was preparing to rise, he had a stroke. Dr. Caporali was summoned. Realizing the gravity of the situation, Caporali called in Professor Pietro Grocco, Italy's most eminent physician, who had treated Verdi in the past. Grocco, who arrived the next day, agreed with Caporali about the prognosis and the treatment. Verdi remained mute, his condition steadily worsening, until 27 January, when he died at 2:50 A.M.

Boito was overwhelmed, and it was only at Easter that he could finally answer a letter from Bellaigue written in March:

> Verdi is dead. He has taken away with him an enormous quantity of light and of vital warmth; we were all brightened by the sunshine of that Olympian old age.
>
> He died magnificently, like a formidable, silenced fighter.
>
> The silence of death had descended on him a week before he died.
>
> Do you know the admirable bust of the Maestro made by Gemito? [. . .] That bust made forty years ago is the image of the Maestro as he was the fourth day before the end. His head bowed on the chest, his eyebrows stern, he looked down and seemed to measure with his gaze an unknown and formidable adversary and to calculate mentally the strength required to oppose him. He also put up a heroic resistance. The breathing of his broad chest sustained him victoriously for four days and three nights. The fourth night still his breathing filled the room, but the effort... poor Maestro! How good and beautiful he was to the very end!
>
> No matter, the old reaper had to carry away his scythe well battered.
>
> [CVB, p. 512]

When Verdi died, Boito was fifty-eight; but he seemed suddenly to become an old man. His broad shoulders were stooped, his gait was shuffling. While he still went through the motions of working on *Nerone,* he was constantly assailed by self-doubt, and apparently erased as much as he wrote.

He was out of sympathy with new developments in music. Hearing Strauss's *Salome* at La Scala, he wrote Bellaigue that it was "a racket of pots and pans," and he was no more generous with Debussy. Though he had played an important role in the launching of Puccini, his interest did not last. He advised the younger man against setting *La bohème,* and had harsh things to say about Puccini's later operas. He did like Riccardo Zandonai, and introduced him to Tito Ricordi; and he showed affection for Antonio Smareglia, a former pupil of Faccio.

But for the most part, his last years were years of loss, as Verdi's death was followed by the deaths of others close to him. In 1906, Giacosa—five years his junior—died. In 1912 it was the turn of Giulio Ricordi, his lifelong friend as well as his publisher. In 1914 came the worst blow of all: the death of his brother Camillo. Though Arrigo had by now a long-established amorous friendship with a younger woman,

Velleda Ferretti, she was a source more of anxiety than of comfort, beset as she was by her own family tragedies and personal ailments.

He continued to serve on committees. He headed the group charged with erecting a bust of Giacosa in the Public Gardens of Milan. In 1913, for the centenary of Verdi's birth, Boito was in constant demand. In 1916, he even lent his name to a Debussy commemoration, not because of any esteem for the composer but to demonstrate his loyalty to France, Italy's ally. Duse, who saw him now on occasion and wrote him, went to call on him one afternoon in 1916, and described him to her daughter:

> I see him, without speaking, sad, very very sad, those beautiful shoulders of long ago—hunched at the top like a tree that refuses to bend. [. . .] There he was with that *sudden* fatigue that strikes the old, as it does children—alone, bewildered, in the midst of the room... with his eyes, coming from afar, afar, looking at an invisible light, alone, his arms hanging at his sides, dejected, and his beautiful head as if forgetting the very thing that was making him suffer so... [. . .] We were silent, the room and the street were peaceful, and the lamp—The portrait of a young woman, of *thirty years ago* (of me, long ago) at his right, and a portrait of Verdi—on his desk, that's all—and some books, books everywhere.
>
> [W. Weaver, *Duse* (London: Harcourt Brace Jovanovich, 1984), p. 315]

The First World War had affected him deeply. In the spring of 1917 he visited the zone of operations in the Monte Santo area, not far from the Austrian border and the front line. Returning to Milan in an army train, he caught cold, and had to take to his bed. It was the beginning of a long period of illness that ended only with his death, of heart attack, on 10 June 1918.

The manuscript of *Nerone* was his chief bequest; the piano-vocal four-act version was complete (he had made sketches for an original fifth act), but it was not fully orchestrated. First Smareglia worked on it, then Vincenzo Tommasini, both under the watchful eye of Toscanini, who conducted the posthumous premiere on 1 May 1924. Officially, the work was a triumph; but it soon vanished from the repertory, leaving Boito's fame to be perpetuated by *Mefistofele* and, more, by his and Verdi's *Otello* and *Falstaff*.

❧ UNDATED LETTERS AND DOCUMENTS

❧Boito to Verdi

4 June

291

Dear Maestro,

Here I am in Milan since yesterday evening, and already eager to receive soon a line from you telling me to come to Sant'Agata. Many greetings to Signora Giuseppina.

> Yours most affectionately,
> A. Boito

292

Dear Maestro,

Today I will have the pleasure of dining with you, and I will bring you the miraculous *elixir* I told you about the other evening. Till we meet.

> Yours,
> A. Boito

❧Verdi to Boito

Monday

293

Dear Boito,

If you come to the theater this evening after 8 you will hear that duet about which there is much to say, whether good or bad I don't know. We will discuss it, and at length.

> Affectionately,
> G. Verdi

❧It is possible that this note dates from the period of the revised *Boccanegra* rehearsals (winter 1881), and the duet is the Simone-Fiesco scene that was the subject of much discussion and revision.

Milan, Wednesday

294 Dear Boito,

If you are passing the Hôtel Milan, be so kind as to climb the stairs...

Read this little article that I am sending you. It is only to tell you to take your precautions when you speak with that Gentleman you introduced me to.

I need not tell you that in the article everything is distorted.

... [?] writes me to reply! Not on your life...

Yours,
G. Verdi

◄In the realm of absolute hypothesis, this letter may date from early May 1890; the article might therefore be Verdi's interview with Destranges, who would be "that Gentleman." See letter no. 146, and the note following it.

295 Ask Boito:

1. After the verses of Falstaff:

T'amo e non è mia colpa	[I love you and it's not my fault
S'io tanta porto vulnerabil polpa	If I carry so much vulnerable
	flesh]

To add two verses for Alice:

Ah!	[Ah!
Ma i sospiri d'amor	But love's sighs
Gonfiano e il cor	Swell both the heart]

FALSTAFF Quand'ero paggio	[When I was the page
Del Duca di Norfolth ero	Of the Duke of Norfolk I
sottile! / *punto.*	was slim! / *period.*]

Cialtron!	[Lout!
Poltron!	Poltroon!
Gorgion!	Greedy!
Beon	Drunkard!
Briccon!	Rogue!
In ginocchion	On your knees]

Later

Ghiotton!		[Glutton!
Gorgion ⎤	Change so as	Greedy!
Beon ⎦	not to repeat	Drunkard!
Perdon		Pardon]

If possible, after the verse: E spiritelli [And spirits]
add another two: . . . -elli
. . . -elli

⌘The document above is not a letter but a reminder Verdi wrote for himself, possibly in view of a visit from Boito. The passages quoted are from *Falstaff,* act 2, part 2, and act 3, parts 1 and 2.

Although it is tempting to place this memorandum in the period when Verdi and Boito exchanged observations on the accentuation of "Windsor" and "Norfolk" (see letters nos. 161 and 162), it is not possible to date the sum of the contents here with precision. Nonetheless, the moment is likely to have been posterior to that of the letters cited above.

296 If you can, come this evening to eat soup with us at 6. If possible even a few moments earlier, for a bit of Falstaffian conversation.

⌘This note, written on a visiting card, may date from the autumn of 1892, when Boito was in Nervi (prior to his transfer to Pegli on 16 November) and Verdi in Genoa.

Hôtel Milan, Monday

297 Dear Boito,

I have read, reread, and studied... the *Basket-Big Belly.*

I have some scruples that I will confess to you, if, leaving your house after 4, you can come to me... and stop here afterwards as well, between six and seven, etc.

G. Verdi

⌘This note seems to date from January 1893, during the *Falstaff* rehearsals, when Verdi was having some second thoughts about the finale of act 2, which he later revised before the opera was performed in Rome in April.

298   Here is the fourth act.
Don't destroy anything of what you had done before.
At the same time I fulfill my little debt and I greet you.
                                              G. Verdi

 ◄ₛThis note probably refers to the final revisions of the French translation of *Otello,* completed shortly before the opera was produced in
Paris in October 1894.

299   When you leave your house, have the kindness to climb the stairs
of the Hôtel Milan. I have a letter from Taffanel.
                                              Verdi

 ◄ₛThis note probably refers to a letter from Taffanel to Verdi dated 21
January 1898, regarding negotiations for the premiere in Paris of the
three *Pezzi sacri.* Verdi answered it on 24 January (see note following
letter no. 254) so the note to Boito was probably written between the
two dates.

300   Dear Boito,
I have been mummified in the house for three days. I want your
news, and I hope the bearer will be able to say this one word to me:
Well.

 ◄ₛNardi transcribed this note from a visiting card, now lost; he tenta-
tively dated it 1898.

301   I wanted to come to you today, but it's a nasty day for me. Give me
your news, and news of your brother.
                                              G.V.

 ◄ₛBoito's biographer Piero Nardi thought this note, which he transcribed from a visiting card, now lost, might date from 1900. The CVB
hypothesizes that this may be the last surviving document of the
Verdi-Boito correspondence. It may also date from the early part of the
year, when Verdi was in Milan, and when both Boito brothers were
unwell. See letter no. 287 above.

❧ APPENDIX

❧The following are libretto-related excerpts from the original texts not included in the translations of the letters: working drafts of libretto passages (with stage directions and occasional comments in longer examples); non-versified paraphrases that maintain a substantial similarity with the final version; and literary quotes influencing development of the libretto. These transcriptions maintain the original orthography, punctuation (except quotation marks and underlining), capitalization, abbreviation, and format as established in the *Carteggio Verdi-Boito*. Repetitions are not included, even when they occur between letters. The abbreviations of character names have been rendered uniform to aid consultation.

Letter No. 1
Demon, be silent
   Demonio taci

No. 6
It is a fine thing to defeat the adversary etc.
   bello è superare l'avversario alla prova del brando; bellissimo è vincerlo per
   magnanimità di cuore
And the helmsman, awed etc.
   ed ammirato il nocchiero alla novità dello spettacolo lasciavasi cadere il
   remo dalle mani e fermava per meraviglia la barca a mezzo il corso

No. 8
I killed Lorenzino etc.
   Ho ucciso Lorenzino perché mi rapìa la sposa
Save my betrothed
   Salva lo sposo mio
Why have you drawn your sword?
   Perché impugni l'acciar?
You had Amelia etc.
              Tu facesti
         rapire Amelia Grimaldi...
         vile Corsaro coronato muori

Doge Ferisci...
Gab.   Amelia
T.   Amelia
Dog. Adorno: tu la vergin difendi; t'ammiro, e t'assolvo...
        Amelia dì come tu fosti rapita
Plebians, Patricians, Populace
    Plebe Patrizi Popolo
Be he cursed!
    Sia maledetto!

No. 9
Consent to our wedding
    A nostre nozze assenti
humble
    Umil
Listen... deep secret
    Ascolta... alto segreto
Fear, O Doge
    Paventa o Doge
Love that angel... But after God... the Fatherland
    ama quell'angelo... Ma dopo Dio... la Patria

No. 10
The new day...
    Il nuovo dì...
Not of regal pride etc.
    Non di regale orgoglio
    L'effimero splendor
    Mi cingerà d'aureola
    Il raggio dell'amor

No. 11
Dawn breaks in the sky etc.
    S'inalba il ciel, ma l'amoroso canto
    Non s'ode ancora...
    Ei mi terge ogni dì, come l'aurora
    La rugiada dei fiori, del ciglio il pianto.

Gabriele *Do you consent etc.*
    Gab.   A nostre nozze assenti?
                                Alto mistero
    Andrea   ~~Un cupo arcano~~
        Sulla vergine incombe.

GAB.   E qual?

AND.   Se parlo
Forse tu più non l'amerai.

GAB.   Non teme
Ombra d'arcani l'amor mio!—T'ascolto.

AND.   Amelia tua d'umile stirpe nacque...

GAB.   La figlia dei Grimaldi?!

AND.   No—la figlia
Dei Grimaldi morì fra consacrate
Vergini in Pisa

AND.   *Devout warrior etc.*

AND.   Pio guerrier, del tempo antico
L'alta fede in te rampolla;
No, la spada tua non crolla
Per nemico odio crudel.

(abbraccian-
dolo)
  Vieni a me,
~~Baldo eroe~~ ti benedico
Nell'amore e nella guerra,
Sii fedele alla tua terra,
L'angiol tuo ti sia fedel.

GAB.   Del tuo labbro il sacro detto
Come balsamo raccolsi,
Saldi son pel brando
~~Forti ho già le vene~~ e i polsi,
M'empie il petto un vasto ardor.
Se da te fui benedetto
L'alma mia più in me non langue,
Freme e m'agita nel sangue
Odio immenso e immenso amor.

SIMONE   *Gentlemen, the king etc.*

SIMONE   Messeri il re di Tartaria vi porge
Pegni di pace e ricchi doni e annunzia
Schiuso l'Eusin alle liguri prore
Acconsentite?

TUTTI   Sì.

SIM.   Ma d'altro voto
(dopo una   Più generoso io vi richiedo.
pausa)

ALCUNI   Parla.

SIM.   La stessa voce che tuonò su Rienzi
Vaticinio di gloria e poi di morte

(s'incomincia ad udire un tumulto lontano)	Or su Genova tuona.—Ecco un messaggio Del romito di Sorga, ei per Venezia Supplica pace...
PAOLO (interrom- pendo)	Attenda alle sue rime Il cantor della bionda Avignonese.
SIM. (con forza)	Messeri!...
	(il tumulto s'avvicina)
PIETRO	Qual clamor?!
ALCUNI	D'onde tai grida?

SIM.   *Why have you drawn etc.*

SIM. (a Gab.)	Perché impugni l'acciar?
GAB.	Ho trucidato Lorenzino.
POPOLO	Assassin.
FIESCHI	Ei la Grimaldi Avea rapita.
SIM.	(Orror!)
POPOLO	Menti!
GAB.	Quel vile Pria di morir disse che un uom possente Al crimine l'ha spinto.
PIE. (a Paolo)	scoperto (Ah! Sei ~~perd~~)
SIM. (con agitazione)	E il nome suo?
GAB. (fissando il Doge con tremenda ironia)	T'aqueta! il reo si spense Pria di svelarlo.
SIM.	Che vuoi dir?
GAB. (terribil- mente)	Pel cielo!! Uom possente tu se!
SIM. (a Gabriel)	Ribaldo!

284

GAB. (al Doge slanciandosi)	Audace Rapitor di fanciulle!
ALCUNI	Si disarmi!
GAB. (disvinco- landosi e correndo con Fiesco per ferire il Doge.)	Empio corsaro incoronato! muori!
AMELIA (entrando e interponendosi fra i due assaltatori e il Doge.)	Ferisci.
SIM. ⎫ FIE. ⎬ GAB. ⎭	Amelia!
TUTTI	Amelia!...
AM.	O Doge! (o padre!) Salva l'Adorno tu.
SIM. (alle guardie che si sono impossessate di Gabriello per disar- marlo)	Nessun l'offenda!! Cade l'orgoglio e al suon del suon dolore Tutta l'anima mia parla d'amore. Amelia dì come tu fosti rapita E come

His heartfelt words etc.

Il suo commosso accento
Sa l'ira in noi calmar;
Vol di soave vento
Che rasserena il mar.

PAO.   *You saw those two? etc.*

PAO.	Quei due vedesti?
PIE.	Sì.
PAO.	Li traggi tosto Dal carcer loro per l'andito ascoso Che questa chiave schiuderá.
PIE.	T'intesi.

I have cursed myself!!...

    Me stesso ho maledetto!!...

    E l'anatema

    M'insegue ancor... e l'aura ancor ne trema!

    Vilipeso... rejetto

    Dal Senato e da Genova, qui vibro

    L'ultimo stral pria di fuggir, qui libro

    La sorte tua, Doge, in quest'ansia estrema.

    Tu che m'offendi e che mi devi il trono

    Qui t'abbandono

    Al tuo destino

    In quest'ora fatale.

(estrae un ampolla, Qui ti stillo una lenta atra agonìa,

ne versa il conte- Là t'armo un'assassino.

nuto nella tazza) Scelga Morte sua via

    Fra il tosco ed il pugnale.

FIE. *Prisoner, in what place etc.*

      m'adduci?

 FIE. Prigioniero, in qual loco ~~mi trovo~~

 PAO. Nelle stanze del Doge, e favella

   A te Paolo.

 FIE.   I tuoi sguardi son truci!

 PAO. Io so l'odio che celasi in te.

   Tu m'ascolta.

 FIE. Che brami?

 PAO.   Al cimento

   Preparasti de' Guelfi la schiera

DOGE *Doge! Shall the two rebels*

 DOGE Doge!—Ancor proveran la tua clemenza

   I due ribelli?—Di paura segno

(versa dall' Fora il castigo.—M'ardono le fauci...

anfora nella Perfin l'onda del fonte è amara al labbro

tazza e beve) Dell'uom che regna... ho l'alma oppressa... infrante

   Dal duol le membra... già... mi vince il sonno...

(s'addormenta) Oh Amelia... ami... un nemico...

No. 13

Dawn breaks in the sky...

 S'inalba il Ciel...

Come to me, I bless you

 Vieni a me ti benedico

On earth and in heaven...
　　In terra e in ciel...
But let not love restrain etc.
　　Ma non rallenti amore
　　La foga in te de cittadini affetti
The Doge is coming. Let us leave
　　Il doge vien. Partiam
O Doge (o father) etc.
　　O Doge (o padre)
　　Salva l'Adorno tu...

No. 16
ANDREA　*You are worthy etc.*
　ANDREA　Di lei sei degno!
　GABRIELLE　　　　　A me fia dunque unita!
　AND.　　In terra e in ciel.
　GAB.　　　　　　Ah! mi ridai la vita!
　(con effusione)
　AND.　　Vieni a me, ti benedico
　　　　　Nella pace di quest'ora;
　　　　　Lieto vivi e fido adora
　　　　　L'angiol tuo, la patria, il ciel.

GAB.　*Pious echo etc.*
　GAB.　　Eco pia del tempo antico
　　　　　La tua voce è un casto incanto;
　　　　　Serberà ricordo santo
　　　　　Di quest'ora il cor fedel.
　(squilli di trombe)
　GAB.　　Ecco il Doge—Partiam. Ch'ei non ti scorga.
　AND.　　Ah! presto il dì della vendetta sorga.

DOGE　*Paolo etc.*
　DOGE　　Paolo.
　PAOLO　　　Signor.
　DOGE　　　　　Ci spronano gli eventi.
　　　　　Di qua partir convien.

AMELIA　*Father, you will see etc.*
　AMELIA　Padre, vedrai la vigile
　　　　　Figlia tua sempre accanto;
　　　　　Nell'ore melanconiche
　　　　　Asciugherò il tuo pianto...
　　　　　Avrem gioje romite

Note soltanto al ciel;
Io la colomba mite
Sarò del regio ostel.

Your voice seems an echo etc.
La tua voce un eco, un canto
Quasi par del tempo antico,
Serberà ricordo santo
De' tuoi detti il cor fedel.

No. 17
To my non-brothers
Ai non fratelli miei
Doge   Paolo! etc.

DOGE   Paolo!

AMELIA   Quel vil nomasti!... Ma a te
buono, generoso devo dire
il vero

~~DOGE   Che~~!

AMELIA   I Grimaldi non sono miei fratelli

DOGE   Ma e tu?

AMELIA   Non sono una Grimaldi

DOGE   E chi sei dumque?.

The singer of the blond Avignonaise
Il cantor della bionda Avignonese
War on Venice! etc.

Guerra a Venezia!

DOGE   È guerra fratricida. Venezia e Genova hanno una patria comune:
Italia.

TUTTI   Nostra patria è Genova

No. 18
of my non-brothers
dei non fratelli miei
Doge   Paolo!

DOGE   Paolo!

AMELIA   Quel vil nomasti... E poiché tanta
Pietà ti move dei destini miei
Vo' svelarti il segreto che mi ammanta:
(dopo breve pausa)
Non sono una Grimaldi.

DOGE   O ciel! chi sei?

PAOLO . . . . . *Let him attend etc.*

PAOLO: . . . . Attenda alle sue rime
(ridendo)   Il cantor della bionda Avignonese.

TUTTI I
CONSIGLIERI Guerra a Venezia!
(poi Paolo ferocemente)

DOGE   E con quest'urlo atroce
Frà due liti d'Italia erge Caìno
La sua clava cruenta!—Adria e Liguria
Hanno patria comune.

TUTTI   È nostra patria
Genova!

PIERO   Qual clamor?

ALCUNI   D'onde tai grida?

No. 20
Peace... forgive... forget... etc.
  Pace... perdono... oblio...
  Sono fratelli nostri!...

No. 21
Peace! Tame your haughty blood etc.
  Pace! l'altero sangue
  Doma e l'orgoglio piega!
  Pace! la patria langue
  Per l'ira tua crudel.
  Col labro mio ti prega
  L'alma fra gli astri assunta
  Della gentil defunta
  Che ti contempla in ciel.

No. 22
Warrior sword
  Brando guerrier

No. 23
Here are the plebeians
  Ecco le plebi
Vengeance!
  Vendetta!
To arms, to arms, Ligurians
  All'armi All'armi Liguri

No. 25
My temples burn
  M'ardon le tempia

No. 26
The dead rise from their graves
  risorgon dalle tombe i morti
Fool, go
  Stolido, va
FIESCO *You dare propose etc.*
  FIESCO Osi a Fiesco proporre un misfatto?
  PAOLO Tu ricusi? (dopo una pausa) Al tuo carcer ten va.

AMELIA *He comes!... love etc.*
  AM.   Ei vien!... l'amor
        M'avvampa in seno. (sen)
        E spezza il freno
        L'ansante cor.

DOGE *Here are the plebians! etc.*
  DOGE   Ecco le plebi!
  LA FOLLA   Vendetta! Vendetta!
           Spargasi il sangue del fiero uccisor!.
  DOGE   Questa è dunque del popolo la voce?!
  (ironicamente) Da lungi tuono d'uragan, da presso
           Gridìo di donne e di fanciulli...

AMELIA *Peace! Restrain, for pity's sake etc.*
  AMELIA   Pace! lo sdegno immenso
  (a Fiesco)   Raffrena per pietà!
         Pace! t'ispiri un senso
         Di patria carità.

No. 28
At his side Fiesco is fighting
  accanto ad esso combatte Fiesco
He had abducted the Grimaldi girl
  Ei la Grimaldi aveva rapita
the two rebels
  i Due ribelli
the traitors
  I traditor
The Doge proclaims you free
  Libero il Doge ti proclama

The Doge pardons all: you are free!
   Il Doge perdona a tutti Tu sei libero!.

No. 29

Beside him a Guelph is fighting
   Accanto ad esso combatte un Guelfo
Beside him an old man is fighting
   accanto ad esso pugna un vegliardo
Beside him a patrician is fighting
   Accanto ad esso pugna un patrizio
the two rebels
   due ribelli
the traitors
   I traditori
the revolutionaries
   i rivoltosi
You are free; here is your sword...
   Libero sei; ecco la spada,...
You are free; this is your weapon...
   Libero sei; quest'è il tuo brando...
At last etc.
                                    alfine
   È giunta l'ora di trovarci a fronte!

No. 35

Let love and jealousy be dispelled together!
   Amore e gelosìa vadan dispersi insieme!
CHORUS   Wherever you look, gleam etc.

                          CORO
(interno)   Dove guardi splendono
avvicinandosi.   avvampan cuori,
                   Raggi, ~~echeggian Cori~~,
                   Dove passi scendono
                   Nuvole di fiori.
                   Qui fra gigli e rose
                   Come a un casto altar,
                   Padri, bimbi, spose
                   Vengono a cantar.

FANCIULLI
(spargendo al suolo fiori di giglio)
T'offriamo il giglio
Soave stel
Che in man degli angeli
Fu assunto in ciel,
Che abbella il fulgido
Manto e la gonna
Della Madonna,
E il santo vel.

DESDEMONA:
Splende il cielo, danza
L'aura intorno ai fior.
Gioja, Amor, Speranza
Cantan nel mio cor.

DONNE E MARINARI
(mentre cantano i fanciulli, accompagnando e armonizzando)
(Mentre all'aure vola
Lieta la canzon,
L'agile mandòla
Ne accompagna il suon)

MARINARI
(offrendo a Desdemona dei monili di corallo e di perle)
A te le porpore
Le perle e gli ostri,
Nella
~~Dalla~~ voragine
Colti del mar.
Vogliam Desdemona
Coi doni nostri
Come un imagine
Sacra adornar.

FANCIULLI E DONNE
(mentre cantano i marinari, accompagnando e armonizzando)

(Mentre all'aure vola
Lieta la canzon,
L'agile mandòla
Ne accompagna il suon.)

LE DONNE
(spargendo rami e fiori)
Per te la
~~La messe~~ florida
~~A te del salice~~
Messe dai
~~Dai nostri~~ grembi
~~La molle fronda,~~
A nembi, a nembi,
~~Amor dell'onda~~

Spargiamo al suol.
~~Dei carmi Amor.~~
L'April circonda
La sposa bionda
~~A te il ciclame~~
~~Tua testa bionda~~
~~Dal fragil stame,~~
D'un etra rorida
~~Dal tenue calice~~
Che vibra al sol
~~D'azzurro e d'or.~~

FANCIULLI E MARINARI
OPPURE MARINARI SOLI,
(mentre le donne cantano accompagnando e armonizzando)
(Mentre all'aure vola
Lieta la canzon,
L'agile mandola
Ne accompagna il suon.)

TUTTI
Dove guardi splendono
     avvampan cuori,
Raggi, ~~echeggian Cori,~~
Dove passi scendono
Nuvole di fiori.
Qui fra gigli e rose,
Come a un casto altar,
Padri, bimbi, spose
Vengono a cantar.

CORO — § Vivi felice! Addio. Qui regna Amor.

DESDEMONA
Splende il cielo, danza
L'aura intorno ai fior
Gioja, Amor, Speranza
Cantan nel mio cor. ∽

There she is! etc.

Eccola!

E JAGO   Vigilate.
(gli mormora)
e gli ripete
mentre canta
il Coro)

E OTELLO   Quel canto mi conquide:
(soavemente   No, no, s'ella m'inganna, il ciel sé stesso irride.
commosso)

I bring you the plea of a man who moans under your scorn...

    D'un uom che geme sotto il tuo disdegno, la preghiera ti porto...

No. 37

JAGO   *In deepest night etc.*

  JAGO   A notte folta io la sua traccia vigilo
               E il varco e l'ora scruto, il resto a te.
               Sarò tua scolta. A caccia, a caccia! Cingiti
               L'arco.
  RODRIGO   Sì. T'ho venduto onore e fè.)

RODRIGO   *(For me the world etc.*

          RODRIGO

  (Per me s'oscura il mondo,
  S'annuvola il destin,
  L'angelo casto e biondo
  Fugge dal mio cammin.)

To the ground! and weep!

  A terra! e piangi!

Flee!

  Fuggite!

Sun, serene and bright etc.

  Sole sereno e vivido
  Che allieti il cielo e il mare,
  Tergi le stille amare
  Che sparge il mio dolor!

No. 38

JAGO   *Hurry! Time is flying! etc.*

  JAGO   T'affretta! Il tempo vola! All'opra ergi tua mira! all'opra sola! Io penso
        a Cassio... L'infame anima ria gli svellerò. Lo giuro. Tu avrai le sue
        novelle a mezzanotte

All flee Otello

  Tutti fuggite Otello

That robs him of all feeling

  Che d'ogni senso il priva

Flee. I loathe you, myself, the whole world...

  Fuggite. Io detesto voi, me, il mondo intero...

I alone am unable etc.

  Fuggirmi io sol non so... Ah l'idra!. Signor
  Vederli insieme avvinti. Ah maledetto
  Pensiero... Sangue Sangue...

un grido e Il fazzoletto.
sviene

Il mio velen lavora

Viva l'eroe di Cipro

Chi può vietar che questa fronte io prema

Col mio tallone

        Gloria

Al Leon di Venezia

            Ecco il Leone!

handkerchief

fazzoletto

fainted, immobile, mute

Svenuto... Immobil... muto

In Cyprus he names a successor... Cassio!

In Cipro elegge un successor... Cassio!.

No. 48

I believe in a cruel God etc.

—— Credo in un Dio crudel che m'ha creato

    Simile a sé, e che nell'ira io nomo.

    ~~E che nell'ira io nomo.~~

—— Dalla viltà d'un germe o d'un atòmo

    Vile son nato;

    Son scellerato

    Perchè son uomo,

    E sento il fango originario in me.

—— Sì! questa è la mia fè!

—— Credo con fermo cuor, siccome crede

    La vedovella al Tempio,

    Che il mal ch'io penso e che da me procede

    Per mio destino adempio.

—— Credo che il giusto è un istrïon beffardo

    E nel viso e nel cuor,

    Che tutto è in lui bugiardo,

    Lagrima, bacio, sguardo,

    Sacrificio ed onor.

             giuoco

—— E credo l'uom ~~gioco~~ d'iniqua sorte

    Dal germe della culla

    Al verme dell'avel.

—— Vien dopo tanta irrisïon la Morte!

—— E poi?—La Morte è il Nulla,
È vecchia fola il Ciel.

No. 53

JAGO   *Don't you fear me? etc.*

JAGO   Ne mi paventi?
EMILIA Uomo crudel
JAGO   A me...
EMILIA   Che tenti!
JAGO   A me quel vel!

No. 54

Give me that veil! etc.

          A me quel vel!

————————

JAGO   (Già la mia brama
(dopo   Conquido, ed ora
d'aver   Su questa trama
carpito il   Jago lavora!)
fazzoletto)

EMILIA   (Vinse l'orrenda   (Vinser gli artigli
          Sua mano impura   Truci e codardi.
          Dio ci difenda   Dio dai perigli
          Dalla sventura.)   Sempre ci guardi.)

JAGO   (Già il laccio l'agile
          Pensier trovò.)

EMILIA   (Muta ma vigile
          Scorta sarò.)

Eм. *No. You are preparing etc.*

Eм.   No. Tu a colpevole
Mister t'accingi.

JAGO   È un mio fuggevole
(quasi   Capriccio.
scherzo-
samente.)

Eм.   Fingi.
(fissandolo)

JAGO   Follie! quel morbido
Lino m'adesca.

Eм.   V'è in te d'un torbido
Fervor la tresca.

JAGO   Cedi.
(incalzando)

Eм.   No.

JAGO   Taci.

Eм.   Punisce il ciel
L'arti mendaci.

JAGO   A me quel vel!

No. 55

CASSIO   *Here I thought to find Desdemona etc.*

CASSIO   Io qui credea di ritrovar Desdemona
Oт.   (Ei la nomò)
CASSIO   Vorrei parlarle ancora
Per saper se la mia grazia è profferta

No. 60

And her eyes wept so much, so much,
  They would have moved stones to pity!

E gli occhi suoi piangevan tanto tanto
  Da impietosir le rupi!.

You love Cassio! etc.

            Ami Cassio!
DESDEMONA No! Sull'anima mia!!
OTELLO   Quel fazzoletto
Ch'io ti donai gli desti
DES.   Non è vero!
Oт.   Io lo vidi nella sua man!
DES.   Fù inganno!.

Oт.	Confessa
Des.	Giuro
Oт.	Bada allo spergiuro!
	Pensa che sei sul tuo letto di morte!
Des.	Non per morir!
Oт.	Per morir tosto
Des.	Aita!
	Cassio non amo... Ch'ei qui venga... ei parli...
Oт.	Più nol vedrai...
Des.	Che dite?...Morto?!
Oт.	Morto!
Des.	Son perduta... Ei tradito!.
Oт.	E pianger l'osi?
Des.	Otello non uccidermi
Oт.	Giù... cadi
	Prostituta
Des.	Pietà
Oт.	Muori
Des.	Ch'io viva
	Questa notte
Oт.	Nò
Des.	Un'ora
Oт.	Nò
Des.	Un istante!
Oт.	No!
Des.	Sol ch'io dica un ave
Oт.	È tardi È tardi... (Pausa lunga)
	Calma... come la tomba
Emilia bussa alla porta	Aprite!
Oт.	Emilia!!
Emilia Entrando... ~~Aprite!...~~	
	Orribile delitto!... Cassio uccise
	Rodrigo
Oт.	E Cassio?
Em.	Vive!
Oт.	Cassio vive?!
Des.	Ingiustamente uccise... ingiustamente
Em.	Ciel qual gemito!. orror
[Des.]	Muojo innocente...
Em.	Chi fù? chi fù?

Marginal notes (right side):

{ Aggiustate come volete questo verso ma evitate una lunga frase come era in prima: "Chiusa per sempre è la sua bocca".

{ Conservate se potete "Otello non uccidermi!" È straziante!

{ A me piacerebbe che Emilia dicesse ancora "Aprite! oh qual delitto!

{ Forse è troppo dire tre volte "Cassio" ma stà tanto bene in Otello il Cassio vive

[DES.] Nissuno... io stessa... al mio...

Signor... mi raccomanda... Addio!... muore

OT. Menti va! trice!

Io l'uccisi

EM. Assassino!

OT. Fù di Cassio

La druda! A Jago il chiedi!...

EM. A Jago?...

OT. A Jago!

EM. Soccorso... ajuto, ajuto!... All'assassinio!.

Entrano Lodovico Cassio Jago e soldati

TUTTI Quai grida... Cielo!... Desdemona uccisa!

EM. a Jago

Jago smentisci quel vile omicida...

Credi la casta
~~Credesti tu~~ Desdemona infida?.

> Mi piace poco in
> questo luogo la parola
> "casta" Non potreste
> dire: Hai tu creduto et.

JAGO Tal la credea

EM. Tu?

JAGO Sì

OT. interrompendo Quel fazzoletto

Che un dì le diedi a Cassio essa donò.

> Questo tratto pare
> lungo, ma in mu-
> sica è riescito ra-
> pido, e breve piú
> che se fosse
> recitato.

EM. Oh potenza divina!

JAGO Taci

EM. Nò

Tutto rivelo

JAGO Taci

EM. Maledetto

Dal Cielo

JAGO Taci

EM. No

JAGO Trema

EM. Costui

Dalla mia man quel fazzoletto colse

A viva forza!

CASSIO E nella mia dimora

Trovai quel velo!

MONTANO entrando grida Rodrigo morente

Svelò di quest'infame opre nefande

Oт. a Jago   Ah! Discolpati

Jago con ~~sprezzo~~ un'urlo   Nò! e fugge

Lod.   S'insegua, e tratto

                Al carcer sia!.

Oт. con grido   E il Ciel non ha piú fulmini!!

Lod. a Otello   Tu sei mio prigionier!.

Oт. pausa lunga   Tutto è finito!...

                La gloria è un lampo, un sogno menzogner!

s'avvicina a Desdemona

                E tù... come sei pallida!—e stanca e muta e bella

                Pia creatura nata—sotto maligna stella

                Fredda, come la casta tua vita e in cielo assorta!

                Desdemona, Desdemona!—Ah!... morta-morta-morta!!

Dopo una lunga pausa corre al tavolo ove aveva deposta la spada...
        lo previene,
Cassio ~~impedisce et~~ e toglie la spada. Allora Otello estrae un pugnale
e dice
~~rapidamente e si uccide~~

                Questo pugnal mi resta!. e si uccide.

Tutti   Ah sciagurato!

                Prima d'ucciderti

No. 66

Honestly I could not. You yourself etc.

                Onestamente nol potrei. Voi stesso

                Il suo contegno colla mente arguta

                Studiate e giudicate

Oт.   Eccolo è desso

                Nell'animo lo scruta

No. 67

. . . warrior etc.

                . . . . guerriero

                . . . .

                È quel ch'Egli è

                        Palesa il tuo pensiero

Jago   Meglio è serbar su ciò la lingua muta

Otel: Eccolo! È lui. Nell'animo lo scruta.

No. 71

And you, how pale you are
　E tu come sei pallida
A kiss, another kiss
　Un bacio un bacio ancora

No. 76

around me a Jago
　d'attorno un Jago
To the oars etc.
　　　　Forza ai remi
　　　　　　Alla riva!!
　　　　Ancorate il vascello
　　　　　　Evviva Evviva!
OTELLO　sbarcato in fondo alla scena: sull'alto...
　　　　Esultate. L'orgoglio Musulmano
　　　　Sepolto è in mar; nostra e del Cielo è gloria
　　　　Dopo l'armi lo vinse ...gano (Entra nel Castello)
TUTTI　　Evviva Otello! Vittoria vittoria!

No. 78

OTELLO　*We will set sail tomorrow. To the ground! and weep!*
　OTELLO　Noi salperem domani—A terra! e piangi!

DESDEMONA　*To the ground!... yes... in the livid etc.*
　　DESDEMONA
　A terra!... sì... nel livido
　Fango... percossa... io giacio...
　Piango... m'agghiaccia il brivido
　Dell'anima che muor.
　E un dì sul mio sorriso
　Fiorìa la speme e il bacio
　Ed or... l'angoscia in viso
　E l'agonìa nel cor.
　　Quel sol sereno e vivido
　Che allieta il cielo e il mare
　Non può asciugar le amare
　Stille del mio dolor.—

EMILIA
Quella innocente un fremito
D'odio non ha ne un gesto
Trattiene in petto il gemito
Con doloroso fren.
La lagrima si frange
Muta sul volto mesto.
No chi per Lei non piange
Non ha pietade in sen.

RODRIGO
(Per me s'oscura il mondo
S'anuvola il destin
L'angiol soave e biondo
Scompar dal mio cammin.)

CASSIO
(L'ora è fatal Un fulmine
Sul mio cammin l'addita
Già mia sorte il culmine
S'offre all'inerte man
L'ebbra fortuna incalza
La fuga della vita
Questa che al ciel m'innalza
È un'onda d'uragan.

LODOVICO
Egli la man funerea
Scuote anelando d'ira
Essa la faccia eterea
Volge piangendo al Ciel
Nel contemplar quel pianto
La carità sospira
E un tenero compianto
Stempra del core il gel

IL CORO
a gruppi dialogando
contemporaneamente ai dialoghi di Jago

DONNE Pietà!

CAV: Mistero!

DONNE Ansia mortal bieca
Ne ingombra anime assorte in lungo orror

CAV: Quell'uomo nero è sepolcrale, e cieca
Un'ombra è in Lui di morte e di terror

DAME Vista crudel! Strazia coll'ugna l'orrido
Petto!

CAV. Figge gli sguardi immoti al suol
Poi sfida il Ciel coll'atra pugna l'ispido
Aspetto ergendo ai dardi alti del Sol

DAME Ei la colpì! Quel viso santo pallido
Blando si china e tace e piange e muor
Piangon così nel Ciel lor pianto gli angeli
Quando perduto giace il peccator—

Jago ad Otello accasciato su d'una sedia

OTEL. Una parola

JAGO E che?
T'affretta! Rapido
Slancia la tua vendetta! Il tempo vola.

OT. Ben parli

JAGO È l'ira inutil ciancia. Scuotiti!
All'opra ergi tua mira! All'opra sola.
Io penso a Cassio. Ei le sue trame espia
L'infame anima ria l'averno inghiotte.
Chi gliela svelle?

OT. Io!

JAGO Tu?

OT. Giurai

JAGO Tal sia
Tu avrai le sue novelle questa notte
abbandona Otello e si dirige verso Rodrigo
I sogni tuoi saranno in mar domani.
E tu sull'aspra terra
Ahi triste!!

ROD. Ahi stolto!

JAGO Stolto! Se vuoi tu puoi sperar, gli umani
Arditi orsù riafferra e m'odi
Ascolto.

ROD. Col primo albor salpa il vascello. Or Cassio

JAGO È il Duce. Eppur se avvien che a questi accada
Sventura... Allor qui resta Otello
Lugubre

ROD. Luce d'altro balen
Mano alla spada!

JAGO A notte folta io la sua traccia seguito
E il varco e l'ora scruto, il resto a te
Sarò tua scolta. A caccia a caccia Cingiti
L'arco
venduto

R. Si t'ho donato[?] onore e fè!

JAGO (Corri al miraggio! Il fragile tuo senno
a parte Ha già confuso un sogno menzogner.
Segui l'astuto ed agile mio cenno
Amante illuso, io seguo il mio pensier
Il dado è tratto! Impavido t'attendo
Ultima sorte, occulto mio destin

ROD. Mi sprona amor, ma un avido tremendo
Astro di morte infesta il mio cammin

No. 79

Jago . . . My Commander etc.

JAGO	. . . . Mio Duce
(s'incammina con Otello verso la porta del fondo. Ma ad un tratto s'arresta.)	Grazie vi rendo. Ecco gli Ambasciatori Andiamo ad essi. Ma... credo opportuno (Anche a sviar sospetti o uggiose inchieste) Che Desdemona accolga quei Messeri.
OTELLO	Sì. Qui l'adduci.
(Jago esce rapidamente dalla porta di sinistra Otello continua ad avviarsi verso il fondo per attendere gli Ambasciatori)	. . . .
LODOVICO	Madonna,
(a Des. che sarà entrata con Jago e seguita a breve distanza da Emilia.)	V'abbia il cielo in sua grazia.
DESDEMONA	E il ciel v'ascolti.
EMILIA	(Come sei mesta.
(a Des. a parte)	
DESDEMONA	Emilia! una gran nube
(a Em. a parte)	Turba il senno d'Otello e il mio destino.)

No. 81

Here are the Ambassadors etc.

Ecco gli Ambasciatori
Li accogliete. Ma ad evitar sospetti
Desdemona si mostri a quei Messeri.
OTELLO Sì, qui l'adduci.

No. 82

Yet here already nests the kindly demon etc.

Pur già qui annida il demone gentil del mal consiglio,
Che il vago avorio allumina del piccioletto artiglio
Mollemente alla prece s'atteggia e al pio fervore
Eppur con questa mano, io v'ho donato il core

———————————

Signor mi raccomanda... Emilia... Addio

No. 83

Let us flee
  fuggiam
They are killing each other
  s'uccidono

No. 87

Beauty and happiness agreeing in sweet song,
I will shatter your tender harmonies.
  Beltà e letizia in dolce inno concordi
  I vostri infrangerò soavi accordi.
Beauty and Love agreeing in sweet song
  Beltà ed Amor in dolce inno concordi

No. 124

MRS. PAGE	*Hold up the jest etc.*
MRS. PAGE	Non spingiamo più oltre la burla.
FALSTAFF	E queste son le Fate?
MRS. FORD	E credete Voi che volendo peccare avressimo scelto un'uomo come Voi?!
FORD	Una balena!
FALS.	Bene!...
ALTRO	Un uomo di crema!
FALS.	Bene!
ALTRO	Un vecchio appassito
FALS.	Molto bene
ALTRO	Maledico come Satana
FALS.	Sempre bene
ALTRI	Povero come Giobbe
[FALS.]	Benissimo
TUTTI	E dedito alle fornicazioni alle taverne, al vino, alle crapule, giurando, spergiurando e bestemmiando Dio...
FALS.	Amen.. e così sia
MRS. [PAGE]	Ed ora Sir Giovanni, come amate le donne di Vindsor?
FALS.	Or incomincio a credere che sono un'asino
TUTTI	Bravo! Ben detto! ben detto! Viva Viva Viva!...

No. 153
Everything in the world is jest etc.

    Tutto nel mondo è burla
    L'uom è nato burlone.
    Nel suo cervello ciurla
    Sempre la sua ragione.
    Tutti gabbati! Irride
    L'un l'altro ogni mortal,
    Ma ride ben chi ride
    La risata final.

ᴥ INDEX